Selected Titles in This Series

55 **Frederick Hoffman, Editor,** Mathematical aspects of artificial intelligence (Orlando, Florida, January 1996)

54 **Renato Spigler and Stephanos Venakides, Editors,** Recent advances in partial differential equations (Venice, Italy, June 1996)

53 **David A. Cox and Bernd Sturmfels, Editors,** Applications of computational algebraic geometry (San Diego, California, January 1997)

52 **V. Mandrekar and P. R. Masani, Editors,** Proceedings of the Norbert Wiener Centenary Congress, 1994 (East Lansing, Michigan, 1994)

51 **Louis H. Kauffman, Editor,** The interface of knots and physics (San Francisco, California, January 1995)

50 **Robert Calderbank, Editor,** Different aspects of coding theory (San Francisco, California, January 1995)

49 **Robert L. Devaney, Editor,** Complex dynamical systems: The mathematics behind the Mandlebrot and Julia sets (Cincinnati, Ohio, January 1994)

48 **Walter Gautschi, Editor,** Mathematics of Computation 1943–1993: A half century of computational mathematics (Vancouver, British Columbia, August 1993)

47 **Ingrid Daubechies, Editor,** Different perspectives on wavelets (San Antonio, Texas, January 1993)

46 **Stefan A. Burr, Editor,** The unreasonable effectiveness of number theory (Orono, Maine, August 1991)

45 **De Witt L. Sumners, Editor,** New scientific applications of geometry and topology (Baltimore, Maryland, January 1992)

44 **Béla Bollobás, Editor,** Probabilistic combinatorics and its applications (San Francisco, California, January 1991)

43 **Richard K. Guy, Editor,** Combinatorial games (Columbus, Ohio, August 1990)

42 **C. Pomerance, Editor,** Cryptology and computational number theory (Boulder, Colorado, August 1989)

41 **R. W. Brockett, Editor,** Robotics (Louisville, Kentucky, January 1990)

40 **Charles R. Johnson, Editor,** Matrix theory and applications (Phoenix, Arizona, January 1989)

39 **Robert L. Devaney and Linda Keen, Editors,** Chaos and fractals: The mathematics behind the computer graphics (Providence, Rhode Island, August 1988)

38 **Juris Hartmanis, Editor,** Computational complexity theory (Atlanta, Georgia, January 1988)

37 **Henry J. Landau, Editor,** Moments in mathematics (San Antonio, Texas, January 1987)

36 **Carl de Boor, Editor,** Approximation theory (New Orleans, Louisiana, January 1986)

35 **Harry H. Panjer, Editor,** Actuarial mathematics (Laramie, Wyoming, August 1985)

34 **Michael Anshel and William Gewirtz, Editors,** Mathematics of information processing (Louisville, Kentucky, January 1984)

33 **H. Peyton Young, Editor,** Fair allocation (Anaheim, California, January 1985)

32 **R. W. McKelvey, Editor,** Environmental and natural resource mathematics (Eugene, Oregon, August 1984)

31 **B. Gopinath, Editor,** Computer communications (Denver, Colorado, January 1983)

30 **Simon A. Levin, Editor,** Population biology (Albany, New York, August 1983)

29 **R. A. DeMillo, G. I. Davida, D. P. Dobkin, M. A. Harrison, and R. J. Lipton,** Applied cryptology, cryptographic protocols, and computer security models (San Francisco, California, January 1981)

28 **R. Gnanadesikan, Editor,** Statistical data analysis (Toronto, Ontario, August 1982)

27 **L. A. Shepp, Editor,** Computed tomography (Cincinnati, Ohio, January 1982)

(*Continued in the back of this publication*)

AMS SHORT COURSE LECTURE NOTES

Introductory Survey Lectures

published as a subseries of

Proceedings of Symposia in Applied Mathematics

Proceedings of Symposia in
APPLIED MATHEMATICS

Volume 55

Mathematical Aspects of Artificial Intelligence

American Mathematical Society
Short Course
January 8–9, 1996
Orlando, Florida

Frederick Hoffman
Editor

American Mathematical Society
Providence, Rhode Island

LECTURE NOTES PREPARED FOR THE
AMERICAN MATHEMATICAL SOCIETY SHORT COURSE
MATHEMATICAL ASPECTS OF ARTIFICIAL INTELLIGENCE
HELD IN ORLANDO, FLORIDA
JANUARY 8–9, 1996

The AMS Short Course Series is sponsored by the Society's Program Committee for National Meetings. The series is under the direction of the Short Course Subcommittee of the Program Committee for National Meetings.

1991 *Mathematics Subject Classification.* Primary 68–xx; Secondary 03–xx, 05–xx, 51–xx, 60–xx, 90–xx.

Library of Congress Cataloging-in-Publication Data

Mathematical aspects of artificial intelligence : American Mathematical Society short course, January 8–9, 1996, Orlando, Florida / Frederick Hoffman, editor.
p. cm. — (Proceedings of symposia in applied mathematics ; v. 55. AMS short course lecture notes)
Includes bibliographical references and index.
ISBN 0-8218-0611-4 (alk. paper)
1. Artificial intelligence—Mathematics—Congresses. I. Hoffman, Frederick, 1937– . II. American Mathematical Society. III. Series: Proceedings of symposia in applied mathematics ; v. 55. IV. Series: Proceedings of symposia in applied mathematics. AMS short course lecture notes.
Q335.M33756 1998
006.3′0151—dc21

98-4693
CIP

∞ The paper used in this book is acid-free and falls within the guidelines
established to ensure permanence and durability.
Visit the AMS home page at URL: http://www.ams.org/

10 9 8 7 6 5 4 3 2 1   03 02 01 00 99 98

Contents

Preface

Artificial Intelligence (AI) is an important and exciting field. It is an active research area and is considered to have enormous research opportunities and great potential for applications. At the same time, AI is highly controversial. There is a history of great expectations, and large investments, with some notable shortfalls and memorable disappointments. We are, of course, most concerned with connections between AI and mathematics. In fact, one of the major controversies regarding AI is the issue of just how mathematical a field it is, or should be. The major research journal in the field, *Artificial Intelligence*, publishes a large number of papers with heavy mathematical content, although many authorities in the field question this emphasis. For one example, the currently hot AI topic of "data mining," obtaining information from incomplete or "noisy" sources, has a necessary mathematical component, and, in general, theoretical AI, like theoretical computer science, is at least arguably a mathematical science. No matter where we come down within the range of "just how mathematical is it?", there is a close enough tie to justify the AMS Short Course, and this volume. We feel that mathematics and mathematicians have a lot to contribute to AI, and that AI has excellent potential for fruitful applications to mathematics. The purpose of the course, and this book, is to introduce mathematicians and others to some of the more mathematical areas within AI, both for the intrinsic value of the material as well as with a view toward stimulating the interest of people who can contribute to the field or use it in their work. We must point out that the AMS has had special sessions and invited talks in the past on AI, so we are in no sense the first to try to draw the community's attention to the field.

This volume begins with a brief introduction to the field of AI, to provide enough general information so that readers can place the remaining chapters in perspective. We provide the necessary definitions and a rather perfunctory outline, with a minimal amount of history. Emphasis within this chapter is somewhat driven by the topics of the remaining chapters.

One of the best known, and most controversial topics of AI is computer chess. Early on in the history of the field, grandiose claims were made for the near-term success of computers as chess champions. The failure of the field to produce an artificial chess champion within the predicted time-line was used to attack AI and its practitioners unmercifully. In reality, while the time-line was unduly optimistic, it now seems that the initial claims have been met, and the attacks on the field because of failures of computer chess will be replaced by controversy about just how intelligent the artificial chess champions really are. In this volume, we present a chapter on computer chess by Monty Newborn. Professor Newborn's comments were featured in news coverage of the famous match in February, 1996, between the program Deep Blue and the human chess champion, and he has written a book on the match. Because of the volatility of the topic, this chapter is "frozen in time" immediately before the February match. The techniques discussed are highly mathematical, involving graph theory, combinatorics and probability and statistics, among others.

Glenn Shafer, whose seminal work on probabilistic reasoning has made him a household word in the AI applications area of expert systems, and in AI in general, continues, in this volume, his development of probability through causal probablity trees. The topic is related to an important practical issue in AI, especially in expert systems; that is, the extent to which causal information, rather than case-based, a posteriori data, should be used in making decisions. His chapter consists of new material, first presented by Professor Shafer in research papers and a 1996 book, with some results appearing here for the first time; at the same time, it has its origins in the early history of probability theory. We find it fascinating that the use of probability in AI has fostered exciting developments in the foundations of probability theory itself, especially since the new insights hark back to the classical beginnings of the field. The chapter is of great interest in its own right, as a contribution to the foundations of probability theory, and also serves as an example both of mathematics serving AI, and of mathematics being developed because of lessons learned from AI.

One of the most difficult problems in reasoning in AI has to do with handling time. Temporal reasoning is part of the huge problem of planning actions to achieve objectives in a dynamic world. It ties into the famous philosophical bugbear of AI–the Frame Problem. Martin Golumbic's chapter explores the topic of temporal reasoning. This is a highly mathematical part of AI, with ties to logic as well as to combinatorics and graph theory. The real-world situations studied in both this chapter and the preceding one provide intriguing settings for the theoretical issues they develop.

Mathematical AI is frequently associated with the "logicist" school within AI, and is heavily based on mathematical logic. The chapter by Golumbic is concerned in large part with logic as well as with graph theory. The next two chapters are even more heavily involved with logic. When an AI system reasons, it generally uses algorithms that are guaranteed to succeed, but require success within certain time frames to be of any real value. While providing a great deal of general information on logical reasoning in AI, Hélène Kirchner explains techniques, using order relations, to make deduction more efficient. These systems are highly mathematical in their strucure, and thus provide another example of synergy–the systems described here are closely related to those used by Larry Wos and his group at Argonne, who devote a lot of their attention to solving problems and proving theorems in pure mathematics. In fact, Dr. Wos and his work have been studied, and honored, by the AMS in the past, and have also been featured in national media regularly, including December, 1996 coverage of new mathematical results by the New York Times.

In general, decision-making in AI involves optimization subject to constraints. In addition, constraints are added to reasoning systems to make them work more efficiently. Once again, AI and mathematics each serve the other. Catherine Lassez's chapter deals with constraint logic programming. The applications of the methods described here range from pure mathematics to optimization in some very applied disciplines, like operations research and financial mathematics. It is unsurprising that the topic is intimately tied to linear programming. The nature of the relationship, and the structure of the theory described here, are fascinating. In fact, the crucial theorems go back to Fourier, the unsung father of linear programming.

Computer vision is obviously necessary for the creation of artificially intelligent beings to function in the real world, thinking robots, as it were. One could argue that, since lower, "unintelligent" animals can see, and blind humans can think and reason, that computer vision is not a legitimate part of the subject of AI. This view has much to commend it, since computer vision presents very difficult problems, and while it is a very mathematical field, the mathematics, at least in part, is both difficult and different from the mathematics used in other parts of AI. Because of the heavy mathematical component of vision, though, and because of image understanding, a part of vision, is part of AI, we have chosen to include a chapter on vision. Vishvjit Nalwa gently guides his readers on a tour of computer vision, giving brief exposure to various facets of the field, and tying it to several areas of mathematics, from combinatorics, probability, and geometry to partial differential equations.

There is much more, and much more that is mathematical, to AI than we are able to touch on here. We sincerely hope that we have provided enough of the flavor of the field to have whetted the appetites of some of our audience, and we look forward to their contributing to and using the results of AI. We welcome comments from our readers.

Proceedings of Symposia in Applied Mathematics
Volume **55**, 1998

Introduction and History

Frederick Hoffman

ABSTRACT. We present a brief introduction and some history along with a structural description of some of the mathematical aspects of artificial intelligence.

1. Introduction

In introducing a book of this type, it would seem natural to begin with definitions. The first definition should be that of artificial intelligence itself. There is, however, no universally accepted definition of either the concept or the field of AI. To get started here, we'll use a fairly standard operational definition of the concept by saying that a computer, with its software, demonstrates artificial intelligence when it exhibits behavior which, were it to be performed by a human, would be considered to require intelligence. We then back down a bit, to eliminate apparently intelligent activity requiring only memory and arithmetic. Something like this last exclusion is necessary to throw out the intelligence of simple calculators. [Except for our including the computer in the definition, we need exceptions to throw out thermos jugs and slide rules.] Then the field can be regarded as the study of the concept, and by extension, also the science which tries to make computers smarter.

The role of mathematics in artificial intelligence is pervasive, but controversial; the role of artificial intelligence in mathematics is relatively small, but growing, and could be larger, to the benefit of both fields. There are aspects of this interplay that should interest both mathematicians wishing to consider working on AI problems and those hoping to apply AI in their mathematical research. I shall first give an overview definition of the field of AI, with a bit of its history, stressing the relations with mathematics, and then try to tie in the coming chapters. I shall then add a little more history, and continue with some introductory information to help the reader get a better picture of the field. The paper by Herbert Simon, "Artificial Intelligence: an empirical science," in the journal, *Artificial Intelligence* (vol 77,1995), has influenced this discussion, because it brings some of the issues involving the relations between AI and mathematics into sharp focus. This is not to say that the views here are in complete agreement with those of Professor Simon, one of AI's founders and its Nobel laureate. He has raised major issues regarding what we are studying here, and his discussion of them adds to our feeling that the mathematical aspects of AI, and the impact of mathematics on AI, are important. Another

1991 *Mathematics Subject Classification.* Primary 90.
Key words and phrases. Artificial Intelligence.

insight into the relation of mathematics and AI can be gained from comparing the early AI texts by Nilsson and Banerji [**31**][**1**]with their later versions[**32**][**2**]. Most fields of applied mathematics gain in rigor as they mature; here, you wonder where the rigor went. Nilsson did collaborate on a more mathematical text later on, however[**17**].

Some of the earliest problems which were attacked in the search for artificial intelligence were problems in mathematics: theorem proving in logic, algebra and geometry; algebra word problems; symbolic integration[**38**]. Symbolic algebra systems like Derive, Macsyma, Maple and Mathematica owe a great deal to AI. An early and continuing challenge was that of discovering and proving a non-trivial mathematical theorem. Some of the efforts in that direction were celebrated when AMS honored 25 years of automated reasoning[**5**]. One of the main tools in AI is and was combinatorial search; hence, one of the knottiest problems is the combinatorial explosion. One of the major applications of AI is in game theory, both in games as games and in games as in the mathematical theory of games. One of the first major successes of AI was Samuel's checkers player, which featured an early "genetic algorithm," and was quite mathematical in nature. For this and many other of the early applications, see [**13**]. Perhaps the most famous of the early quests was the attempt to create a champion chess player; one of the most celebrated boasts was that this quest would meet with relatively early success; the biggest failure of the field, at least according to many of its critics, was the failure to achieve this goal anywhere near its target date. A computer did become world checkers champion, but only because the world's greatest checkers player, combinatorial mathematician Marion Tinsley, had to resign from a tournament because of illness. While chess was a major failure for AI in a period of crisis for the field, and a long-term irritation, this all changed on May 11, 1997, when IBM's Deep Blue defeated Garry Kasparov, the reigning human chess champion of the world, and a man said by many to be the greatest chess player who ever lived[**20**]. Kasparov said in a press conference after the match that he would be able to beat Deep Blue after he got the chance to study its play, and criticized the fact that Deep Blue's progam had been tailored to play him. On the other hand, he had earlier complimented the computer on some moves which seemed human-like to him. We shall learn from Monty Newborn about some of the mathematical techniques used to propel AI to the goal of an artificial chess champion. He has also pointed out, in a lecture January 4, 1996, to the AI and mathematics community, some lessons for the field, and for computer science and mathematics in general, from the long quest. The questions of whether brute force or human-type cleverness is most important is one of the issues addressed, and takes us back to the question of what it means for a program to be intelligent.

After early successes, which generated a lot of attention and a lot of government funding, in the 1960's and into the 1970's, AI came upon a bad period, its "dark ages," partly from failed promises like that of creating an artificial chess champion. The field moved from an early stress on generality in problem solving, to programs which demonstrated intelligence by being fed enormous amounts of knowledge about a limited, but important field, together with the ability to reason logically about this field. These programs, the expert systems, came to the fore in the 1980's. Many of the most important expert systems required a calculus of probabilities to simulate the decision-making ability of domain experts. It seemed to many practitioners that the usual rules of probability were inappropriate to handle the sort of reasoning real experts use when dealing with uncertainty. Two methods of probabilistic calculation developed for expert systems are the system of certainty factors, developed for the EMYCIN family of systems, and a method based on the Dempster-Shafer theory, which one of our authors described in his *Mathematical Theory of Evidence*. This contribution made him a household word in the field. In this volume, he is presenting an answer to another major need in the field, a causal theory of probability [**36**]. In this effort, he is returning to the early roots of probability theory to do something new. His new theory, using probability trees, was influenced by artificial intelligence, and he sees AI as a natural field of application for the theory. Beyond this, it shows promise for the field of mathematical probability in general. Among other intriguing aspects of the theory is its treatment of martingales without measure theory.

Causal probability is strongly related to temporal considerations. In fact, many critical difficulties in AI arise from problems with time. Human beings can frequently neglect the effects of time on a situation when they reason; thinking computers must take explicit notice of time. This is part of the famous "frame problem" in AI, and temporal reasoning is the topic of Martin Golumbic's chapter. Golumbic began his research career as a combinatorialist, and now emphasizes problems in combinatorial mathematics interacting with real world problems in computer science and artificial intelligence. His approach presented here is very combinatorial, and algorithmic, in nature. One aspect involves interval graphs, a very active field of inquiry in applied combinatorics. The situation here again is one in which mathematics is employed in the service of AI; also, again, the investigations made on this topic should be important in computational complexity, and in applications of AI techniques in combinatorial design theory. There is a strong tie-in with satisfiability, the NP-complete problem of greatest interest among mathematicians, and one which figures in a wide range of AI applications.

I should add in passing that AI techniques have been used to great effect in the search for combinatorial designs of many sorts. Genetic algorithms, synthetic annealing (which I have always considered an AI technique), as well as basic hill-climbing algorithms have been used to great effect in the past, and will be used more in the future, and software developed to attack satisfiability problems, important in theoretical computer science as well as in AI, appear to have great promise in design theory.

Logic is both an early area of study and application of the field of AI and a major tool in the field. Expert systems and other AI software obviously must reason logically. In fact, logic programming languages, most notably Prolog, are used to develop expert systems. The series of mathematical problem-solving tools developed at Argonne Labs by Larry Wos and his team, AURA, Otter and EQP, can be viewed as mechanized mathematical logic. This situation makes what might seem to be arcane questions in mathematical logic or theoretical computer science turn out to be questions in applications-oriented artificial intelligence. In a nutshell, the discovery of resolution refutation and the unification algorithm made it possible to do "all" first order predicate calculus by computer; of course, subject to the limitations of the combinatorial explosion. Hélène Kirchner's chapter deals with improving the efficiency of algorithms of this type. She uses rewrite rules in logic to make efficient some of the important types of search in machine logic, and handles some of the difficulties in dealing with the relation of "equals." This is an important case in which mathematical logic is used to solve AI problems, but in turn, the AI problems to which the method is applied include proofs in group theory and other parts of mathematics. Interestingly, we see again underlying ideas which predate computers and AI.

Herbert Simon, in the paper mentioned earlier, as he tries to convince his audience that AI is worrying too much about theoretical mathematical issues, raises linear programming as an example in which results are more important than theoretical mathematics. I would point out that the fact that the simplex algorithm, which is provably "bad," is used much more than provably "good" interior point algorithms, aligns the field very well with AI. Constraint logic programming and linear programming are tools for solving similar types of problems. Catherine Lassez's chapter deals with constraint logic programming. It is closely related to Hélène Kirchner's chapter, but brings in a new set of techniques, some of which owe their origins to the same work by Fourier which forms the basis for linear programming. This topic, which involves both "old-fashioned" and highly mathematical techniques, has many important current applications.

If one tries to specify the field of AI, one has a dilemma about computer vision. Since animals see, and blind people think, why should one include computer vision as a part of AI? On one hand, since the mathematical problems associated with vision are perhaps harder than those associated with any other part of AI, and involve "hard analysis," which is not seen elsewhere in the field, it would seem reasonable to eliminate computer vision from artificial intelligence. On the other hand, image understanding, including interpretation of raw visual impulses using tools like perspective, as well as character recognition for reading, would seem to be a very important part of artificial intelligence, and is a part of computer vision. In addition, the field has excited many eminent researchers in the last few years. On balance, it would seem that we should include computer vision in AI. Since, if included in AI, computer vision is one of the most mathematical parts of the field, we included it for the purposes of this volume. This keeps us in the mainstream of AI; the journal, *Artificial Intelligence*, came out in October, 1995 with a 550-page volume on computer vision. Appropriately, the editors of that volume drew analogies between our first topic, chess, and our last topic, vision. We shall be guided by Vic Nalwa, who has successfully introduced many readers to vision. His chapter will touch on many aspects of the field, involving many types of mathematics.

This volume barely scratches the surface of the field. We have not dealt with the issues of knowledge representation, language understanding, or languages for artificial intelligence, among other things, and we have only briefly referred to expert systems. We hope that the material here will entice some of you to pursue AI further. We hope that, among other things, interest in AI from the mathematics community will help keep the theory side of AI on equal standing with the experimental side. We feel very strongly that each field can benefit greatly from collaborative efforts between the communities.

2. History

This brief sketch of the history of AI will be arranged topically.

AI was "established" as a named discipline at a conference held at Dartmouth College in 1956, but it has a long "pre-history," in which mathematics, along with some of the topics in this volume, plays a role. A mechanical chess player, which turned out to have a man inside, is a comical part of the prehistory. More interesting is the device developed by the intriguing rogue, Ramón Lull, who used combinatorial techniques to provide the necessary uncertainty in an artificial advice system in the thirteenth century. See, e.g., [**16**]. Many of the tasks assigned to the precursors of computers could be said to fall under the AI classification, and one of the earliest arguments against AI, the assertion that, "The computer can only do what it is programmed to do, and thus AI is not possible," is credited to Ada, Lady Lovelace, the "first computer programmer." The attempts to mechanize human thought seem quite natural, then, and AI, with its mathematical components, is a natural addition to the sciences. Thus, symbolic and algebraic logic, and the work of Charles Dodgson and George Boole are precursors of AI. Russell and Whitehead's *Principia Mathematica* was a natural target for AI. The Logic Theory Machine, or Logic Theorist, of Newell, Shaw and Simon was already at work on theorems of logic in 1956[**13**], and Hao Wang made a great breakthrough in 1960 with his method[**43**], which was a computerization of Gentzen's 1934 technique[**18**]. The most important breakthrough in doing logic by machine was the development of resolution refutation as a proof method, and the unification algorithm to make it work for the first-order predicate calculus[**34**]. This is the principle underlying Prolog[**6**] (as well as Carl Hewett's previously proposed language, Planner[**23**]).

Other mathematical targets of early AI research were algebra word problems, integral calculus and geometry. Successes in these ventures led to attempts to generalize. The most important and influential of these programs was the General Problem Solver of Newell, Shaw and Simon, starting about 1959[**12**]. A descendant of the Logic Theory Machine and a later chess-playing program, it epitomized the ideal of problem solving in AI–the computer as a symbolic manipulator rather than a number cruncher, using heuristics to get results in a wide range of problems. It was not the breakthrough it was cracked up to be, and this and other failures to generalize led many people to conclude that general problem solving was not the way to go. Meanwhile, progress continued to be made in many mathematical areas. The integration programs led to Macsyma, a general symbolic algebra program. MuMath and its successor Derive also had roots in AI, as did Scratchpad and its successor, Axiom, while the other major programs of that type, Reduce, SAC, Maple and Mathematica, were developed outside the AI community, as were special purpose symbolic algebra programs like Cayley/Magma, GAP and Macauley. Meanwhile, AURA, Argonne's AUtomated Reasoning Assistant, was developed to help mathematicians prove theorems and test conjectures[**47**]. It had some successes in universal algebra, and was also applied successfully to logic puzzles. Its successor program, Otter, has seen recent success, as we shall see later. As suggested earlier, AI techniques, like hill-climbing and simulated annealing, have been used to search for solutions to combinatorial problems, over a number of years. In fact, Jean-Louis Laurière created his declarative language, ALICE, to search for solutions to combinatorial problems, in the mid-1970's

Language handling was another of the early AI tasks. Terry Winograd's program, SHRDLU, was a great success[**46**]. Weizenbaum's Eliza is another highly-regarded language-handling program. When attempts are made to deal with unrestricted communication, ambiguity and anaphora cause problems. Typical examples of hard to handle sentences include, "Time flies like an arrow," "The boy saw the girl on the hill with the telescope," and "The pen was in the bag; the bag was in the pen." Machine translation was an early goal, and a well-publicized failure.

Here the much cited example is the translation of the chestnut, "The spirit was willing, but the flesh was weak," to "The wine was all right, but the meat was rotten." A much-told tale is that IBM put a lot of effort and money into translation, in the 1950's, and then gave up on it, and on AI, because of the failure of machine translation. While translation done completely by machine has never enjoyed great commercial success, IBM did not end its research in the area in the way the story goes. It is true that IBM was not in AI in early days of the field on a scale commensurate with its size, but then, it wasn't in personal computers early, either. An interesting account of industrial experience with AI can be found in [**14**].

After the failure to generalize its successes, along with some cuts in government and industrial funding, AI needed something to get it out of the doldrums. The answer was the expert systems. These programs use relatively large amounts of data about limited application areas to produce expert performance. Expert systems, with the mantra, "In the knowledge is the power," led the AI resurgence in the 80's, although the systems go back to the early 70's. Stanford's DENDRAL, for identification of molecular compounds, was actually started in 1969, and is still in wide use today, including over the Internet. Stanford's MYCIN, for diagnosis of bacterial infections of the blood, was never put to practical use, but may be the most influential system. Carnegie-Mellon's R1, aka DEC's XCon, an expert system to configure large computer installations, was the first major commercial success. As an interesting aside, Douglas Lenat's expert system, AM–Artificial Mathematician–was programmed to make discoveries in mathematics, using heuristics supplied by the programmer, serving as "domain expert." The project was not continued, and no new mathematics was discovered, but it was an influential program in the development of expert systems[**10**]-.

In the early 80s, it was possible to list and describe essentially all the expert systems in use or in serious stages of development[**21**]. By the end of the decade, there were individual corporations with more than one hundred expert systems in use. Today, the novelty is gone; expert systems are simply an important industrial technology. See [**26**] and [**14**].

Game-playing has always played a fairly large role in AI. Assumptions and rules are generally as in the mathematical theory of games. Most games are zero-sum games of perfect information, and the analysis is based on minmax–assume the oponent will make the best available move. Power comes from being able to evaluate a large number of possibilities quickly. An evaluation system is used, and the backed-up evaluation is speeded up by a form of pruning of the game tree. These techniques are used in ubiquitous commercial software and shareware available for such games as checkers, chess, battleships, gomoku, backgammon and Othello/reversi. There are bridge programs out there, and Windows 95 plays hearts. Go is a tougher target, but work is being done. We've mentioned the current situation in chess. More progress is due to machine improvement than theoretical developments. AI is also being used in other applications of the mathematical theory of games. Negotiation is an important example.

Vision has always been a very tough problem for AI. The techniques for identifying objects for, say, robots working on an assembly line, have changed little from the early days of the field. Identification for more exciting purposes, like reconnaissance, involves methods like those in some expert systems, and has benefitted from research in that area–blackboard architecture, intelligent agents, etc. Optical character recognition meets the criteria for AI, and has been an area of steadily improving technology, but is generally classified as part of the separate field of "pattern recognition." Theoretical work on vision is heavily mathematical, and will be mentioned briefly a bit later.

Speech recognition, understanding of "connected" speech, and artificial production of speech have always figured prominently in the public perception of artificial intelligence. Machines that read aloud from the printed page, or from keyboarded input, go back decades, and involve little that can be called artificial intelligence. The reading ability depends, of course, on optical character recognition. Speech understanding, on the other hand, is a very hard task, and is done rather poorly, even today, as most of us have experienced personally, when conversing on the telephone with machines. A lot of the successful speech understanding is done by machines trained to one speaker's voice, with no relation to connected speech. This is analagous to the handling of cursive writing by hand-held computers. It is a form of machine learning, though, and machine learning is an important part of artificial intelligence. Systems for understanding connected speech figure importantly in the history of expert systems. Harpy, HWIM (Hear What I Mean), and Hearsay I, II and III were ARPA funded speech understanding projects, and Hearsay III evolved into a general purpose expert systems building tool, using the blackboard architecture.

The use of artificial intelligence in education has a spotty history. Much computer aided instruction is little more than (pre-computer) programmed instruction, implemented on a computer. AI can enter in a number of ways. The system can attempt to build a model of the student, as in BUGGY, which teaches arithmetic. An expert system can essentially act as master to a student apprentice, as in STEAMER, an engine expert. A student can use the explanation facility provided in virtually all expert systems to analyze expert decision-making. The system can function in a more traditional teaching role: answering questions, working examples, critiquing student solutions, suggesting references, etc.

This broader approach to education brings in the use of "intelligent agents," the same sort of constructs that are now being put forward as the answer to today's information overload. Just as they can teach, they can select the articles you want to read for you from your newspaper or magazine (on the web), summarize those of more limited interest, and deep-six the rest. They can follow your investments, the sports teams you root for, and on and on. They're new; they're exciting. They are being hailed by some as another salvation for the field of AI. The mathematical aspects of these applications are in their learning and search functions.

Artificial creativity is somewhat controversial. There is a strong argument that there are things that computers shouldn't do, even if they can[**44**]. But computer-composed music goes back to the early days of AI, and can take the form of attempts to originate, or attempts to compose "ala" a real composer. In both cases, there are rules and randomness, and a strong mathematical component. There have been presentations of computer music at mathematical meetings. Computer created music seems closer to most human-created music than does the work of such moderns as John Cage. The computer artist, Aaron, the creation of the human artist, Harold Cohen, is quite successful[**27**]. The question most often raised in this case is whether Aaron is an artificial artist, or merely an extension of his creator. We won't enter this controversy.

We also won't dwell for long on the programming language and hardware aspects of AI. While AI programs have been written in virtually all high level languages, as well as assembly and machine languages, LISP and Prolog, although not the first, have been the most popular development languages. LISP, as first developed by the AI pioneer, John McCarthy, was very mathematical, and very simple, in structure. The basic data structure was the list; the basic operation was function evaluation. The language was interpreted and not compiled, and programs could act on programs. "Functional programming" is viewed by some as a synonym for programming in LISP. Eventually, every major AI center had its own version of LISP, and these became more and more elaborate, and bigger and bigger. Some LISP implementations could compile at least parts of their programs. It's amusing to compare the LISP 1.5 manual [**25**]with Xerox's Interlisp manual[**41**]. Eventually, the US Department of Defense stepped in and contracted for a standard version of LISP, Common LISP[**40**]. Prolog, from *programmation logique*, is another declarative (i.e., non-procedural) language, which was not compiled, and Prolog programs can act on themselves as data[**6**]. To over-simplify, Prolog implemented resolution with unification in the first-order predicate calculus, restricted to "Horn clauses," $p_1 \wedge p_2 \wedge \cdots \wedge p_n \to q$. Eventually, compiled forms of Prolog became available, as well as attempts to parallelize it. There have been many special-purpose languages within AI, most notably the expert-systems shells. Today, many AI programs developed in LISP or Prolog, or with special-purpose tools, are eventually implemented in C.

Early AI work was done on whatever machines were available. The DEC 10 and DEC 20 and Xerox Alto are machines which are well known as early AI platforms. Then came the LISP machines, by LMI, Symbolics, TI and Xerox. They used versions of LISP essentially as assembly languages. Now, AI is done on whatever hardware is available, or on custom chips.

Early in the history of AI, there was a question as to whether artificial intelligence should try to duplicate human thought processes at the neural level[**28**]. The proponents of this approach lost the early battles, but developments in computer hardware, including parallel processing, gave new impetus to this "low level" approach, and neural networks are an important, and mathematical, area of current research. There are important applications of neural networks in AI, including hybrid systems, involving neural nets along with more traditional AI techniques.

3. Structure

Usually, the first task encountered in solving a problem by machine is the task of representing the problem. Sometimes, the right representation makes all the difference in the world in solving the problem. A typical example of this case is the famous "mutilated checkerboard" problem: Thirty-two dominoes, each the size of two checkerboard squares, can cover the checkerboard. Can the board resulting from the removal of two diagonally opposite corner squares be covered with thirty-one dominoes? The solution is clear, if we think of the squares as colored in the usual fashion.

Much of Artificial Intelligence problem solving consists of searching graphs for solution paths. Suppose we want to solve the old, "missionaries and cannibals" problem. We begin with three missionaries and three cannibals on one bank of a river, with a boat that can carry one or two people and can be rowed by one.

We want to get the group across the river as efficiently as possible, and assume cooperation of all concerned, subject to the constraint that at no time may there be on either bank a group with both missionaries and cannibals in which the cannibals outnumber the missionaries. We solve the problem by constructing a graph, with nodes representing each "viable" arrangement of people and boat, and connecting nodes by arcs which represent "moves" of the boat. We then seek a shortest path from our starting node to the node representing a crossing by everyone.

For another example, consider the problem of getting exactly four quarts of a liquid into an unmarked five quart jug, using only it and a three quart jug to measure. Here, our nodes would represent ordered pairs of integers, corresponding to the contents of the jugs, and directed arcs would represent filling, emptying and decanting. Again, we seek a (preferably shortest) path from a starting node to a goal node.

In the two examples just given, it is easy to generate the whole graph in the computer. In the case of more complicated problems, the graph may be too large, or may even be potentially infinite, and the program generates portions of the graph as needed.

We can illustrate the most important classical AI search algorithm, the A*-algorithm of Hart, Nielssen and Raphael, for attacking the general problem of finding a shortest path from start to goal with the most basic of scenaria[**31**]. Suppose we wish to plan a road trip from, say, Orlando to Providence. We wish to use interstate highways, and minimize total distance. We have a map giving road distances between junctions of interstates, and a means of measuring "crow flight" distances on our map. We build a path from start to goal by dynamically estimating, for each node on the graph, the minimum distance from start to goal on a path passing through that node. Note that, if this information were available exactly, we could find the desired path easily. Our heuristic procedure is to begin with the starting node, estimating the optimal distance as the straight-line distance. We place on a stack, OPEN, the nodes adjacent to the start node, together with pointers back to the start node, and with the minimum distance function estimated as the sum of the distance from the start and the straight line distance to the goal. We then continue our work on the node on OPEN with the smallest value for this function. The algorithm continues with estimates as the sum of "best distance from start so far" and straight-line distance to goal. The search terminates when the goal node is on OPEN with the smallest minimum distance function of all nodes on OPEN. It is guaranteed to find a shortest path, if any path exists, and is usually better than less selective algorithms, like breadth-first or depth-first search. It is a form of best-first search. In general graphs, the algorithm works this successfully, if the estimate of distance remaining to goal is an underestimate of true distance which respects the triangle inequality. Versions of the algorithm which violate these rules may be less efficient or may fail to find the shortest path, but are sometimes used in practice.

Sometimes the "state-space graph" to be searched is obvious; sometimes finding the right graph to search is the main step to a solution. Some problems must be approached hierarchically; that is, in searching the graph, we find that we must replace an arc with a new graph to be searched. When solving the problem of, "How do I go to Baltimore from my home in Boca Raton?", I start out with a graph that has arcs from Boca Raton to each of the three airports which I take planes out of. After I solve that planning problem, I create a new graph with a start at my home, and a goal at the airport I have decided on, and solve the smaller problem it represents. The ability to split a problem into subproblems of different "granularity" is an important aspect of human problem-solving which must be captured in successful machine problem-solvers. The use of this technique, as well as an approach which tried to find paths by working in both directions, using "operators" to reduce differences between start and goal, called, "means-end analysis," figures importantly in the General Problem Solver of Newell, Shaw and Simon.

In some cases, AND-OR graphs are used to represent the subdivision of a problem into sub-problems. Here the graph is a rooted tree, with the root representing the whole problem. AND nodes represent sets of problems which must all be solved to solve the node; at OR nodes, only one successor must be solved. Game trees are essentially a restricted type of AND-OR graphs. Let us consider a game with two players, the maximizer and the minimizer. [This is a way of looking at zero-sum two person games.] Let us assume the maximizer is to play first, and that we are playing the role of the maximizer. Arcs from the start node represent the maximizer's possible first moves. At each successor node, arcs represent moves of the minimizer. According to the conventions of the mathematical theory of games, we assume that the minimizer will always make the best move, and we seek best moves for the maximizer. The standard method is to generate a prescribed number of levels of the graph at each stage of play. Some "static evaluation function" is used to evaluate the nodes at the base of the subtree that has been generated, and the value is propagated upward to the choice node by using the assumption of each player's making the best possible move. In general, some sort of pruning method is used to cut down on the number of nodes at bottom level which must be evaluated. The most common method, alpha-beta pruning, involves carrying upper and lower bound information on the value of the function at the choice node, and using this information to avoid considering parts of the subtree that cannot figure in the optimal solution. In general, the quality of play is determined by the depth of the subtree and the quality of the evaluation function. In Samuel's checker playing program, the evaluation function is improved by a genetic algorithm, one which learns from experience. In both chess and checkers, the game is split into stages, beginning with a prescribed start, and with possibly different depths at different stages, but the main ingredients of machine game playing remain fairly similar, game to game.

Another direct application of mathematical structure to AI is the use of conceptual graphs, developed by John Sowa and others[**39**].

Wang [**43**] programmed his computer to prove assertions in the propositional calculus through the orderly application of a few simple rules. Essentially, the method works like this:

Consider a proposition of the form (expression 1) $\vee$ (expression 2) $\Rightarrow$ (expression 3).

Obviously, this is equivalent to (expression 1) $\Rightarrow$ (expression 3), together with (expression 2) $\Rightarrow$ (expression 3). Similarly, a proposition of the form (expression 1) $\Rightarrow$ (expression 2) $\wedge$ (expression 3) is equivalent to the pair of propositions (expression 1) $\Rightarrow$ (expression 2) and (expression 1) $\Rightarrow$ (expression 3). These equivalencies are used to reduce a proposition to prove to a set of propositions without $\vee$ on the left or $\wedge$ on the right. If only $\vee$, $\wedge$ and $\neg$ occur, and the terms appearing are all atoms, the statements can only be proved if the same atom appears on both sides, or appears on the same side both with and without a $\neg$. The actual method is a bit more complicated, since it also handles $\rightarrow$, $\leftarrow$ and $\leftrightarrow$, and allows manipulation of $\neg$. It was impressively effective when it was introduced.

We shall first illustrate resolution in the propositional calculus, and then in the predicate calculus. First, let p, q and r be propositions. It is clear that $\neg p \vee q$ and $p \vee r$ together imply $q \vee r$. This sort of "cancellation" is used to derive consequences of sets of assumptions. It is clear that it can be used to handle the usual forms of syllogisms. We give three classical syllogisms, each followed by the equivalent application of resolution.

$p \rightarrow q$	$\neg p \vee q$	$p \rightarrow q$	$\neg p \vee q$	$p \rightarrow q$	$\neg p \vee q$
p	p	$q \rightarrow r$	$\neg q \vee r$	$\neg q$	$\neg q$
q	q	$p \rightarrow r$	$\neg p \vee r$	$\neg p$	$\neg p$

The method becomes resolution refutation when assumptions and the negation of the desired conclusion are used to arrive at the null clause. The method becomes a complete proof method when "factoring," replacing $p \vee p$ with p, is added. To extend the method to the first order predicate calculus, one must, of course, allow substitution of variables and constants for universally quantified variables. In fact, the method is applied to a proof of a theorem in first order predicate calculus, by first reducing the task to deriving the empty, or null clause from a conjunction of clauses, including the negation of the conclusion of the theorem. The clauses are each disjunctions of individual terms, some of which may be negated. All variables are universally quantified, and each clause's variables are distinct from the variables in all other clauses. The reduction may be accomplished algorithmically, by eliminating implication (converting $p \rightarrow q$ to $\neg p \vee q$), moving $\neg$ inwards with DeMorgan's laws, using different variables for different quantifiers, moving quantifiers outwards, replacing existentially quantified variables with so-called Skolem constants or functions (e.g., in the domain of integers, the fact that there is an integer greater than 4, $\exists x(x > 4)$, may be replaced with $A > 4$, where A is an unknown constant; and the fact that there is no largest integer, $\forall y \exists x(x > y)$, may be replaced with $A(y) > y$, where $A(y)$ is an unknown function of y), and then applying distributive and associative laws to get a conjunction of disjunctive expressions.

Automation of this procedure required finding a good way of choosing substitutions for variables of different clauses, in order to apply resolution. This was accomplished by J. A. Robinson in 1965 with the unification algorithm[**34**]. That still left major strategic difficulties in applying resolution: how to choose the clauses to resolve. This is still an important issue, and is addressed in Hélène Kirchner's paper in this volume, as well as in a vast number of books and papers. Choice strategies and indexing systems for clauses in storage are ways in which automated reasoning systems differ.

Expert systems come in a wide variety. We shall discuss some of the "pure" forms, and then briefly indicate the sorts of combinations that have been used. Let us begin with rule-based systems[**22**]. Such a system's knowledge is contained in its rules. We first illustrate some of the features and mechanisms with a toy "freshman mathematics advisor," which does not work well, but is not worse than all human advisors. The system is to help a student select a single mathematics course.

Here are some of the rules:

R1: If the student has a 4 or a 5 in AP Calculus BC, and is a mathematics, physics, computer science or engineering major, the student should take matrix theory.

R2: If the student has a 4 or a 5 in AP Calculus BC, the student should take no mathematics.

R3: If the student has a 3 in AP Calculus BC, or a 4 or a 5 in AP Calculus AB, and is a mathematics, physics or engineering major, the student should take Calculus 3.

R4: If the student has a 3 in AP Calculus BC, or a 4 or a 5 in AP Calculus AB, and is a computer science major, the student should take matrix theory.

R5: If the student has a 3 in AP Calculus BC, or a 4 or a 5 in AP Calculus AB, the student should take no mathematics.

R6: If the student has a 3 in AP Calculus AB, and is a mathematics, physics, chemistry, computer science or engineering major, the student should take Calculus 2.

R7: If the student has a 3 in AP Calculus AB, and is a business, biology, psychology, geology, nursing, social science or education major, the student should take idiot statistics.

R8: If the student has a 3 in AP Calculus AB, and is an arts and letters major, the student should take Math for Poets 1 or 2.

R9: If the student has taken AP Calculus, or other high school calculus, and is a mathematics, physics, chemistry, computer science or engineering major, the student should take Calculus 1.

R10: If the student has taken AP Calculus, or other high school calculus, and is a business, biology or geology major, the student should take Business Calculus.

[We omit the next ten rules; the reader can certainly supply them.]

R21: If the student has passed intermediate algebra (or algebra for college students) with a C or better, and is an arts and letters major, the student should take Math for Poets 1 or 2.

R22: If the student has passed intermediate algebra (or algebra for college students) with a C or better, the student should take college algebra.

R23: If the student has passed algebra 1 with a C or better, the student should take intermediate algebra.

This rather overlong list will serve to illustrate several features of rule-based systems. First, we shall consider the system as a forward-chaining system, (also called bottom-up, or data-directed), with the rules attempted in order, and we shall require it to give a single answer. That is, we begin with R1. If the premises of R1 are satisfied, we give the advice in the conclusion; otherwise we go to R2 and repeat. Once we have given advice, we leave the system. Thus, there is no conflict, for example, between R21 and R22. If the premises of R21 are satisfied, then R22 will not be tested. The reader may wonder what would be done with a student for whom no rule "fired." Kick him or her out? Only if it were ascertained that the student had passed no course essentially equivalent to one on the list. And anyway, the system is just a toy! One question that arises is, what do you do about information looked at when considering one question, which is relevant to another? This is a question of efficiency, with the answer varying according to features of the system, if the information on the premises is stored before the system is activated. On the other hand, if the information must be asked of the student, or looked up in a separate database, one would think that the answers would be kept active for use in subsequent questions. Perhaps, there could be links between rules, so that, if one rule failed because a certain precondition failed, no subsequent rule with that precondition would be examined. Another approach is to arrange premises of rules in a graph, and traverse the graph to reach the goal of giving advice. This is the idea of a decision tree; it is not always classed as a part of artificial intelligence. In fact, the system of rules given here could be dismissed as being simply a standard computer algorithm for course selection. The same argument has been raised against some well-known, successful expert systems.

The second major way of applying a set of rules like those just given is backward-chaining (also called top-down, or goal-directed). In backward-chaining, instead of immediately applying the rules in the order given, one gives an order to the "goals," (here the, "the student should..." parts). For example, we might take the frequently held view that the highest goal should be, the student should take no math. Then we would try R2 and R5. We would tell a math major who had a 5 in AP Calculus BC to take no math. Oops! Better make taking matrix theory the highest goal. Then Calculus 3. Again, the issue of how to handle information from applying previous rules is a big one.

The reader can probably construct systems which have more personal appeal; the points to be noted include the versatility of the idea. Rule-based systems like this one can be constructed to make decisions in taxonomy, food or wine selection, choice of motels, etc. Note that in taxonomy systems, the rules probably would create a hierarchy of classifications, creating a "subgoaling" approach. The famous MYCIN system made clinical diagnoses of infectious diseases of the blood. It was a backward chaining system. MYCIN had another feature, though. The rules supplied by human experts, MD's specializing in the types of infections under consideration, are not absolute. They involve the representation of degrees of belief in certain diagnoses, based on symptoms. This adds two major complications. First, there must be a way of calculating with the "certainty factors." It turns out that they do not correspond exactly to ordinary mathematical probabilities. The developers of the system felt that they could not simply use Bayes' Theorem to calculate, and derived their own rules for the calculation. Second, even though the system works on the assumption that the symptoms are generated by a single disease, the uncertainty forces the system to consider other diseases after it has given one answer. As was suggested earlier, there are many schemes for handling uncertain data, or uncertainty in rules themselves, in expert systems, including Bayes' Theorem, the MYCIN scheme, Dempster-Shafer Theory and others[**11**] [**35**][**33**].

Some expert systems simply involve the use of a given set of rules to make decisions. There are many "shells" available to build such systems. The shells generally have a rule acquisition and editing language, a dialogue facility and an explanation mechanism. Some have a probability calculus. There are several families of shells that have their origins in MYCIN; others are descendants of such early expert systems as Prospector or Caduceus.Some shells were built up from scratch. Many use LISP as the development language; a smaller number use prolog; other languages are used, too. In some cases, the system may be armed with causal knowledge–systems making diagnoses of machine failures would be of this type, for example. Here the causal probability described by Glenn Shafer is quite applicable. Other systems create rules statistically from data. Metadendral, a major part of the early and still active DENDRAL system, learned from data. Forecasting systems, such as weather forecasting systems, are of this type. Again, there are shells available, several evolving from the work of Donald Michie. Some systems are "production systems," which have their roots in psychology. Facts and rules are both subject to orderings, to determine what facts are checked to see if what rules fire. The most famous and important tool for building production systems is OPS, Carnegie-Mellon University's "Our Production System," which actually exists in several versions. The most famous and important system built with OPS is R1/XCON, which configures computer systems for DEC. It and descendants and offshoots are in constant use.

Uncertainty in artificial intelligence (in expert systems and elsewhere) is sometimes handled through the use of modal logic, or of fuzzy logic, where degrees of truth are possible[**15**][**48**]. While the necessity of handling inexact concepts (bright, when you are taking pictures, for example) is an obvious complication for human reasoning, and hence for machine reasoning, most of the advertised breakthroughs for fuzzy logic represent human applications of common sense, rather than theoretical progress. This sort of "application of AI" appears in ads for TV sets and for cameras.

One important factor in human intelligence is the ability to learn. It then follows that machine learning is an important part of AI. We have noted one sort of learning in the discussion of expert systems. This is an instance of "case-based reasoning," an important part of AI in its own right. Another form of machine learning is genetic algorithms, which behave like the evaluation functions in Samuel's checker player. Thomas Mitchell's version spaces provide a way of building decision trees from positive and negative examples, and form an important learning technique, which is quite mathematical in structure[**30**]. Neural networks are another example of systems which learn, and are felt by some proponents to model human learning in a more direct fashion than other systems.

We should again mention the concept of planning, and the frame problem. Let us consider the problem of planning the motions of a robot which needs to sort and put away a number of objects. We assume that the robot is capable of all the physical actions, as well as all the object identifications which are necessary. We are then faced with identifying pre- and post-conditions for all the operations which the robot must perform. It is thus necessary to identify all those conditions relevant to the task which are subject to change when operations are performed. In general, human beings can make this sort of distinction very easily, although we occasional make mistakes. [My then teen-age son and I had a big argument once over whether or not I had left my itinerary for a trip where he couldn't miss it. It turned out that the draft from my closing the door upon my departure had released the itinerary from its refrigerator magnet, and it had moved out of sight.] The major problem is cataloging everything that can change, and then handling the effects of the operations, as well as accounting for changes that could occur with the passing of time. The ideas of pre- and post-conditions for operations are part of all planning programs, going back to early AI; working with time figures prominently in recent attacks on treating the frame problem, and is the topic of Martin Golumbic's chapter in this book.

4. Examples

We shall sketch a selection of examples which fall under the heading of mathematical aspects of artificial intelligence, in order to give a better indication of the breadth of the field.

The search for combinatorial structures of various sorts, for design of experiments, coding and cryptography, graph theory, geometry and topology, among others, has a long history, and was an obvious and early application of computers in mathematics. Blind search, of course, is subject to the combinatorial explosion, so heuristic search was employed very early in this area, although not always classified as artificial intelligence. Jean-Louis Lauriere's program and language for a number of problems in combinatorics was cited earlier. "Hill-climbing"–searching a state-space by moving to adjacent nodes whenever some figure of merit is improved–is a very natural approach to search for solutions to design problems, and has been used on a variety of such problems. Simulated annealing, an improvement on hill-climbing, in which moves away from local optima are permitted or forbidden according to the values of a random variable whose probabilities are influenced by heuristic weights[**24**], was used to get new results on the famous "football pool" problem in the 1980's[**42**], and has been employed in other search problems since[**45**]. Refinements of simulated annealing, using expert systems techniques to "tweak" the probabilities further, would seem to offer much promise for this type of application. The idea would be to employ heuristics which a human expert would use to direct a search, either by paper-and-pencil or by computer. Hantao Zhang and others have used machine theorem-provers to construct latin squares and related designs[**49**]. Other uses of AI methods figured in the development of the CRC Handbook of Combinatorial Designs[**8**].

It is apparent that the chances for success of programs conducting searches in large state-spaces would be improved by restricting the size of the space, as long as the solutions were still there. An analogy from a "toy" AI application frequently taught in elementary courses: Let us solve the game of tic-tac-toe. We may as well assume that the first move is by x, and is in (a)the upper left corner, (b)upper center or (c)the center. In case (a), we assume the first move by o to be (i)upper center, (ii)upper right corner, (iii)center, (iv)right center or (v)lower right corner. In case (b), we assume the second move in (i)upper left corner, (ii)left center, (iii)center, (iv)lower left corner or (v)lower center. In case (c), o's possibilities are (i)upper left corner or (ii)upper center. Continuing in this manner, we get a much more manageable graph for the game. A group of researchers in AI and mathematical computing at the University of Oregon is engaged in a promising effort to exploit group theory to develop "symmetry-breaking predicates" to accomplish this sort of reduction in search in various satisfiability problems[**9**]. This is a very interesting project, relating AI and mathematics in several ways.

The automated reasoning group at Argonne National Lab, under the leadership of Larry Wos, has a long history in using automated mathematics to solve, or help humans solve, problems in many areas, including mathematics. The three Argonne products, AURA, Otter and EQP, are all, in some sense, resolution-based theorem provers, with varying strategies[**47**][**29**]. They have been promoted to the mathematics community through workshops and through open invitations to mathematicians to present conjectures to be checked, as well as through texts, research monographs and journal articles. We mention two recent developments.

W. McCune and A. D. Sands presented some new single implicative axioms for groups and for abelian groups, discovered and proved by Otter, in the December, 1996 *American Mathematical Monthly*, and in the same month, McCune, using EQP, proved the "Robbins Conjecture," a result in Boolean algebra, which had eluded mathematicians since the 1930's. While it is possible to exaggerate the significance of these results, they are exciting, and bode well for the future of automated reasoning in mathematics.

Learning was mentioned earlier, and we cited Mitchell's version spaces as a rather mathematical construct for a machine learning program. In the September, 1997 issue of *Artificial Intelligence*, C. A. Gunter, T-H Ngair and D. Subramanian use the theory of partially ordered sets, in particular, employing the concept of an anti-chain, to make progress in the use of version spaces, as well as to analyze assumption-based truth maintenance systems.

Vic Nalwa's chapter on vision introduces us to many important aspects of machine vision. David Mumford's review of Jean-Michel Morel and Sergio Solimini's book, *Variational methods in image segmentation*, in the April, 1996 issue of the *Bulletin of the American Mathematical Society,* discusses more technical, "hard analysis" aspects of machine vision, and would be a good starting point for someone wanting to venture out in that direction. The theory is rich, and deep, and there are exciting new results.

5. Conclusion

This volume is meant to introduce readers to the fascinating interplay between mathematics and artificial intelligence. It can only scratch the surface, and this chapter is meant to provide a little background for readers new to AI, whet their appetities, and provide some directions for future investigations. The authors of this volume feel strongly that the fields of AI and mathematics have much to offer each other, and hope that we have made a contribution to future efforts at collaboration between the practitioners of the two areas.

We provide a somewhat sketchy bibliography, which should, however, contain enough pointers to enable readers to find material on everything we discussed here. The texts by Bender [**4**]and Ginsberg[**19**] would probably be the most appropriate to our readers. We also list the *Handbook* and the *Encyclopedia of Artificial Intelligence* [**3**][**7**][**37**]. We have mentioned the most important research journal in the field of AI, *Artificial Intelligence.* We should also cite the newer journal, *Annals of Mathematics and Artificial Intelligence,* published by Baltzer Science Publishers, with more than 22 volumes since 1990. The journal is described as "devoted to reporting significant contributions on the interaction of mathematical and computational techniques reflecting the evolving disciplines of artificial intelligence...The scope of AMAI is intended to represent a wide range of topics of concern to scholars applying quantitative, combinatorial, logical, algebraic and algorithmic methods to AI areas as diverse as decision support, automated deduction, reasoning, knowledge-based systems, machine learning, computer vision, robotics and planning. These include applied logicians, algorithms and complexity researchers, AI theorists, and applications specialists using mathematical methods. In this way, we hope to influence the spawning of new areas of applied mathematics and the strengthening of the scientific underpinnings of artificial intelligence."

Among symposia devoted to the interplay of AI and the mathematical sciences are the series of International Symposia on Artificial Intelligence and Statistics, held biennially since 1987, and the International Symposia on Artificial Intelligence and Mathematics, held since 1990. The Symposium in January, 1998 in Fort Lauderdale, Florida, is the fifth of this biennial series. The Symposium's goal is to foster interactions among mathematics, theoretical computer science, and artificial intelligence. The meeting includes paper presentation, invited speakers, and special topic sessions. Topic sessions in the past have covered computational learning theory, nonmonotonic reasoning, and computational complexity issues in AI. The editorial board of the *Annals of Mathematics and Artificial Intelligence* serves as the permanent Advisory Committee for the AI and Mathematics series.

References

[1] R. B. Banerji, *Theory of Problem-Solving: An Approach to Artificial Intelligence*, Elsevier Science Publishing, New York, 1969

[2] R. B. Banerji, *Artificial Intelligence: A Theoretical Approach*, North Holland, Amsterdam, 1980

[3] A. Barr And E. Feigenbaum, *The Handbook of Artificial Intelligence, v1-2*, Morgan-Kaufmann, San Mateo, CA, 1981

[4] E. A. Bender, *Mathematical Methods in Artificial Intelligence*, IEEE Computer Society Press, Piscataway, NJ, 1996

[5] W. W. Bledsoe and D. Lovelands, eds, *Automated Theorem Proving: After 25 Years*, AMS, Providence, 1984

[6] W. F. Clocksin and C. S. Melish, *Programming in Prolog*, Springer-Verlag, New York, 1981

[7] P. R. Cohen and E. Feigenbaum, *The Handbook of Artificial Intelligence, v3*, Morgan-Kaufmann, San Mateo, CA, 1982

[8] C. Colbourn and J. Dinitz, eds, *The CRC Handbook of Combinatorial Designs*, CRC Press, Boca Raton, 1996

[9] J. M. Crawford, M. Ginsberg, E. Luks and A. Roy, *Symmetry Breaking Predicates for Search Problems*, Fifth International Conference on Principles of Knowledge Representation and Reasoning (1996)

[10] R. Davis and D. B. Lenat, *Knowledge-Based Systems in Artificial Intelligence*, McGraw-Hill, San Francisco, 1982

[11] A. P. Dempster, *A Generalization of Bayesian Inference*, J. Roy. Stat. Soc. B **30** (1968) 205-247

[12] G. E. Ernst and A. Newell, *GPS: A Case Study in Generality and Problem-Solving*, Academic Press, New York, 1969

[13] E. Feigenbaum and J. Feldman, eds, *Computers and Thought*, McGraw-Hill, New York, 1963

[14] E. Feigenbaum, P. McCorduck and H. P. Nii, *The Rise of the Expert Company*, Random House, New York, 1988

[15] M. Fitting, *Proof Methods for Modal and Intuitionistic Logics*, D. Reidel, Boston, 1983

[16] K. Ford, C. Glymour and P. Hayes, *Android Epistemology*, MIT Press, Cambridge, MA, 1995

[17] M. R. Genesereth and N. J. Nilsson, *Logical Foundations of Artificial Intelligence*, Morgan-Kaufmann, San Mateo, CA, 1987

[18] G. Gentzen, *Untersuchungen über das logische Schliessen*, Math Z. **39** (1935)176-210, 405-431

[19] M. Ginsberg, *Essentials of Artificial Intelligence*, Morgan-Kaufmann, San Mateo, CA, 1993

[20] D. Goodman and R. Keene, *Man Versus Machine*, H3 Publications, 1997

[21] P. Harmon and D. King, *Expert Systems–Artificial Intelligence in Business*, John Wiley and Sons, New York, 1985

[22] F. Hayes-Roth, D. A. Waterman and D. B. Lenat, eds, *Building Expert Systems*, Addison-Wesley, Reading, MA 1983

[23] C. Hewett, *PLANNER: A Language for Proving Theorems in Robots*, Proceedings of the First IJCAI, Morgan-Kaufmann, San Mateo, CA (1969) 295-301

[24] S. Kirkpatrick, Jr, C. D. Gelatt and M. P. Vecchi, *Optimization by simulated annealing*, Science **220** (1983) 4598

[25] J. McCarthy et al, *LISP 1.5 Progammer's Manual*, MIT Press, Cambridge, MA, 1962

[26] P. McCorduck, *Machines Who Think*, W. H. Freeman, San Francisco, 1979
[27] P. McCorduck, *Aaron's Code*, W. H. Freeman, New York, 1991
[28] W. McCulloch and W. Pitts, *A Logical Calculus of the Ideas Imminent in Nervous Activity*, Bull Math. Biophys. (1943)
[29] W. McCune, *OTTER 2.0 Users Guide*, Argonne National Laboratory, Argonne, IL, 1990
[30] T. M. Mitchell, *Version Spaces: An Approach to Concept Learning*, PhD Thesis, Stanford University, Stanford, CA, 1977
[31] N. J. Nilsson, *Problem-Solving Methods in Artificial Intelligence*, McGraw-Hill, New York, 1971
[32] N. J. Nilsson, *Principles of Artificial Intelligence*, Tioga, Palo Alto, CA 1980
[33] J. Pearl, *Probabalistic Reasoning in Intelligent Systems*, Morgan-Kaufmann, San Mateo, CA, 1988
[34] J. A. Robinson, *A machine-oriented logic based on the resolution principle*, JACM **12** (1965) 23-41
[35] G. Shafer, *A Mathematical Theory of Evidence*, Princeton University Press, Princeton, 1976
[36] G. Shafer, *The Art of Causal Conjecture*, MIT Press, Cambridge, MA, 1996
[37] S. C. Shapiro, *Encyclopedia of Artificial Intelligence, 2d Ed*, John Wiley and Sons, New York, 1992
[38] J. A. Slagle, *A Heuristic Program that Solves Symbolic Integration Problems in Freshman Calculus*, JACM 10 (1963) 507-520
[39] J. F. Sowa, *Conceptual Structures: Information Processing in Mind and Machine*, Addison-Wesley, Reading, MA 1984
[40] G. L. Steele, Jr. et al, *Common LISP: The Language*, Digital, Burlington, MA, 1984
[41] W. Teitelman et al, *InterLisp Reference Manual*, Xerox PARC, Palo Alto, CA, 1978
[42] P. J. van Laarhoven, E. H. L. Aarts, J. H. van Lint and L. T. Wille, *New upper bounds for the football pool problem for 6, 7 and 8 matches*, J Combin. Theory, Ser A, **52** (1989) 304-312
[43] H. Wang, *Towards Mechanical Mathematics*, IBM J. Res. Devel. 4 (1960) 224-268
[44] J. Weizenbaum, *Computer Power and Human Reason*, W. H. Freeman, San Francisco, 1976
[45] L. T. Wille, *Improved binary code coverings by simulated annealing*, Congressus Numerantium 73 (1990) 53-58
[46] T. Winograd, *Understanding Natural Language*, Academic Press, New York, 1972
[47] L. Wos, *Automated Reasoning: Introduction and Applications*, Prentice-Hall, Englewood cliffs, NJ, 1984
[48] L. A. Zadeh, *Fuzzy logic and approximate reasoning*, Symthese **30** (19750 407-428
[49] H. Zhang and F. E. Bennett, *Existence of Some (3,2,1)-HCOLS and (3,2,1)-ICOILS*, J. Comb. Math. and Comb. Comp. **22** (1996) 13-22

Department of Mathematical Sciences, Florida Atlantic University, Boca Raton, FL 33431

E-mail address: Hoffman@fau.edu

Proceedings of Symposia in Applied Mathematics
Volume **55**, 1998

Reasoning About Time

MARTIN CHARLES GOLUMBIC
BAR-ILAN UNIVERSITY, RAMAT-GAN, ISRAEL
GOLUMBIC@CS.BIU.AC.IL

1. INTRODUCTION

Reasoning about time is essential for applications in artificial intelligence and in many other disciplines. Given certain explicit relationships between a set of events, we would like to have the ability to infer additional relationships which are implicit in those given. For example, the transitivity of "before" and "contains" may allow us to infer information regarding the sequence of events. Such inferences are essential in story understanding, planning and causal reasoning. There are a great number of practical problems in which one is interested in constructing a time line where each particular event or phenomenon corresponds to an interval representing its duration. These include seriation in archeology, behavioral psychology, temporal reasoning, scheduling, and combinatorics. Other applications arise in non-temporal contexts, for example, in molecular biology, where arrangement of DNA segments along a linear DNA chain involves similar problems.

A system to reason about time should have a knowledge base consisting of temporal and other information, a mechanism for determining consistency of temporal data, and routines for answering queries and discovering or inferring new facts. We will present several formal models to represent temporal knowledge which can be used in reasoning systems. Our interests are in the mathematical and computation properties of these models and the algorithms which can be applied to effectively solve temporal problems.

Example 1. *Fred was reading the Orlando Sentinel* while *eating breakfast in the hotel restaurant. Shortly* before he finished *Marty joined him. Fred put the paper down, and they discussed the plans for publishing the volume of papers from the AMS short course. The waitress took Marty's order. Glenn and Vic's papers* were taken care of *but* before *deciding who should referee Catherine's paper,* they saw *Helene enter the restaurant, and Fred asked her to join the discussion. He wondered if the others would be coming too, but Helene said* she saw *Monty sitting in the lobby at* 7 o'clock *when she went out jogging. He had eaten breakfast at* 6 am, *the first customer of the day. No one had heard from Jean-Louis, but he rarely eats breakfast. The three of them made the* final *decisions. It was a* half hour before *the first morning lectures*

1991 *Mathematics Subject Classification.* Primary 68T99, 68R10.

would begin. *Fred drank the last of his coffee and left to go for a walk* just as *Marty's bagel and lox was being served. Helene filled her plate at the buffet and saw Fred at the phone, probably calling Jean-Louis to be sure he was awake. (He was, and he had eaten breakfast with Monty!) At* 9 am *the lectures* started, *and everyone was* present. *That is, everyone except Catherine, Glenn and Vic, who were* still *snowed in up North.*

This example illustrates many of the issues that arise in temporal reasoning. First, there is the *chronology* of the story which takes place in the restaurant during a certain "window of time": Fred is eating, Marty enters, they discuss, Helene enters, they conclude the discussion, Fred leaves and Marty is served, Helene fills her plate and Fred phones, lectures start, etc. The narrative follows a time line reporting actions in the order in which they happen. Second, the story provides *temporal information* on other actions which have occurred outside its "window of time": Monty ate at 6 am, was in the lobby at 7am, and Jean-Louis was with him at breakfast. Third, the story gives *temporal clues* through the use of words and expressions: just as, before finishing, 7 o'clock, they saw, everyone was present, half hour before, etc.

All of these allow one to reconstruct a portion of a temporal scenario, that is, what happened, when or in what order, and by whom. It does not help us determine if Jean-Louis was preparing transparencies for his talk or sleeping or working on some research with Monty between breakfast and the lectures, but we can determine that he had no input on who would referee Catherine's paper. Detectives and puzzle enthusiasts, consultants and strategic planners, chefs and building contractors, politicians and college students all reason about time in this way.

There are at least three major approaches to reasoning about time. The first is *quantitative* where we treat the duration of an event in a numerical fashion. The temporal range of the starting point and finishing point, the length of time between disjoint events, and so forth, are numbers which may satisfy specified inequalities or various measurable constraints. Methods used in the quantitative approach may be based on constraint propagation, heuristic search, mathematical programming, and other techniques from artificial intelligence and operations research. The second is *qualititative* where events are represented by abstract time points and time intervals, and we process and deduce "relationships" between them, such as pairs intersecting each other, one preceding, following or containing another, etc. The techniques used in the qualitative approach often involve combinatorial and graph theoretic methods. The third is *logical* where the truth of predicates and propositions vary with time. This approach gives rise to a host of temporal, non-monotonic logics for reasoning about world states which change over time. We can think of other approaches as well, such as statistical or probabilistic temporal reasoning.

It is our belief that no single approach will ever be adequate to handle the diversity of all forms of temporal reasoning problems. Neither will an integrated solution method ever satisfy the virtually unbounded complexity that temporal situations can exhibit. Nevertheless, major strides have been made, and will continue to be made, to handle larger classes of useful problems and to give effective and efficient solutions in important application areas.

Mathematical and computational properties of the time line are intrinsically interwoven. We may not want to rely upon a program for updating and maintaining a database of financial transactions without providing a provably consistent representation for it at any point of time. We may find that the behavior of a hardware circuit depends on timing properties which can be optimized mathematically. Coordinating independent, distributed systems in a changing environment may call for communication protocols satisfying temporal conditions. Underlying mathematical structure of time intervals may give rise to algorithms for scheduling a sequence of actions to achieve a set of goals. The classical Yale Shooting Problem, to determine whether a gun is loaded at time T_n, given the fact that it was loaded at T_0 and a sequence of events (such as firing, reloading, jamming, various uncertainties, etc.), could mean the difference between life and death.

In this article, we provide background reading material for entering the field of temporal reasoning. It is not a complete survey, and it is biased by the author's particular interests. However, it should be a good (qualitative) starting point for anyone new to the field, and may even have some continuing value for the more familiar reader.

1.1. Events in Time: Points and Intervals. An *event* in time may be thought of as an interval $[s, t]$ on the time line where s is its starting endpoint and t is its terminal or finishing endpoint and having a *duration* given by $t - s \geq 0$. The special case where $s = t$ is called a *point event* since it has no duration, and otherwise it will be called an *interval event.*

Explosions, birth, and burial are typical examples of point events, at least from the point of view of an historian; however, they might be treated as interval events by the physicist, midwife or grave digger. Therefore, the granularity of the time line will depend on the context of the application. We will usually treat time as being linearly ordered discrete units, such as minutes, seconds, years, hours, millenia, nanoseconds, etc. Although we may use closed, half open or open intervals to represent temporal events, we generally use closed intervals.

Point events are easier to deal with than interval events, but the latter are more interesting. Consider the following statements:

S_1: Paul dived into the swimming pool before Ringo.

S_2: John finished swimming laps while George was still swimming laps.

We think of diving as a point event, so S_1 has the meaning $dive(Paul) < dive(Ringo)$. But swimming laps has a duration, so while S_2 tells us that $start\_laps(George) < finish\_laps(John) < finish\_laps(George)$, we have no information about who started swimming laps first.

With interval events we have twice as many points to reason about. But that is *not* the reason for the higher complexity. When a statement relates two point events, it is a binary relation. When a statement relates two interval events, it can be a 4-way constraint. For example, S_2 gave us two binary constraints, but S_3 (below) gives a relation among 4 points which cannot be expressed using simple binary relations.

> S_3: Carole and Carly each drove the school bus around town for a few hours today.

The relationship in S_3 requires the 4-way constraint:

$$finish\_bus(Carole) < start\_bus(Carly) \vee finish\_bus(Carly) < start\_bus(Carole)$$

since a bus can have only one driver at a time.

We shall see later that as we add more expressiveness to our relations, we pay for it by increased computational complexity.

1.2. Quantitative Approaches. In Section 2 we will present a model for metric temporal constraint problems (MTCPs) consisting of variables representing time points and sets of inequalities on their differences. Example 2 tells a story about Allan and Judy and Figure 1.1 shows the corresponding temporal constraint network whose edges are labelled by the intervals of possible values for the pairwise differences. Thus, an edge $i \to j$ labelled by $[a, b]$ represents the inequality $a \leq x_j - x_i \leq b$. It is worthwhile noting that two of the edges in the network are labelled by more than one interval indicating a disjunction, that is, the difference for such a pair can be in either interval. As an exercise, the reader may analyse the temporal constraints, ad hoc, and find a consistent solution, i.e., values assigned to the variables x_i such that all the inequalities are satisfied. A formal technique will be given in Section 2.

Example 2. *Allan spent two hours in the library solving the exercises at the end of his chapter. After finishing, he planned to go swimming at the pool for at least 45 minutes but no more than one hour. It is 25 minutes walking from the library to the pool, but by bus it takes only 5 to 15 minutes. Afterwards, he would meet Judy at her house and go to a party. Since Allan lives next door to the pool, he can go to her house by bicycle which is more fun, and takes 45 to 55 minutes. Going by taxi is more expensive, but faster, no more than 10 minutes. Judy had called Allan on his cellular telephone to make the arrangements, and he told her that he was already* *in the library solving the exercises for the past 45 minutes. She told him that she was catching the next train which would get her home in one hour. Then she would change clothes and watch a video movie taking 135 to 140 minutes altogether, but she would wait for him no more than 10 minutes after it finished. Could Allan ride his bicycle to Judy's house and be sure not to miss her?*

The variables and their constraints, as extracted from the story, are the following:

x_0 - Allan started solving the Exercises
x_1 - Allan finished the Exercises

$$120 \leq x_1 - x_0 \leq 120$$

x_2 - Allan started swimming

$$5 \leq x_2 - x_1 \leq 15 \quad \text{or} \quad 25 \leq x_2 - x_1 \leq 25$$

x_3 - Allan finished swimming

$$45 \leq x_3 - x_2 \leq 60$$

x_4 - Allan arrived at Judy's home

$$45 \leq x_4 - x_3 \leq 55 \quad \text{or} \quad 0 \leq x_4 - x_3 \leq 10$$

x_5 - Judy called Allan

$$45 \leq x_5 - x_0 \leq 45$$

x_6 - Judy arrived home

$$60 \leq x_6 - x_5 \leq 60$$

x_7 - Judy finished watching the movies

$$135 \leq x_7 - x_6 \leq 140$$

x_8 - Judy left her house

$$0 \leq x_8 - x_7 \leq 10$$

Allan's goal:

$$0 \leq x_8 - x_4 \leq \infty$$

Remark 1. *Presumably Allan can control the swimming time, but not the bus time. This model does not make such a distinction.*

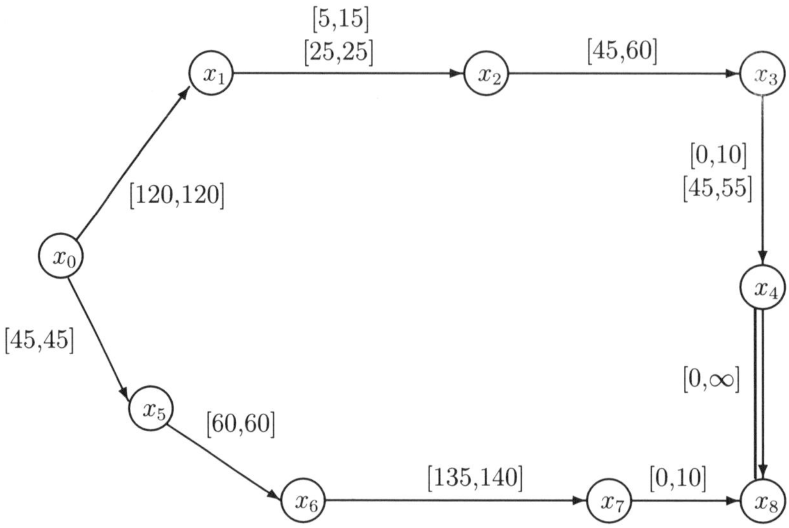

Figure 1.1. The temporal constraint network for Example 2.

1.3. Qualitative Approaches. Some temporal reasoning problems make no mention of numbers, clock times, dates, durations, etc. Rather, only qualitative relations such as *before*, *during*, *after* or *not after* are given between pairs of events. This is often the case in story telling, where we get clues from the natural language text about temporal relationships without specific times stated.

The *seriation problem* asks for a mapping of the events onto the time line such that all the given relations are satisfied, that is, a consistent scenerio. Unlike the metric temporal constraint problems (MTCPs) where numerical methods, including shortest path algorithms and constraint based methods are useful, here a more combinatorial, graph theoretic approach is needed. This reconstruction of the events on the time line from qualitative data is similar to DNA mapping problems in molecular biology where the true DNA sequence of the gene must be built up using overlap data of clone fragments.

One of the techniques most useful with qualitative problems is the propagation of constraints between pairs of events. We will illustrate this on a simple example and postpone a full development of the method to Section 3.

Example 3. *Once upon a time there were four bears, Papa bear, Mama bear, Baby bear and Teddy Bear. Each bear sat at the table to eat his morning porridge, but since there were only two chairs (the third chair was broken in a previous story), the bears had to take turns eating. Baby and Teddy always ate together sharing the* *same chair, and on this day Mama was seated for part of Baby bear's meal when the door opened and in walked their new neighbor, Goldie.*

"What a great aroma," she said. "Can I join for a bowl?" Mama replied, "Sure, but you will have to wait for a chair!" "Yeah, I know all about chairs," said Goldie. So Goldie sat down when Baby and Teddy got up.

Papa entered the kitchen. Looking at Mama he said, "I wouldn't sit at the same table with that girl." Mama answered, "Then it's good you ate already."

In this story, we assume that each character sat at the table for an interval of time without interruption. Let's call these intervals I_B, I_G, I_M, I_P, I_T, subscripts indicating the first initial of the character's name. Since Baby and Teddy always eat together, we have $I_B = I_T$, so there are only four intervals that we have to place on the time line.

Here are some questions to ask:

1. Could Papa and Baby both be at the table together?

2. Could Papa and Mama both be at the table together?

3. Could Papa have spent some time at the table with both Baby and Mama?

4. Did anyone sit at the table with Goldie?

Consider the three relations $\prec$, $\cap$, $\succ$ between intervals, where $I \prec J$ (equiv. $J \succ I$) denotes that I and J are disjoint intervals with I occurring before J, and $I \cap J$ denotes that I and J intersect. We can represent the interval events of our story as the vertices of an oriented graph with edges labelled by the possible relations between pairs of events. For example, if $I \prec J$ or $I \cap J$ are both possible, and the edge $e = (I, J)$ is oriented from I to J, then e will be labelled $\prec \cap$. The graph for our example appears in Figure 1.2.

Our story provides the following facts:

(a) Only two chairs (This is not temporal but resource information.)

(b) $I_B \cap I_M$ Mama and Baby seated when the door opened.

(c) $I_B \prec I_G$ Goldie sat down when Baby got up.

(d) $I_P \prec I_G$ Papa ate before Goldie.

(e) $I_M \cap I_G$ Language clue Papa to Mama, "I wouldn't sit ... with that girl."

Although no relation is stated between I_P and I_B or I_M, we could "reason" that $I_P \prec \cap I_M$, that is, Papa could not eat *after* Mama since that would contradict the last paragraph of the story. Let's formalize that reasoning process using constraint propagation.

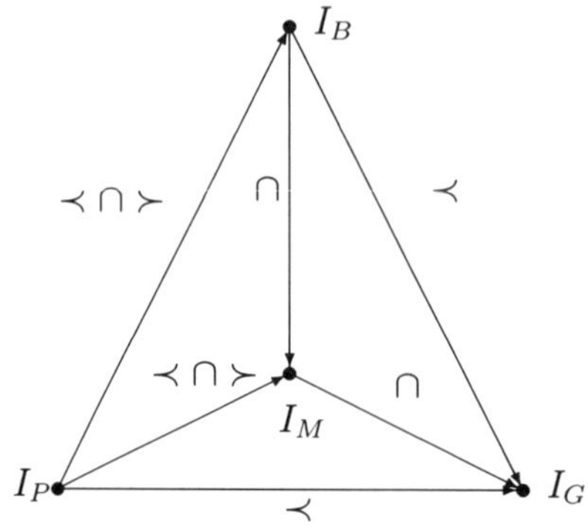

Figure 1.2. The constraint graph before propagation.

The simplest form of propagation is ordinary transitivity, namely if $I \prec J$ and $J \prec K$, then $I \prec K$. But we can define other implications as well between three intervals, for example, $I \prec J$ and $J \cap K$ implies $I \prec \cap K$, which can easily be seen by trying to draw the intervals I, J, K on the time line. This is precisely the rule we used combining facts (d) and (e) to deduce $I_P \prec \cap I_M$. These generalized transitivity rules are given in the multiplication table in Figure 1.3, and illustrates one of the *interval algebras*, namely A_3, which will be studied further in Section 3. This language is limited, as it cannot express the idea that one interval contains another. More complex interval algebras A_6, A_7, A_{13} and ord-Horn allow containment and other primitive relations.

	$\prec$	$\cap$	$\succ$
$\prec$	$\prec$	$\prec \cap$	$\prec \cap \succ$
$\cap$	$\prec \cap$	$\prec \cap \succ$	$\cap \succ$
$\succ$	$\prec \cap \succ$	$\cap \succ$	$\succ$

Figure 1.3. The multiplication table for A_3 constraint propagation.

1.4. Logical Approaches and Related Topics. Logic and logic programming are used widely to express temporal information and to automate reasoning about time. In Section 4, we briefly introduce temporal logic and provide references. Temporal reasoning issues also arise in distributed artificial intelligence with the coordination of multiple agents, and in the area of temporal databases which must maintain a repository of non-static facts and knowledge and answer temporal queries. We provide some motivation and references in Section 5 for these topics.

2. Metric Temporal Constraint Problems - A Qualitative Approach

Constraint networks are frequently used in artificial intelligence to represent sets of values which may be assigned to variables, subject to binary restrictions that may apply between pairs of variables. The temporal constraint networks presented in this section are an important example of this, and we shall use them to formalize methods for solving quantitative problems.

2.1. Metric Temporal Constraint Networks. Let $x_1, x_2, \ldots, x_n$ be variables which represent time *points* and let x_0 be an arbitrary fixed point in time which we call the *origin*. A *constraint* between x_i and x_j consists of a set of inequalities on their difference, namely

$$C_{i,j} = \begin{cases} a_1 \leq x_j - x_i \leq b_1 \\ \vdots \\ a_r \leq x_j - x_i \leq b_r \end{cases}$$

A constraint $C_{i,j}$ is *satisfied* by an assignment $x_i = c_i$ and $x_j = c_j$ if *one* of its inequalities holds for this assignment. The bounds $a_1, b_1, \ldots, a_r, b_r$ may be negative, zero or positive.

A *metric temporal constraint problem* (MTCP) consists of the set of variables $X = \{x_0, x_1, \ldots, x_n\}$ and a constraint set $C_{i,j}$ (possibly empty) for each i and j $(i \neq j)$. A *solution* to the MTCP is an assignment of real numbers to each of the variables $x_0, x_1, \ldots, x_n$ such that each of the constraints $C_{i,j}$ is satisfied. Unary constraints, like $a \leq x_i \leq b$, are easily handled by expressing them as binary constraints with the origin, namely, $a \leq x_i - x_0 \leq b$.

Example 4.

$$C_{1,2} = \begin{cases} -3 \leq x_2 - x_1 \leq 2 \\ 10 \leq x_2 - x_1 \leq 12 \end{cases}$$

The first inequality is interpreted as "either x_2 occurs after x_1 with a distance of at most 2 apart or they are equal or x_2 occurs before x_1 at a distance of at most 3 apart." The second inequality adds the additional possibility that "x_2 occurs after x_1 separated by a distance of between 10 and 12." For example, $x_1 = 40$, $x_2 = 60$ does not satisfy $C_{1,2}$, however, $x_1 = 40$, $x_2 = 51$, and $x_1 = 40$, $x_2 = 39$ both satisfy $C_{1,2}$.

Example 5. *By setting the origin $x_0 = 0$ to mean 8:00 am, we can express other time points. For example, $30 \leq x_5 - x_0 \leq 30$, or more simply $x_5 = 30$, is interpreted as "x_5 occurs at exactly 8:30 am." We can also express unary constraints such as "x_6 occurs between 7:45 am - 8:15 am or between 10:00 am - 10:30 am" by the two inequalities: $-15 \leq x_6 - x_0 \leq 15$ or $120 \leq x_6 - x_0 \leq 150$.*

Example 6. *We cannot express ternary constraints (on three variables) such as in the statement, "Peter finished 15 minutes after Paul and Mary had both finished", since we don't know which of Paul or Mary finished second.*

Let $D_{i,j}$ denote the union of the constraint intervals for $x_j - x_i$ given by $C_{i,j}$, namely

$$D_{i,j} = [a_1, b_1] \cup \cdots \cup [a_r, b_r]$$

Thus, $D_{i,j}$ represents the *domain* of the difference $x_j - x_i$ over all possible permitted values according to the *input* of the problem. However, in a solution the pair x_i and x_j must satisfy both $x_j - x_i \in D_{i,j}$ and $x_i - x_j \in D_{j,i}$, so that for simplicity we combine $D_{i,j}$ and $D_{j,i}$ as follows:

Noting that $a \leq x_j - x_i \leq b$ if and only if $-b \leq x_i - x_j \leq -a$, we define the *reversal* of a constraint set as

$$D_{i,j}^{-1} = [-b_r, -a_r] \cup \cdots \cup [-b_1, -a_1]$$

We define the intersection sets

$$T_{i,j} = D_{i,j} \cap D_{j,i}^{-1} \text{ (for all } i \neq j).$$

It is easy to show that $T_{i,j} = T_{j,i}^{-1}$, so with these sets it is sufficient to have only one of them for each pair (i, j), the other being implicit. Furthermore, one can calculate $T_{i,j}$ from $C_{i,j}$ and $C_{j,i}$ in linear time. Doing this for each pair (i, j), combining intervals that overlap, we construct an equivalent version of the problem which we call its canonical form.

A temporal constraint problem is in *canonical* form if we are given the constraints as the union of disjoint intervals

$$T_{i,j} = [a_1, b_1] \cup \cdots \cup [a_r, b_r]$$

satisfying $T_{i,j} = T_{j,i}^{-1}$. Thus, a tuple $< c_0, c_1, \ldots, c_n >$ is a solution if and only if $c_j - c_i \in T_{i,j}$ for all $i < j$. We call $T_{i,j}$ the *canonical constraint set* for i and j.

Example 7.

$$C_{2,1} = \begin{cases} 2 \leq x_1 - x_2 \leq 5 \\ -1 \leq x_1 - x_2 \leq 0 \\ -6 \leq x_1 - x_2 \leq -3 \\ -11 \leq x_1 - x_2 \leq -11 \end{cases}$$

Combining $C_{2,1}$ with $C_{1,2}$ from Example 4, we have

$$\begin{aligned} D_{1,2} &= [-3,2] \cup [10,12] \\ D_{2,1}^{-1} &= [-5,-2] \cup [0,1] \cup [3,6] \cup [11,11] \end{aligned}$$

whose intersection gives the canonical form

$$T_{1,2} = [-3,-2] \cup [0,1] \cup [11,11]$$

Thus, $x_1 = 40$, $x_2 = 51$ is still a possible solution, but $x_1 = 40$, $x_2 = 39$ is no longer possible.

Temporal constraint problems are often represented in a graphical form called a *temporal constraint network*. The network has vertices corresponding to the variables $x_0, x_1, \ldots, x_n$ and a directed arc from i to j labelled by its constraint set $D_{i,j}$. If there is no constraint for a pair, the arc is usually omitted.[1] The *canonical network* labels arc (i,j) with the set $T_{i,j}$ and omits the arc (j,i). We denote by $T_e = \{I_e^1, \ldots, I_e^r\}$ the set of disjoint intervals labeling the arc $e = (i,j)$. From our experience, we always recommend using the canonical network.

In general, metric temporal constraint problems are intractible, that is, their computational complexity is NP-hard, as is the case with all general forms of constraint satisfiability problems. However, in practice, certain heuristic algorithms work well with real temporal data, and one simplified version, the simple temporal problems where each constraint $T_{i,j}$ consists of a single interval, have a well known polynomial time algorithm. These computational aspects are presented in Sections 2.2-2.3.

The quantitative approach to temporal reasoning offers convenient mechanisms for expressing and dealing with metric information which are important and useful in managing and understanding the timing of events. They form the basis for several implemented systems, and may be combined with other approaches.

2.2. Simple Temporal Problems and Distance Constraints. A metric temporal constraint problem (MTCP) in which at most one inequality $x_j - x_i \leq c_{i,j}$ is specified for each *ordered* pair (i,j) is called a *simple temporal problem* (STP). Alternatively, the constraint can be expressed on the *unordered* pair (i,j) by the inequality $-c_{j,i} \leq x_j - x_i \leq c_{i,j}$ or as the single canonical interval $T_{i,j} = [-c_{j,i}, c_{i,j}]$. Simple temporal problems can be solved using the efficient techniques available for finding shortest paths in a directed graph with weighted edges. These have been studied for many years as simple distance or difference constraints.

A system S of *simple distance* (or *difference*) *constraints* on a set of variables $\{x_i\}$ is a collection of weak and strict inequalities of the form

$$x_j - x_i \leq c_{i,j} \qquad \text{or} \qquad x_j - x_i < c_{i,j}$$

[1] Although we could include it with the label $[-\infty, \infty]$.

with at most one inequality for each ordered pair (i, j). By convention, we assign $c_{i,i} = 0$, and if no constraint is specified for a pair (i, j), then we may assign $c_{i,j} = \infty$. Clearly, any STP can be regarded as a system of simple difference constraints.

The problems that are studied here are concerned with the existence of a solution to the system of constraints; i.e., is S feasible? Bellman's notion of a *distance graph* is used to solve these problems[2]:

Construct a directed weighted graph G_S with directed edge $i \to j$ labelled by the *weight* $c_{i,j}$ and marked *solid* or *dotted* depending upon whether the inequality is weak or strict. Figure 2.1 shows the distance graph for a set of inequalities, with edges labelled ∞ omitted, and its corresponding edge distance matrix. Besides the immediate constraint $x_j - x_i \leq c_{i,j}$, each path $\pi = [i = i_0, i_1, \ldots, i_k = j]$ in G_S from i to j induces a constraint on the distance $x_j - x_i$ by summing the weights on the path, namely

$$x_j - x_i \leq weight(\pi) = \sum_{t=1}^{k} c_{i_{t-1}, i_t}$$

Bellman [1958] was the first to show that when all inequalities are weak, S is feasible if and only if G_S has no negative cycle. The more general result is the following.

Theorem 8. *A system S of simple distance constraints is feasible if and only if its distance graph G_S has no negative weight cycle and any zero weight cycle consists of $\leq$ edges only.*

The proof of Thereom 8 can be found in several references including Pe'er and Shamir [1995]. For completeness, we provide a proof which will also have the added benefit of leading us to the algorithms for finding a solution or a forbidden cycle.

Proof. Suppose there was a negative weight cycle $C = [i_0, i_1, \ldots, i_k = i_0]$ in G_S. Then $x_{i_0} - x_{i_0} \leq weight(C) < 0$ which cannot be satisfied. Next, suppose C is a zero weight cycle with at least one strict inequality. Then

$$x_{i_0} - x_{i_0} = \sum_{t=1}^{k} (x_{i_t} - x_{i_{t-1}}) < \sum_{t=1}^{k} c_{i_{t-1}, i_t} = weight(C) = 0$$

which is not feasible.

Conversely, if G_S has no negative cycle, then the minimum weight $d_{i,j}$ over all paths from i to j is well defined for every pair of vertices. However, this alone will not distinguish between weak and strict inequalities, which must be taken into account when constructing a feasible solution. Therefore, we consider two cases:

[2]Simple difference constraints are a special case of linear programming (LP); however, they can be solved by algorithms which are more efficient than a general LP algorithm.

- *All edges have labels* $\leq$. Choose a variable x_0 to be the origin. Since $d_{0,j} \leq d_{0,i} + d_{i,j}$ and $d_{i,j} \leq c_{i,j}$, we have $d_{0,j} - d_{0,j} \leq c_{i,j}$. Therefore, by assigning $x_k = d_{0,k}$, we obtain a feasible solution.

Remark 2. *Most books assume all inequalities are weak* ($\leq$) *and conclude the proof here.*

- *Some edges are labelled* $<$. We solve this case by constructing a slightly perturbed but equivalent system S' on the same set of variables as S. Let n be the number of variables and fix ε such that $0 < \varepsilon < c/n$ where c is the granularity of the weights, (e.g., if all weights are integers, then $c = 1$, or if weights are decimals with 4 significant digits to the right of the decimal point, then $c = 0.0001$, etc.) Define S' to include (1) every weak inequality $x_j - x_i \leq c_{i,j}$ in S, and (2) a weak equality $x_j - x_i \leq c_{i,j} - \varepsilon$ for every strict inequality $x_j - x_i < c_{i,j}$ in S. Thus, all edges in $G_{S'}$ have labels $\leq$, since all constraints of S' are weak inequalities.

Claim: S is feasible iff S' is feasible.

Clearly, a feasible solution to S' also satisfies S. Suppose S' is not feasible but S is feasible. Then $G_{S'}$ must contain a negative weight cycle C. If all edges in C were labelled by $\leq$ in G_S, then the constraints on C would be identical in S and S', so C would also be a negative cycle in G_S, contradicting the feasibility of S. Therefore, we may assume that C does not consist of only $\leq$ edges in G_S, and so $weights_S(C) > 0$. On one hand, by the choice of c as the granularity of the edge weights, we must have $weights_S(C) > c$. On the other hand, the weight in G_S of each edge in C differs from the weight in $G_{S'}$ by no more than ε, and since C contains at most n edges, we have

$$weights_S(C) \leq weights_{S'}(C) + n\varepsilon < n\varepsilon < c$$

which is a contradiction. This proves the *Claim.*

Finally, we have shown that to solve a system S of weak and strict constraints, it is sufficient to solve the system S' of weak constraints, which can be done according to the first case above. The solution obtained for S' is also a solution for S, and the infeasibility of S' would imply the infeasibility of S. This concludes the proof of Theorem 8. ■

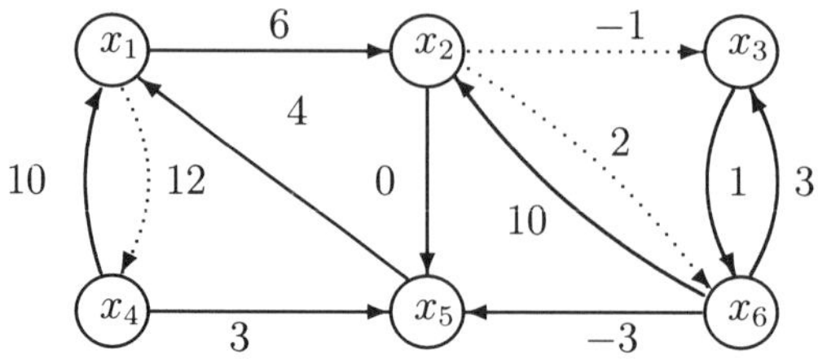

$$\begin{array}{lll} x_1 - x_4 \leq 10 & x_2 - x_1 \leq 6 & x_3 - x_2 < -1 \\ x_4 - x_1 < 12 & x_5 - x_4 \leq 3 & x_1 - x_5 \leq 4 \\ x_5 - x_2 \leq 0 & x_6 - x_2 < 2 & x_6 - x_3 \leq 1 \\ x_5 - x_6 \leq -3 & x_2 - x_6 \leq 10 & x_3 - x_6 \leq 3 \end{array}$$

	1	2	3	4	5	6
1	0	6	∞	**12**	∞	∞
2	∞	0	**−1**	∞	0	**2**
3	∞	∞	0	∞	∞	1
4	10	∞	∞	0	3	∞
5	4	∞	∞	∞	0	∞
6	∞	10	3	∞	−3	0

Figure 2.1. The distance graph for a set of inequalities, and its corresponding distance matrix. *Weak inequalities are indicated by solid arcs in the graph and normal font entries in the matrix and strict inequalities by dotted arcs and bold font entries.*

We have just seen that finding the minimum weight $d_{i,j}$ of a path from i to j, for all pairs i, j, allows us to construct a solution. This problem, often called the "all-pairs shortest path problem", can be solved by the Floyd-Warshall algorithm (Figure 2.2), the repeated matrix squaring algorithm or the Donald Johnson algorithm.

In the case where all edges represent weak inequalities, the solution $x_k = d_{0,k}$, for all k and an arbitrary x_0 is obtained immediately as in the proof of the Theorem. In the case of a mix of strict and weak inequalities, the appropriate ε can be calculated and the solution will be obtained by slightly perturbing the distances $d_{0,k}$.

An alternative method for constructing a solution uses the Bellman-Ford algorithm for solving the "single-source shortest path" problem. Here the origin x_0 is a *new* variable added to the problem and the corresponding new vertex 0 added to G_S serves as the source node with an edge weighted zero directed from 0 to each other vertex.

The complexity of the Floyd-Warshall algorithm is $O(n^3)$ and that of the Bellman-Ford algorithm is $O(mn)$ where n is the number of variables and m is the number of constraints (or edges).[3] Repeated matrix squaring is $O(n^3 \log n)$ and Johnson's

[3] Dijkstra's algorithm could also be used if all edge weights were non-negative, a very unlikely situation in our temporal problems.

algorithm is $O(n^2 \log n + mn)$ but is rather complicated. For further reading on these well-known algorithms, see the book by Cormen, Leiserson and Rivest [1990]. Figure 2.2 gives our version of the Floyd-Warshall algorithm. $M^{(k)}$ indicates the distance matrix after iteration k, hence, $m_{i,j}^{(0)} = c_{i,j}$ and $m_{i,j}^{(n)} = d_{i,j}$. To apply the algorithm to the example in Figure 2.1, we could choose $\varepsilon = 0.1$ and modify the three boldface entries in the original distance matrix accordingly to start the algorithm with $M^{(0)}$ as input.

Floyd-Warshall (M, n) [Input: the $n \times n$ distance matrix M]
$M^{(0)} \leftarrow M$
for $k \leftarrow 1$ **to** n **do**
    for $i \leftarrow 1$ **to** n **do**
        for $j \leftarrow 1$ **to** n **do**
            $m_{i,j}^{(k)} \leftarrow \min(m_{i,j}^{(k-1)}, m_{i,k}^{(k-1)} + m_{k,j}^{(k-1)})$
        endfor
    endfor
endfor
for $i \leftarrow 1$ **to** n **do**
    if $m_{i,i}^{(n)} < 0$ **then**
        print (Not feasible. Negative weight cycle.)
        exit
    endif
endfor
return $M^{(n)}$ [Output: the shortest distance matrix $M^{(n)}$]

Figure 2.2. The Floyd-Warshall algorithm to compute all-pairs shortest paths and test feasibility.

2.3. Solving General Temporal Problems. The general metric temporal constraint problem (MTCP) is known to be a computationally hard problem (Dechter, Meiri and Pearl [1991]). It is NP-complete even if there are at most two constraints per edge (pair of variables). Thus, all known algorithms to find a solution will have exponential complexity in the worst case (unless $P = NP$). Nevertheless, there is good reason to be optimistic because in practice many real world MTCPs can be solved by an increasing number of heuristic search algorithms using constraint propagation and intelligent backtracking. (The same statement can be made for many NP-complete problems which are important for applications.)

In this section we describe several techniques for guiding an otherwise arbitrary backtracking algorithm, teaching it to become smarter and smarter. Among these, we mention backjumping, forward checking, variable ordering, value ordering and learning schemes. Additional methods include path consistency and topologically motivated algorithms for exploiting the constraint network as a preprocessing step before applying backtracking.

Brute Force Backtracking. Let $T = (X, \{T_e\}_{e \in E})$ be a general MTCP given in canonical form, and let $G = (X, E)$ be its associated constraint network. Each edge $e \in E$ is labelled by a set of disjoint intervals $T_e = \{I_e^1, \dots, I_e^r\}$. Selecting exactly one of these intervals for each edge gives an instance of a simple temporal problem (STP) which can be solved in polynomial time using the Floyd-Warshall algorithm for example (Section 2.2). By iterating over all possible selections and solving each of the STPs, we could (in principle) find all possible solutions to T. A brute force backtracking algorithm for doing this is given in Figure 2.3.

Since the number of possibilities is potentially exponential, we must be clever in how we perform this iteration. Even though in the worst case we cannot avoid the exponential complexity, it is possible to *guide* the search for a solution using techniques developed for constraint satisfaction problems and other combinatorially explosive problems.

choose an ordering of the edges of $E : e_1, e_2, \cdots, e_m$
for all $I_{e_1} \in T_{e_1}$ **do**
    for all $I_{e_2} \in T_{e_2}$ **do**
        ⋮
            for all $I_{e_m} \in T_{e_m}$ **do**
                call Floyd-Warshall with labels $(I_{e_1}, I_{e_2}, \dots, I_{e_m})$
            endfor
        ⋮
    endfor
endfor

Figure 2.3. Brute force backtrack algorithm

Variable ordering, value ordering and testing partial instantiations. The order of the edges chosen in the first line of Figure 2.3 is called the *instantiation order*. The instantiation order of the interval variables $I_{e_1}, \dots, I_{e_m}$ was chosen arbitrarily in the brute force algorithm. However, if the algorithm were to be stopped as soon as Floyd-Warshall finds a solution, then some instantiation orders would lead us to a solution faster than others.

One of the simplest heuristics that is usually profitable is ordering the edges according to number of intervals in their canonical constraint domains, from fewest to most. Other more complicated rules for ordering could also be considered. This is known as *variable ordering.*

A second degree of freedom ignored by the brute force algorithm is the order in which the domain intervals $I_{e_i}^1, \ldots, I_{e_i}^r$ are selected for each edge e_i. Again there may be more favorable orders within T_{e_i}, namely, choosing first those intervals whose likelihood of being in a solution is greatest. This is known as *value ordering*, but unfortunately it is usually difficult to predict in advance which domain intervals are more favorable.

A third opportunity of speeding up the brute force algorithm is by noting that it is not necessary to generate a full instantiation $I_{e_1}, \ldots, I_{e_m}$ before running Floyd-Warshall. Rather, it can be called to test a partial instantiation to find inconsistencies in a subgraph, and thus may rule out a large number of full instantiations early on. After all, *adding* additional constraints as the instantiation proceeds never adds new solutions, but instead usually cuts off many dead branches in the search tree.

In summary, we want to intelligently order the variables, and if possible the values within the domains, and then test partial instantiations periodically - either after every instantiation or at certain points during the search. There may also be an interaction between the variable ordering and the frequency of testing. Both theoretical and experimental studies have been carried out on variable and value ordering and alternative search methods, and the interested reader should consult the constraint satisfiability literature, for example, Mackworth [1977, 1992], Mackworth and Freuder [1985], Mohr and Henderson [1986], Nadel [1989], Nudel [1983] and their forward citations.

3. Interval and Point Temporal Algebras - A Qualitative Approach

Interval consistency problems deal with events, each of which is assumed to be an interval on the real line or on any other linearly ordered set. Allen [1983] defined a fundamental model for temporal reasoning using the thirteen *primitive interval relations*, expressing the relative positions between two intervals, obtained by considering all possible relations between their four endpoints (see Figure 3.1). We call this 13-valued interval algebra A_{13}.

RELATION	NOTATION	INTERPRETATION
x before y	$\prec$	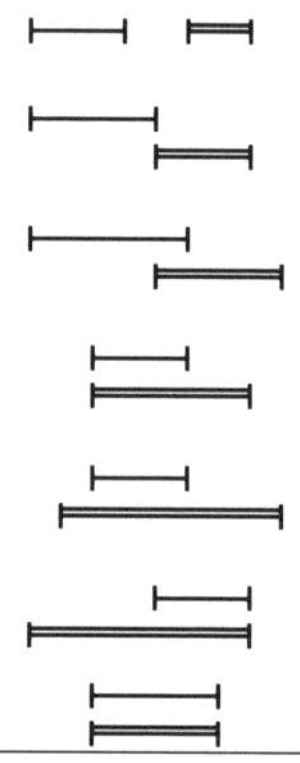
y after x	$\succ$	
x meets y	m	
y met-by x	m^{-1}	
x overlaps y	o	
y overlapped-by x	o^{-1}	
x starts y	s	
y started-by x	s^{-1}	
x during y	d	
y includes x	d^{-1}	
x finishes y	f	
y finished-by x	f^{-1}	
x equals y	$\equiv$	

Figure 3.1. The 13-valued interval algebra A_{13}.
Thin line: x interval. Thick line: y interval.

These thirteen primitive relations represent all possible configurations between two intervals. However, in order to represent partial or nonexact information, we allow a disjunction of primitive relations to express the explicit knowledge we have about a pair of intervals.

Example 9. *$I_x\{\prec, m, d^{-1}\}I_y$ represents the disjunction*

$$I_x \textit{ before } I_y \quad \text{or} \quad I_x \textit{ meets } I_y \quad \text{or} \quad I_x \textit{ includes } I_y$$

Allen allows any nonempty subset of the 13 primitive relations to hold between a pair of intervals, that is, any of the 8191 possible disjunctions of A_{13}.

The approach of Golumbic and Shamir [1993] has been to simplify Allen's model in order to study its complexity using graph theoretic techniques. The first of the two lines of specialization which we study here is macro relations. Macro relations refers to partitioning the 13 primitive relations into more coarse relations by regarding a subset of primitive relations as a new basic relation. We let

$$\begin{aligned} \cap &= \{m, m^{-1}, o, o^{-1}, s, s^{-1}, f, f^{-1}, d, d^{-1}, \equiv\} \\ \alpha &= \{m, o\}, \qquad \alpha^{-1} = \{m^{-1}, o^{-1}\} \\ \subset &= \{s, f, d\}, \qquad \subset^{-1} = \{s^{-1}, f^{-1}, d^{-1}\} \end{aligned}$$

From these we define the 3-valued and 7-valued interval algebras A_3 and A_7 whose elements are called its *atomic relations*, respectively,

$$A_3 : \{\prec, \succ, \cap\} \qquad\qquad A_7 : \{\prec, \succ, \alpha, \alpha^{-1}, \subset, \subset^{-1}, \equiv\}$$

For certain applications it is convenient to assume that all interval endpoints are distinct. This simplification generates the 6-valued algebra

$$A_6 : \{\prec, \succ, o, o^{-1}, d, d^{-1}\}$$

The choice of which of these algebras A_i to use depends on the nature of the application, data, constraints and on the type of complexity result being proved. We have already seen one example of using A_3 in the story of the Four Bears in Section 1.3. We shall present applications in archaeology and molecular biology later in this section.

We use the term 'algebra' here since the set of atomic relations in each A_i forms a Boolean algebra, and in certain cases, together with an additional composition operation, forms a *relation algebra*, in the sense defined by Tarski (see Ladkin & Maddux [1989]).

An even simpler specialization of Allen's model is the point algebra introduced by Vilain and Kautz [1986], in which each event is regarded as a single point rather than an interval. We denote the point algebra by P_3; its primitive relations are simply $\{<, =, >\}$. The point algebra has much more efficient algorithmic properties than the interval algebras, but has much less expressive power for modeling a temporal scenario. We study the point algebra P_3 in Section 3.3. **We cannot emphasize too strongly that P_3 and A_3 are very different**, stemming from the fact that equality between points is not at all like intersection between intervals.

3.1. Interval Satisfiability Problems. The input to all temporal reasoning problems which will be studied here is a set of events, and for each pair of events x and y, a set $D(x, y)$ of atomic relations in a fixed algebra A_i. The semantics here is that we do not know precisely the relationship between x and y, but it must be one of those in the set $D(x, y)$. For example, we read $D(x, y) = \{\prec, \subset\}$ (or, equivalently, $x\{\prec, \subset\}y$) as 'x is either before or contained in y'; and $D(x, y) = \{\prec, d^{-1}, \equiv\}$ and $x\{\prec, d^{-1}, \equiv\}y$ both mean 'either x ends before y starts, or y is during x, or the two are equal'. We also call a set of atomic relations a *relation set*. We omit braces when there is no ambiguity, e.g., $x \prec y$ or $x \cap y$. Without loss of generality, we assume that all relation sets are non-empty, and that for each pair of elements x and y, the relation sets $D(x, y)$ and $D(y, x)$ given as input are consistent, i.e., for each atomic relation R, $R \in D(x, y) \iff R^{-1} \in D(y, x)$. This corresponds to our canonical form for the MTCP in Section 2.1.

An *interval realization* (or *representation*) is an assignment of intervals on the real line to events. Since all the algebras discussed here are concerned with topological properties only, a realization can be viewed also as a complete weak order of the interval endpoints, thereby identifying all realizations which differ in metric only. A realization is *consistent* with the input $\{D(x,y)\}$ if for each pair of events, one of the atomic relations in their relation set holds. Two realizations are *distinct* if for at least one pair of events, the atomic relations which hold between them differ in the two realizations. The input data $\{D(x,y)\}$ is *consistent* (or *satisfiable*) if it admits a consistent realization.

The *interval satisfiability problem* (ISAT) is to determine if the input data $\{D(x,y)\}$ is consistent, and to find one consistent realization in case it is. The *minimal labeling problem* (MLP) is to determine the minimal sets $D'(x,y) \subseteq D(x,y)$ such that the set of consistent interval realizations is unchanged, and every remaining atomic relation holds in some realization.

Example 10. *For the input* $x\{\prec, m, o\}y$, $y\{\prec, \equiv, \succ\}z$, $z\{f, s\}x$, *two consistent realizations are shown in Figure 3.2. The relations* $y \prec z$ *and* $z \equiv y$ *are impossible. The minimal labeling for this problem is* $x\{\prec, m, o\}y$, $y \succ z$, $z\{f, s\}x$.

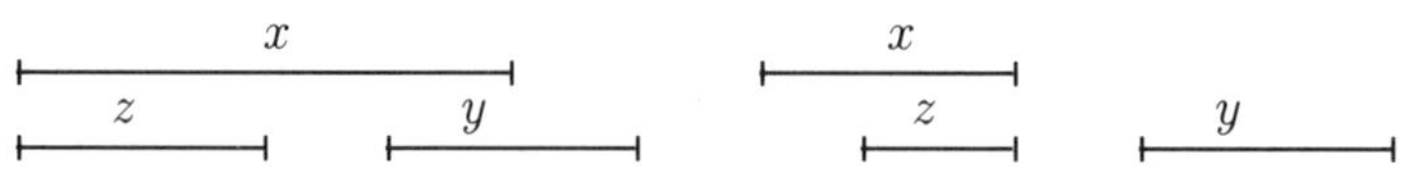

I: $x\, o\, y,\ y \succ z,\ z\, s\, x$ II: $x \prec y,\ y \succ z,\ z\, f\, x$

Figure 3.2. Two interval realizations for Example 10.

The *all consistent solutions problem* (ACSP) is that of enumerating all the combinations of atomic relations which are consistent with the given data. This problem arises since not all tuples of the cross product of a minimal labeling are consistent. The number of combinations may, of course, be exponential, and the goal here is to construct a *polynomial representation structure* $\sum$ requiring $O(p(n))$ space and from which k distinct solutions can be produced in $O(q(n,k))$ time, where n is the number of variables, p and q are polynomial functions, and k is any number less than or equal to the number of solutions. The closely related *endpoint sequence problem* (ESP) is that of enumerating all the distinct interval realizations which are consistent with the given data. For A_{13}, the last two problems are equivalent, but in the smaller algebras there may be several (or many) distinct endpoint sequences which realize the same combination of atomic relations.

Allen [1983] originally provided a heuristic approach for solving the MLP in A_{13}. It is a constraint propagation approach using a 13×13 composition or multiplication table for atomic relations, analogous to what we presented in Section 1.3 for A_3. That algorithm is polynomial but does not always provide a minimal solution, and may give a false positive answer to ISAT. Vilain and Kautz [1986] have shown that MLP is in fact NP-complete for A_{13}. Golumbic and Shamir [1993] obtain a stronger result using macro relations to reduce the number of atomic relations from thirteen to three. Our first main result is that even in A_3, the interval satisfiability problem is NP-complete. Consequently, all four problems ISAT, MLP, ACSP and ESP are intractable for all four interval algebras A_i, $i = 3, 6, 7, 13$.

To prove that ISAT is NP-complete for A_3, we introduced a new combinatorial problem, the interval graph sandwich problem (IGSP), which we proved to be NP-complete. The IGSP is shown to be a special case of ISAT. Recall that an undirected graph $G = (V, E)$ is called an *interval graph* if its vertices can be represented by intervals on the real line such that two vertices are adjacent if and only if their intervals intersect (see Golumbic [1980]). The interval graph sandwich problem (IGSP) is the following:

INTERVAL GRAPH SANDWICH PROBLEM:

INPUT: Two disjoint edge-sets, E^1 and E^2 on the same vertex set V.

QUESTION: Is there a graph $G = (V, E)$ satisfying $E^1 \subseteq E \subseteq E^1 \cup E^2$ which is an interval graph?

Denote $E^3 = V \times V - \{E^1 \cup E^2\}$. When $E^1 = \phi$ or $E^3 = \phi$, the answer is trivially yes. When $E^2 = \phi$, the problem is polynomial by the algorithm of Booth and Lueker [1976]. We show that in the general case, the problem is NP-complete.

An application in molecular biology: In physical mapping of DNA, information on intersection or non-intersection of pairs of segments originating from a certain DNA chain is known from experiments, without knowledge of the nucleotide sequences of the segments or the chain. The goal is to find out how the segments can be arranged as intervals along a line (the DNA chain), so that their pairwise intersections in that arrangement match the experimental data. (This question, raised by the famous biologist Seymour Benzer, was one of the original motivations for the study of interval graphs. In fact, Benzer raised the *decision version* of this question, since at the time the linearity of the DNA was only a hypothesis.) In the graph presentation, vertices correspond to segments and two vertices are connected by an E^1-edge (resp., E^3-edge) if their segments are known to intersect (resp., not to intersect). E^2-edges correspond to the case where the experimental information on the intersections is inconclusive, or simply unavailable. The decision problem is thus equivalent to the IGSP.

Theorem 11. *The interval graph sandwich problem is NP-complete.*

Proof. One proof (omitted in this paper) relies on a reduction from the Not-All-Equal 3-Satisfiability problem and the fact that an interval graph cannot contain an asteriodal triplet of vertices. The detailed proof is given in Golumbic and Shamir [1993]. An alternate (and shorter) proof based on a reduction from the Betweenness problem is given in Golumbic, Kaplan and Shamir [1995a].

Theorem 12. *ISAT is NP-complete for A_3.*

Proof. For a given instance of the IGSP problem, construct an instance of ISAT on A_3 as follows: For each edge $(x, y) \in E^1, E^2$ or E^3, let $D(x, y) = \cap, \prec \cap \succ$ or $\prec\succ$, respectively. It is clear that this ISAT problem has a solution if and only if the IGSP has one.

Corollary 13. *ISAT, MLP, ACSP and ESP are NP-hard for A_3, A_6, A_7 and A_{13}.*

Proof. This follows from the observation that the algebra A_3 is contained in each A_i and that for any $i = 3, 6, 7, 13$, ISAT has a solution if and only if MLP has a non-empty solution if and only if ACSP has a non-empty solution if and only if ESP has a non-empty solution. ■

3.2. Restricted Domains and Tractable Fragments. Due to the intractability of the general versions of ISAT, MLP and ACSP, attention has been focused on (1) polynomial time heuristic algorithms for approximate MLP solutions on A_{13} followed by efficient (albeit exponential) backtrack search, Allen [1983] and vanBeek [1989, 1991], and (2) exact polynomial time solutions to several restricted cases of the interval satisfiability problem, Golumbic and Shamir [1993]. In the latter, by suitably restricting the input domain of an NP-complete problem, one can often obtain a special class which admits a polynomial time algorithm, which is the topic of this section.

Solutions to several restricted cases of ISAT have been known for a long time, and many of these cases correspond to other applications. These will be extended by the new results presented here, and lead us to our second line of specialization, namely, restricted domains. In the general case for an interval algebra A_i, each relation set $D(x, y)$ may take any of $2^i - 1$ possible values. We may restrict this by designating a *fragment* or *restricted domain* Δ to denote a particular family of relation sets in A_i and requiring that each relation set $D(x, y)$ be a member of Δ. We represent each relation set in A_3 by a concatenation of its atomic relations, omitting braces. Hence, $\prec\cap$ represents $\{\prec, \cap\}$, $\prec$ represents $\{\prec\}$, etc. The seven possible relation sets in A_3

in this notation are: $\prec$, $\succ$, $\cap$, $\prec\cap$, $\cap\succ$, $\prec\succ$, $\prec\cap\succ$. Thus, the NP-completeness of the interval graph sandwich problem shows that even when all relation sets are restricted to be from the fragment $\Delta_0 = \{\cap, \prec\succ, \prec\cap\succ\}$ (meaning *intersect, disjoint* or *don't care*), ISAT remains NP-complete. The tractible and intractible fragments for A_{13} are fully characterized below.

In the temporal reasoning literature, polynomial algorithms have been developed for ISAT and MLP on special restrictions of A_{13}; e.g., by assuming that all events are points instead of intervals, Ladkin and Maddux [1994] and vanBeek [1989, 1991], or by assuming that the restricted domain satisfies certain convexity conditions, Nökel [1989, 1991]. Nebel and Burckert [1995] introduce a fragment of A_{13} called the 'ORD-Horn algebra' which they prove to be the maximal tractable fragment of A_{13} containing all the 13 atomic relations.

A number of well-known recognition problems in graph theory and partially ordered sets may be viewed as restricted interval satisfiability problems. Five of these, all of which have polynomial time solutions, are given in Figure 3.3 along with their appropriate Δ, (see Golumbic [1980]).

Class	Restricted Domain Δ
Interval orders	$\{\prec, \succ, \cap\}$
Interval graphs	$\{\prec\succ, \cap\}$
Circle (or overlap) graphs	$\{\alpha, \alpha^1, \equiv\}, \{\prec, \succ, \subset, \subset^{-1}\}\}$
Interval containment graphs	$\{\{\subset, \subset^{-1}\}, \{\prec, \succ, \alpha, \alpha^{-1}, \equiv\}\}$
Posets of dimension 2	$\{\{\subset\}, \{\subset^{-1}\}, \{\prec, \succ, \alpha, \alpha^{-1}, \equiv\}\}$

Figure 3.3. Polynomial interval satisfiability problems in graph theory.

We describe the results of a systematic study on the complexity of the restricted domains in A_3. Since we can assume that two converse relations sets ($\prec$ and $\succ$, or $\prec\cap$ and $\succ\cap$) always appear together in a restricted domain, there are 31 possible fragments. All of these cases have now been classified as either polynomial or NP-complete. For certain restricted domains special polynomial algorithms have been devised. An interesting example is the restricted domain $A_3 - \prec\succ$: By excluding only one out of the seven relation sets, ISAT becomes linearly solvable. For lack of space, we only state here the results for restricted domains without proofs or algorithms, and refer the interested reader to Golumbic and Shamir [1993] for fragments Δ_1–Δ_3 and Webber [1995] for Δ_4 in the theorems below. Another positive result is that the polynomiality of ISAT implies the polynomiality of MLP and the existence of a polynomial representation structure for ACSP. These results apply to each of the algebras A_i $(i = 3, 6, 7, 13)$ and also to any restricted domain in these algebras.

Theorem 14. *Let Δ_1 be the restricted domain $A_3 - \prec\succ$, that is*

$$\Delta_1 = \{\prec, \succ, \cap, \prec\cap, \cap\succ, \prec\cap\succ\}.$$

(1) ISAT(Δ_1) is solvable in linear time.

(2) MLP(Δ_1) is solvable in $O(mn)$ steps for a problem with n events and m explicit relation sets.

(3) There exists a polynomial representation structure which facilitates the solution of ESP on Δ_1 in $O(n)$ steps per realization.

Theorem 15. *ISAT is solvable in $O(n^3)$ time for $\Delta_2 = \{\prec, \succ, \cap, \prec\succ\}$.*

Theorem 16. *ISAT is solvable in linear time for $\Delta_3 = \{\prec, \succ, \prec\cap\succ, \prec\succ\}$.*

Theorem 17. *ISAT is NP-complete for $\Delta_4 = \{\prec\cap, \cap\succ, \prec\succ\}$.*

Since every subset of a polynomially solvable restricted domain is polynomial, and every superset of an NP-complete fragment is NP-complete, the above results resolve the complexity of all 31 possible restricted domains in A_3.

An application in archaeology: The *seriation* problem in archaeology attempts to place a set of artifact types in their proper chronological order. This problem was formulated by Flinders Petrie, a well-known archaeologist at the turn of the century, while studying 800 types of pottery found in 900 Egyptian graves. To each artifact type there corresponds a time interval (unknown to us) during which it was in use. To each grave there is a point in time (also unknown) when its contents were interred. Each grave provides the intersection data for the intervals corresponding to its contents.

3.3. Point Algebras. Villain and Kautz [1986] have suggested an alternate model, which they have called the *point algebra* (PA), to simplify and cope with the computational limitations of IA, the Interval Algebra A_{13}. The point algebra, which we denote by P_3, deals only with the sets of *point relations*, namely, the 7 non-empty subsets of $\{<, =, >\}$:

$$<, =, >, \leq, \geq, \neq, ?$$

where $\leq, \geq, \neq, ?$ stand for $\{<, =\}$, $\{=, >\}$, $\{<, >\}$, $\{<, =, >\}$, respectively. All the computational problems which we have studied for the interval algebras are polynomial for point algebras. For further reading on this and their applications, see Nökel [1991] and vanBeek [1992].

4. Temporal Logic

The approach to temporal reasoning perhaps most familiar to the mathematics community is the study of temporal logics. Temporal logic is not simply a variation of predicate or propositional logic, but rather, a very special family of logics centered upon a distinguished variable t which ranges over a *flow of time.* What makes the logic special is that the truth of axioms and propositions involving the time parameter t are dictated by its particular properties. How we choose to view time, as distinct time points 0,1,2,3,..., as a continuous total order, as a multiple time flow with linear past and branching futures, etc., imposes its unique attributes on the logical model.

Some temporal examples are quite easy to express in logical form. The sentence, *"Fred is driving the carpool today and will continue to drive the carpool every three days,"* could be represented as

$$\begin{aligned}&Drive(\underline{\text{now}}, \text{Fred, Carpool})\\ &\quad\&(\forall t, s \geq \underline{\text{now}})\\ &\qquad[Drive(t,\text{Fred,Carpool}) \ \& \ (t+2=s) \longrightarrow Drive(s,\text{Fred, Carpool})]\end{aligned}$$

But very quickly we can get to sentences whose predicate logic forms are increasingly unreadable. Consider the following example, which describes a situation which will continue until another situation finishes:

> *"Since B became University President (Pres) the value of the endowment fund (Value) has steadily been going down, and it will continue to go down for as long as he or she remains President."*

$$\begin{aligned}&\exists t < \underline{\text{now}}[Pres(t, B)\\ &\quad\& \ \exists s < t\forall u[s < u < t \longrightarrow \neg Pres(u, B)]\\ &\quad\& \ \forall u[t < u < \underline{\text{now}} \longrightarrow Pres(u, B)]\\ &\quad\&\forall u, v, x, y[t < u < v < \underline{\text{now}} \ \& \ Value(u, x) \ \& \ Value(v, y) \longrightarrow x > y]]\\ &\& \ \forall s > \underline{\text{now}}[\forall u[\underline{\text{now}} < u < s \longrightarrow Pres(u, B)]\\ &\quad\longrightarrow \forall u, v, x, y[\underline{\text{now}} < u < v < s \ \& \ Value(u, x) \ \& \ Value(v, y) \longrightarrow x > y]]\end{aligned}$$

We could model the temporal dependence between our incumbent President and the financial decline of the Endowment using the qualitative approach of interval algebra in Section 3. A concise *temporal logic* solution to such an example is also possible. Temporal logics add special operators, constructs and rules to a standard propositional or predicate logic in order to enhance its expressibility and capacity for reasoning about time. The examples above are patterned after those in the recent book by Gabbay, Hodkinson and Reynolds [1994] which may be consulted for a comprehensive treatment of the subject.

Constraints of space and time do not permit us here to give an extensive survey of the logical approach to temporal reasoning, nor the use of logic programming as a computational tool for automated reasoning about time. The chapters by Kirchner and Lassez in this book deal with some of these aspects. A further source of material can be found in the *Journal of Logic and Computation*, the survey by Emerson [1990] and other similar publications. For the remainder of this section we will highlight some of the main issues and obstacles in this field.

One complication that arises is when we need to express a difference between the *planned* future and the *actual* future. For example, *"Glenn took a flight to Orlando, but the plane landed in Tampa instead."* Although our common notion of time is linear, here we see the need for branching of time between various possible outcomes. Another matter of difficulty is incorporating *functional* dependence, as with the loaded gun in the Yale shooting problem which may jam or backfire. Even when the order of events is determined and unambiguous, there remain past-future relationships which must be constrained by *causality* or *closeness.* An example illustrating this is given in Gabbay et al. [1994], *"Last year, every time I went to London I came back with a headache."*

There is no one single temporal logic, as we have alluded to before, which can capture even a majority of the concepts of time one can imagine. Specialized temporal logics are needed to neatly express each such set of relationships. We have mentioned before the choice of how to view the flow of time, as integers, reals, poset, etc., and the units of time, as points, intervals, or infinite subsequences. Other factors include restrictions of finiteness, events being true 'once only' or multiple times, temporal connectives like 'X true until Y' or 'true tomorrow' and descriptive durations such as 'sometimes true', 'usually true', 'forever more true', 'occasionally true'.

There are many philosophical aspects to temporal reasoning which further complicate logical representation. Consider the following example.

Example 18. *A construction site which at time t_i is 'building a factory' but which at a later time t_j has changed to 'building a supermarket' without any changes whatsoever in the plans. The truth of 'what' is being built is only in the mind of the current owner. Or to make things even more interesting, suppose a sales representative at time t_k ($t_i < t_k < t_j$) has two other potential customers, a skating rink operator and a bowling alley chain. What is the construction site for them?*

These and other considerations make temporal reasoning a major challenge for artificial intelligence.

5. Temporal Issues in Other Areas

5.1. Distributed Artificial Intelligence: A Handful of Autonomous Agents.

Five Golumbic women, each with a mind of her own, each pursuing her individual goals, usually self-motivated, share a common shortage of resources. There is no centralized decision maker (i.e., dictator). An environment for conflict! An opportunity for cooperation!

Arguments, persuasive counter-arguments, negotiation

This is what *Distributed Artificial Intelligence* (DAI) is all about: establishing (relative) cooperation and coordination between autonomous agents. Through communication and techniques for executing negotiations all disputed subjects are to be resolved. Moreover, since cooperation between the agents is usually needed in advance to accomplish their goals, it should be planned ahead. The DAI literature is young and growing rapidly and raises many temporal issues.

Example 19. *It's 6:45 pm and three women need reasonable shares of the remaining hot water and individual six minute time slots in the shower. Two of them need seven minute time slots with the hair dryer (presumably after their showers). All five have to eat something, but none of them has any time to throw together a quiche and salad. Four have to access the ironing board, and one has to spend a few quiet moments with the author. There is ample dressing and mirror space, but only two sinks. Two must have use of the one computer with a printer, and three will require vehicular support. All have a deadline of 7:30 pm.*

In distributed AI, one agent tries to persuade another agent to change its intentions and to increase its will to cooperate. *'You don't really need the station wagon; it's only two kilometers to the Teen Ween Campfire Rockathon and there is no parking.'* The negotiation process influences the other agent's mental state. *'I can skip that shower; why break a long standing precedent?'* During each phase of negotiation, the agent has the ability to generate any type of argument or justification that will convince its counterpart to cooperate. *'When I was your age, I could whip up a salmon mousse and Minute Rice in less than a minute.'*

After repeated encounters, the agents will analyze their opponent's behavior, learn from past events, and gather experience. *'Let's let A dry her hair first; last time, she (i) kept pulling the plug on us, (ii) kept making those teary faces at us, (iii) almost missed her 7:30 deadline, (iv) all the above.'* The agents 'learn' to execute more effective negotiation in future conflicts. *'Somebody order a pizza.'*

The goal of distributed AI is to successfully accomplish all of this by setting down a number of inference rules based on a formal logic. This model simulates the negotiations. The more realistic the rules and the better the logical methodology, the greater the chance of actually providing an automated solution. Further reading on DAI can be found in Bond and Gasser [1988], O'Hare and Jennings [1996].

5.2. Temporal Databases, Query Languages and Discovery. Databases often contain information which have temporal attributes, e.g., when the information was stored, when it became valid, when it ceased to be valid, etc. It is of increasing importance to be able to represent this temporal data in a manner that facilitates answering temporal queries.

One approach has been to extend large programming methodologies for this purpose, and this has led researchers to design such languages as Templog, temporal extensions of Datalog, Temporal Deductive Databases, Tempur, TL1, THLP, TQuel, HRDM, TSQL2 and others, for the purpose of expressive and efficient temporal query processing. In the design of such a language or methodology, many of the same issues of representation which we have discussed earlier arise, namely, time model options (discrete, continuous, point-based, interval-based), explicit representation of a set of values (lists of dates, times, etc. such as a printed train schedule) or implicit representation (deduction rules, repetition formulas, constraints, etc., such as, *true at* t_0 and *true* $\forall t = t_0 + 24n$ for $1 \leq n \leq 10$, n integer).

Another approach extends database systems by adding temporal operations and queries, and others by building totally new data models and languages. Surveys of the issues being studied for temporal databases can be found in Chomicki [1994], Roddick and Patrick [1992] and the articles appearing in Tansel, et al. [1993]. For further reading in this area, see references [1, 11, 14–19, 23–26, 47, 51, 62, 64, 78, 81, 84, 86].

6. Conclusion

We have briefly explored some of the main themes of temporal reasoning through qualitative, quantitative and logical methods. It is a vast topic on which many volumes have been written. We wish the reader success in following a few of the ideas presented here, pursuing a path through those volumes, and building upon them new results, theories, structures and algorithms for reasoning about time.

Acknowledgements

I am pleased to acknowledge my colleague Ron Shamir for our collaborative work relating combinatorial and temporal results on interval relations, and Itay Meiri for his work on constraint-based temporal reasoning which appeared in the working notes. My thanks to Fred Hoffman and Glenn Shafer for their careful reading and helpful comments on this paper.

A personal remark: My research in the area of applied combinatorial algorithms during the past twenty years has taken me into many disciplines within computer science and discrete applied mathematics. While maintaining my longstanding interest in perfect graphs and algorithmic graph theory, a collage of related topics has emerged: constraint based scheduling from artificial intelligence, compiler and software optimization, VLSI circuit problems, physical mapping of DNA, and many mathematical results on classes of intersection graphs and their applications.

This eclectic collection has an algorithmic commonality whose properties have been the focus of this researcher's work. "Reasoning about time" has entered almost all of these areas. Planning the efficient use of resources, scheduling meetings, analyzing a sequence of events which have happened, ordering a list of instructions to minimize wasted processor time or to meet a deadline, designing timing driven algorithms for early delay estimation, applying the same temporal interval results to genetic patterns in molecular biology, are all examples of *time* playing a central role in every aspect of our lives.

It is my hope that this article will provide an introduction to the field of temporal reasoning and opportunities for further research.

References

[1] M. Abadi and Z. Manna, Temporal logic programming, *Journal of Symbolic Computation* **8** (1989).

[2] A. V. Aho, J. E. Hopcroft, and J. D. Ullman, *The Design and Analysis of Computer Algorithms*, Addison-Wesley, Reading, MA, 1974.

[3] J. F. Allen, Maintaining knowledge about temporal intervals, *Communications of the ACM* **26** (1983), 832-843.

[4] J. F. Allen, Towards a general theory of action and time, *Artificial Intelligence* **23** (1984), 123-154.

[5] J. F. Allen and P. J. Hayes, A common-sense theory of time, *Proc. IJCAI-85*, Los Angeles, CA, pp. 528-531, 1985.

[6] J. F. Allen and P. J. Hayes, Moments and points in an interval-based temporal logic, *Computational Intelligence* **5** (1989), 223-238.

[7] M. J. Almeida, *Reasoning About the Temporal Structure of Narrative*, Ph.D. thesis, State University of New York, Buffalo, NY, 1987.

[8] S. Arnborg, D. G. Corneil and A. Proskurowski, Complexity of finding embeddings in a k-tree, *SIAM Journal of Algebraic Discrete Methods* **8** (1987), 177-184.

[9] B. Aspvall and Y. Shiloach, A polynomial time algorithm for solving systems of linear inequalities with two variables per inequality, *SIAM Journal of Computing* **9** (1980), 827-845.

[10] R. C. Backhouse and B. A. Carre, Regular algebra applied to path-finding problems, *J. Inst. Math. Applications* **15** (1975), 161-186.

[11] M. Baudinet, On the expressiveness of temporal logic programming, *Information and Computation* **117** (1995), 157-180.

[12] U. Bertelé and F. Brioschi, *Nonserial Dynamic Programming*, Academic Press, New York, 1972.

[13] A.H.Bond and L.Gasser, eds., *Readings in Distributed Artificial Intelligence*, Morgan Kaufmann Publishers, San Mateo, CA, 1988.

[14] B. C. Bruce, A model for temporal references and its application in a question answering program, *Artificial Intelligence* **3** (1972), 1-25.

[15] J. Chomicki, Temporal query languages: a survey, *Kansas State University Report*, Jan. 1995. An earlier version appears in *Lecture Notes in Artificial Intelligence* **827** (1994).

[16] J. Chomicki, Efficient checking of temporal integrity constraints using bounded history encoding, *ACM Trans. on Database Systems* **20** (1995), 149-186.

[17] J. Chomicki and D. Niwinski, On the feasibility of checking temporal integrity constraints, *J. Computer System Sciences* **51** (1995), 523-535.

[18] J. Chomicki and D. Toman, Implementing temporal integrity constraints using an active DBMS, *IEEE Trans. Knowledge and Data Engr.* **7** (1995), 566-582.

[19] J. Clifford and D. S. Warren, Formal semantics for time in databases, *ACM Transactions on Database Systems* **8** (1983), 214-254.

[20] T. H. Cormen, C. E. Leiserson and R. L. Rivest, *Introduction to Algorithms*, MIT Press, Cambridge, MA, 1990.

[21] G. B. Dantzig, *Linear Programming and Extensions*. Princeton University Press, Princeton, NJ, 1962.

[22] E. Davis, Constraint propagation with interval labels, *Artificial Intelligence* **32** (1987), 281-331.

[23] T. Dean, Large-scale temporal data bases for planning in complex domains, *Proc. IJCAI-87*, Milan, Italy, pp. 860-866, 1987.

[24] T. Dean, Using temporal hierarchies to efficiently maintain large temporal databases, *Journal of the ACM* **36** (1989), 687-718.

[25] T. Dean, J. Firby and D. Miller, Hierarchical planning involving deadline, travel time and resources, *Computational Intelligence* **4** (1990), 381-398.

[26] T. L. Dean and D. V. McDermott, Temporal data base management, *Artificial Intelligence* **32** (1987), 1-55.

[27] R. Dechter, Enhancement schemes for constraint processing: backjumping, learning, and cutset decompositions, *Artificial Intelligence* **41** (1990), 273-312.

[28] R. Dechter, Constraint networks, in: *Encyclopedia of Artificial Intelligence, 2nd Edition*, S. Shapiro, editor, John Wiley, New York, 1992.

[29] R. Dechter, I. Meiri and J. Pearl, Temporal constraint networks, *Artificial Intelligence* **49** (1991), 61-95.

[30] R. Dechter and J. Pearl, Network-based heuristics for constraint satisfaction problems, *Artificial Intelligence* **34** (1987), 1-38.

[31] R. Dechter and J. Pearl, Tree clustering for constraint networks, *Artificial Intelligence* **38** (1988), 353-366.

[32] Y. Deville and P. Van Hentenryck, An efficient arc consistency algorithm for a class of CSP problems. *Proc. IJCAI-91*, Sydney, Australia, 1991, pp. 325-330.

[33] E. A. Emerson, Temporal and modal logic, in: *Handbook of Theoretical Computer Science,* J. van Leeuwen, editor, Elsevier/MIT Press, 1990, pp. 995-1072.

[34] S. Even, *Graph Algorithms*, Computer Science Press, Rockville, MD, 1979.

[35] C. Freksa, Temporal reasoning based on semi-intervals, *Artificial Intelligence* **54** (1992), 199-227.

[36] E. C. Freuder, Synthesizing constraint expressions, *Communications of the ACM* **21** (1978), 958-965.

[37] E. C. Freuder, A sufficient condition of backtrack-free search, *Journal of the ACM* **29** (1982), 24-32.

[38] D. M. Gabbay, I. Hodkinson and M. Reynolds, *Temporal logic: Mathematical Foundations and Computational Aspects (vol. 1)*, Oxford University Press, 1994.

[39] M. R. Garey and D. S. Johnson, *Computers and Intractability: A Guide to the Theory of NP-Completeness*, W. H. Freeman, San Francisco, CA, 1979.

[40] M. C. Golumbic, *Algorithmic Graph Theory and Perfect Graphs*, Academic Press, New York, 1980.

[41] M. C. Golumbic, H. Kaplan and R. Shamir, On the complexity of DNA physical mapping, *Advances in Applied Mathematics* **15** (1994), 251-261.

[42] M. C. Golumbic and R. Shamir, Complexity and algorithms for reasoning about time: a graph-theoretic approach, *J. Assoc. Comput. Mach.* **40** (1993), 1108-1133.

[43] J. Y. Halpern and Y. Shoham, A propositional modal logic of time intervals, *Journal of the ACM* **38** (1991), 935-962.

[44] I. Hamlet and J. Hunter, A representation of time for medical expert systems, *Lecture Notes in Medical Informatics* **33**, Springer-Verlag, 1987, 112-119.

[45] S. Hanks and D. V. McDermott, Default reasoning, nonmonotonic logics, and the frame problem. *Proc. AAAI-86*, Philadelphia, PA, pp. 328-333, 1986.

[46] R. M. Haralick and G. L. Elliott, Increasing tree search efficiency for constraint satisfaction problems, *Artificial Intelligence* **14** (1980), 263-313.

[47] C. S. Jensen, and R. T. Snodgrass, Temporal specialization and generalization, *IEEE Trans. on Knowledge and Data Engr.* **6** (1994), 954-974.

[48] K. Kahn and G. A. Gorry, Mechanizing temporal knowledge, *Artificial Intelligence* **9** (1977), 87-108.

[49] H. Kautz and P. B. Ladkin, Integrating metric and qualitative temporal reasoning, *Proc. AAAI-91*, Anaheim, CA, pp. 241-246, 1991.

[50] D. G. Kendall, Incidence matrices, interval graphs and seriation in archaeology, *Pacific J. Math* **28** (1969), 565-570.

[51] M. Koubarakis, Database models for infinite and indefinite temporal information, *Information Systems* **19** (1994), 141 174.

[52] P. B. Ladkin, Time representation: a taxonomy of interval relations, *Proc. AAAI-86*, Philadelphia, PA, pp. 360-366, 1986.

[53] P. B. Ladkin, Metric constraint satisfaction with intervals, Technical Report TR-89-038, International Computer Science Institute, Berkeley, CA, 1989.

[54] P. B. Ladkin and R. D. Maddux, The algebra of constraint satisfaction problems and temporal reasoning, Technical Report, Kestrel Institute, Palo Alto, CA, 1988.

[55] P. B. Ladkin and R. D. Maddux, On binary constraint problems, *Journal of the ACM* **41** (1994), 435-469.

[56] P. B. Ladkin and A. Reinefeld, Effective solutions of qualitative interval constraint problems, *Artificial Intelligence* **57** (1992), 105-124.

[57] C. E. Leiserson and J. B. Saxe, A mixed-integer linear programming problem which is efficiently solvable, *Proc. 21st Annual Allerton Conference on Communication, Control, and Computing*, pp. 204-213, 1983.

[58] Y. Z. Liao and C. K. Wong, An algorithm to compact a VLSI symbolic layout with mixed constraints, *IEEE Transactions on Computer-Aided Design of Integrated Circuits and Systems*, **CAD-2** (1983), 62-69.

[59] A. K. Mackworth, Consistency in networks of relations, *Artificial Intelligence* **8** (1977), 99-118.

[60] A. K. Mackworth, Constraint satisfaction, in: *Encyclopedia of Artificial Intelligence, 2nd Edition*, S. Shapiro, editor, John Wiley, New York, 1992.

[61] A. K. Mackworth and E. C. Freuder, The complexity of some polynomial network consistency algorithms for constraint satisfaction problems, *Artificial Intelligence* **25** (1985), 65-74.

[62] R. Maiocchi and B. Pernici, Temporal data management systems: A comparative view, *IEEE Trans. on Knowledge and Data Engr.* **3** (1991), 504-524.

[63] J. Malik and T. O. Binford, Reasoning in time and space, *Proc. IJCAI-83*, Karlsruhe, Germany, pp. 343-345, 1983.

[64] L. E. McKenzie, Jr. and R. T. Snodgrass, Evaluation of relational algebras incorporating the time dimension in databases, *ACM Computing Surveys* **23** (1991), 501-543.

[65] D. V. McDermott, A temporal logic for reasoning about processes and plans, *Cognitive Science* **6** (1982), 101-155.

[66] I. Meiri, Combining qualitative and quantitative constraints in temporal reasoning, *Artificial Intelligence* (to appear 1996).

[67] R. Mohr and T. C. Henderson, Arc and path consistency revisited, *Artificial Intelligence* **28** (1986), 225-233.

[68] U. Montanari, Networks of constraints: Fundamental properties and applications to picture processing, *Information Sciences* **7** (1974), 95-132.

[69] B. A. Nadel, Constraint satisfaction algorithms, *Computational Intelligence* **5** (1989), 188-224.

[70] B. Nebel and H.-J. Bürckert, Reasoning about temporal relations: A maximal tractable subclass of Allen's interval algebra, *J. ACM* **42** (1995), 43-66.

[71] K. Nökel, Temporal matching: Recognizing dynamic situations from discrete measurements, *Proc. IJCAI-89*, Detroit, MI, pp. 1255-1260, 1989.

[72] K. Nökel, Temporally distributed symptoms in technical diagnosis, *Lecture Notes in Artificial Intelligence* **517**, Springer-Verlag, 1991.

[73] B. Nudel, Consistent-labeling problems and their algorithms: expected-complexities and theory-based heuristics, *Artificial Intelligence* **21** (1983), 135-178.

[74] G. O'Hare and N. Jennings, *Foundations of Distributed Artificial Intelligence*, John Wiley, 1996.

[75] C. H. Papadimitriou and K. Steiglitz, *Combinatorial Optimization: Algorithms and Complexity*, Prentice-Hall, Englewood Cliffs, NJ, 1982.

[76] M. Poesio and R. J. Brachman, Metric constraints for maintaining appointments: dates and repeated activities, *Proc. AAAI-91*, Anaheim, CA, pp. 253-259, 1991.

[77] P. W. Purdom, Search rearrangement backtracking and polynomial average time, *Artificial Intelligence* **21** (1983), 117-133.

[78] J. F. Roddick and J. D. Patrick, Temporal semantics in information systems - a survey, *Information Systems* **17** (1992), 249-267.

[79] Y. Shoham, *Reasoning About Change: Time and Causation from the Standpoint of Artificial Intelligence*, MIT Press, Cambridge, MA, 1988.

[80] R. Shostak, Deciding linear inequalities by computing loop residues, *Journal of the ACM* **28** (1981), 769-779.

[81] R. T. Snodgrass, Temporal databases, in: *Theories and Methods of Spatio-Temporal Reasoning in Geographic Space*, Springer-Verlag, *LNCS* **639**, 1992.

[82] F. Song and R. Cohen, The interpretation of temporal relations in narrative, *Proc. AAAI-88*, St. Paul, MN, pp. 745-750, 1988.

[83] F. Song and R. Cohen, Temporal reasoning during plan recognition, *Proc. AAAI-91*, Anaheim, CA, pp. 247-252, 1991.

[84] A. Tansel, J. Clifford, S. Gadia, S. Jajodia, A. Segev and R. Snodgrass, eds., *Temporal Databases: Theory, Design and Implementation*, Benjamin/Cummings, 1993.

[85] A. Tarski, On the calculus of relations, *J. Symbolic Logic* **6** (1941), 73-89.

[86] C. I. Theodoulidis and P. Loucopoulos, The time dimension in conceptual modelling, *Information Systems* **16** (1991), 273-300.

[87] R. E. Valdés-Pérez, The satisfiability of temporal constraint networks, *Proc. AAAI-87*, Seattle, WA, pp. 256-260, 1987.

[88] P. VanBeek, Approximation algorithms for temporal reasoning, *Proc. IJCAI-89*, Detroit, MI, pp. 1291-1296, 1989.

[89] P. VanBeek, Temporal query processing with indefinite information, *Artificial Intelligence Med.* **3** (1991), 745-750.

[90] P. VanBeek, Reasoning about qualitative information, *Artificial Intelligence* **58** (1992), 297-326.

[91] P. VanBeek and R. Cohen, Exact and approximate reasoning about temporal relations, *Computational Intelligence* **6** (1990), 132-144.

[92] J. F. A. K. VanBenthem, *The Logic of Time, 2nd Edition*, D. Reidel, 1991.

[93] S. A. Vere, Planning in time: Windows and durations for activities and goals, *IEEE Transactions on Pattern Analysis and Machine Intelligence* **5** (1983), 246-267.

[94] M. Vilain, A system for reasoning about time, *Proc. AAAI-82*, Pittsburgh, PA, pp. 197-201, 1982.

[95] M. Vilain and H. Kautz, Constraint propagation algorithms for temporal reasoning, *Proc. AAAI-86*, Philadelphia, PA, pp. 377-382, 1986.

[96] A. B. Webber, Proof of the interval satisfiability conjecture, *Annals of Mathematics and Artificial Intelligence* **15** (1995), 231-238.

[97] B. C. Williams, Doing time: Putting qualitative reasoning on firmer ground, *Proc. AAAI-86*, Philadelphia, PA, pp. 105-113, 1986.

Proceedings of Symposia in Applied Mathematics
Volume **55**, 1998

Orderings in Automated Theorem Proving

Hélène Kirchner

ABSTRACT. This paper is intended to give an introduction to several techniques used in automated theorem proving, and based on the concept of ordering on terms and more generally on formulas. Different orderings and their automation are presented and several applications are considered. We show how orderings provide a way to incorporate equality decision procedures in theorem provers. We also illustrate their fundamental role to automatise proofs by induction and proofs by refutation. Finally, we explain how they allow pruning the search space of a theorem prover by defining strategies to restrict application of inference rules.

1. Introduction

Automated theorem proving in its broad sense covers a wide variety of proof systems. Proof assistants help the mathematician to verify all steps of a user driven proof. In systems like NuPrl [**24**], CoQ [**25**], Nqthm [**19**], HOL [**36**], Isabelle [**87**] or LP [**38**], parts of the deduction process are automatic, but the user interaction remains important to guide the general development of the proof. Often tactics can be programmed to encapsulate subproof development. In contrast, in automated theorem provers like RRL [**61**], Otter [**77, 82**], or the Prolog Technology Theorem Prover [**107**], the user interaction is minimised and the proof development is fully automatic on some logical fragments. One main problem there is to prune the search space and to eliminate redundant subproofs. In this paper, the goal is not to give a survey of all these provers, but rather to focus on the automation problem and to see how the notion of ordering on terms and derived techniques can be used for this purpose in the context of automated deduction. The use of orderings will be illustrated on various applications in first-order theorem proving: equality decision, proof by induction, proof by refutation, ordered and basic strategies.

Once it is recognised that orderings on terms and more generally on formulas are of primary use in automated theorem proving, a main challenge is then to design orderings that can be automated too, so that the computer can prove automatically that a term is greater than another. Automation of the ordering process is thus a key point to go from proof assistants to automated theorem provers. The ordering process itself may be either fully automatic when it is based on a syntactic analysis of terms, or partially automated when supported by an interpretation provided by

---

1991 *Mathematics Subject Classification.* Primary 68T15, 03B35, 68Q42; Secondary 06F99.

This work was partially supported by the Esprit Basic Research Working Groups 6112 (COMPASS) and 6028 (CCL).

the user. In Section 3, several methods are presented that have been integrated in various automated theorem provers.

Incorporating equality decision in theorem provers has been one of the most challenging problems in automated deduction, and in the past thirty years, a number of methods have been proposed. The term rewriting method, a refinement of replacement of equals by equals, has been one of the most successful approaches for this problem. Rewrite systems are sets of directed equalities (two ordered terms), called rewrite rules, that are used for replacements in a given direction only. They induce a relation on terms that is often required to have two properties: termination and confluence. With these properties, finite rewrite systems provide decision procedures for their underlying equational theories, and therefore are of particular interest in automated deduction. For most interesting proofs in mathematical structures, set and graph theory, or geometry, the ordering on terms needs to be extended to quotient sets modulo some axioms, like associativity and commutativity laws for functions. The previous concepts and methods can be adapted to incorporate such axioms. Section 4 presents rewrite systems and their use for equality decision.

When there exists a terminating rewrite system (i.e. without infinite rewrite sequence), the corresponding rewrite relation is a well-founded ordering over terms and can be considered as the basis for induction in a Nœtherian induction principle. Intuitively, to prove a theorem by induction, its variables are instantiated by a set of significant terms, then these instances are reduced to produce smaller conjectures in the well-founded ordering induced by the rewrite system. Each conjecture is simplified until becoming trivial, using rewrite rules, previously proved conjectures, and smaller instances of the conjecture itself. Section 5 shows how these ideas are implemented to automatise proofs by induction.

In proofs by refutation, the negation of the formula to be proved is asserted and the goal is then to derive a contradiction. Negated equalities are introduced and involved in the deduction process. Even when equalities are not orientable with a given ordering, some orientable instances of them are allowed to be used to simplify and prune the search space. Section 6 presents these techniques and illustrates them on several examples involving associative and commutative operators.

Term rewriting techniques have also been widely used to incorporate equality in resolution-style theorem provers, for instance in the form of paramodulation and superposition inferences. They are quite important to reduce the search space and eliminate redundant equations. They are combined with ordered strategies that consist in choosing at each inference step, maximal subformulas with respect to a given ordering. These techniques are applied to theorem proving in Horn logic with the equality predicate, or in general to the full first-order logic with equality. Section 7 addresses some work done in this direction.

It has appeared since the 1990s that ordering conditions are better handled via constraints on formulas. So ordering and equality constraints were proposed for improving the deduction processes in first-order logic with equality both from the point of view of expressivity and efficiency. Section 8 shows how ordering constraints can be used in automated theorem provers to design complete and efficient strategies.

2. Preliminaries

The material included in this survey is strongly inspired from the literature on term rewriting and automated deduction and more specifically from [**46, 68**]. The notations used in this paper are consistent with [**30**], which the reader may refer to for the concepts of terms, substitution and rewrite systems.

A first-order signature $\Sigma = (\mathcal{F}, \mathcal{P})$ is composed of a set of function symbols $\mathcal{F}$ and a set of predicate symbols $\mathcal{P}$, both with arities. $\mathcal{T}(\mathcal{F}, \mathcal{X})$ denotes the set of terms built on $\mathcal{F}$ (i.e. involving function symbols $\mathcal{F}$) and variables $\mathcal{X}$. $\mathcal{T}(\mathcal{F})$ is the set of ground terms, i.e. without variables. $\mathcal{V}ar(t)$ denotes the set of variables of a term t, $t_{|\omega}$ the subterm of t at position ω, and $t[u]_\omega$ the term t that contains the subterm u at position ω (ω may be omitted). Atoms $p(t_1, \dots, t_n)$ are built from terms $t_1, \dots, t_n$ and a predicate $p \in \mathcal{P}$, and are also called positive literals. Negative literals are of the form $\neg p(t_1, \dots, t_n)$. Clauses are formulas of the form $\neg L_1 \vee \dots \vee \neg L_n \vee M_1 \vee \dots \vee M_m$ where L_i and M_j are atoms. In general $C[t]_\omega$ indicates that the expression C (that can be a term, an atom, a literal or a clause) contains t as subexpression at some position ω (often omitted).

We use Greek letters $\sigma, \theta, \dots$ to denote substitutions, that are completely defined by a mapping of variables to terms written $\sigma = (x_1 \mapsto t_1) \dots (x_n \mapsto t_n)$ when $\sigma(x_i) = t_i$ for $i = 1, \dots, n$. The term t_i is called the instantiation of x_i. The *domain* of the substitution σ is the finite set of variables $\mathcal{D}om(\sigma) = \{x \mid x \in \mathcal{X} \text{ and } \sigma(x) \neq x\}$, the *range* of σ is the set of terms $\mathcal{R}an(\sigma) = \cup_{x \in \mathcal{D}om(\sigma)} \sigma(x)$. A substitution σ is *ground* if $\mathcal{R}an(\sigma) \subseteq \mathcal{T}(\mathcal{F})$. Composition of σ and ρ is denoted $\rho\sigma$. An expression C (that can be a term, an atom, a literal or a clause) is an instance of another expression D when there exists a substitution σ such that $C = \sigma(D)$.

In equational logic [**39, 99, 108, 109**], a formula is a universally quantified equality on terms. *Equational theorems* are deduced from a set A of *equational axioms* by an inference rule called *replacement of equals by equals*. It consists of replacing, in a term t, an instance $\sigma(l)$ of a left-hand side of an axiom $(l = r)$ by the same instance of its right-hand side $\sigma(r)$, thus producing another term s. This is denoted by $t \longleftrightarrow_A s$, while $\overset{+}{\longleftrightarrow}_A$ and $\overset{*}{\longleftrightarrow}_A$ denote respectively the transitive and the reflexive transitive closure of this replacement relation. Such proofs are called *equational proofs*. A model of a set of axioms A is an algebra satisfying A. From a completeness theorem due to Birkhoff [**15**], it follows that the inference rule of replacing equals by equals is sufficient to prove equalities valid in all models of A.

3. Orderings on terms and formulas

A binary relation $\mathcal{R}$ on a set $\mathcal{T}$ is reflexive if $(\forall t \in \mathcal{T},\ t\, \mathcal{R}\, t)$; antisymmetric if $(\forall t, t' \in \mathcal{T},\ t\, \mathcal{R}\, t'$ and $t'\, \mathcal{R}\, t$ implies $t = t')$; transitive if $(\forall t, t', t'' \in \mathcal{T},\ t\, \mathcal{R}\, t'$ and $t'\, \mathcal{R}\, t''$ implies $t\, \mathcal{R}\, t'')$. Composition of relations is denoted by $\circ$.

A *(partial) ordering* is a reflexive, antisymmetric and transitive relation on a set $\mathcal{T}$, denoted $\geq$. Its symmetric relation is denoted $\leq$. A *total ordering* satisfies moreover: $\forall t, t' \in \mathcal{T},\ t \geq t'$ or $t' \geq t$. The equivalence relation associated to an ordering $\geq$ on a set $\mathcal{T}$, denoted $\simeq$, is defined as usual as the intersection of $\geq$ and its symmetric relation $\leq$: $\forall t, t' \in \mathcal{T}, t \simeq t'$ if $t \geq t'$ and $t \leq t'$.

The associated *strict ordering* $>$ is defined by: $t > t'$ if $t \geq t'$ and $t \not\simeq t'$.

DEFINITION 3.1. A strict partial ordering $>$ on a set $\mathcal{T}$ is *well-founded* if there exists no infinite descending chain $t_1 > t_2 > \dots$ of elements of $\mathcal{T}$.

For a given ordering, two kinds of extensions will be used in the following, namely the multiset and lexicographic extensions. A multiset over a set $\mathcal{T}$ is a function M from $\mathcal{T}$ to the natural numbers. Intuitively for any element x in $\mathcal{T}$, $M(x)$ specifies the number of occurrences of x in M. A multiset is finite if $M(x) = 0$ for all but finitely many x.

Let $>$ be a strict partial ordering on $\mathcal{T}$.

- Its multiset extension $>^{mult}$ is the transitive closure of the following relation on finite multisets over $\mathcal{T}$:

$$\{s_1, \ldots, s_{i-1}, s_i, s_{i+1}, \ldots, s_n\} >^{mult} \{s_1, \ldots, s_{i-1}, t_1, \ldots, t_k, s_{i+1}, \ldots, s_n\}$$

  if for some element s_i, there exist k elements, $k \geq 0$, such that $s_i > t_j$ for any $j = 1, \ldots, k$.
  If $>$ is well-founded on $\mathcal{T}$, its multiset extension $>^{mult}$ is well-founded on finite multisets over $\mathcal{T}$.
- Its lexicographical extension $>^{lex}$ is defined on the cartesian product $\mathcal{T}^n$ by:

$$(s_1, \ldots, s_n) >^{lex} (t_1, \ldots, t_n)$$

  if there exists i, $1 \leq i \leq n$ such that $s_i > t_i$, and $\forall j, 1 \leq j < i,\ s_j = t_j$.
  If $>$ is well-founded on $\mathcal{T}$, so is $>^{lex}$ on $\mathcal{T}^n$, but this result does not extend to tuples of arbitrary length: for example if $\mathcal{T} = \{a, b\}$ with $b > a$, then $(b) >^{lex} (a, b) >^{lex} (a, a, b) >^{lex} (a, a, a, b) >^{lex} \ldots$

When $\mathcal{T}$ is a set of terms, orderings which are closed under context and substitution, are the most interesting ones.

DEFINITION 3.2. A *reduction ordering* $>$ is an ordering on terms, such that for any term t and any substitution σ, if $u > s$ then $t[u] > t[s]$ and $\sigma(u) > \sigma(s)$.

There are essentially two classes of well-founded reduction orderings on terms that have been automated in theorem provers, and that may be combined to produce more complex and powerful ones.

- *Syntactical orderings* are based on an analysis of the term structure. Among these orderings are for instance the *recursive path ordering* [**26**], the *lexicographic path ordering* [**58**] and the *recursive decomposition ordering* [**57, 76**]. These orderings are convenient, since they rely on the simple concept of precedence, which is a partial order on the signature. Moreover the precedence can be built incrementally when increasing sets of ordering problems are handled.
- Another family consists of *semantical orderings*, that interpret terms in another structure where a well-founded ordering is known. For such a purpose, two common well-ordered sets are the natural numbers and the terms ordered by a syntactical ordering. The first choice enables one to consider functions over natural numbers which are stable by substitutions. The most frequently used are polynomials [**73, 13, 103, 23, 35**]. The set of terms ordered by a syntactical ordering may also be chosen as a target for the "semantics" [**3, 12**].
- Both methods may be combined, as in [**69**] that uses a semantical ordering (polynomial interpretation of degree 1) and a syntactical ordering. A general ordering dealing with semantical as well as syntactical aspects has more recently been proposed in [**29**].

Here we just illustrate each of the first two families with specific examples.

Syntactical orderings contain the important family of simplification orderings. In addition to being reduction orderings, simplification orderings enjoy the so-called *subterm property* which means that a term is greater than any of its subterms. In other words:

DEFINITION 3.3. A *simplification ordering* is a reduction ordering that satisfies $t > u$ for any term t and any subterm u of t, different from t.

The last subterm condition suffices for ensuring well-foundedness of simplification orderings, provided that the signature is finite.

Simplification orderings can be built from a well-founded ordering on the function symbols $\mathcal{F}$ called a *precedence.* A powerful example is the following *multiset path ordering* also called *recursive path ordering*:

DEFINITION 3.4. Let $>_{\mathcal{F}}$ be a precedence on $\mathcal{F}$. The *multiset path ordering* $>_{mpo}$ is defined on ground terms by $s = f(s_1, .., s_n) >_{mpo} t = g(t_1, \dots, t_m)$ if one at least of the following conditions holds:

1. $f = g$ and $\{s_1, \dots, s_n\} >_{mpo}^{mult} \{t_1, \dots, t_m\}$
2. $f >_{\mathcal{F}} g$ and $\forall j \in \{1, \dots, m\}$, $s >_{mpo} t_j$
3. $\exists i \in \{1, \dots, n\}$ such that either $s_i >_{mpo} t$ or $s_i \sim t$ where $\sim$ means equivalent up to permutation of subterms.

The precedence on $\mathcal{F}$ does not need to be total, and the condition $f = g$ can be replaced by $f \sim_{\mathcal{F}} g$, where $\sim_{\mathcal{F}}$ is the equivalence induced on $\mathcal{F}$ by $>_{\mathcal{F}}$. Taking into account the fact that a variable may be replaced by any term, the definition of the multiset path ordering can be extended to terms with variables by adding the following conditions: two different variables are incomparable, and a function symbol and a variable are incomparable.

THEOREM 3.5. **[26]** *The multiset path ordering is a simplification ordering.*

EXAMPLE 3.6. Let $\mathcal{F} = \{f, p, h\}$ be a set of function symbols with respective arities 2, 2 and 1. Clearly by the subterm property, we can deduce:

$$h(p(x, y)) >_{mpo} p(x, y) >_{mpo} y.$$

Assuming $f >_{\mathcal{F}} p$, in order to show:

$$f(p(x, y), z) >_{mpo} p(x, f(z, y))$$

we verify:

$$f(p(x, y), z) >_{mpo} x \text{ and } f(p(x, y), z) >_{mpo} f(z, y).$$

The first condition uses the subterm property and the latter holds since

$$p(x, y) >_{mpo} y.$$

Instead of comparing the multisets of subterms, the next ordering compares them lexicographically.

DEFINITION 3.7. Let $>_{\mathcal{F}}$ be a precedence on $\mathcal{F}$. The *lexicographic path ordering* $>_{lpo}$ is defined on terms by $s = f(s_1, .., s_n) >_{lpo} t = g(t_1, \dots, t_m)$ if one at least of the following condition holds:

1. $f = g$ and $(s_1, \dots, s_n) >_{lpo}^{lex} (t_1, \dots, t_m)$ and $\forall j \in \{1, \dots, m\}, s >_{lpo} t_j$
2. $f >_{\mathcal{F}} g$ and $\forall j \in \{1, \dots, m\}, s >_{lpo} t_j$
3. $\exists i \in \{1, \dots, n\}$ such that either $s_i >_{lpo} t$ or $s_i = t$.

Again, the condition $f = g$ can be replaced by $f \sim_{\mathcal{F}} g$ where $\sim_{\mathcal{F}}$ is the equivalence induced by $>_{\mathcal{F}}$.

THEOREM 3.8. [**58**] *The lexicographic path ordering is a simplification ordering.*

It is extended to terms with variables in the same way as the multiset path ordering.

EXAMPLE 3.9. Let $\mathcal{F} = \{ack, s, 0\}$ be a set of function symbols with respective arities 2, 1 and 0. Assuming the precedence $ack >_{\mathcal{F}} s$, it is easy to show that:

$$\begin{array}{rcl} ack(0,y) & >_{lpo} & s(y) \\ ack(s(x),0) & >_{lpo} & ack(x,s(0)) \\ ack(s(x),s(y)) & >_{lpo} & ack(x,ack(s(x),y)). \end{array}$$

Interpreting 0 as the zero of natural numbers, s as the successor function and ack as the Ackermann's function, the three following equalities recursively define the Ackermann's function.

$$\begin{array}{rcl} ack(0,y) & = & s(y) \\ ack(s(x),0) & = & ack(x,s(0)) \\ ack(s(x),s(y)) & = & ack(x,ack(s(x),y)). \end{array}$$

As further explained in Section 4, the termination of the Ackermann's function is proved by the three inequalities above.

In contrast to this syntactic approach, the construction of a semantical reduction ordering relies on the definition of homomorphisms mapping ground terms into another algebra in which a well-founded ordering is known.

Let τ be an homomorphism from ground terms in $\mathcal{T}(\mathcal{F})$ to an $\mathcal{F}$-algebra $\mathcal{A}$ with a well-founded ordering $>$. Let f_τ denote the image of $f \in \mathcal{F}$ using τ; τ and $>$ are required to satisfy the monotonicity condition:

$$\forall a, b, a_1, \ldots, a_{k-1}, a_{k+1}, \ldots, a_n \in \mathcal{A}, \forall f \in \mathcal{F},$$

$a > b$ implies $f_\tau(a_1, \ldots, a_{k-1}, a, a_{k+1}, \ldots, a_n) > f_\tau(a_1, \ldots, a_{k-1}, b, a_{k+1}, \ldots, a_n)$.

Then the ordering $>_\tau$ defined by:

$$\forall s, t \in \mathcal{T}(\mathcal{F}),\ s >_\tau t \text{ if } \tau(s) > \tau(t),$$

is well-founded.

To compare terms with variables, the ordering $>_\tau$ is extended by defining:

$$\forall s, t \in \mathcal{T}(\mathcal{F}, \mathcal{X}), s >_\tau t \text{ if } \nu(\tau(s)) > \nu(\tau(t))$$

for all instantiations ν of variables of $\tau(s)$ and $\tau(t)$ by values in $\mathcal{A}$. Then $>_\tau$ is well-founded.

In the following example, $\mathcal{A}$ is the algebra of natural numbers with its usual ordering $>$, together with polynomial interpretations [**73**].

EXAMPLE 3.10. Assume that we need to prove that $i(f(x,y)) >_\tau f(f(i(x),y),y)$. Let us interpret i and f respectively by the square and the sum functions on positive natural numbers:

$$\begin{array}{rcl} \tau(i(x)) & = & \tau(x)^2 \\ \tau(f(x,y)) & = & \tau(x) + \tau(y) \end{array}$$

In addition, let $\tau(x) = x$ and $\tau(y) = y$.

The monotonicity condition $a > b$ implies $f_\tau(a) > f_\tau(b)$ is clearly satisfied, since the considered functions are increasing on natural numbers. Now,

$$\begin{aligned}\tau(i(f(x,y))) &= (x+y)^2 = x^2 + y^2 + 2xy \\ \tau(f(f(i(x),y),y)) &= x^2 + 2y.\end{aligned}$$

and for any instantiation of variables x and y by positive natural numbers n and m, we get $n^2 + m^2 + 2nm > n^2 + 2m$. So $i(f(x,y)) >_\tau f(f(i(x),y),y)$.

In order to build more powerful orderings, a natural idea is to combine existing ones. For instance, lexicographic and multiset arguments may be combined to get the recursive path ordering with status, in which each symbol f in the signature has a status which can be either lexicographic or multiset [**27**].

Another direction is to combine two well-founded orderings by taking their union. But it is not true that the union of two well-founded orderings is still well-founded, even if the function symbols are disjoint.

EXAMPLE 3.11. Consider the smallest reduction ordering relation on terms with function symbols $\mathcal{F}_1 = \{a, b, f\}$ which contains

$$f(a,b,x) >_1 f(x,x,x).$$

This relation is well-founded [**110**]. Consider on the other hand the smallest reduction ordering relation on terms with function symbols $\mathcal{F}_2 = \{g\}$ which contains

$$\begin{aligned}g(x,y) &>_2 x \\ g(x,y) &>_2 y.\end{aligned}$$

Again one can prove that this relation is well-founded, intuitively because no finite term can contain an infinite number of symbols g. However in the disjoint union of both signatures, there is a cycle:

$$\begin{aligned}f(g(a,b),g(a,b),g(a,b)) &>_1 \cup >_2 f(a,g(a,b),g(a,b)) \\ &>_1 \cup >_2 f(a,b,g(a,b)) \\ &>_1 \cup >_2 f(g(a,b),g(a,b),g(a,b))\end{aligned}$$

Another difficulty for automated deduction is to extend these orderings on equivalence classes of terms modulo an equality relation. Let A be any set of axioms with a decidable A-equivalence relation $\overset{*}{\longleftrightarrow}_A$.

DEFINITION 3.12. A reduction ordering $>$ is *A-compatible* if

$$\overset{*}{\longleftrightarrow}_A \circ > \circ \overset{*}{\longleftrightarrow}_A \subseteq > .$$

Such orderings have been described for associative-commutative axioms in [**83, 96**]. Well-founded A-compatible reduction orderings do not exist when A contains an axiom like idempotency $(x + x = x)$ where a lone variable occurs on one side and several times on the other. If l, r are two terms such that $l > r$, this implies since $>$ is a reduction ordering, $\sigma(l) > \sigma(r)$ for any substitution σ. But then a contradiction to well-foundedness of $>$ may be built as follows :

$$\sigma(l) \overset{*}{\longleftrightarrow}_A \sigma(l)+\sigma(l) > \sigma(r)+\sigma(l) \overset{*}{\longleftrightarrow}_A \sigma(r)+(\sigma(l)+\sigma(l)) > \sigma(r)+(\sigma(r)+\sigma(l))\ldots$$

Other axioms that prevent the existence of a well-founded strict A-compatible reduction ordering are equalities like $(x * 0 = 0)$ where a variable occurs on one side and not on the other. Then if $l > r$,

$$0 \longleftrightarrow_A \sigma(l) * 0 > \sigma(r) * 0 \longleftrightarrow_A 0$$

provides the contradiction $0 > 0$.

To compare atoms in first-order logic, one can make abstraction of some predicates. For instance, to compare two equalities $(l_1 = r_1)$ and $(l_2 = r_2)$, the multisets $\{l_1, r_1\}$ and $\{l_2, r_2\}$ are compared with the multiset extension of a chosen ordering on terms. One can also use a precedence $>_{\mathcal{P}}$ on the set of predicate symbols $\mathcal{P}$ [**49**].

4. Rewrite systems and equality decision

A first application of orderings on terms is the development of terminating rewriting techniques. The section illustrates how these techniques have evolved from the beginning of their formal study in the 80's [**53**]. Their development corresponds to an increasing applicability to more and more complex mathematical theories and has been supported by implementations.

For each rewrite relation $\longrightarrow$ defined in this paper on a set $\mathcal{T}$ whose elements are denoted by $t, t', \ldots$, we also define:

$$\begin{array}{lll} t \longleftarrow t' & \text{if} & t' \longrightarrow t \\ t \longleftrightarrow t' & \text{if} & \text{either } t \longrightarrow t' \text{ or } t' \longrightarrow t \\ t \overset{*}{\longleftarrow} t' & \text{if} & t' \overset{*}{\longrightarrow} t \\ t \overset{+}{\longleftarrow} t' & \text{if} & t' \overset{+}{\longrightarrow} t \end{array}$$

4.1. Rewriting and completion. Rewrite rules are pairs of patterns (here terms) and operationally behave as follows: given a term which is the subject to reduce, try to recognise the first pattern somewhere in the term, using a matching algorithm. Usually when the pattern contains variables, this phase provides instantiations for them. Then at the place where the first pattern has been recognised, the second pattern is substituted with the same instantiation of common variables. Such a reduction process appears as a programming paradigm in expert systems and in functional languages. We shall see here how rewrite rules and reduction are used in automated theorem proving.

DEFINITION 4.1. A *rewrite rule* is a pair of terms denoted $(l \rightarrow r)$ with the additional assumption that the set of variables of r is included into the set of variables of l. The term l is called the left-hand side and the term r is the right-hand side of the rule. A *rewrite system* R is a set of rewrite rules.

Rewriting a term with a rewrite system R consists in replacing a subterm which matches a left-hand side of a rewrite rule by the right-hand side whose variables are bound to values computed by the matching algorithm.

DEFINITION 4.2. Given a rewrite system R, a term t *rewrites* to a term t', if there exists a rule $l \rightarrow r$ of R, a position ω in t, a substitution σ, satisfying $t_{|\omega} = \sigma(l)$ and called a *match* from l to $t_{|\omega}$, such that $t' = t[\sigma(r)]_\omega$.

The rewrite relation is denoted by $\longrightarrow_R$ and a rewriting step is denoted by $t[\sigma(l)]_\omega \longrightarrow_R t[\sigma(r)]_\omega$ or simply $t \longrightarrow_R t'$.

EXAMPLE 4.3. With the rewrite rule $s(x)+y \rightarrow s(x+y)$, the term $s(s(0))+s(0)$ rewrites at top to $s(s(0) + s(0))$ with the matching substitution $(x \mapsto s(0))(y \mapsto s(0))$. This last term rewrites at position 1 to $s(s(0 + s(0)))$ with the matching substitution $(x \mapsto 0)(y \mapsto s(0))$.

Iterating this process is called *reducing*. If two terms can be reduced to a same one, a special proof is obtained, called a *rewrite proof.* A term which cannot be rewritten is said to be in *normal form.*

The rewrite relation $\longrightarrow_R$ is well-founded if it is included into a well-founded ordering. This is the case whenever there exists a well-founded reduction ordering $>$ on terms such that any rewrite rule $(l \to r) \in R$ satisfies $l > r$. This ensures that all rewriting sequences issued from any term terminate, and R is said to be *terminating.* The reader should note that we abusively identify the rewrite system R and the associated rewrite relation $\longrightarrow_R$ when we express the properties of this relation.

Termination is in general undecidable, but the tools presented in the previous section to build well-founded reduction orderings provide sufficient conditions for proving termination. A survey can be found in [**27**]. The ordering used for the termination proof of a rewrite system is related to the complexity of computations performed with R. Several results have been obtained in this direction for polynomial interpretations [**42, 75, 23**] and for multiset path orderings [**41**].

Another property required for a rewrite system is the uniqueness of the normal form for any term. This is crucial for applications where computing normal forms must be independent of the strategy of rule application. Uniqueness of the normal form is implied by another property called *confluence.* A rewrite system is confluent when two rewrite sequences beginning from the same term can always be extended to end with the same term. Local confluence is a special case of confluence.

DEFINITION 4.4. A rewrite system R is *confluent* if the relation $\longrightarrow_R$ satisfies on $\mathcal{T}(\mathcal{F},\mathcal{X})$:

$$\overset{*}{\longleftarrow}_R \circ \overset{*}{\longrightarrow}_R \subseteq \overset{*}{\longrightarrow}_R \circ \overset{*}{\longleftarrow}_R .$$

R is *locally confluent* if the relation $\longrightarrow_R$ satisfies on $\mathcal{T}(\mathcal{F},\mathcal{X})$:

$$\longleftarrow_R \circ \longrightarrow_R \subseteq \overset{*}{\longrightarrow}_R \circ \overset{*}{\longleftarrow}_R .$$

Confluence (which may be defined as an abstract property of relations, not specifically of rewriting relations) is equivalent to the *Church-Rosser property* that relates equational theorems and rewrite proofs: a rewrite system is Church-Rosser if every equational theorem $(t = t')$ has a rewrite proof, i.e. a proof of the form $t \overset{*}{\longrightarrow}_R \circ \overset{*}{\longleftarrow}_R t'$.

DEFINITION 4.5. The rewrite system R is *Church-Rosser* if the relation $\longrightarrow_R$ satisfies on $\mathcal{T}(\mathcal{F},\mathcal{X})$:

$$\overset{*}{\longleftrightarrow}_R = \overset{*}{\longrightarrow}_R \circ \overset{*}{\longleftarrow}_R$$

So deciding whether an equational theorem holds, amounts to reduce both its sides to a same normal form. A rewrite system R provides a decision procedure for an equational theory defined by a set of axioms E if R is finite, confluent, terminating and $\overset{*}{\longleftrightarrow}_R$ coincides with $\overset{*}{\longleftrightarrow}_E$.

The Church-Rosser property is equivalent to the local confluence property, under the termination assumption. These results are summarised by the following theorem.

THEOREM 4.6. *If the rewrite system R is terminating, the following properties are equivalent:*

1. *R is Church-Rosser,*
2. *R is confluent,*
3. *R is locally confluent,*
4. *for any* $t, t' \in \mathcal{T}(\mathcal{F}, \mathcal{X})$, $t \overset{*}{\longleftrightarrow}_R t'$ *if and only if* t *and* t' *have the same normal forms.*

Local confluence itself is equivalent to the convergence of *critical pairs* [**69, 51**]. Critical pairs are consequences that can be derived from the application of two overlapping rewrite rules on the same term. Their computation relies on the unification process:

DEFINITION 4.7. A *unifier* of two terms s and t is a substitution σ that makes them equal, i.e. satisfies $\sigma(s) = \sigma(t)$. When such a substitution exists, the two terms are said unifiable, and then any instance of σ is again a unifier. A unifier σ of s and t is the *most general unifier* if for every unifier θ of s and t, there exists a substitution ρ such that $\theta = \rho\sigma$.

The most general unifier is unique up to variable renaming [**95**].

The set $CP(R)$ of critical pairs of a rewrite system R is computed by unifying, in all possible ways, a left-hand side l_1 with a non-variable subterm u of another left-hand side l_2. We always assume that rules have disjoint sets of variables, which can be easily satisfied with a renaming substitution. Note also that u may be a variable renaming of l_1. If σ is the most general unifier of l_1 and u (denoted $mgu(u, l_1)$ for short), the term $\sigma(l_2)$ can be rewritten in two different ways leading to a critical pair.

DEFINITION 4.8. Let $(l_1 \to r_1)$ and $(l_2 \to r_2)$ be two rewrite rules with disjoint sets of variables. If there exists a position ω in l_2 such that $l_{2|\omega}$ is not a variable, and $l_{2|\omega}$ and l_1 are unifiable with a most general unifier σ, then

$$\sigma(l_2[r_1]_\omega = r_2)$$

is a *critical pair* of $(l_1 \to r_1)$ into $(l_2 \to r_2)$ at position ω. $CP(R)$ denotes the set of critical pairs between all rules in R.

Although undecidable in general, confluence is decidable for terminating finite rewrite systems, which only have finite sets of critical pairs.

Now the question is: given a set of axioms E, is it possible to find a confluent and terminating rewrite system that generates the same equational theory? The answer is given by a *completion procedure* which transforms a pair (E, R) made of a set of equalities E and a set of rewrite rules R. Often initialised with the given set of axioms E defining the theory of interest and an empty set of rules R, completion computes critical pairs, orients equalities into rewrite rules and keeps terms in normal form for the current set of rewrite rules. Following [**6, 2**], completion is described through transition rules which transform a set of equalities E and a set of rewrite rules R. They are given below. *Deduce* adds to E equational consequences of R obtained by critical pairs computation. *Orient* transforms an equality of E into a rewrite rule, taking into account a given reduction ordering in order to ensure termination. *Delete* and *Simplify* respectively removes and reduces equalities in E. *Compose* and *Collapse* reduce the terms in the rewrite rules of R. When a left-hand side is reduced, orientation has to be reconsidered, so the obtained equality goes back to E. In addition each rule can be reduced only by another rule which is smaller in some sense. This is the reason for the condition in *Collapse*.

$$\begin{array}{llcll}
\textit{Deduce:} & E, R & \mapsto\!\!\!\rightarrow & E \cup \{s = t\}, R & \text{if } (s = t) \in CP(R) \\
\textit{Orient:} & E \cup \{s = t\}, R & \mapsto\!\!\!\rightarrow & E, R \cup \{s \rightarrow t\} & \text{if } s > t \\
\textit{Delete:} & E \cup \{s = s\}, R & \mapsto\!\!\!\rightarrow & E, R & \\
\textit{Simplify:} & E \cup \{s = t\}, R & \mapsto\!\!\!\rightarrow & E \cup \{s = u\}, R & \text{if } t \longrightarrow_R u \\
\textit{Compose:} & E, R \cup \{s \rightarrow t\} & \mapsto\!\!\!\rightarrow & E, R \cup \{s \rightarrow u\} & \text{if } t \longrightarrow_R u \\
\textit{Collapse:} & E, R \cup \{s \rightarrow t\} & \mapsto\!\!\!\rightarrow & E \cup \{u = t\}, R & \text{if } s \longrightarrow_R u \text{ by a rule} \\
 & & & & l \rightarrow r \in R \text{ with } s \gg l
\end{array}$$

where $>$ is a reduction ordering and $\gg$ is the *encompassment ordering* on terms, defined by $s \gg l$ if there exists a subterm of s which is an instance of l and not conversely.

A *derivation* is a sequence

$$(E_0, R_0) \mapsto\!\!\!\rightarrow (E_1, R_1) \mapsto\!\!\!\rightarrow \dots \mapsto\!\!\!\rightarrow (E_i, R_i) \dots$$

such that (E_{i+1}, R_{i+1}) is computed from (E_i, R_i) by applying one of the transition rules given above for completion.

Let $R_* = \bigcup_{i\geq 0} R_i$ be the set of all generated rules and $E_* = \bigcup_{i\geq 0} E_i$ the set of all generated equalities. Let R_∞ and E_∞ be respectively the set of persisting rules and equalities, i.e. the sets effectively generated by completion starting from a set of axioms E_0. Formally:

$$E_\infty = \bigcup_{i\geq 0} \bigcap_{j>i} E_j \quad \text{and} \quad R_\infty = \bigcup_{i\geq 0} \bigcap_{j>i} R_j.$$

Completion has three possible outcomes: either it terminates, or fails with a non-orientable equality, or diverges, i.e. generates infinitely many new rules. When the completion ends up with an empty set of equalities in E, if all critical pairs of R have been computed, R contains a Church-Rosser and terminating rewrite system.

THEOREM 4.9. *Let us assume given a well-founded reduction ordering used to orient equalities. If the derivation* $(E_0, R_0) \mapsto\!\!\!\rightarrow (E_1, R_1) \mapsto\!\!\!\rightarrow \dots$ *satisfies* $CP(R_\infty)$ *is a subset of* E_* *and* E_∞ *is empty, then* R_∞ *is Church-Rosser and terminating. Moreover* $\overset{*}{\longleftrightarrow}_{E_0 \cup R_0}$ *and* $\overset{*}{\longleftrightarrow}_{R_\infty}$ *coincide on terms.*

The proof of this theorem relies on a proof theoretic interpretation of completion given in [**2**]. Completion can be understood as a proof simplification process, where each step decreases the complexity of some equational proofs. The minimal (i.e. less complex) proofs in this setting are rewrite proofs.

EXAMPLE 4.10. The group example studied by Knuth and Bendix is now folklore in the term rewriting community. Consider the signature $\mathcal{F}$ composed of three operators $e, i, *$ taking respectively $0, 1$ and 2 arguments. Consider the following set, called *Groups*, of axioms for groups.

$$\begin{array}{rcl}
x * e & = & x \\
x * i(x) & = & e \\
(x * y) * z & = & x * (y * z)
\end{array}$$

An equational proof of $i(x) * x = e$ in *Groups* is given below:

$$\begin{array}{rcl}
i(x) * x & = & i(x) * (x * e) = i(x) * (x * (i(x) * i(i(x)))) \\
& = & i(x) * ((x * i(x)) * i(i(x))) \\
& = & i(x) * (e * i(i(x))) = (i(x) * e) * i(i(x)) = i(x) * i(i(x)) = e
\end{array}$$

Equational proofs of equational theorems are not easy to construct: at each step an axiom and an orientation to apply it have to be chosen. Considering axioms as rewrite rules:

$$\begin{aligned} x * e &\rightarrow x \\ x * i(x) &\rightarrow e \\ (x * y) * z &\rightarrow x * (y * z) \end{aligned}$$

we get the following proof, which is not a rewrite proof:

$$\begin{gathered} i(x) * x \leftarrow i(x) * (x * e) \leftarrow i(x) * (x * (i(x) * i(i(x)))) \leftarrow i(x) * ((x * i(x)) * i(i(x))) \\ \rightarrow i(x) * (e * i(i(x))) \leftarrow (i(x) * e) * i(i(x)) \rightarrow i(x) * i(i(x)) \rightarrow e. \end{gathered}$$

There are peaks, i.e. terms like $(i(x) * e) * i(i(x))$, from which two sequences of rewritings are issued, and terms where rewriting is not applied any more. Such terms, for instance $i(x) * x$, $i(x) * (e * i(i(x)))$, e are in normal form for the rewrite system. To get a rewrite system able to prove $(i(x) * x = e)$ with a rewrite proof, the completion process has to be applied. For instance a critical pair is computed between the second and third rules: unifying $x * i(x)$ and the variable renamed subterm $x' * y'$ of associativity, we get an overlapped term $(x * i(x)) * z$ on which both rules can be applied.

$$e * z \longleftarrow (x * i(x)) * z \longrightarrow x * (i(x) * z).$$

The new equality $(e * z = x * (i(x) * z))$ obtained by rewriting the overlapped term with each rule, is a critical pair of this system. It is added to the set of equalities and the completion process goes on. The following rewrite system

$$\begin{aligned} x * e &\rightarrow x \\ e * x &\rightarrow x \\ x * i(x) &\rightarrow e \\ i(x) * x &\rightarrow e \\ i(e) &\rightarrow e \\ i(i(x)) &\rightarrow x \\ i(x * y) &\rightarrow i(y) * i(x) \\ (x * y) * z &\rightarrow x * (y * z) \\ x * (i(x) * y) &\rightarrow y \\ i(x) * (x * y) &\rightarrow y \end{aligned}$$

can be obtained by completion from *Groups*. Then we get a very simple rewrite proof in one step $i(x) * x \longrightarrow e$. A rewrite proof for $\forall x,\ i(x * i(x)) = i(x) * i(i(x))$ is

$$i(x * i(x)) \longrightarrow i(i(x)) * i(x) \longrightarrow x * i(x) \longrightarrow e \longleftarrow i(x) * x \longleftarrow i(x) * i(i(x)).$$

Even when the process diverges, completion can nevertheless semi-decide validity of an equational theorem [**52**] in the following way: if a rewrite system produced at some step by the completion procedure reduces both terms of the theorem to a same one, then the theorem is valid.

EXAMPLE 4.11. [**28**] The theory of idempotent semi-groups (sometimes called bands) is defined by a set E of two axioms, associativity and idempotency of $*$:

$$\begin{aligned}(x*y)*z &= x*(y*z)\\ x*x &= x\end{aligned}$$

From E, the completion generates an infinite set of rewrite rules:

$$\begin{aligned}(x*y)*z &\rightarrow x*(y*z)\\ x*x &\rightarrow x\\ x*(x*z) &\rightarrow x*z\\ x*(y*(x*y)) &\rightarrow x*y\\ x*(y*(x*(y*z))) &\rightarrow x*(y*z)\\ &\;\;\ldots\\ x*(y*(z*(y*(x*(y*(z*x)))))) &\rightarrow x*(y*(z*x))\\ &\;\;\ldots\end{aligned}$$

Although this completion does not terminate, it can be used as a semi-decision procedure for proving for instance the theorem:

$$((x*((y*z)*x))*x)*((y*z)*x) = (x*y)*(y*((x*y)*(z*x)))$$

The partial system shown above reduces both terms of the theorem to $x*(y*(z*x))$. Of course, it is not possible to prove that a theorem is not valid with this method because one cannot prove that there is no step where both terms of the theorem reduce to a same one. So this is only a semi-decision method.

4.2. Class rewriting and completion. Some equalities, for instance commutativity, cannot be oriented into rules without loosing termination of the rewriting relation. Typically, with a rewrite rule $(x*y \rightarrow y*x)$, the term $a*b$ can be indefinitely rewritten $a*b \longrightarrow b*a \longrightarrow a*b\ldots.$ Associativity in presence of commutativity produces the same problem. Such equalities cause a failure of the completion process, more precisely of the orientation rule. A solution to this problem was proposed in [**90**] and consists in incorporating these equalities into the rewriting process itself, more precisely in the matching algorithm. A related problem occurs when completion diverges. It is sometimes possible to isolate some axioms A causing this divergence, and then work in equivalence classes modulo A, if A-equivalence is decidable. The idea of extending rewriting and completion by working in equivalence classes can be traced back to [**90, 20, 72**] and led to the definition of class rewrite systems and rewriting modulo A.

DEFINITION 4.12. A *class rewrite system* R/A is defined by a set R of rewrite rules and a set A of equalities. Rewriting in equivalence classes modulo A is defined as the compound relation

$$\longrightarrow_{R/A} = \overset{*}{\longleftrightarrow}_A \circ \longrightarrow_R \circ \overset{*}{\longleftrightarrow}_A .$$

R/A is *Church-Rosser modulo* A if the relation $\longrightarrow_{R/A}$ on terms satisfies:

$$\overset{*}{\longleftrightarrow}_{R\cup A} = \overset{*}{\longrightarrow}_{R/A} \circ \overset{*}{\longleftrightarrow}_A \circ \overset{*}{\longleftarrow}_{R/A}$$

The class rewrite system is *terminating modulo* A if $\longrightarrow_{R/A}$ terminates.

Whenever the class rewrite system R/A is Church-Rosser and terminating modulo A, $\overset{*}{\longleftrightarrow}_{R\cup A}$ is decidable by checking A-equivalence of R/A-normal forms. This gives a method for proving equational theorems in a theory described by a class rewrite system. Then to be effective, this method assumes two conditions: A-equivalence must be decidable and R/A-normal forms must be computable. Since this is not always true with the relation $\longrightarrow_{R/A}$, other computable rewrite relations must be considered.

In practice it is easier to compute with the *rewriting modulo A* relation $\longrightarrow_{R_A}$ using a matching modulo A algorithm and defined as follows:

DEFINITION 4.13. Given a class rewrite system R/A, a term t (R_A)-*rewrites* to a term t', which is denoted by $t \longrightarrow_{R_A} t'$ if there exists a rule $l \to r$ of R, a position ω in t, a substitution σ satisfying $t_{|\omega} \overset{*}{\longleftrightarrow}_A \sigma(l)$ and called a *match modulo A* from l to $t_{|\omega}$, such that $t' = t[\sigma(r)]_\omega$.

EXAMPLE 4.14. Let us consider three constant symbols a, b, c and

$$\begin{aligned} A &= \{a + (b + c) = (a + b) + c\} \\ R &= \{(a + b) \to c\} \end{aligned}$$

Then $a + (b + b) \longrightarrow_{R/A} c + b$, since $(a + (b + b)) \overset{*}{\longleftrightarrow}_A ((a + b) + b) \longrightarrow_R (c + b)$. But $a + (b + b)$ is R_A-irreducible, since associativity may only be applied below the position where the rule matches.

Let us consider now

$$\begin{aligned} A &= \{a + b = b + a\} \\ R &= \{(a + b) \to c\} \end{aligned}$$

Then $a + (b + a) \longrightarrow_{R_A} a + c$, since $(b + a) \overset{*}{\longleftrightarrow}_A (a + b)$.

Confluence of R_A is not enough to be equivalent to the Church-Rosser property, as in the case where $A = \emptyset$. Coherence, another diamond property, is needed.

DEFINITION 4.15. Let R/A be a class rewrite system and $\longrightarrow_{R_A}$ the rewriting modulo A relation defined on $\mathcal{T}(\mathcal{F}, \mathcal{X})$.

- R_A is *confluent modulo A* if
$$\overset{*}{\longleftarrow}_{R_A} \circ \overset{*}{\longrightarrow}_{R_A} \subseteq \overset{*}{\longrightarrow}_{R_A} \circ \overset{*}{\longleftrightarrow}_A \circ \overset{*}{\longleftarrow}_{R_A}.$$
- R_A is *coherent modulo A* if
$$\overset{*}{\longleftarrow}_{R_A} \circ \overset{*}{\longleftrightarrow}_A \subseteq \overset{*}{\longrightarrow}_{R_A} \circ \overset{*}{\longleftrightarrow}_A \circ \overset{*}{\longleftarrow}_{R_A}.$$
- R_A is *locally coherent with R modulo A* if
$$\longleftarrow_{R_A} \circ \longrightarrow_R \subseteq \overset{*}{\longrightarrow}_{R_A} \circ \overset{*}{\longleftrightarrow}_A \circ \overset{*}{\longleftarrow}_{R_A}.$$
- R_A is *locally coherent with A modulo A* if
$$\longleftarrow_{R_A} \circ \longleftrightarrow_A \subseteq \overset{*}{\longrightarrow}_{R_A} \circ \overset{*}{\longleftrightarrow}_A \circ \overset{*}{\longleftarrow}_{R_A}.$$

The next theorem relates the different properties.

THEOREM 4.16. [**56**] *If R/A is terminating, the following properties are equivalent:*

1. *R_A is Church-Rosser modulo A.*
2. *R_A is confluent and coherent modulo A.*
3. *R_A is locally coherent with R and with A modulo A.*

4. $\forall t, t'$, $t \overset{*}{\longleftrightarrow}_{R \cup A} t'$ *if and only if* t *and* t' *have* A*-equivalent normal forms for* R_A.

Equational completion procedures generalise the standard case [**74, 89, 56, 5**], but they must be carefully studied to minimise sources of inefficiency, which comes from rewriting modulo A and from the computation of sets of critical pairs modulo A: equational completion assumes the existence of an equational unification algorithm for the subtheory defined by the non-oriented axioms A. A-unification is undecidable in general.

DEFINITION 4.17. An *A-unifier* of two terms s and t is a substitution σ such that $\sigma(s) \overset{*}{\longleftrightarrow}_A \sigma(t)$. A *complete set of A-unifiers* of s and t, denoted $CSU_A(s,t)$, is a set of A-unifiers such that for every A-unifier θ of s and t, there exist $\sigma \in CSU_A(s,t)$ and a substitution ρ satisfying $\theta(x) \overset{*}{\longleftrightarrow}_A \rho(\sigma(x))$ for every variable x of s and t.

Now a superposition between two rewrite rules produces a set of new equational consequences. This set can even be infinite in some theories A, as simple as the associativity axiom.

DEFINITION 4.18. Let $(l_1 \rightarrow r_1)$ and $(l_2 \rightarrow r_2)$ be two rewrite rules with disjoint sets of variables. If there exists a position ω in l_2 such that $l_{2|\omega}$ is not a variable, and $l_{2|\omega}$ and l_1 are A-unifiable with a complete set $CSU_A(l_{2|\omega}, l_1)$ of A-unifiers, then

$$\{\sigma(l_2[r_1]_\omega = r_2) \mid \sigma \in CSU_A(l_{2|\omega}, l_1)\}$$

is the *set of critical pairs modulo A* of $(l_1 \rightarrow r_1)$ into $(l_2 \rightarrow r_2)$ at position ω.

$CP_A(R)$ denotes the set of critical pairs modulo A between all rules in R.

In order to check local coherence of R_A with both R and A, other critical pairs between rules in R and axioms in A have to be computed too [**56**]. An alternative is to add so-called extended rules (or extensions).

DEFINITION 4.19. Consider a rule $l \rightarrow r$ and an axiom $g = d$ in A with disjoint sets of variables such that $g_{|\omega}$ is a non-variable subterm A-unifiable with l. The *extended rule* of $l \rightarrow r$ with respect to $g = d$ at position ω is the rule $(g[l]_\omega \rightarrow g[r]_\omega)$.

Note that computing an extended rule only needs to know the position ω for which l and $g_{|\omega}$ are A-unifiable, but does not need to compute A-unifiers. Moreover such a rule denoted by $g[l] \rightarrow g[r]$ for short, satisfies $g[l] > g[r]$, and its adjunction does not violate the termination property.

EXAMPLE 4.20. Assume that A contains the associativity axiom of $+$,

$$x + (y + z) = (x + y) + z.$$

A rule $l \rightarrow r$, in which the top symbol of l is $+$, has two extended rules $z + l \rightarrow z + r$ and $l + z \rightarrow r + z$ where $z \notin \mathcal{V}ar(l)$.

Whenever a new rule is introduced, its extensions with axioms in A are computed. Recursively extensions of extensions are also computed. An extended rule is never simplified and can only disappear if the initial rule itself disappears. A general approach to deal with class rewrite systems with extended rules when A is any set of axioms with a decidable unification problem is proposed in [**56**].

Significant examples of theories with associativity and commutativity axioms have been handled with these techniques.

EXAMPLE 4.21. [**89, 63**]. Starting from the two axioms

$$\begin{aligned} x + 0 &= x \\ x + (-x) &= 0 \end{aligned}$$

and the fact that + is associative and commutative, an equational completion procedure generates an equational rewrite system for abelian groups, given by the following sets of rewrite rules and equalities:

$$\begin{aligned} x + 0 &\rightarrow x \\ -0 &\rightarrow 0 \\ - - x &\rightarrow x \\ x + (-x) &\rightarrow 0 \\ -(x + y) &\rightarrow (-x) + (-y) \end{aligned}$$

$$\begin{aligned} x + y &= y + x \\ (x + y) + z &= x + (y + z) \end{aligned}$$

EXAMPLE 4.22. Boolean ring and algebra . A boolean algebra is built on a set of function symbols $\mathcal{F} = \{0, 1, \wedge, \vee, \neg\}$ that satisfies the following equalities.

$$\begin{array}{lcl@{\qquad}lcl} x \vee 0 & = & x & (x \vee y) \wedge y & = & y \\ x \wedge 1 & = & x & (x \wedge y) \vee y & = & y \\ x \wedge (y \vee z) & = & (x \wedge y) \vee (x \wedge z) & x \vee (\neg x) & = & 1 \\ x \vee (y \wedge z) & = & (x \vee y) \wedge (x \vee z) & x \wedge (\neg x) & = & 0 \end{array}$$

$$\begin{array}{lcl@{\qquad}lcl} x \wedge y & = & y \wedge x & x \vee y & = & y \vee x \\ (x \wedge y) \wedge z & = & x \wedge (y \wedge z) & (x \vee y) \vee z & = & x \vee (y \vee z) \end{array}$$

Since the 1950s it is known that any term of the boolean algebra (i.e. any boolean formula) admits a normal form, which is called *the set of prime implicants* and can be produced algorithmically. Such algorithms have been proposed by Quine [**91, 92**] or by Slagle, Chang and Lee [**101**]. But surprisingly, attempts to find a Church-Rosser class rewrite system for Boolean algebra using a completion procedure failed to terminate in all experiments reported by [**54, 89**]. Only in 1991, a formal proof on the non-existence of a confluent and terminating system for boolean algebra was given in [**102**].

In 1985, J. Hsiang observed that there exists, however, a class rewrite system for boolean rings in an extended signature $\mathcal{F} = \{0, 1, \wedge, \vee, \neg, \oplus\}$, where the conjunction $\wedge$ and the exclusive-or $\oplus$ are associative and commutative. It is given by the following sets of rewrite rules and equalities, denoted BR/AC:

$$\begin{aligned} x \oplus 0 &\rightarrow x \\ x \oplus x &\rightarrow 0 \\ x \wedge 0 &\rightarrow 0 \\ x \wedge 1 &\rightarrow x \\ x \wedge x &\rightarrow x \\ x \wedge (y \oplus z) &\rightarrow (x \wedge y) \oplus (x \wedge z) \end{aligned}$$

$$\begin{array}{lcl@{\qquad}lcl} x \wedge y & = & y \wedge x & x \oplus y & = & y \oplus x \\ (x \wedge y) \wedge z & = & x \wedge (y \wedge z) & (x \oplus y) \oplus z & = & x \oplus (y \oplus z) \end{array}$$

Using this class rewrite system, we get for example:

$$\begin{array}{l} (p(x) \wedge p(x)) \oplus p(x) \oplus (q(y) \wedge r(x,y) \wedge 1) \oplus (p(x) \wedge 0) \oplus 1 \\ \quad \stackrel{*}{\longrightarrow}_{BR/AC} \quad q(y) \wedge r(x,y) \oplus 1. \end{array}$$

In order to deal with Boolean algebras notations, one may add four more rules for defining implication $\Rightarrow$, equivalence $\equiv$, negation $\neg$ and disjunction $\vee$. A class rewrite system for computing normal forms in Boolean algebras with the extended signature is as follows:

$$\begin{array}{rcl} x \vee y & \rightarrow & (x \wedge y) \oplus x \oplus y \\ x \Rightarrow y & \rightarrow & (x \wedge y) \oplus x \oplus 1 \\ x \equiv y & \rightarrow & x \oplus y \oplus 1 \\ \neg x & \rightarrow & x \oplus 1 \\ x \oplus 0 & \rightarrow & x \\ x \oplus x & \rightarrow & 0 \\ x \wedge 0 & \rightarrow & 0 \\ x \wedge 1 & \rightarrow & x \\ x \wedge x & \rightarrow & x \\ x \wedge (y \oplus z) & \rightarrow & (x \wedge y) \oplus (x \wedge z) \end{array}$$

$$\begin{array}{lcl@{\qquad}lcl} x \wedge y & = & y \wedge x & x \oplus y & = & y \oplus x \\ (x \wedge y) \wedge z & = & x \wedge (y \wedge z) & (x \oplus y) \oplus z & = & x \oplus (y \oplus z) \end{array}$$

The well-known properties of operators $\wedge, \vee, \neg$ can easily be proved by this class rewrite system:

$$\begin{array}{lcl@{\qquad}lcl} 1 \vee x & = & 1 & \neg(x \vee y) & = & (\neg x) \wedge (\neg y) \\ x \vee x & = & x & \neg(x \wedge y) & = & (\neg x) \vee (\neg y) \\ 0 \wedge x & = & 0 & \neg(\neg x) & = & x \\ x \wedge x & = & x & & & \end{array}$$

This axiomatisation has given rise to a specific technique for first-order theorem proving which transforms first-order predicate logic into a special case of equational logic. This transformation is achieved through the canonical system for Boolean rings presented above. In first-order logic, one first converts the negation of the sentences into rewrite rules, then applies superpositions and reductions as in other completion procedures until $1 = 0$ is generated, which indicates a contradiction and provides a refutation, or until there are no more critical pairs left [**45, 43, 44**]. A related method, inspired by the Gröbner basis generation in polynomial rings [**21**], was presented in [**60**] and implemented in the system RRL. The completeness of a refined procedure was proved in [**4**].

Thanks to a refinement of rewriting modulo A, called normalising rewriting [**80**], more results have been obtained for reasoning modulo various theories A: axioms like a unity element, idempotency or nilpotency, can be added to associativity and commutativity of operators. With this method also, abelian group, boolean ring or finite field theory may be incorporated in deduction as built-in theories A.

4.3. Conditional rewriting. Rewriting techniques have been extended to conditional equalities, written $\Gamma \Rightarrow s = t$, where Γ is a conjunction of equalities $\bigwedge_{i=1,\dots,n}(s_i = t_i)$. Their meaning is that s and t are equal *if* the condition Γ is satisfied. In a conditional rewrite rule, the equality is oriented and denoted $\Gamma \Rightarrow s \rightarrow t$.

DEFINITION 4.23. A *conditional rewrite rule* is a formula $\Gamma \Rightarrow s \rightarrow t$ where s and t are terms and Γ is a conjunction of equalities, with the additional assumption that every variable occurring either in the condition or in the right-hand side of a rule also occurs in the left-hand side, i.e. $\mathcal{V}ar(\Gamma) \cup \mathcal{V}ar(r) \subseteq \mathcal{V}ar(l)$. A *conditional rewrite system* R is a set of conditional rewrite rules.

Applying a conditional rewrite rule requires checking that the condition is satisfied in the theory generated by the conditional rewrite system.

DEFINITION 4.24. Given a conditional rewrite system R, a term t rewrites to a term t' if there exist a conditional rewrite rule $\Gamma \Rightarrow l \rightarrow r$ of R, a position ω in t, a substitution σ, satisfying $t_{|\omega} = \sigma(l)$, and $\sigma(s_i) \overset{*}{\longleftrightarrow}_R \sigma(t_i)$ for every equality $(s_i = t_i)$ in the condition Γ. Then $t' = t[(\sigma(r)]_\omega$.

Let us illustrate by a simple example the application of conditional rewrite rules.

EXAMPLE 4.25. [**14**] Consider the conditional rewrite system:

$$\begin{array}{rcrcl} & & f(a) & \rightarrow & a \\ x = f(x) & \Rightarrow & f(x) & \rightarrow & c \end{array}$$

and the two terms $f(a)$ and $f(f(a))$. Since $a \overset{*}{\longleftrightarrow}_R f(a)$, $f(a) \longrightarrow c$ by applying the second rule. In a similar way, $f(f(a)) \longrightarrow c$ with the same rule, since $f(a) \overset{*}{\longleftrightarrow}_R f(f(a))$. But neither c nor $f(c)$ are reducible.

For terminating unconditional rewrite systems, with a finite number of rules, the equivalence $\overset{*}{\longleftrightarrow}_R$ is decidable. With conditional rewrite systems, this is no more the case, even for finite terminating ones [**59**]. In this situation again, orderings on terms provide a possible solution. Additional ordering conditions can be added to get back decidable properties. One of them is the notion of reductive system [**31**]. A conditional rewrite rule $\bigwedge_{i=1,\dots,n}(s_i = t_i) \Rightarrow l \rightarrow r$ is *reductive* if there exists a well-founded reduction ordering $>$ such that for each substitution σ, $\sigma(l) > \sigma(r)$, $\sigma(l) > \sigma(s_i)$ and $\sigma(l) > \sigma(t_i)$, for all indices i, $1 \leq i \leq n$. A conditional rewrite system is *reductive* if each rule is reductive. It has been proved in [**31**] that when R is reductive, the relations $\longrightarrow_R$, $\overset{*}{\longrightarrow}_R$ and $\overset{*}{\longleftrightarrow}_R$ are all decidable.

As for unconditional rewrite systems, a conditional rewrite system R is *Church-Rosser on ground terms* if the relation $\longrightarrow_R$ satisfies on $\mathcal{T}(\mathcal{F})$:

$$\overset{*}{\longleftrightarrow}_R = \overset{*}{\longrightarrow}_R \circ \overset{*}{\longleftarrow}_R$$

EXAMPLE 4.26. The next example is an axiomatisation of integers with a constant 0, two functions s for successor, p for predecessor, and the usual predicate *less than*, denoted $\prec$.

$$\begin{array}{rrcl}
 & s(p(x)) & = & x \\
 & p(s(x)) & = & x \\
 & 0 \prec 0 & = & false \\
 & 0 \prec s(0) & = & true \\
 & s(x) \prec y & = & x \prec p(y) \\
 & p(x) \prec y & = & x \prec s(y) \\
(y \prec x) = true \Rightarrow & y \prec s(x) & = & true \\
(y \prec x) = false \Rightarrow & y \prec p(x) & = & false
\end{array}$$

A completion process can be performed with the system CEC [**34**] on this set of formulas and produces the following set of rewrite rules:

$$\begin{array}{rrcl}
 & s(p(x)) & \rightarrow & x \\
 & p(s(x)) & \rightarrow & x \\
 & 0 \prec 0 & \rightarrow & false \\
 & 0 \prec s(0) & \rightarrow & true \\
 & s(x) \prec y & \rightarrow & x \prec p(y) \\
 & p(x) \prec y & \rightarrow & x \prec s(y) \\
(y \prec x) = true \Rightarrow & y \prec s(x) & \rightarrow & true \\
(y \prec x) = false \Rightarrow & y \prec p(x) & \rightarrow & false
\end{array}$$

Two additional conditional equalities are also derived by the system and simplified:

$$\begin{array}{rrcl}
y \prec s(x) = false \Rightarrow & y \prec x & = & false \\
y \prec p(x) = true \Rightarrow & y \prec x & = & true
\end{array}$$

A precise description of the computations performed by CEC and their justifications can be found in [**34**].

5. Proofs by induction

Equational deduction and rewrite proofs are not sufficient to prove all theorems that hold in the initial algebra of an equational theory E defined by a rewrite system R. This initial algebra is the quotient algebra of ground terms $\mathcal{T}(\mathcal{F})$ by the equivalence $\stackrel{*}{\longleftrightarrow}_E$.

EXAMPLE 5.1. Let us consider the axiomatisation of natural numbers, with the constant 0, the successor function s and the addition $+$ defined by the following rewrite system R:

$$\begin{array}{rcl}
x + 0 & \rightarrow & x \\
x + s(y) & \rightarrow & s(x + y)
\end{array}$$

The commutativity of $+$, $x+y = y+x$, cannot be deduced by equational replacement or rewriting with R as described in Section 4. However this is a property which holds for any instantiations of variables x and y by natural numbers. Choosing for instance $x = s(0)$ and $y = s(s(0))$, we can prove by rewriting with R that $s(0) + s(s(0)) = s(s(0)) + s(0)$.

The difficulty encountered here is that the proof of such theorems needs an induction principle. A first approach of proof assistants like Nqthm [**19**] is to provide induction schemas and some tactics to transform the theorem to prove into easier lemmas. Another approach tries to minimise user interaction and to automatise the proof as much as possible. The concept of ordering is again useful here. The essential idea underlying this induction technique is that, when a (conditional or unconditional) rewrite system R is terminating, then the corresponding rewrite relation is a well-founded ordering on terms and can be used as support for inductive reasoning.

Inductive theorems are equalities that hold in the initial algebra, which means that for all instantiations of variables by ground terms, we get equal ground terms.

DEFINITION 5.2. An equality $(t = t')$ is an *inductive theorem of* E if for any ground substitution σ, $\sigma(t) \overset{*}{\longleftrightarrow}_E \sigma(t')$. This is denoted $E \models_{ind} (t = t')$.

Let $>$ be a well-founded ordering closed under substitution, and $(t = t')$ be a formula with some variables $x, y, z \ldots$. The proof method relies on several steps: first, find a finite set of terms $\{t_i\}$ such that every ground term is an instance of some t_i. Second, select induction variables in the formula to prove and instantiate them with these terms $\{t_i\}$. Third, reduce each instance to get a smaller formula and prove it inductively.

When R is a terminating rewrite system, the set of terms t_i is given by computing a cover set, which provides a finite description of the set of R-irreducible ground terms: any R-irreducible ground term is an instance of some element in the cover set. The notion was introduced in [**93, 116**].

DEFINITION 5.3. A *cover set* for a (conditional) rewrite system R is a finite set $CS(R)$ of R-irreducible terms that satisfies: for any R-irreducible ground term u, there exists a term t in $CS(R)$ and a ground substitution σ such that $\sigma(t) = u$.

Further work has been done for improving this notion of cover set by restricting the set of terms used to build instances of a theorem, and also by choosing more carefully induction variables to be instantiated [**16, 17**]. In particular, *test sets* are refinements of cover sets that are needed for disproving theorems.

Cover sets are used to build substitutions σ that instantiate variables by terms of $CS(R)$ appropriately renamed. $CSS(R)$ denotes this set of cover set substitutions σ built from $CS(R)$.

EXAMPLE 5.4. In Example 5.1, the cover set is $CS(R) = \{0, s(z)\}$. For an induction variable x for instance, the set of cover set substitutions is $CSS(R) = \{(x \mapsto 0),\ (x \mapsto s(z))\}$.

The *rewriting induction* process, described below in the equational case, is based on the expansion of an equality to be proved, using cover sets and rewriting. Intuitively, an expansion is a reduced instance of an equality. Rewriting is performed on the greatest term of the instantiated equality or on both terms if they are incomparable in the ordering.

DEFINITION 5.5. The *expansion set* of an equality $(p = q)$ such that $q \not> p$, with respect to a cover set $CS(R)$, is the set of equalities $Exp(p = q)$ defined as

$$
\begin{aligned}
Exp(p = q) &= \{p' = \sigma(q) \mid \sigma \in CSS(R) \text{ and } \sigma(p) \longrightarrow_R p'\} \\
&\quad \text{if } p > q, \\
Exp(p = q) &= \{p' = q' \mid \sigma \in CSS(R) \text{ and } \sigma(p) \longrightarrow_R p',\ \sigma(q) \longrightarrow_R q'\} \\
&\quad \text{if } p \text{ and } q \text{ are incomparable.}
\end{aligned}
$$

Given a set R of rewrite rules, the rewriting induction process is parameterised by a reduction ordering and transforms two sets of equalities: C contains the set of equalities to be proved (the conjectures), and H records the conjectures that, once expanded, can be used as inductive hypotheses. The method combines simplification by rewriting with selection of significant terms selected in cover sets. The powerful simplification strategy uses not only rewrite rules in R, but also conjectures, as soon as they have been reduced to other equalities in C. Redundant formulas may be eliminated. For instance, an equality $(p = p)$ trivially holds and thus may be deleted. The process is described by the set of rules given below.

Expand:	$C \cup \{p = q\}, H$	$\mapsto\!\!\!\twoheadrightarrow$	$C \cup Exp(p = q), H \cup \{p = q\}$	
Delete:	$C \cup \{p = p\}, H$	$\mapsto\!\!\!\twoheadrightarrow$	C, H	
Simplify:	$C \cup \{p = q\}, H$	$\mapsto\!\!\!\twoheadrightarrow$	$C \cup \{p' = q\}, H$	if $p \longrightarrow_{R \cup H} p'$

We get the following result:

THEOREM 5.6. [**93, 16**] *Assume given a well-founded reduction ordering used to compute expansion sets. If there is a derivation starting from* $(C, \emptyset)$ *and ending in* $(\emptyset, H)$ *for some set* H*, then all equalities in* C *are inductive consequences of* R.

EXAMPLE 5.7. An easy illustration of the method is provided by the proof of the commutativity of $+$ on natural numbers, where $+$ is defined by the following set of rules.

$$\begin{array}{rcl} x + 0 & \rightarrow & x \\ x + s(y) & \rightarrow & s(x + y) \end{array}$$

The chosen ordering is the multiset path ordering induced by $+ > s > 0$. Note that $CS(R) = \{0, s(z)\}$.

Let $C_0 = \{u + v = v + u\}$. The equality is first expanded, giving

$$\begin{array}{rcl} C_1 & = & \{u = 0 + u,\ s(u + z) = s(z) + u\} \\ H_1 & = & \{u + v = v + u\}. \end{array}$$

Again the first equality in C_1 is expanded.

$$\begin{array}{rcl} C_2 & = & \{0 = 0,\ s(y) = 0 + s(y),\ s(u + z) = s(z) + u\} \\ H_2 & = & \{u + v = v + u,\ u = 0 + u\}. \end{array}$$

The first equality in C_2 is deleted and the second is simplified using the orientable equality $0 + u \rightarrow 0$ in H_2 to $s(y) = s(y)$ that can be deleted too. We are left with

$$\begin{array}{rcl} C_3 & = & \{s(u + z) = s(z) + u\} \\ H_3 & = & \{u + v = v + u,\ u = 0 + u\}. \end{array}$$

Again the first equality in C_3 is expanded.

$$\begin{array}{rcl} C_4 & = & \{s(0 + z) = s(z),\ s(s(y) + z) = s(s(z) + y)\} \\ H_4 & = & \{u + v = v + u,\ u = 0 + u,\ s(u + z) = s(z) + u\}. \end{array}$$

$s(0 + z) = s(z)$ is simplified (by $0 + u \rightarrow u$) and deleted. $s(s(y) + z) = s(s(z) + y)$ is simplified twice by $s(z) + u \rightarrow s(z + u)$ and yields $s(s(y + z)) = s(s(z + y))$. Using then $u + v = v + u$ to simplify again, we eventually get a trivial equality which is deleted. We end up with

$$C_5 = \emptyset \text{ and } H_5 = \{u + v = v + u,\ u = 0 + u,\ s(u + z) = s(z) + u\}.$$

Using these ideas, a general system to perform induction in conditional and equational theories is proposed in [**16**] and implemented in the SPIKE theorem prover [**17**]. It is important to note that confluence of R is not needed for proving that a theorem is inductively valid. However, it is necessary if one wants to extend the method to refute invalid properties. The interested reader can refer to [**17, 18**] for the description of a refutationally complete procedure in confluent conditional (or equational) theories.

6. Proofs by refutation

In a *proof by refutation* (or contradiction), one assumes the negation of the formula to be proved and then derives a contradiction. A proof process is said refutationally complete when from the negation of any valid theorem, the process always generates a contradiction.

In the context of equational theories, negation of an equality is called a *disequality* and denoted $(s \neq t)$. A contradiction is found when a disequality $(s \neq s)$ is generated. Moreover, instead of requiring that each equality be oriented into a rewrite rule, the idea of working with orientable instances of an equality emerged in 1985, and was further developed in [**7**]. For instance, the commutativity axiom $(x * y = y * x)$ may have an instance such as $(f(x) * x = x * f(x))$ or $(a * b = b * a)$ that can be oriented with a lexicographic path ordering. Such an instance reduces the term $(f(a)*a)$ into $(a*f(a))$, or $a*b$ into $b*a$ provided $a >_{\mathcal{F}} b$. This method requires a reduction ordering $>$ which can be extended to an ordering total on ground terms. Polynomial orderings mentioned in Section 3 satisfy this requirement. Also, any total precedence on operators can be used to define a lexicographic path ordering total on ground terms. This restriction can be somewhat relaxed, since the reduction ordering needs only to be total on ground terms which are equivalent with respect to the considered equational theory, as proved in [**2**].

Given a set of equalities E, and a well-founded reduction ordering $>$ satisfying the previous requirement, $E^>$ denotes the set of all orientable instances of equalities in E:

$$E^> = \{\sigma(l) \to \sigma(r) \mid (l = r) \in E, \sigma(l) > \sigma(r)\}.$$

The *ordered rewriting* relation is just rewriting with orientable instances. Note that $s \longrightarrow_{E^>} t$ implies $s \longleftrightarrow_E t$ and $s > t$.

The ideas of a completion process can be naturally adapted to this context. In 1985, an *ordered completion* (also called unfailing) was proposed in which orientable instances of an equality can be used to perform reductions, even if the equality itself is not orientable.

Deduction of new equalities needs the definition of *ordered critical pairs* between two equalities of E, obtained by unifying one term of an equality with a non-variable subterm of the other one. Such deduced equalities must cover all cases of peaks for ordered rewriting, which eliminates some unifying substitutions. The notation $\sigma(l) \not\leq \sigma(r)$ means that this instance of $l = r$ satisfies either $\sigma(l) > \sigma(r)$ or $\sigma(l)$ and $\sigma(r)$ are two incomparable (non ground) terms.

DEFINITION 6.1. Let $(l_1 = r_1)$ and $(l_2 = r_2)$ be two equalities with disjoint sets of variables. If there exists a position ω in l_2 such that $l_{2|\omega}$ is not a variable, $l_{2|\omega}$ and l_1 are unifiable with a most general unifier σ such that $\sigma(l_2) \not\leq \sigma(r_2)$ and

$\sigma(l_1) \not\leq \sigma(r_1)$, then

$$\sigma(l_2[r_1]_\omega = r_2)$$

is an *ordered critical pair* of $(l_1 = r_1)$ into $(l_2 = r_2)$ at position ω.

$OCP(E)$ denotes the set of ordered critical pairs between all equalities in E.

Let E be a set of equalities and $(t = t')$ an equational theorem to be proved in the theory generated by E, with $t, t' \in \mathcal{T}(\mathcal{F}, \mathcal{X})$. Given a term t with universally quantified variables, let the Skolem form of t be the term t_0 where each variable is replaced by a new constant that does not belong to $\mathcal{F}$. Assume that t_0 and t'_0 are the Skolem forms of respectively t and t'. Let us introduce also a new commutative binary function symbol $\neq$ which stands for the negation of equality. Then let us eventually define

$$E' = E \cup \{t_0 \neq t'_0\}.$$

In this enriched signature, we now have to deal with disequalities $(t \neq t')$. Another kind of critical pairs must be computed.

DEFINITION 6.2. Let $(l_1 = r_1)$ be an equality and $(l_2 \neq r_2)$ a disequality in E with disjoint sets of variables. If there exists a position ω in l_2 such that $l_{2|\omega}$ is not a variable, $l_{2|\omega}$ and l_1 are unifiable with a most general unifier σ, and if in addition $\sigma(l_1) \not\leq \sigma(r_1)$, then

$$\sigma(l_2[r_1]_\omega \neq r_2)$$

is an *ordered critical disequality* of $(l_1 = r_1)$ into $(l_2 \neq r_2)$ at position ω.

$OCD(E)$ denotes the set of ordered critical disequalities between all equalities and disequalities in E.

As for completion, a set of transition rules is given for ordered completion. Again *Deduce* adds in E equational consequences of E obtained by ordered critical pair computation and *Narrow* adds critical disequalities. *Delete* removes trivial equalities in E. *Collapse* reduces the terms in equalities. Each equality can be reduced only by another one which is smaller in some sense. This is the reason of the condition in *Collapse.*

Deduce:	E	$\mapsto\!\!\!\!\twoheadrightarrow$	$E \cup \{s = t\}$	if $(s = t) \in OCP(E)$
Narrow:	E	$\mapsto\!\!\!\!\twoheadrightarrow$	$E \cup \{s \neq t\}$	if $(s \neq t) \in OCD(E)$
Delete:	$E \cup \{s = s\}$	$\mapsto\!\!\!\!\twoheadrightarrow$	E	
Collapse:	$E \cup \{s = t\}$	$\mapsto\!\!\!\!\twoheadrightarrow$	$E \cup \{s = u\}$	if $t \longrightarrow_{E^>} u$ by an equality $l = r \in E$ with $t \gg l$ or $t = l$ and $s > r$

where $\gg$ is again the encompassment ordering.

When no disequality is introduced, ordered completion behaves like an unfailing completion that can only terminate or diverge. If all ordered critical pairs have been fairly computed, the resulting set of equalities $E^{>}_{\infty}$ is Church-Rosser and terminating on ground terms. Moreover ordered completion has been proved refutationally complete [**6, 48, 97, 7, 2**]. In this context, a contradiction is produced by a disequality $(s \neq s')$ where s and s' are unifiable. This contradicts the trivial equality $(x = x)$ always assumed to be present in the axiomatisation. The refutational completeness of ordered completion is expressed in the following result:

THEOREM 6.3. [**97, 2**] *Let E be a set of equalities and $>$ be a well-founded reduction ordering that can be extended to an ordering total on ground terms. Then* *the equality* $(t = t')$ *is valid in* E *(i.e.* $t \overset{*}{\longleftrightarrow}_E t'$*) if and only if there exists a derivation*

$$E_0 = E \cup \{t_0 \neq t'_0\} \mapsto\!\!\!\!\rightarrow E_1 \mapsto\!\!\!\!\rightarrow \ldots$$

for which E_* *contains a disequality* $(s \neq s')$ *with* s *and* s' *unifiable and* $OCP(E_\infty)$ *is a subset of* E_*.

The next example illustrates this method.

EXAMPLE 6.4. An entropic groupoid is defined by two axioms:

$$\begin{aligned} (x * y) * (z * w) &= (x * z) * (y * w) \\ (x * y) * x &= x \end{aligned}$$

The first one cannot be oriented in any reduction ordering, so a standard completion procedure as described in Section 4 would fail on this example. The ordered completion applied with the lexicographic path ordering, uses first the rules *Deduce*, *Delete* and *Collapse*, to produce the following set of equalities [**7**]:

$$\begin{aligned} (x * y) * x &= x \\ z * (y * x) &= z * x \\ ((x * y) * z) * w &= x * w \\ (x * y) * w &= (x * z) * w. \end{aligned}$$

For proving a universally quantified equational theorem like

$$\forall x, y, u, v, \ \ (x * (y * u)) * v = (x * x) * v$$

its negated Skolem form

$$(cx * (cy * cu)) * cv \neq (cx * cx) * cv$$

is added to the axioms. The ordering is extended to take into account the new constants. We may consider now the lexicographic path ordering with the following precedence: $* >_{\mathcal{F}} cx >_{\mathcal{F}} cy >_{\mathcal{F}} cu >_{\mathcal{F}} cv$. Each side of the theorem matches with the left-hand side of the fourth rule. Instantiating z in the right-hand side of this rule by the smallest symbol cv, two ordered rewriting steps can be applied. The normal form of each side of the theorem is $(cx * cv) * cv$. This achieves the proof.

In the rest of this section, we sketch how an ordered completion process for class rewrite systems can be designed, and focus on the special case where A is composed of associativity and commutativity (AC for short) axioms only. These theories are interesting in practice, since a unification algorithm is known [**105**], and extended rules can be systematically built: for each $(l = r) \in E$, such that the top symbol f in l is associative and commutative, the extended equality is $(f(l, z) = f(r, z))$ where z is a new variable (distinct from variables in l and r). From now on, an equality $(f(l, z) = f(r, z))$ implicitly denotes an extended equality of $(l = r)$ where the top symbol of l is an AC-operator f. For such l, it is sufficient to compute critical pairs at positions ω that are not immediately below another f.

Since the syntactic form of extended equalities are known in this specific case of AC-theories, AC-critical pairs between equalities and extended equalities can be computed without explicitely introducing extended equalities. This is the purpose of the next definition, where the first case corresponds to AC-critical pairs between two ordinary equalities, the second case corresponds to AC-critical pairs between an ordinary equality and an extended equality, and the third case corresponds to

AC-critical pairs between two extended equalities. All are obtained from the more general Definition 4.18.

DEFINITION 6.5. Let $(l_1 = r_1)$ and $(l_2 = r_2)$ be two equalities with disjoint sets of variables, and let ω be a non-variable position of l_2.

1. If $l_{2|\omega}$ and l_1 are AC-unifiable with a complete set $CSU_{AC}(l_{2|\omega}, l_1)$ of AC-unifiers, then

$$\{ \sigma(l_2[r_1]_\omega = r_2) \mid \begin{array}{l} \sigma \in CSU_{AC}(l_{2|\omega}, l_1) \\ \sigma(l_1) \not\leq \sigma(r_1),\ \sigma(l_2) \not\leq \sigma(r_2) \ \} \end{array}$$

is the set of *Eq-Eq-Superpositions modulo AC* of $(l_1 = r_1)$ into $(l_2 = r_2)$ at position ω.

2. If $l_{2|\omega}$ and $f(l_1, z)$ are AC-unifiable with a complete set $CSU_{AC}(l_{2|\omega}, f(l_1, z))$ of AC-unifiers, then

$$\{ \sigma(l_2[f(r_1, z)]_\omega = r_2) \mid \begin{array}{l} \sigma \in CSU_{AC}(l_{2|\omega}, f(l_1, z)) \\ \sigma(l_1) \not\leq \sigma(r_1),\ \sigma(l_2) \not\leq \sigma(r_2) \ \} \end{array}$$

is the set of *Ext-Eq-Superpositions modulo AC* of $(l_1 = r_1)$ into $(l_2 = r_2)$ at position ω.

3. If $f(l_1, z)$ and $f(l_2, z')$ are AC-unifiable with a complete set of AC-unifiers $CSU_{AC}(f(l_1, z), f(l_2, z'))$, then

$$\{ \sigma(f(r_1, z) = f(r_2, z')) \mid \begin{array}{l} \sigma \in CSU_{AC}(f(l_1, z), f(l_2, z')) \\ \sigma(l_1) \not\leq \sigma(r_1),\ \sigma(l_2) \not\leq \sigma(r_2) \ \} \end{array}$$

is the set of *Ext-Ext-Superpositions modulo AC* of $(l_1 = r_1)$ into $(l_2 = r_2)$ at position ω.

Then the set $OCP_{AC}(E)$ of ordered critical pairs of E modulo AC is the set of all Eq-Eq-Superpositions, Ext-Eq-Superpositions, Ext-Ext-Superpositions modulo AC for all equalities in E.

The notion of ordered critical disequalities is extended in a similar way to handle AC axioms. Refutational completeness of ordered completion modulo AC can be obtained as a consequence of more general results in first-order theorem proving in [**8**].

To illustrate the ordered completion modulo AC technique, we present two additional examples.

EXAMPLE 6.6. Ring Commutativity Problems
A ring is defined by the following set of axioms $RING$:

$$\begin{array}{lcllcl}
x + y & = & y + x & (x * y) * z & = & x * (y * z) \\
(x + y) + z & = & x + (y + z) & x * (y + z) & = & (x * y) + (x * z) \\
x + 0 & = & x & (x + y) * z & = & (x * z) + (y * z) \\
x + i(x) & = & 0 & 0 * x & = & 0 \\
i(x + y) & = & i(x) + i(y) & x * 0 & = & 0 \\
i(0) & = & 0 & i(x) * y & = & i(x * y) \\
i(i(x)) & = & x & x * i(y) & = & i(x * y)
\end{array}$$

In 1945 the mathematician Jacobson proved that the next theorem holds in (associative) rings:

$$(\forall x, \exists n > 1, x^n = x) \Rightarrow \forall x, y, (x * y = y * x)$$

As such, this theorem has not been proved automatically up to now, nor even checked, but one could hope to automatically prove a weaker form:

$$(\exists n > 1, \forall x, x^n = x) \Rightarrow \forall x, y, (x * y = y * x)$$

Actually, instances of this weaker form have been proved using rewrite techniques. They correspond to specific values of n in the next theorem:

$$(\forall x, x^n = x) \Rightarrow \forall x, y, (x * y = y * x).$$

The case $n = 2$ is rather easy: adding to the set of axioms $RING$ the equality $x * x = x$ and running completion modulo associativity and commutativity results in a rewrite system for boolean rings and produces the equality $x * y = y * x$.

The case $n = 3$ was given as a challenge problem in [**114**]. The first mechanical proof was done in 1981 by Veroff [**111**] using the Argonne National Laboratory theorem prover based on resolution and paramodulation (see Section 7). In 1984, Stickel produced a proof using exclusively rewrite techniques [**106**]. Adding to the set of axioms $RING$ the equality $x * x * x = x$, and running completion modulo associativity and commutativity of $+$, generate the equality $x * y = y * x$ as well as a complete set of rewrite rules. The proof was reproduced and optimised in RRL [**61**] using a careful selection of critical pairs. RRL proceeds by refutation, that is in addition to the $RING$ equalities and to the hypothesis $x * x * x = x$, the negation of commutativity with existential variables replaced by new constants, is added: $cx * cy \neq cy * cx$. RRL has been able to prove the commutativity of rings in which every element satisfies $x^n = x$ for a large class of even numbers $n < 2^{50000}$. For instance for $n = 6$, the system first generates the equality $x * x = x$ and thus reduces the problem to the previous case $n = 2$ [**62**]. However the problem is still open for odd numbers n.

EXAMPLE 6.7. Moufang's Identities in Alternative Rings
Alternative rings are non-associative rings that satisfy the following set of axioms.

$$\begin{array}{lcllcl}
0 + x & = & x & 0 * x & = & 0 \\
i(x) + x & = & 0 & x * 0 & = & 0 \\
i(x + y) & = & i(x) + i(y) & x * (y + z) & = & (x * y) + (x * z) \\
i(i(x)) & = & x & (x + y) * z & = & (x * z) + (y * z) \\
i(0) & = & 0 & (x * y) * y & = & x * (y * y) \\
(x + y) + z & = & x + (y + z) & (x * x) * y & = & x * (x * y) \\
x + y & = & y + x & i(x) * y & = & i(x * y) \\
 & & & x * i(y) & = & i(x * y)
\end{array}$$

The identities below have been proved by R. Moufang, in 1933.

$$\begin{array}{rcl}
(x * y) * x & = & x * (y * x) \\
x * ((y * z) * x) & = & (x * (y * z)) * x \\
x * (y * (x * z)) & = & ((x * y) * x) * z \\
((z * x) * y) * x & = & z * (x * (y * x)) \\
(x * y) * (z * x) & = & (x * (y * z)) * x
\end{array}$$

A first automated proof has been reported in 1990 by S.Anantharaman and J.Hsiang in [**1**] using the system SBREVE. Let us briefly look at the proof of the first identity

$$(y * x) * y = y * (x * y).$$

It is first negated and existentially quantified variables x, y are replaced by constants cx, cy. The following disequality is added to the set of equalities defining alternative rings:

$$((cy * cx) * cy) \neq (cy * (cx * cy)).$$

The completion process generates, among others, the following critical pair:

$$x * ((y + z) * (y + z)) = ((x * (y + z)) * y) + ((x * (y + z)) * z)$$

It is simplified to produce:

$$\begin{gathered} x * (y * y) + x * (z * z) + x * (y * z) + x * (z * y) \\ = \\ x * (y * y) + x * (z * z) + (x * y) * z + (x * z) * y \end{gathered}$$

Regularity of $+$ is used thanks to the application of a cancellation transition rule introduced in the system. This gives an ordered equality

$$((x * y) * z) + ((x * z) * y) \rightarrow (x * (y * z)) + (x * (z * y)).$$

Then a new critical pair is computed between this last rule and the extended rule of $i(x) + x \rightarrow 0$:

$$(x * (y * z)) + (x * (z * y)) + i((x * z) * y) = (x * y) * z.$$

The goal equality $((cy * cx) * cy) \neq (cy * (cx * cy))$ can now be simplified into:

$$cy * (cx * cy) \neq cy * (cx * cy)$$

using the orientable instance

$$(cy * cx) * cy \rightarrow (cy * (cx * cy)) + (cy * (cy * cx)) + i((cy * cy) * cx).$$

To perform this proof, the system has computed 67 critical pairs and 15 ordered equalities.

7. Ordered strategies in first-order theorem proving

The impact of ordering and rewriting techniques in first-order theorem proving is two-fold: first, rewriting techniques have been used to improve the treatment of equality, and second, orderings have led to powerful proof strategies. In this section we give a brief overview of these two aspects.

First-order theorem proving manipulates general clauses with any predicate symbols. Validity of a formula in the class of all first-order models can be checked by considering only Herbrand models, which are interpretations whose domain is the set of ground terms built from functional symbols [**40**]. The proof of a formula can again proceed by refutation: the formula is first negated and a contradiction is derived by applying inference rules. In 1965, Robinson proposed *resolution* as a complete inference rule [**95**]. Let $C_1 = L_1 \vee D_1$ and $C_2 = \neg L_2 \vee D_2$ be two clauses such that L_1 and L_2 are unifiable with a most general unifier σ. Then $D = \sigma(D_1 \vee D_2)$ is deduced by *resolution* from C_1 and C_2. The resolution method does not deal directly with equality and an axiomatisation of equality must be added explicitly. The replacement of equals by equals has been generalised in [**94**] from equational logic to first-order logic with equality, in order to improve the efficiency of resolution theorem provers. This goes with the introduction of another inference rule called *paramodulation*. Let $C_1 = (s = t) \vee D_1$ and $C_2[r]$ be two clauses such that s and r are unifiable with a most general unifier σ. Then $D = \sigma(C_2[t] \vee D_1)$ is deduced by *paramodulation* of C_1 into C_2. Several inference rules have been designed in order to reduce the size of formulas handled at each step of deduction. Tautology elimination and subsumption are well-known. Term rewriting is also used sometimes under the name of *demodulation* [**115**]. Let $C_1 = (s = t) \vee D_1$ and $C_2 = L_2[u] \vee D_2$ be two clauses such that there exists a substitution σ satisfying $\sigma(s) = u$, $\sigma(s) > \sigma(t)$ and $\sigma(D_1)$ is a subset of D_2. Then $D = L_2[\sigma(t)] \vee D_2$ is the result of the demodulation of C_2 with C_1.

It has been observed since 1975 [**20, 72, 100**] that the computation of critical pairs is a restriction of paramodulation to the case where equalities can be oriented. However, until the eighties, very few theoretical results were known about the effect of simplifying during deduction. An extension of the classical *semantic trees* method was designed in [**88, 47, 97**] to show the refutational completeness of several refinements of the resolution and paramodulation rules. In particular the literals which are resolved are restricted to be maximal within each clause. The common feature of these refinements is that they allow free interleaving of deduction steps with simplification steps without losing completeness. Another approach with a different proof technique is developed in [**9**]. Various refutationally complete calculi for first-order logic with equality allowing elimination of redundant formulas are presented there. In particular, a superposition rule on first-order clauses is obtained as a refinement of the paramodulation rule, with restrictions formulated thanks to a well-founded ordering on terms and atomic formulas.

In [**9**], a clause $\neg L_1 \vee \ldots \vee \neg L_n \vee M_1 \vee \ldots \vee M_m$ is written as $\Gamma \Rightarrow \Delta$, where $\Gamma = L_1 \wedge \ldots \wedge L_n$ and $\Delta = M_1 \ldots \vee M_m$. Since predicates can be encoded as boolean functions, without lost of generality, we can restrict to equational clauses with only one predicate, which is equality. Then, an ordering on equational clauses is built as follows. Clauses $\Gamma \Rightarrow \Delta$ are thought of as finite multisets of occurrences of equalities. An occurrence of an equality $(s = t)$ in the antecedent Γ of a clause is identified with the multiset $\{\{s, t\}\}$, and an occurrence in the succedent Δ of a clause with the multiset $\{\{s\}, \{t\}\}$. A well-founded (total) reduction ordering $>$ on (ground) terms gives by multiset extensions a well-founded (total) ordering on clauses, denoted by $>_C$.

Thanks to such orderings, it is possible to extend results obtained in Section 6 to the case where E is a set of equational clauses [**9**]. Instead of developing here this general case, let us restrict to the simpler case of equational Horn clauses, i.e. clauses $\Gamma \Rightarrow \Delta$ where Δ is reduced to only one positive literal. This restricted case has the advantage to require less inference rules, while being a significant illustration of the general techniques.

In ordered completion, the superposition rule *Deduce* for ordered equalities was the only one producing new equalities. In equational Horn clause logic, we need three rules instead: superposition, narrowing and reflection. In order to limit the set of useful deductions and implement an ordered strategy, some ordering restrictions are imposed in the conditions of these rules.

DEFINITION 7.1. Let $\Delta \Rightarrow g = d$ and $\Gamma \Rightarrow l = r$ be two conditional equalities with disjoint sets of variables, such that l and g unify at a non-variable position ω of g with the most general unifier σ, satisfying moreover

- $\sigma(d) \not\geq \sigma(g)$, $\sigma(r) \not\geq \sigma(l)$,
- for all $(u_i = v_i) \in \Delta$, $\sigma(u_i = v_i) \not\geq \sigma(g = d)$,
- for all $(s_i = t_i) \in \Gamma$, $\sigma(s_i = t_i) \not\geq \sigma(l = r)$.

Then the term $\sigma(g)$ produces by *ordered superposition* the *conditional ordered critical pair*

$$\sigma(\Delta \wedge \Gamma) \Rightarrow \sigma(g[r]_\omega = d).$$

Let $SUP(E)$ be the set of conditional ordered critical pairs obtained from all conditional equalities in E.

Beyond the computation of ordered conditional critical pairs, conditions must be partially solved when they are more complex than the conclusion. This motivates the introduction of the set of *conditional narrowings* computed from E, in which the left-hand side l of a conditional equality is unified with a non-variable subterm occurring in the condition of another one.

DEFINITION 7.2. Let $(\Delta \wedge s = t) \Rightarrow g = d$ and $\Gamma \Rightarrow l = r$ be two conditional equalities with disjoint sets of variables, such that l and s unify at a non-variable position ω of s with the most general unifier σ, satisfying moreover

- $\sigma(t) \not\geq \sigma(s)$, $\sigma(r) \not\geq \sigma(l)$,
- for all $(u_i = v_i) \in \Delta \cup \{g = d\}$, $\sigma(u_i = v_i) \not> \sigma(s = t)$,
- for all $(s_i = t_i) \in \Gamma$, $\sigma(s_i = t_i) \not\geq \sigma(l = r)$.

Then the *conditional ordered narrowing* obtained from these two equalities is the conditional equality

$$\sigma(\Gamma \wedge \Delta \wedge s[r]_\omega = t) \Rightarrow \sigma(g = d).$$

Let $NAR(E)$ be the set of conditional ordered narrowings obtained from all conditional equalities in E.

In addition to conditional critical pairs and conditional narrowings, the notion of reflexive resolvent is also needed. When one of the conditions of a rule can be immediately solved by syntactic unification, a *reflexive resolvent* can be built.

DEFINITION 7.3. Let $\Delta \wedge s = t \Rightarrow g = d$ be a conditional equality, such that s and t unify with the most general unifier σ, satisfying moreover

- $\sigma(g = d) \not> \sigma(s = t)$,
- for all $(u_i = v_i) \in \Delta$, $\sigma(u_i = v_i) \not> \sigma(s = t)$.

Then the *reflexive resolvent* obtained from this equality is the conditional equality

$$\sigma(\Delta) \Rightarrow \sigma(g = d).$$

Let $REF(E)$ be the set of reflexive resolvents obtained from all conditional equalities in E. An essential property of the above newly generated formulas is that they are each smaller for the ordering $>_C$ than one of the initial formulas.

In this first-order setting, the notion of *saturation of a set of clauses*, in the sense that all non-redundant inferences are computed, generalises completion processes. Let us make these notions more precise. A clause is *redundant* if all its ground instances can be proved from smaller clauses. A set of equational Horn clauses E is said *saturated* if all conditional equalities in $SUP(E) \cup NAR(E) \cup REF(E)$ are redundant in E.

EXAMPLE 7.4. Given constants 0 and *true*, function symbols s and f, and a simplification ordering $>$, the following set of conditional equalities is saturated:

$$\begin{array}{rcrcl} & & f(0) & = & true \\ f(x) = true & \Rightarrow & f(s(x)) & = & true \end{array}$$

Note that there is no superposition between the two conditional equalities and no narrowing because $f(x) < f(s(x))$ in any simplification ordering. Forgetting ordering restrictions would lead to the generation of an infinite set of equalities of the form

$$f(s^k(0)) = true, \text{ for } k = 1, 2, \ldots$$

With these definitions, the next result can be stated:

THEOREM 7.5. **[9]** *A saturated set of equational Horn clauses E has a model if and only if it does not contain the empty clause* $\Rightarrow$.

When E is not saturated, a saturation process can be applied. A refutationally complete set of rules for Horn clause logic with equality has been proposed already in **[70]** and is a direct extension of ordered completion.

This work was further improved to handle associative and commutative axioms with techniques similar to those developed in Section 6. Let us just illustrate them on a last example.

EXAMPLE 7.6. A Kleene algebra K is axiomatised in **[71]** with the following set of axioms stating that $(K, +, 0)$ is an idempotent commutative monoid, $(K, \cdot, 1)$ is a monoid, $(K, +, \cdot, 0, 1)$ is an idempotent semi-ring.

$$\begin{array}{lcl} x_1 + 0 & = & x_1 \\ x_1 + x_1 & = & x_1 \\ x_1 \cdot (x_2 \cdot x_3) & = & (x_1 \cdot x_2) \cdot x_3 \\ 1 \cdot x_1 & = & x_1 \\ x_1 \cdot 1 & = & x_1 \\ x_1 \cdot (x_2 + x_3) & = & (x_1 \cdot x_2) + (x_1 \cdot x_3) \\ (x_1 + x_2) \cdot x_3 & = & (x_1 \cdot x_3) + (x_2 \cdot x_3) \\ 0 \cdot x_1 & = & 0 \\ x_1 \cdot 0 & = & 0 \end{array}$$

Associativity and commutativity of $+$ are implicit. The star operator $*$ of Kleene is defined by four axioms.

$$\begin{array}{rcrcl} & & 1 + (x_1 \cdot x_1^*) & = & x_1^* \\ & & 1 + (x_1^* \cdot x_1) & = & x_1^* \\ (x_1 \cdot x_2) + x_2 = x_2 & \Rightarrow & (x_1^* \cdot x_2) + x_2 & = & x_2 \\ (x_1 \cdot x_2) + x_1 = x_1 & \Rightarrow & (x_1 \cdot x_2^*) + x_1 & = & x_1 \end{array}$$

In order to prove the property $x_1^* \cdot x_1^* = x_1^*$ in Kleene's algebras, the Skolem form of the negation of this property is added to the previous system:

$$cx_1^* \cdot cx_1^* = cx_1^* \Rightarrow$$

The ordering used in this example is an extension to associative and commutation theories of a recursive path ordering defined in **[11]**. The system DATAC **[112, 98]** applies a saturation process generalised to AC-theories to generate the following sequence of deductions and simplifications of initial clauses.

$$
\begin{array}{rcll}
 & & 1+(x_1 \cdot x_1^*) & = \quad x_1^*+1 \\
 & & x_1^*+1 & = \quad x_1^* \\
 & & x_1^*+(x_2 \cdot x_2^*) & = \quad x_2^*+x_1^* \\
 & & (x_2^* \cdot x_1)+(1 \cdot x_1) & = \quad x_2^* \cdot x_1 \\
 & & (x_2^* \cdot x_1)+x_1 & = \quad x_2^* \cdot x_1 \\
(x_1 \cdot x_2)+x_2 = x_2 & \Rightarrow & (x_1^* \cdot x_2) & = \quad x_2 \\
cx_1^* = cx_1^* \wedge (cx_1 \cdot cx_1^*)+cx_1^* = cx_1^* & \Rightarrow & & \\
(cx_1 \cdot cx_1^*)+cx_1^* = cx_1^* & \Rightarrow & & \\
cx_1^*+cx_1^* = cx_1^* & \Rightarrow & &
\end{array}
$$

Conditional ordered narrowing applied to $(\Rightarrow x_1+x_1 = x_1)$ and $(cx_1^*+cx_1^* = cx_1^* \Rightarrow)$ generates $(cx_1^* = cx_1^* \Rightarrow)$. The empty clause is then obtained by computing its reflexive resolvent.

8. Ordering constraints in automated theorem proving

Constraints have been introduced as a general paradigm in automated deduction since the 1990s [**64**], although one could find similar ideas in theory resolution [**104**] and in higher-order resolution [**50**]. The idea is to distinguish two levels of deduction and to use adequate and efficient tools at each level. When, for instance for syntactic reasons, these two levels do not interfere, this idea leads to an interesting modularisation of provers. This is a case similar to the CLP framework [**55**] which has been studied in the context of knowledge representation for instance by [**22, 33**]. But we are interested here in using formulas defined with the equality predicate (possibly among others) at both levels. This induces an additional difficulty and we focus here on this kind of problems.

A first motivation for introducing constraints in equational deduction processes arises when considering the problem of completion modulo a set of axioms A as in Section 4.2. A main drawback of this class of completion procedures is an inherent inefficiency, due to the computation of A-unifiers. For example, the unification of the terms $x * x * x * x$ and $y_1 * y_2 * y_3 * y_4$ where $*$ is associative commutative and x, y_1, y_2, y_3, y_4 are variables, produces a complete set of solutions with 34 359 607 481 unifiers [**32**]. A natural idea is to use constraints to record unification problems in the theory A and to avoid solving them immediately. For instance, the set of critical pairs modulo A at position ω between $(l_1 \rightarrow r_1)$ and $(l_2 \rightarrow r_2)$ in R will be represented by the constrained equality

$$(l_2[r_1]_\omega = r_2 \parallel l_{2|\omega} =_A^? l_1)$$

where the *equational constraint* $l_{2|\omega} =_A^? l_1$ expresses the unification problems and schematises the set of its solutions, which is assumed to be non-empty. Since constraints are just checked for satisfiability, this is, in general, much simpler than finding a complete set of solutions or a solved form, especially in equational theories.

A second motivation is brought by ordered completion, as in Section 6, where the set of orientable instances of an equality $(l = r)$ can be represented as an *ordering constraint* $l >^? r$ and an ordered critical pair between $(l_1 = r_1)$ and $(l_2 = r_2)$ at position ω in l_2 by

$$(l_2[r_1]_\omega = r_2 \parallel (l_1 >^? r_1) \wedge (l_2 >^? r_2) \wedge (l_1 =^? l_{2|\omega}))$$

provided the constraint is satisfiable.

More generally, there are several advantages in using constraints in automated deduction. They provide a way to make explicit every symbolic computation step, especially unification and ordering problems to check while applying a deduction step. Moreover they keep track of choices made along a derivation and this is a way to avoid a new choice inconsistent with previous ones. They help to modularise deduction and in particular to design better controls by delaying complex problem solving and pruning some parts of the search tree. Constraints also schematise (infinitely) many objects, especially substitutions or ground instances in our context, and thus give theorem provers more expressive power. Last, equational and ordering constraints very elegantly express basic and ordered strategies in automated theorem proving. Basic strategies avoid applying inference rules in parts of the formulas which have been introduced by substitutions in previous steps. Ordered strategies select maximal terms or literals in formulas to apply inference steps.

In this context, the constraint language is defined as follows. Elementary *constraints* are equations $(t =^? t')$ and inequations $(t >^? t')$ with $t, t' \in \mathcal{T}(\mathcal{F}, \mathcal{X})$. The constraint language contains conjunctions of elementary constraints and two additional symbols $\top$ (for *true*) and $\bot$ (for *false*).

The equality and ordering predicates are interpreted in the ground term algebra $\mathcal{T}(\mathcal{F})$. The equality predicate is interpreted in $\mathcal{T}(\mathcal{F})$ by syntactic equality and the ordering predicate by a simplification ordering $>$ total on ground terms.

Symbolic solutions of constraints c are substitutions σ on $\mathcal{T}(\mathcal{F}, \mathcal{X})$, such that $\sigma(c)$ holds in the interpretation $\mathcal{T}(\mathcal{F})$. The set of all symbolic solutions of c is denoted $SS(c)$. Two constraints are equivalent if they have the same set of solutions.

Instead of considering any constrained first-order formula, let us focus again on equalities, for simplicity.

DEFINITION 8.1. A *constrained equality*, denoted $(l = r \parallel c)$, is given by two terms l and r in $\mathcal{T}(\mathcal{F}, \mathcal{X})$ and a constraint c such that $\mathcal{V}ar(c) \subseteq \mathcal{V}ar(l) \cup \mathcal{V}ar(r)$. The constrained equality $(l = r \parallel c)$ schematises on $\mathcal{T}(\mathcal{F}, \mathcal{X})$ the set of equalities $\mathcal{S}(l = r \parallel c) = \{\sigma(l) = \sigma(r) \mid \sigma \in SS(c)\}$.

The definitions of confluence and termination generalise to sets of constrained equalities. A set $E = \{(l = r \parallel c)\}$ of constrained equalities is said to be *terminating and confluent on ground terms* if the corresponding set of rewrite rules

$$R^E = \{\sigma(l) \to \sigma(r) \mid (l = r \parallel c) \in E,\ \sigma \in SS(c)\}$$

is terminating and confluent on $\mathcal{T}(\mathcal{F})$.

EXAMPLE 8.2. [**81**] The following set E of constrained equalities

$$\begin{array}{l}(x * y) * z = x * (y * z) \parallel \top \\ x * y = y * x \parallel x >^? y \\ x * (y * z) = y * (x * z) \parallel x >^? y\end{array}$$

allows deciding the word problem for associativity and commutativity of $*$. If $>$ is the lexicographic path ordering and a, b, c are constants such that $c > b > a$:

$$\begin{array}{l}b * (c * (b * a)) \longrightarrow_{R^E} b * (c * (a * b)) \longrightarrow_{R^E} b * (a * (c * b)) \\ \qquad \longrightarrow_{R^E} a * (b * (c * b)) \longrightarrow_{R^E} a * (b * (b * c)).\end{array}$$

In the context of constrained equalities, the superposition rule and the notion of critical pair must be adapted to handle constraints. New constrained equalities are computed by *constrained superposition* at non-variable positions.

DEFINITION 8.3. Let $(l_1 = r_1 \parallel c_1))$ and $(l_2 = r_2 \parallel c_2)$ be two constrained equalities with disjoint sets of variables. If there exists a position ω in l_2 such that $l_{2|\omega}$ is not a variable, and the conjunction of constraints

$$c_1 \wedge c_2 \wedge \ (l_{2|\omega} =^? l_1) \ \wedge \ (l_1 >^? r_1) \ \wedge \ (l_2 >^? r_2)$$

is satisfiable, then

$$(l_2[r_1]_\omega = r_2 \parallel c_1 \wedge c_2 \wedge (l_{2|\omega} =^? l_1) \wedge (l_1 >^? r_1) \wedge (l_2 >^? r_2))$$

is a *constrained critical pair* of $((l_1 = r_1 \parallel c_1)$ into $(l_2 = r_2 \parallel c_2)$ at position ω.

$CCP(E)$ denotes the set of constrained critical pairs between all constrained equalities in E.

This definition is already sufficient to explain how constraints can improve inference systems.

- Here the constraint $(l_{2|\omega} =^? l_1)$ is crucial to implement the basic strategy, since considering this equation as a constraint prevents further deductions to be applied elsewhere than in the part $l_2[r_1]$ in the deduced formula. Positions in $l_2[r_1]$ correspond to basic positions. The ordering constraint $(l_1 >^? r_1)$ expresses a part of an ordered strategy that states that inference steps are applied to bigger terms. We could also add an additional constraint to c_3, namely $(\{l_2, r_2\} >^? \{l_1, r_1\})$, to achieve another refinement of the ordered strategy.
- Constraints c_1 and c_2 are inherited in the constraint of the deduced formula, and thus a trace is kept from previous choices, in particular in the ordering process.
- The decomposition between the equational part and the constraint part allows a clear separation of the constraint solving that may be delayed. However, satisfiability has to be checked in order to avoid unnecessary inference steps.

In standard (i.e. without constraints) completion procedures, superposition is combined with simplifications that eliminate redundant equalities or rewrite rules. But using simplification in conjunction with constrained superposition may lead to loose completeness, as in the next example.

EXAMPLE 8.4. [**84**] Let $\mathcal{F} = \{f, g, a, b\}$ with $f >_\mathcal{F} g >_\mathcal{F} a >_\mathcal{F} b$ and assume given the following equalities:

$$\begin{aligned} a &= b \\ f(g(x)) &= g(x) \\ f(g(a)) &= b \end{aligned}$$

Constrained superposition of the two first equalities leads to $(g(x) = b \parallel x =^? a)$. Using a naive notion of simplification, we could say that the third equality is simplified into $(f(b) = b)$. Constrained superposition yields again $(f(b) = g(x) \parallel x =^? a)$. But $(g(b) = b)$ has no rewrite proof.

One possible solution is to use propagation [**64**]. This amounts to weakening the constraints by partially solving them and propagating the values of variables in the equality. We denote by $\hat{\theta}$ the equational form $(\bigwedge_{i=1}^n (x_i = t_i))$ of the substitution $\theta = (x_1 \mapsto t_1) \dots (x_n \mapsto t_n)$. If $(l = r \parallel c)$ is a constrained equality and if c is equivalent to $c' \wedge \hat{\theta}$, then $(\theta(l = r) \parallel \theta(c'))$ is a *weakened form* of $(l = r \parallel c)$. The constraint $\theta(c')$ is called a *weakening* of c.

EXAMPLE 8.5. For instance in Example 8.4, propagation generates $g(a) = b$. Then superposition with $a = b$ yields $g(b) = b$.

Another possibility is to define an appropriate notion of redundancy as in [**9**]. But in the constraint context, all instances by solutions of constraints must be taken into account for redundancy definition. As a first example of redundant equalities, one can prove that, if a constrained equality of the form $(l = r \parallel \hat{\sigma})$ is reducible in the range of σ, it is redundant. More work is needed to obtain satisfactory criteria for elimination of redundancies, and further hints can be found in [**10, 84, 85, 78, 66**].

A completion process for constrained equalities applies superposition and elimination of redundant constrained equalities, possibly interleaved with propagation. It is expressed in the same formalism as previous completion processes. *Deduce* adds in E consequences of E obtained by constrained critical pair computation. *Delete* removes redundancies in E. *Propagate* weakens some constraints to make possible more elimination of redundancies, and is usually applied lazily.

$$\begin{array}{llcl}
\textit{Deduce:} & E & \mapsto\!\!\!\!\twoheadrightarrow & E \cup \{(s = t \parallel c)\} \\
 & & & \text{if } (s = t \parallel c) \in CCP(E) \\
\textit{Delete:} & E \cup \{(s = t \parallel c)\} & \mapsto\!\!\!\!\twoheadrightarrow & E \\
 & & & \text{if } (s = t \parallel c) \text{ is redundant.} \\
\textit{Propagate:} & E \cup \{(s = t \parallel c)\} & \mapsto\!\!\!\!\twoheadrightarrow & E \cup \{(\theta(s = t) \parallel \theta(c'))\} \\
 & & & \text{if } \theta(c') \text{ is a weakening of } c.
\end{array}$$

A set of equational axioms E without constraints can, of course, be considered as a set of constrained equalities with the trivial constraint $\top$. For such theories, the result of a fair completion with constraints produces a set E_∞ which is confluent on ground terms and generates the same congruence as E.

THEOREM 8.6. [**84**] *Let E be a set of equational axioms without constraints. Let us assume given a well-founded reduction ordering $>$ which can be extended to an ordering total on ground terms. If the derivation $E_0 = E \mapsto\!\!\!\!\twoheadrightarrow E_1 \mapsto\!\!\!\!\twoheadrightarrow \dots$ satisfies $CCP(E_\infty)$ is a subset of E_*, then the set of constrained equalities E_∞ is terminating and confluent on ground terms. Moreover $\xleftrightarrow{*}_{E_0}$ and $\xleftrightarrow{*}_{R^{E_\infty}}$ coincide on ground terms.*

This result does not hold any more if in the initial set of equalities E, some of them have non trivial constraints. Let us consider $\mathcal{F} = \{a, b, f, g\}$ and a simplification ordering $>$ induced by the precedence $f > g > a > b$. Let E be the set of two constrained equalities: $(g(a) = b \parallel \top)$ and $(f(x) = a \parallel x =^? g(y))$. No rule applies, although the proof

$$a \xleftrightarrow{*}_E f(g(a)) \xleftrightarrow{*}_E f(b)$$

contradicts confluence of R_E.

The problem comes from the fact that there is a superposition in the constraint part which is not taken into account. A first idea is to look for cases where superposition into constraints is useless. Using a hierarchical approach in which constraints are restricted to a sub-signature is enough to recover completeness. This is done with so-called built-in constraints in [**67**]. An alternative initially proposed in [**64**] is again to use propagation. Coming back to our example, the propagation applies straightforwardly and yields the (unconstrained) equality $(f(g(y)) = a)$. It generates with $(g(a) = b)$ the equality $(f(b) = a)$.

To close this section, let us give a simple example to illustrate the completion process with equality and ordering constraints.

EXAMPLE 8.7. [**64**] Let $\mathcal{F} = \{0, +\}$ and two initial equalities:

$$\begin{array}{lcl} x + 0 & = & 0 + x \\ (x + y) + z & = & x + (y + z) \end{array}$$

Let us consider as simplification ordering a lexicographic path ordering induced by the precedence $+ >_{\mathcal{F}} 0$. Superposition of the first equality at position 1 in the second creates a new constrained equality

$$((0 + x) + z' = x' + (y' + z') \parallel c)$$

where $c = (x + 0 >^? 0 + x) \wedge ((x + y) + z >^? x + (y + z)) \wedge (x + 0 =^? x' + y')$.

Another superposition at top gives:

$$(0 + x = x' + (y' + z') \parallel c)$$

where $c = (x{+}0 >^? 0{+}x) \wedge ((x'{+}y'){+}z' >^? x'{+}(y'{+}z')) \wedge (x{+}0 =^? (x'{+}y'){+}z')$.

After some simplification of constraints and propagation, we get

$$\begin{array}{lclcl} (0 + x) + z & = & x + (0 + z) & \parallel & x >^? 0 \\ 0 + (x + y) & = & x + (y + 0) & \parallel & (x + y) >^? 0 \end{array}$$

The final system is

$$\begin{array}{lclcl} x + 0 & = & 0 + x & \parallel & x >^? 0 \\ (x + y) + z & = & x + (y + z) & \parallel & \top \\ x + (0 + y) & = & 0 + (x + y) & \parallel & x >^? 0 \end{array}$$

Similar techniques have been used for first-order theorem proving with constraints in the systems Saturate [**86**] and DATAC [**112, 98**].

9. Conclusion

We focussed our attention in this survey on theorem proving techniques using orderings on terms and rewriting techniques. Their interest in equality decision procedures, proofs by refutation and proofs by induction has been emphasised and illustrated by examples. In these different proof methods, we have shown how orderings can be handled either implicitly or explicitely through constraints. We would like to conclude this presentation by mentioning some current investigations in the domain of automated theorem proving.

Practical implementations are faced with the problem of efficiency. There is certainly a tradeoff to find between applying inferences fast and applying complex techniques for eliminating redundant formulas. But efficiency can also be improved through dedicated data structures, especially graphs as those defined in [**79, 65**]. There, the initial problem is stored in a graph with terms represented as directed acyclic graphs (dags). The edges of the dags are called subterm edges, and the graph has also edges for equalities, called rewrite edges. Inferences are transformations on the graph, which create new subterm and rewrite edges, labelled with the ordering or unification constraint and the substitution used in the inference. Thanks to this shared structure, first performance results look very promising.

Theorem proving often needs to design strategies and heuristics. Good heuristics in proofs by induction are quite important to avoid divergence and the generation of an infinity of useless lemmas. A current effort is to design a system that can help to discover useful new lemmas, using for instance generalisation techniques, when an automatic deductive prover fails to produce them [**113**].

We have seen in this survey how some useful strategies have been encoded through constraints, and those can be completely automated. But in general, a real language for expressing tactics or strategies is needed, as in most proof assistants. This will provide the capability to combine user-given proof plans with automatic techniques like simplification or completion.

To integrate decision procedures in proof assistants would have the great advantage to release the user from large parts of proofs for which the method to be applied is completely automatic. This would link automated deduction to work on logical frameworks and higher-order logic. Interesting new problems arise there, especially in the direction of incorporating types and higher-order functions.

References

[1] S. Anantharaman and J. Hsiang. An automated proof of the Moufang identities in alternative rings. *Journal of Automated Reasoning*, 6:79–109, 1990.

[2] L. Bachmair. *Canonical equational proofs.* Computer Science Logic, Progress in Theoretical Computer Science. Birkhäuser Verlag AG, 1991.

[3] L. Bachmair and N. Dershowitz. Commutation, transformation and termination. In J. Siekmann, editor, *Proceedings 8th International Conference on Automated Deduction, Oxford (UK)*, volume 230 of *Lecture Notes in Computer Science*, pages 5–20. Springer-Verlag, 1986.

[4] L. Bachmair and N. Dershowitz. Inference rules for rewrite-based first-order theorem proving. In *Proceedings 2nd IEEE Symposium on Logic in Computer Science, Ithaca (N.Y., USA)*, pages 331–337, 1987.

[5] L. Bachmair and N. Dershowitz. Completion for rewriting modulo a congruence. *Theoretical Computer Science*, 67(2-3):173–202, October 1989.

[6] L. Bachmair, N. Dershowitz, and J. Hsiang. Orderings for equational proofs. In *Proceedings 1st IEEE Symposium on Logic in Computer Science, Cambridge (Mass., USA)*, pages 346–357. IEEE, 1986.

[7] L. Bachmair, N. Dershowitz, and D. Plaisted. Completion without failure. In H. Aït-Kaci and M. Nivat, editors, *Resolution of Equations in Algebraic Structures, Volume 2: Rewriting Techniques*, pages 1–30. Academic Press inc., 1989.

[8] L. Bachmair and H. Ganzinger. Associative-Commutative superposition. Technical Report MPI-I-93-250, Max-Planck-Institut für Informatik, Saarbrücken, 1993.

[9] L. Bachmair and H. Ganzinger. Rewrite-based equational theorem proving with selection and simplification. *Journal of Logic and Computation*, 4(3):1–31, 1994.

[10] L. Bachmair, H. Ganzinger, C. Lynch, and W. Snyder. Basic paramodulation and superposition. In *Proceedings 11th International Conference on Automated Deduction, Saratoga Springs (N.Y., USA)*, pages 462–476, 1992.

[11] L. Bachmair and D. A. Plaisted. Termination orderings for associative-commutative rewriting systems. *Journal of Symbolic Computation*, 1:329–349, 1985.

[12] F. Bellegarde and P. Lescanne. Transformation orderings. In *12th Coll. on Trees in Algebra and Programming, TAPSOFT*, volume 249 of *Lecture Notes in Computer Science*, pages 69–80. Springer-Verlag, 1987.

[13] A. Ben Cherifa and P. Lescanne. Termination of rewriting systems by polynomial interpretations and its implementation. *Science of Computer Programming*, 9(2):137–160, October 1987.

[14] J. A. Bergstra and J. W. Klop. Conditional rewrite rules: Confluency and termination. *Journal of Computer and System Sciences*, 32(3):323–362, 1986.

[15] G. Birkhoff. On the structure of abstract algebras. *Proceedings Cambridge Phil. Soc.*, 31:433–454, 1935.

[16] A. Bouhoula. *Preuves automatiques par récurrence dans les théories conditionnelles.* Thèse de Doctorat d'Université, Université Henri Poincaré – Nancy 1, March 1994.

[17] A. Bouhoula and M. Rusinowitch. Automatic case analysis in proof by induction. In Ruzena Bajcsy, editor, *Proceedings 13th International Joint Conference on Artificial Intelligence, Chambéry (France)*, volume 1, pages 88–94. Morgan Kaufmann, August 1993.

[18] A. Bouhoula and M. Rusinowitch. Implicit induction in conditional theories. *Journal of Automated Reasoning*, 14(2):189–235, 1995.

[19] R. S. Boyer and J. S. Moore. *A Computationnal Logic*. ACM monograph series. Academic Press, Inc, 1979.

[20] T. Brown. *A structured design-method for specialized proof procedures*. PhD thesis, California Institute of Technology, Pasadena, California, 1975.

[21] B. Buchberger. History and basic features of the critical-pair / completion approach. In *Proceedings 1st Conference on Rewriting Techniques and Applications, Dijon (France)*, volume 202 of *Lecture Notes in Computer Science*. Springer-Verlag, 1985.

[22] H.-J. Bürckert. *A Resolution Principle for a Logic with Restricted Quantifiers*, volume 568 of *Lecture Notes in Artificial Intelligence*. Springer-Verlag, 1991.

[23] E. A. Cichon and P. Lescanne. Polynomial interpretations and the complexity of algorithms. In D. Kapur, editor, *Proceedings 11th International Conference on Automated Deduction, Saratoga Springs (N.Y., USA)*, volume 607 of *Lecture Notes in Computer Science*, pages 139–147. Springer-Verlag, June 1992.

[24] R. L. Constable et al. *Implementing Mathematics with the Nuprl Proof Development System*. Prentice Hall, Inc., Englewood Cliffs, New Jersey 07632, 1986.

[25] T. Coquand and G. Huet. The Calculus of Constructions. *Information and Computation*, 76, 1988.

[26] N. Dershowitz. Orderings for term-rewriting systems. *Theoretical Computer Science*, 17:279–301, 1982.

[27] N. Dershowitz. Termination of rewriting. *Journal of Symbolic Computation*, 3(1 & 2):69–116, 1987.

[28] N. Dershowitz. Completion and its applications. In H. Aït-Kaci and M. Nivat, editors, *Resolution of Equations in Algebraic Structures, Volume 2: Rewriting Techniques*, pages 31–86. Academic Press inc., 1989.

[29] N. Dershowitz and C. Hoot. Natural termination. *Theoretical Computer Science*, 142(2):179–207, May 1995.

[30] N. Dershowitz and J.-P. Jouannaud. Rewrite Systems. In J. van Leeuwen, editor, *Handbook of Theoretical Computer Science*, chapter 6, pages 244–320. Elsevier Science Publishers B. V. (North-Holland), 1990.

[31] N. Dershowitz and M. Okada. A rationale for conditional equational programming. *Theoretical Computer Science*, 75:111–138, 1990.

[32] E. Domenjoud. A technical note on AC-unification. the number of minimal unifiers of the equation $\alpha x_1 + \cdots + \alpha x_p \doteq_{AC} \beta y_1 + \cdots + \beta y_q$. *Journal of Automated Reasoning*, 8:39–44, 1992.

[33] A. Frisch and R. Scherl. A general framework for modal deduction. In J. A. Allen, R. Fikes, and E. Sandewall, editors, *Principles of Knowledge Representation and Reasoning: Proceedings of the Second International Conference*, San Mateo, CA, USA, 1991.

[34] H. Ganzinger. A completion procedure for conditional equations. *Journal of Symbolic Computation*, 11:51–81, 1991.

[35] J. Giesl. Generating polynomial orderings for termination proofs. In J. Hsiang, editor, *Rewriting Techniques and Applications, 6th International Conference, RTA-95*, LNCS 914, pages 426–431, Kaiserslautern, Germany, April 5–7, 1995. Springer-Verlag.

[36] M.-J.-C. Gordon and T.-F. Melham. *Introduction to HOL: a theorem proving environment for higher order logic*. Cambridge University Press, 1993. ISBN 0-521-44189-7.

[37] G. Grätzer. *Universal Algebra*. Springer-Verlag, second edition, 1979.

[38] J. V. Guttag, J. J. Horning, S. J. Garland, K. D. Jones, A. Modet, and J. M. Wing. *Larch: Languages and Tools for Formal Specification*. Springer-Verlag, 1993.

[39] L. Henkin. The logic of equality. *American Mathematical Monthly*, 84(8):597–612, 1977.

[40] J. Herbrand. Recherches sur la théorie de la démonstration. *Travaux de la Soc. des Sciences et des Lettres de Varsovie, Classe III*, 33(128), 1930.

[41] D. Hofbauer. Termination proofs by multiset path orderings imply primitive recursive derivation lengths. *Theoretical Computer Science*, 105(1):129–140, October 1992.

[42] D. Hofbauer and C. Lautemann. Termination proofs and the length of derivations. In N. Dershowitz, editor, *Proceedings 3rd Conference on Rewriting Techniques and Applications, Chapel Hill (N.C., USA)*, volume 355 of *Lecture Notes in Computer Science*, pages 167–177. Springer-Verlag, April 1989.

[43] J. Hsiang. Refutational theorem proving using term rewriting systems. *Artificial Intelligence*, 25(1):255–300, 1985.

[44] J. Hsiang. Rewrite methods for theorem proving in first order theory with equality. *Journal of Symbolic Computation*, 3(1 & 2):133–151, 1987.

[45] J. Hsiang and N. Dershowitz. Rewrite methods for clausal and non-clausal theorem proving. In *Proceedings of 10th International Colloquium on Automata, Languages and Programming*, volume 154 of *Lecture Notes in Computer Science*, pages 331–346, Barcelona (Spain), 1983. Springer-Verlag.

[46] J. Hsiang, H. Kirchner, P. Lescanne, and M. Rusinowitch. The term rewriting approach to automated theorem proving. *Journal of Logic Programming*, 14(1&2):71–99, October 1992.

[47] J. Hsiang and M. Rusinowitch. A new method for establishing refutational completeness in theorem proving. In J. Siekmann, editor, *Proceedings 8th International Conference on Automated Deduction, Oxford (UK)*, volume 230 of *Lecture Notes in Computer Science*, pages 141–152. Springer-Verlag, 1986.

[48] J. Hsiang and M. Rusinowitch. On word problem in equational theories. In Th. Ottmann, editor, *Proceedings of 14th International Colloquium on Automata, Languages and Programming, Karlsruhe (Germany)*, volume 267 of *Lecture Notes in Computer Science*, pages 54–71. Springer-Verlag, 1987.

[49] J. Hsiang and M. Rusinowitch. Proving refutational completeness of theorem proving strategies: The transfinite semantic tree method. *Journal of the ACM*, 38(3):559–587, July 1991.

[50] G. Huet. *Constrained Resolution: A Complete Method for Higher Order Logic.* PhD thesis, Case Western Reserve University, 1972.

[51] G. Huet. Confluent reductions: Abstract properties and applications to term rewriting systems. *Journal of the ACM*, 27(4):797–821, October 1980. Preliminary version in 18th Symposium on Foundations of Computer Science, IEEE, 1977.

[52] G. Huet. A complete proof of correctness of the Knuth and Bendix completion algorithm. *Journal of Computer and System Sciences*, 23:11–21, 1981.

[53] G. Huet and D. Oppen. Equations and rewrite rules: A survey. In R. V. Book, editor, *Formal Language Theory: Perspectives and Open Problems*, pages 349–405. Academic Press inc., 1980.

[54] J.-M. Hullot. *Compilation de Formes Canoniques dans les Théories équationelles.* Thèse de Doctorat de Troisième Cycle, Université de Paris Sud, Orsay (France), 1980.

[55] J. Jaffar and J.-L. Lassez. Constraint logic programming. In *Proceedings of the 14th Annual ACM Symposium on Principles Of Programming Languages, Munich (Germany)*, pages 111–119, 1987.

[56] J.-P. Jouannaud and H. Kirchner. Completion of a set of rules modulo a set of equations. *SIAM Journal of Computing*, 15(4):1155–1194, 1986. Preliminary version in Proceedings 11th ACM Symposium on Principles of Programming Languages, Salt Lake City (USA), 1984.

[57] J.-P. Jouannaud, P. Lescanne, and F. Reinig. Recursive decomposition ordering. In D. Bjørner, editor, *Formal Description of Programming Concepts 2*, pages 331–348, Garmisch-Partenkirchen, Germany, 1982. Elsevier Science Publishers B. V. (North-Holland).

[58] S. Kamin and J.-J. Lévy. Attempts for generalizing the recursive path ordering. *Inria, Rocquencourt*, 1982.

[59] S. Kaplan. Conditional rewrite rules. *Theoretical Computer Science*, 33:175–193, 1984.

[60] D. Kapur and P. Narendran. An equational approach to theorem proving in first-order predicate calculus. In *Proceedings of the International Joint Conference on Artificial Intelligence*, Los Angeles (USA), 1985.

[61] D. Kapur and H. Zhang. RRL: A rewrite rule laboratory. In *Proceedings 9th International Conference on Automated Deduction, Argonne (Ill., USA)*, volume 310 of *Lecture Notes in Computer Science*, pages 768–769. Springer-Verlag, 1988.

[62] D. Kapur and H. Zhang. A case study of the completion procedure: ring commutativity problems. In Jean-Louis Lassez and G. Plotkin, editors, *Computational Logic. Essays in*

honor of Alan Robinson, chapter 10, pages 360–394. The MIT press, Cambridge (MA, USA), 1991.

[63] C. Kirchner and H. Kirchner. Reveur-3: Implementation of a general completion procedure parametrized by built-in theories and strategies. *Science of Computer Programming*, 20(8):69–86, 1986.

[64] C. Kirchner, H. Kirchner, and M. Rusinowitch. Deduction with symbolic constraints. *Revue d'Intelligence Artificielle*, 4(3):9–52, 1990. Special issue on Automatic Deduction.

[65] C. Kirchner, C. Lynch, and C. Scharff. A fine-grained concurrent completion procedure. In H. Ganzinger, editor, *Proceedings of RTA'96*, volume 1103 of *Lecture Notes in Computer Science*, pages 3–17. Springer-Verlag, September 1996.

[66] H. Kirchner and P.-E. Moreau. Prototyping completion with constraints using computational systems. In J. Hsiang, editor, *Proceedings 6th Conference on Rewriting Techniques and Applications, Kaiserslautern (Germany)*, volume 914 of *Lecture Notes in Computer Science*, pages 438–443. Springer-Verlag, 1995.

[67] H. Kirchner and C. Ringeissen. Constraint solving by narrowing in combined algebraic domains. In P. Van Hentenryck, editor, *Proc. 11th International Conference on Logic Programming*, pages 617–631. The MIT press, 1994.

[68] H. Kirchner. On the use of constraints in automated deduction. In A. Podelski, editor, *Constraint Programming: Basics and Trends*, volume 910 of *Lecture Notes in Computer Science*, pages 128–146. Springer-Verlag, 1995.

[69] D. E. Knuth and P. B. Bendix. Simple word problems in universal algebras. In J. Leech, editor, *Computational Problems in Abstract Algebra*, pages 263–297. Pergamon Press, Oxford, 1970.

[70] E. Kounalis and M. Rusinowitch. On word problem in Horn logic. In J.-P. Jouannaud and S. Kaplan, editors, *Proceedings 1st International Workshop on Conditional Term Rewriting Systems, Orsay (France)*, volume 308 of *Lecture Notes in Computer Science*, pages 144–160. Springer-Verlag, July 1987. See also the extended version published in Journal of Symbolic Computation, 11(1 & 2), 1991.

[71] D. Kozen. A completeness theorem for Kleene algebras and the algebra of regular events. In *Proc. 6th IEEE symposium on Logic in Computer Science (LICS)*, pages 214–225. IEEE Computer Society Press, Los Alamitos, July 1991.

[72] D. S. Lankford. Canonical inference. Technical report, Louisiana Tech. University, 1975.

[73] D. S. Lankford. On proving term rewriting systems are noetherian. Technical report, Louisiana Tech. University, Mathematics Dept., Ruston LA, 1979.

[74] D. S. Lankford and A. Ballantyne. Decision procedures for simple equational theories with associative commutative axioms: complete sets of associative commutative reductions. Technical report, Univ. of Texas at Austin, Dept. of Mathematics and Computer Science, 1977.

[75] C. Lautemann. A note on polynomial interpretation. *Bulletin of European Association for Theoretical Computer Science*, 1(36):129–131, October 1988.

[76] P. Lescanne. On the recursive decomposition ordering with lexicographical status and other related orderings. *Journal of Automated Reasoning*, 6:39–49, 1990.

[77] E. Lusk, W. McCune, R. Overbeek, S. Winker, and L. Wos. Automated reasoning contributes to mathematics and logic. In M. E. Stickel, editor, *Proceedings 10th International Conference on Automated Deduction, Kaiserslautern (Germany)*, volume 449 of *Lecture Notes in Computer Science*, pages 485–499. Springer-Verlag, July 1990.

[78] C. Lynch and W. Snyder. Redundancy criteria for constrained completion. In C. Kirchner, editor, *Proceedings 5th Conference on Rewriting Techniques and Applications, Montreal (Canada)*, volume 690 of *Lecture Notes in Computer Science*, pages 2–16. Springer-Verlag, 1993.

[79] C. Lynch. Goal directed completion using sour graphs. In *Proceedings of the CCL'95 Workshop*, Rottach-Egern, September 1995.

[80] C. Marché. Normalised rewriting and normalised completion. In S. Abramsky, editor, *Proceedings 9th IEEE Symposium on Logic in Computer Science, Paris (France)*, pages 394–403, 1994.

[81] U. Martin and T. Nipkow. Ordered rewriting and confluence. In M. E. Stickel, editor, *Proceedings 10th International Conference on Automated Deduction, Kaiserslautern (Germany)*, volume 449 of *Lecture Notes in Computer Science*, pages 366–380. Springer-Verlag, 1990.

[82] W. W. McCune. Otter 3.0: Reference manual and guide. Technical Report 6, Argonne National Laboratory, 1994.

[83] P. Narendran and M. Rusinowitch. Any ground associative-commutative theory has a finite canonical system. In R. V. Book, editor, *Proceedings 4th Conference on Rewriting Techniques and Applications, Como (Italy)*, volume 488 of *Lecture Notes in Computer Science*, pages 423–434. Springer-Verlag, April 1991.

[84] R. Nieuwenhuis and A. Rubio. Basic superposition is complete. In B. Krieg-Brückner, editor, *Proceedings of ESOP'92*, volume 582 of *Lecture Notes in Computer Science*, pages 371–389. Springer-Verlag, 1992.

[85] R. Nieuwenhuis and A. Rubio. Theorem proving with ordering constrained clauses. In D. Kapur, editor, *Proceedings 11th International Conference on Automated Deduction, Saratoga Springs (N.Y., USA)*, volume 607 of *Lecture Notes in Computer Science*, pages 477–491. Springer-Verlag, 1992.

[86] P. Nivela and R. Nieuwenhuis. Saturation of first-order (constrained) clauses with the *Saturate* system. In C. Kirchner, editor, *Proceedings 5th Conference on Rewriting Techniques and Applications, Montreal (Canada)*, volume 690 of *Lecture Notes in Computer Science*, pages 436–440. Springer-Verlag, 1993.

[87] L. C. Paulson. The foundation of a generic theorem prover. *Journal of Automated Reasoning*, 5:363–397, 1989.

[88] G. Peterson. A technique for establishing completeness results in theorem proving with equality. *SIAM Journal of Computing*, 12(1):82–100, 1983.

[89] G. Peterson and M. E. Stickel. Complete sets of reductions for some equational theories. *Journal of the ACM*, 28:233–264, 1981.

[90] G. Plotkin. Building-in equational theories. *Machine Intelligence*, 7:73–90, 1972.

[91] W. V. Quine. The problem of simplifying truth functions. *American Math. Monthly*, 59:521–531, 1952.

[92] W. V. Quine. On cores and prime implicants of truth functions. *American Math. Monthly*, 66:755–760, 1959.

[93] U. S. Reddy. Term rewriting induction. In M. E. Stickel, editor, *Proceedings 10th International Conference on Automated Deduction, Kaiserslautern (Germany)*, volume 449 of *Lecture Notes in Computer Science*, pages 162–177. Springer-Verlag, 1990.

[94] G. A. Robinson and L. T. Wos. Paramodulation and first-order theorem proving. In B. Meltzer and D. Mitchie, editors, *Machine Intelligence 4*, pages 135–150. Edinburgh University Press, 1969.

[95] J. A. Robinson. A machine-oriented logic based on the resolution principle. *Journal of the ACM*, 12:23–41, 1965.

[96] A. Rubio and R. Nieuwenhuis. A precedence-based total AC-compatible ordering. In C. Kirchner, editor, *Proceedings 5th Conference on Rewriting Techniques and Applications, Montreal (Canada)*, volume 690 of *Lecture Notes in Computer Science*, pages 374–388. Springer-Verlag, 1993.

[97] M. Rusinowitch. *Démonstration automatique-Techniques de réécriture*. InterEditions, 1989.

[98] M. Rusinowitch and L. Vigneron. Automated Deduction with Associative-Commutative Operators. *Applicable Algebra in Engineering, Communication and Computation*, 6(1):23–56, January 1995.

[99] J. R. Schoenfield. *Mathematical logic*. Addison-Wesley Publishing Company, 1970.

[100] J. R. Slagle. Automated theorem-proving for theories with simplifiers, commutativity and associativity. *Journal of the ACM*, 21(4):622–642, 1974.

[101] J. R. Slagle, C. L. Chang, and R. C. T. Lee. A new algorithm for generating prime implicants. *IEEE Transactions on Computing*, 19(4):304–310, 1970.

[102] R. Socher-Ambrosius. Boolean algebra admits no convergent term rewriting system. In R. V. Book, editor, *Proceedings 4th Conference on Rewriting Techniques and Applications, Como (Italy)*, volume 488 of *Lecture Notes in Computer Science*, pages 264–274. Springer-Verlag, April 1991.

[103] J. Steinbach. AC-termination of rewrite systems — A modified Knuth-Bendix ordering. In H. Kirchner and W. Wechler, editors, *Proceedings 2nd International Conference on Algebraic and Logic Programming, Nancy (France)*, volume 463 of *Lecture Notes in Computer Science*, pages 372–386. Springer-Verlag, 1990.

[104] M. E. Stickel. Automated deduction by theory resolution. *Journal of Automated Reasoning*, 1(4):285–289, 1985.
[105] M. E. Stickel. A unification algorithm for associative-commutative functions. *Journal of the ACM*, 28:423–434, 1981.
[106] M. E. Stickel. A case study of theorem proving by the Knuth-Bendix method: Discovering that $x^3 = x$ implies ring commutativity. In R. Shostak, editor, *Proceedings 7th International Conference on Automated Deduction, Napa Valley (Calif., USA)*, volume 170 of *Lecture Notes in Computer Science*, pages 248–258. Springer-Verlag, 1984.
[107] M. E. Stickel. A PROLOG technology theorem prover: implementation by an extended PROLOG compiler. In J. Siekmann, editor, *Proceedings 8th International Conference on Automated Deduction, Oxford (UK)*, volume 230 of *Lecture Notes in Computer Science*, pages 573–587. Springer-Verlag, 1986.
[108] A. Tarski. Equational logic and equational theories of algebras. In K. Schütte, editor, *Contributions to Mathematical Logic*, pages 275–288. Elsevier Science Publishers B. V. (North-Holland), Amsterdam, 1968.
[109] W. Taylor. Equational logic. *Houston Journal of Mathematics*, 1979. Appears also in [**37**], Appendix 4.
[110] Y. Toyama. Counterexamples to termination for the direct sum of term rewriting systems. *Information Processing Letters*, 25(3):141–143, May 1986.
[111] R. L. Veroff. Canonicalization and demodulation. Internal Report ANL-81-6, Argonne National Laboratory, Argonne,IL, 1981.
[112] L. Vigneron. Associative-Commutative Deduction with Constraints. In A. Bundy, editor, *Proceedings 12th International Conference on Automated Deduction, Nancy (France)*, volume 814 of *Lecture Notes in Artificial Intelligence*, pages 530–544. Springer-Verlag, June 1994.
[113] T. Walsh. A divergence critic. In A. Bundy, editor, *Proceedings 12th International Conference on Automated Deduction, Nancy (France)*, volume 814 of *Lecture Notes in Artificial Intelligence*, pages 14–28. Springer-Verlag, June/July 1994.
[114] L. Wos. *Automated Reasoning: 33 basic research problems.* Prentice Hall, Inc., Englewood Cliffs, NJ, 1988.
[115] L. Wos, G. A. Robinson, D. F. Carso, and L. Shalla. The concept of demodulation in theorem proving. *Journal of the ACM*, 14(4):698–709, 1967.
[116] H. Zhang, D. Kapur, and M. S. Krishnamoorthy. A mechanizable induction principle for equational specifications. In E. Lusk and R. Overbeek, editors, *Proceedings 9th International Conference on Automated Deduction, Argonne (Ill., USA)*, volume 310 of *Lecture Notes in Computer Science*, pages 162–181. Springer-Verlag, 1988.

CRIN-CNRS & INRIA-Lorraine
Current address: BP 239, 54506 Vandœuvre-lès-Nancy Cedex, France
E-mail address: `Helene.Kirchner@loria.fr`

Proceedings of Symposia in Applied Mathematics
Volume 55, 1998

Programming with Constraints:
Some Aspects of The Mathematical Foundations

Catherine Lassez
Department of Computer Science
New Mexico Institute of Mining and Technology,
Socorro, New Mexico 87825
classez@sphinx.cs.nmt.edu

Abstract

In this paper, we present the mathematical foundations of constraint programming. A program is a set of constraints, i.e. a mathematical formula. A set of constraints is viewed as an implicit representation of the set of all constraints that it entails. There is a query system such that an answer to a query is a relationship that is satisfied if and only if the query is entailed by the system. And most importantly there exists a SINGLE algorithm to answer all queries (an oracle). In the case of logic programming, the constraint domain is Horn clauses and the algorithm is resolution. The soundness and completeness of resolution guarantees a well-defined programming system.

In the domain of arithmetic constraints, the algorithm is quantifier elimination, and Tarski's theorem provides the counterpart to the soundness and completeness of resolution. As the cost of implementation in the general case is prohibitive, we restrict ourselves to the linear case. A program is a conjunction of linear constraints which represents a polyhedral set. Fourier's algorithm, the counterpart of Tarski's for the linear case, provides the parametric query answering mechanism.

Interestingly, in this framework, classic linear programming results are interpreted in a new light. In particular, duality is given a quantifier elimination interpretation rather than the usual economic one,

1991 *Mathematics Subject Classification.* Primary 68T27.

and a link between the simplex algorithm and the ubiquitous Helly's theorem is shown.

Note that proofs are not included in the following presentation. The interested reader is referred to the literature.

1 Introduction

Much work has been done in AI on constraint satisfaction problems based on the pioniering papers by Freuder, Macworth, Montanari and Pearl (see [Davis 87] and [Pearl 88] for references). The main thrust of that work is algorithmic and heuristic, trying to solve hard combinatorial problems. Languages have been designed specifically to solve constraint problems; see [Borning 88] [Steele 82].

More recently, a somewhat orthogonal approach has been developed: instead of designing languages to solve constraint satisfaction problems, constraints are used as primitive elements in the design of programming systems. For instance, constraints handling techniques have been incorporated in a number of programming systems, including CLP($\Re$), CHIP, CAL, CIL, Prolog III, BNR-Prolog, 2LP, Mathematica and Trilogy.

From Logic Programming.....

One will find in [Chang and Lee 73] a review of the early works of Black, Darlington, Slagle, Green and Raphael, Waldinger and Lee, on the use of theorem proving for the design of deductive question answering systems. A more systematic approach and a restriction to Horn clauses led to logic programming and its associated languages and databases. The fundamental ideas and results that make logic formulae suitable for such systems are:

- A logic formula is viewed as an implicit and concise representation of its set of logical consequences. That is viewed as a database or a program possessing knowledge.
- A query $Q(x, y)$ is answered by a set of substitutions (or constraints in

the case of CLP) which establish a relationship between the variables, satisfied if and only if $Q(x, y)$ is a logical consequence of the formula. In other words the query-answer system allows the extraction of all knowledge implicitly stored in the formula.

- A SINGLE algorithm, resolution, is sufficient to answer all queries.
- The semantics of the system are easily described through model theory which accommodates the declarative aspects, while proof theory describes the operational aspects. The results on soundness and completeness guarantee the correctness of the system.
- In the case of CLP, which takes constraints as input as well as output, the language used to describe input and output may be lifted to the same level as the programming language itself.

The key concept in terms of programming paradigm is the use of resolution. A confusion is often made between *declarative programming language* and *specification language.* (**What** is to be computed as opposed to **How** it is to be computed). A specification language does not need to be executable, or could be executable through a package of thousands of subroutines. What makes logic based languages *declarative* is resolution. Its universal power, since it can handle all computable functions, relieves (at least IN PRINCIPLE) the user from much programming.

The last point above also needs some emphasis. The language of logic is very expressive, but the output of a standard logic programming language is restricted to substitutions. We can specify very complex objects, but we can get only a very restrictive and primitive output, which is most frustrating. The introduction of constraints helps alleviate this problem, as illustrated in [Lassez 87] [Jaffar and Lassez 87(1)]

....to Lazy Programming

The properties of logic formulae have counterparts in other domains, in particular in those most important from a computational point of view. Certainly a candidate is real arithmetic. The reader is referred to [Van Den Vries

89] for a high level exposition of Tarski's elimination theory for real closed fields.

Tarski proved the following theorem:

Theorem 1 *(Tarski) To any formula* $\phi(X_1, X_2, \ldots, X_m)$ *in the vocabulary* $\{0, 1, +, \cdot, =, <\}$ *one can effectively associate two objects: (i) a quantifier free formula* $\theta(X_1, \ldots, X_m)$ *in the same vocabulary, and (ii) a proof of the equivalence* ϕ–θ *that uses only the axioms for real closed fields.*

What it means is that we can view an arithmetic formula (multivariate polynomials, inequalities, and, or, not, disjunction, conjunction, existential and universal quantifiers) as representing the set of all its *logical* consequences, that is, the set of all arithmetic formulae that it entails. And that in order to obtain one of these consequences, a SINGLE algorithm, QUANTIFIER ELIMINATION, is needed, in analogy with logic formulae and resolution.

From a semantic point of view we have the same advantage as in the case of logic, since we are dealing with the very old and well understood language of mathematics. A very simple and familiar example is the equation of degree two:

$$\exists x \; ax^2 + bx + c = 0 \quad a \neq 0$$

We all know from high school that an equivalent formula is:

$$b^2 - 4ac \geq 0$$

This formula may be obtained by eliminating the existential quantifier (or equivalently eliminating the variable x) from the equation. All such consequences of arithmetic formulae can indeed be obtained by eliminating quantifiers (or variables).

Another example is a typical problem in geometry: how to find the convex hull of a given set of points. A point of coordinates $(x_1, \ldots, x_n)$ is in the convex hull of a set of m points iff there exist λ_j's such that the system:

$$\begin{cases} x_1 = \Sigma\alpha_1^j\lambda_j \\ \vdots \\ x_n = \Sigma\alpha_n^j\lambda_j \\ \Sigma\lambda_j = 1 \\ \lambda_j \geq 0, \;\; j = 1, ..., m \end{cases}$$

is satisfied, where $\{(\alpha_1^j, \;\; ..., \;\; \alpha_n^j)\}$ are the coordinates of the points. The representation of the convex hull is an equivalent set of relations solely among the x_i's. It is obtained by eliminating all λ_j's from the system.

Example 1 *Given the points:*

$$\begin{cases} (1, 0, 0) \\ (0, 1, 0) \\ (0, 0, 1) \end{cases}$$

we write the system:

$$\begin{cases} x_1 = \lambda_1 \\ x_2 = \lambda_2 \\ x_3 = \lambda_3 \\ \lambda_1 + \lambda_2 + \lambda_3 = 1 \\ \lambda_i \geq 0 \end{cases}$$

Eliminating the λ's, we obtain

$$\begin{cases} x_1 + x_2 + x_3 = 1 \\ x_1 \geq 0, \;\; x_2 \geq 0, \;\; x_3 \geq 0 \end{cases}$$

which represents the convex hull of the points. □

An interesting side effect is that this gives a trivial proof of the classic theorem that

the convex hull of a finite set of points is a polyhedral set, since Gauss-Jordan reduction and Fourier elimination do not introduce nonlinearities or disjunctions.

Elimination theory was a very active area at the turn of the century; modern work on algebraic geometry was more directed towards abstraction and *declarative* aspects. However, with the recent applications to robotics and CAD/CAM [Canny 87], elimination theory is making a strong comeback in algebraic geometry under the influence of Abhyankar (see [Kapur and Mundy 93]). What remains to be shown is that one can develop a rich querying system along the lines of the one for logic formulae.

Another domain of interest is Boolean algebra. We will not elaborate on it here, but just show through a simple example that it is another area where fundamental results allow for a possible systematic treatment of a querying system along lines similar to those of logic or arithmetic formulae. See [Brown 90] for further information. Our remarks on Boolean algebra come from that book. C.I. Lewis in 1918 stated that

> *For purpose of application of the algebra to ordinary reasoning, elimination is a process more important than solution, since most processes of reasoning take place through the elimination of middle terms.*

We consider the following simple example.

Example 2 *An* **AND** *gate has 2 inputs* x_1 *and* x_2 *and* z_1 *as output. The output of the* **AND** *gate is connected to the input of an* **OR** *gate whose second input is labeled* x_3 *and whose output is labelled* z_2.
The equations:

$$\begin{cases} z_1 = x_1 \cdot x_2 \\ z_2 = x_3 + z_1 \end{cases}$$

define the circuit by reflecting its structure. But the functionality of the circuit is better expressed by a relationship solely between input and output variables.
Boole showed that this is achieved simply by eliminating the other variable:

$z_2 = x_3 + x_1 \cdot x_2$ □

So the paradigmatic aspects of reasoning or programming with logic formulae also apply to other important domains and mathematical objects.

To summarize, the three main points for a given domain are:

- A set of constraints is viewed as an implicit representation of the set of all constraints that it entails.
- There is a query system such that an answer to a query $Q(x, y)$ is a relationship that is satisfied if and only if the query is entailed by the system.

  And most importantly:
- There exists a SINGLE algorithm to answer all queries (an oracle).

As mentioned in the case of resolution, it is these oracles that can answer any query about an important area that lead to really high level languages. In other words, what is described here is the opposite situation to conventional programming, where the primitive elements are small objects and high level is achieved bottom up by creating macros and a large collection of subroutines. Here the approach is top down, where the primitive elements of the language are as powerful as possible, and the number of basic algorithms is kept to a minimum. The effect is striking: a logic based language can be described rigorously and succinctly in a few words: the syntax is Horn clauses, the interpreter is SLD resolution. For standardization purposes one would need more details, but nevertheless these few words provide an accurate description. To achieve a similar description capturing the essence of ADA would require substantially more text! Since the use of these oracles is to avoid programming unless it is absolutely necessary, it seems appropriate to call *lazy programming*, this approach to programming with constraints. So in lazy programming, one queries a constraint based formulation of the problem at hand, and oracles (resolution, various forms of quantifier elimination, etc.) perform the computation.

Before we address the *real* problems and see how hard it is to be lazy, let us mention research directions that are important in our context.

One is to develop query systems for numeric and boolean constraints. For reasons that will be made clearer in the next section, specialized cases should be considered. The one we present later shows that if symbolic computation is very appropriate at the specification level, in order to achieve efficiency we have to consider and synthesize results and algorithms from linear programming and computational geometry as well.

Another direction which could be explored is the relationship between the oracle algorithms, as an ad hoc collection is not what is warranted. The analogy between the intended querying systems should be reflected in the algorithms on which they are based. Clearly all elimination algorithms are conceptually at least very closely related. By looking again at resolution, we see also a notion of elimination: at each step we eliminate the occurence of a predicate. Two powerful algorithms which are quite relevant to constraint programming are Knuth-Bendix and Buchberger's algorithm for constructing Grobner bases. Their relationship has been studied and a synthesis established [Kandri-Rody and Kapur 83] [Kapur et al. 89]. Buchberger studies the relationships between the two aforementioned algorithms and resolution. In [Buchberger 87], he proposes to establish certain basic *algorithm types* as a natural analogue to the concept of *datatype*. The oracles we discuss would form one of these types.

A problem that we do not address here is how to integrate the various modules corresponding to different domains of constraints. The CLP scheme is certainly a candidate, giving to logic formulae a predominant role. Another promising work in this direction can be found in [Kirchner and Ringeissen 94]. An object oriented framework could be also be considered which could provide more flexibility.

.... Computers do not run (only) on Principles

When they do they have a tendency to blow up.

The advent of resolution in the mid-sixties raised (wild) hopes that automatic reasoning systems would be immediately available. The enormous difficulties met by the first attempts at implementation led a major part of the community to reject resolution with the same fervor as it praised it initially. We now know that in order to obtain really practical logic based systems a number of substantial compromises had to be made. A major one was to restrict the domain to Horn clauses. Further major work was also essential at the design and implementation level. For other domains of constraints we are at present in a situation similar to the situation of resolution in the late sixties. The hopes have been raised of a revolution in applications such as robotics, graphics, constructive solid geometry, etc. But the attempts at creating really practical systems have met with enormous difficulties, far more severe than in the case of logic formulae.

We briefly describe some of the problems next. We refer the reader to the book [Hoffman 89], and papers [Arnon 89] [Arnon 90] [Buchberger 87] [Kapur and Mundy 89] for applications of symbolic computation methods. Also M. Coste in [Boissonat and Laumond 88] provides a high level introduction to quantifier elimination.

Problems with Quantifier Elimination

- SIZE of output and intermediate swell

  If the main problem with resolution was speed, with quantifier elimination we have a far worse problem: the size of the output can be exponential (see [Davenport and Heintz 88]). So it seems that there is really no point in going further, since even if by magic we were able to obtain the output, we would be so overwhelmed that it would be useless. However, one should realize that much of the complexity of the output may be due to the method of elimination. Indeed, there is no canonical form for arithmetic constraints; equivalent expressions may have widely differing sizes. The elimination methods will not necessarily provide the shortest one; there is no clear notion of simplification to guide the methods. The recent work of Renegar (see [Kapur and Mundy 93]) gives a thorough comparison of the various methods as well as very significant new bounds. Now, even in the case where the output size is reasonable, we may still have intermediate computation of doubly exponential size. The two problems are of course linked, as the output of a variable elimination problem may well represent an intermediate computation in a further elimination process.

- Finite and infinite precision arithmetic

  Another major problem discussed in [Davenport et al. 88] is finite precision arithmetic. Consider the polynomial:

  $$P(x) = (x+1)(x+2)\dots(x+20)$$

  Let us change one coefficient of $P(x)$ by adding a tiny perturbation, so tiny that it seems negligible:

  $$Q(x) = P(x) + 2^{-23}x^{19}$$

  If $P(x)$ has twenty obvious real roots, $Q(x)$ has only ten real roots, and the imaginary part of the other roots is comparatively very big. Therefore, we can see that round off errors can create instabilities unacceptable in a solver. One can, of course, resort to infinite precision arithmetic. But then, the problem comes that first computations are considerably slowed down, and worse, the size of the representation of coefficients can grow arbitrarily, aborting the computation.

2 Parametric Queries

Let S be the set of constraints representing the program in store. The question to address is: what type of information do we want to extract from S, during execution of the program or at output time? First examples are queries of the type $S \Rightarrow Q$? where Q can be:

- $x = 3$
- $x + y - z = 1$
- $x - y + 3z \leq 0$

Such queries require a simple yes/no answer which can be obtained by showing that the constraint $S \wedge \neg Q$ is not solvable. This is the standard technique for subsumption in theorem proving.

In logic programming one goes a level higher: unless the query is ground (that is has no variables), it requires more than a yes/no answer. The answer to a general query is a set of substitutions which form a finite representation of the set of answers. It is obtained as a side effect of the solvability test.

So the examples above correspond to ground queries in a logic program, despite the presence of variables. A trivial case of a query that would correspond to the more powerful queries in logic programs is:

Do the constraints in store imply that the variable x has a fixed value?

More formally

$$\exists \alpha \forall x : S \Rightarrow x = \alpha ?$$

Clearly here, if the answer to the existential question is *yes*, we want to know the value of α.

More generally, linear relationships among the program variables may be implied by the constraints in store. This information is essential for representing constraints in a canonical form, for output standardization, constraint propagation, and the elimination of redundancy in parallel (see [Lassez et al. 89], [Lassez and McAloon 88], [Lassez and McAloon 90] for details). In CLP ($\Re$), a non-linear expression such as $z = log(x - y)$ is delayed. The knowledge that $x - y$ has a fixed value α for some α will resolve the delay.

Let us consider now inequality queries. In CLP($\Re$) the output should represent the relationships between the input variables only. However, the constraints in store contain auxiliary variables introduced during the execution of the rules in the program. For example, let x, y be the input variables and u, v be the auxiliary variables in $S = \{x + 2y + u \leq 1, -y - u + v \leq 2, x + u - v \leq 0\}$. After eliminating u and v we obtain $\{x - y \leq 2\}$ as the output. A related situation occurs in order to resolve guards in committed choice languages [Maher 87], [Saraswat 93]. The guards contain existential queries, and their execution leads to a similar problem of variable (or quantifier) elimination.

These problems can be formalized as answering *parametric queries* of the form:

$$\exists \alpha, \beta, \gamma, ... \forall x, y, ... : S \Rightarrow \alpha x + \beta y + ... \leq (or =) \gamma \wedge R(\alpha, \beta, ..., \gamma)?$$

where $R(\alpha, \beta, ..., \gamma)$ is a set of linear relations on the parameters such as $(\alpha = 0,\ \beta \leq 2\gamma)$.

A parametric query asks under what conditions on the parameters $\alpha, \beta, \ldots, \gamma$, the constraint in the query is implied by the constraints in store. What we request is a finite representation of the set of answers.

By varying the parameters, specific queries can be formulated in this framework.

- *Is x bound to a specific value a?*

  $$\exists \alpha, \beta, \ldots, \gamma, \forall x, y, \ldots, S \Rightarrow \alpha x + \beta y + \ldots = \gamma \wedge \alpha = 1, \beta = 0, \delta = 0, \ldots, \gamma = a?$$

- *Is x ground?*
  same as above but with γ unconstrained.

- *Does S imply $2x + 3y \leq 0$?*

  $$\exists \alpha, \beta, \ldots, \gamma, \forall x, y, \ldots, S \Rightarrow \alpha x + \beta y + \ldots = \gamma \wedge \alpha = 2, \beta = 3, \ldots, \gamma = 0$$

- *What are the constraints implied by the projection of S in the x,y-plane?*
  All parameters set to 0 except α, β, γ.

The test for solvability and the classic optimization problem of linear programming can also be expressed in this way:

- *Is S solvable?*
  all the parameters are set to 0 except γ and R is reduced to $\gamma \geq 0$
  This is a direct application of Fourier's theorem, which states that if the elimination of all the variables results in a tautology then S is solvable.

- *What are the upper and lower bounds of $x + y + z$?*
  as above, all parameters are set to 0 except those of x, y and z and $R = \{\gamma \geq 0, \alpha = 1, \beta = 1, \delta = 1\}$. The answer gives the range of values for γ that correspond to the minimum and maximum of the expression.

Parametric queries generalize both logic programming queries, which ask if there exists an assignment of values to the variables in the query so that the query becomes a logical consequence of the program clauses, and CSP's, which are restricted to constraints of the type $x = a$. What we now request is a finite representation of the set of answers. The novelty and the apparent technical difficulty come from the fact that we quantify over coefficients of an arithmetic expression, not over its variables. The method to obtain answers to parametric queries is derived from a direct corollary to Fourier's theorem. It is rarely mentioned and does not seem to have been used in this form at least, but it is in fact equivalent to the fundamental Duality Theorem in Linear Programming [Achmanov 84]. It provides a simple characterization of the set of constraints implied by S, and forms the basis for our approach. (For the sake of simplicity, we will use the word combination for non-negative combination unless specifically stated).

A constraint C is a *quasi-linear combination* of constraints of $S = \{C_1, ..., C_n\}$ if and only if C is obtained by adding a positive number to the right hand side of a non-negative linear combination of constraints of S.

Theorem 2 (The Subsumption Theorem) *A constraint C is implied by a set of constraints S if and only if C is a quasi-linear combination of constraints in S.*

In other words, given $S = \{a_1x + b_1y + ... \leq c_1, a_2x + b_2y + ... \leq c_2, ...\}$, the constraint $\alpha x + \beta y + ... \leq \gamma$ is implied by S if and only if the following system is solvable:

$$\begin{array}{l} \sum \lambda_i a_i = \alpha \\ \sum \lambda_i b_i = \beta \\ \vdots \\ \sum \lambda_i c_i + q = \gamma \\ \lambda_1 \geq 0, \lambda_2 \geq 0 \ldots, q \geq 0 \end{array}$$

The answer to the query is the set of relations on the parameters obtained by the elimination of the λ's and q from the above system.

Example 3 *Let* $S = \{2x + 3y - z \leq 1, x - y + 2z \leq 2, x - y + z \leq 0\}$ *and* $Q = \exists \alpha, \beta, \forall x, y, S \Rightarrow \alpha x + \beta y \leq 1$?
The derived system is:

$$\begin{array}{l} 2\lambda_1 + \lambda_2 + \lambda_3 = \alpha \\ 3\lambda_1 - \lambda_2 - \lambda_3 = \beta \\ -\lambda_1 + 2\lambda_2 + \lambda_3 = 0 \\ \lambda_1 + 2\lambda_2 + q = 1 \\ \lambda_1 \geq 0, \lambda_2 \geq 0, \lambda_3 \geq 0, q \geq 0 \end{array}$$

(the λ*'s are the multipliers of the constraints in* S*).*
The answer Q *is* $\{2\alpha - 3\beta \leq 0, -\alpha = +\beta \leq 0, -3\alpha + 7\beta \leq 5\}$ □

Note that if the projection on the parameter space is empty, then the associated query is satisfied for all values of the parameters.

In the next section we show that Fourier's variable elimination procedure and associated elementary theorems allow us to derive directly from their specification a number of interesting sets. For instance, we obtain the subsumption cone of S, which characterizes the set of all constraints implied by a set S of linear constraints. From the subsumption cone we can also derive information about the set of hyperplanes cutting S or the set of supporting hyperplanes of S. We can also obtain executable specifications for the convex hull of a collection of polyhedral sets, the separability set which characterizes the hyperplanes separating two given polyhedral sets, and, of course, the set of answers to a given parametric query. We see here that variable elimination is a very simple and powerful tool to reason about linear constraints.

Unfortunately, Fourier's procedure which is of great significance for historical and theoretical reasons in linear programming [Dantzig 73], is essentially not meaningful practically. It generates incrementally sets of constraints of exponentially growing size. Furthermore, these constraints are mostly redundant [Lassez et al. 89]. So in the third section we propose another method for variable elimination. We present the problem of variable elimination as a problem of answering a particular parametric query. The minimal set of generators of the set of answers to the query represents the set of constraints resulting from variable elimination. The formulation of the problem is a simple and natural generalization of the classical linear programming problem. This method is more efficient than Fourier's, as it bypasses the costly intermediate steps, and generates far less redundancy.

Using the preceding framework and an extension to Fourier's theorem [Lassez and Maher 88], we provide a formulation which is a variant of duality theory in linear programming. From this, we can derive algorithms to determine the existence of answers to the equality query as a side effect of solvability without the overhead inherent in other methods.

We conclude with a few remarks concerning implementation issues and the possibility of extending the techniques presented in this paper to related problems, for instance, the determination of causes of unsolvability. Also, we mention how one can efficiently provide approximations to the answers in the hard case, where the answers have an exponential or otherwise unmanageable size.

3 Fourier's Method

In the 1820's, Fourier [Fourier 1824] proposed the first algorithm for solving sets of linear arithmetic inequalities. Although classic, this algorithm is not well-known, and its relevance is often dismissed as only historical because of its computational complexity. However, apart from its historical interest, it has important theoretical properties. For instance, quoting Dantzig and Eaves [Dantzig 73]:

> *... from it one can derive easily (by trivial algebraic manipulations) the fundamental Duality Theorem of linear programming, Farkas Lemma, the various theorems of the alternatives, and the well-known Motzkin Transportation Theorem.*

Fourier's Algorithm tests the solvability of a finite set of linear inequalities with a simple variable elimination procedure that we shall refer to as *Fourier's elimination.*

Let $S = \{Ax \leq b\}$ be a set of linear inequalities where $A = (a_{ij})$ is an $m \times n$ matrix of real numbers (m and n are finite positive integers), $x = (x_i)$ is a variable vector of R^n and $b = (b_j)$ is a real constant vector of R^m.

3.1 Fourier's elimination

To eliminate a variable $x_k \in x$ from S, all the inequalities containing x_k are paired so that the signs of the coefficient of x_k in each pair are opposite. To see how the procedure works, it is convenient to arrange the inequalities in a slightly different form: if the variable x_k appears in an inequality C with a negative sign, C is re-written so that x_k appears alone on the right-hand side and conversely on the left-hand side if the sign is positive, giving:

$$\frac{b}{a_k} - \sum_{\substack{j=1 \\ j\neq k}}^{m-1} \frac{a_j x_j}{a_k} a_j \leq x_k \quad \text{or} \quad x_k \leq \frac{b}{a_k} - \sum_{\substack{j=1 \\ j\neq k}}^{m-1} \frac{a_j x_j}{a_k} a_j$$

For simplicity sake, the left-hand side and the right-hand side are renamed l_i and r_j respectively. S is partitioned into the three sets:

$$\begin{aligned} T = &\ \{l_i \leq x_k, \quad i = 1, \ldots, p\} \\ U = &\ \{x_k \leq r_j, \quad j = 1, \ldots, q\} \\ V = &\ \{d_l \leq 0, \quad l = 1, \ldots, s\} \end{aligned}$$

with $0 \leq p, q, l \leq n$ and no l_i, r_j or d_l contain x_k. T (resp. U) is the set of inequalities of S in which x_k has a negative (resp. positive) coefficient. V is the set that does not contain x_k.

A *Fourier step eliminating* x_k is the transformation which produces the new set:

$$S' \left\{ \begin{array}{ll} l_i \leq r_j & \forall i = 1, \ldots, p \quad \forall j = 1, \ldots, q \\ d_l \leq 0 & \forall l = 1, \ldots, s \end{array} \right.$$

In case either T or U is empty, that is, the variable x_k always appears with the same sign in S, all constraints containing x_k are removed. We say that the Fourier step is *trivial.*

Example 4 $S = \{2x_1 + 3x_2 - x_3 \leq 1, -x_1 + 2x_2 \leq 2, x_1 - x_2 + 2x_3 \leq -1, x_2 + x_3 \leq 3\}$ *and the variable to eliminate is* x_1.

$$\begin{aligned} T &= \{2x_2 - 2 \leq x_1\} \\ U &= \{x_1 \leq \tfrac{1}{2} - \tfrac{3}{2}x_2 + \tfrac{1}{2}x_3, x_1 \leq -1 + x_2 - 2x_3\} \\ V &= x_2 + x_3 \leq 3 \end{aligned}$$

After elimination of x_1, $S' = \{7x_2 - x_3 \leq 5, x_2 + 2x_3 \leq 1, x_2 + x_3 \leq 3\}$. □

The geometric interpretation of Fourier's elimination is the projection. The following lemma, essentially due to Fourier, verifies that a Fourier elimination step computes a projection of the polyhedron represented by the inequalities of S.

$S \rightarrow S'$ denotes that S implies S' and $S \rightarrow_F S'$ denotes that S' is the result of one Fourier step on S.

Lemma 1 (Projection lemma) *Let* S *be a set of inequalities and* x *a variable of* S. *If* $S \rightarrow_F S'$ *by the elimination of the variable* x *then* $\exists x S \leftrightarrow S'$.

3.2 Fourier's algorithm

Fourier's algorithm consists in the repeated application of Fourier's procedure until all variables are eliminated or a contradiction is generated.

Fourier's theorem states that:

> *If all the variables of* S *can be eliminated in this way without generating a contradiction, then* S *is solvable.*

The algorithm has three possible outcomes:

1. A contradiction.
   At one point during the variable elimination, an inequality $c \leq 0$ where c is a positive constant is generated. As this is a contradiction, S is found to be unsolvable, and the algorithm stops.

2. A non-empty set of tautologies.
   The remaining inequalities are tautologies of the form $c_k \leq 0$ where c_k is a negative constant for all k. The algorithm stops as all variables have been eliminated. No contradiction has been generated, therefore S is solvable.

3. The empty set.
   All inequalities have been eliminated and the resulting set is empty. The algorithm stops and as no contradiction was generated, S is solvable.

The distinction between the two cases when S is solvable is important. The fact that the elimination of all the variables gives the empty set means that the solvability of S is independent of the left-hand-side constants of the inequalities.

Also, in case 2 if one of the tautologies is of the form $0 \leq 0$ it indicates the presence of hidden equalities in S. These remarks are examples of Fourier's *hidden properties* and what additional information, both algebraic and geometric, can be extracted from the algorithm. This is discussed in detail in the next section.

Example 5 *Continuing from the previous example, we eliminate x_2 from*

$$\{7x_2 - x_3 \leq 5,\ x_2 + 2x_3 \leq 1,\ x_2 + x_3 \leq 3\}$$

As x_2 appears with a positive coefficient in all the inequalities, the result is the empty set and S is solvable. □

It is important to note that Fourier's algorithm is independent of the order in which the variables are eliminated. The numbers of steps necessary to eliminate all variables, however, may vary depending on this order.

Example 6 *Elimination of x_3 instead of x_2 in the example above gives:* $\{15x_2 \leq 11,\ 8x_2 \leq 8\}$. *An additional step is required to eliminate the last variable, but as previously, the result is the empty set.* □

The correctness of Fourier's algorithm is a direct consequence of the projection lemma. It establishes the equivalence between the algebraic operation of variable elimination and the geometric operation of projection.

3.3 Fourier's hidden properties

The output of applying Fourier's algorithm to a set of linear inequalities contains more than the proof of solvability or unsolvability of that set.

In the case of solvability, algebraic information, for instance the presence of hidden equalities and whether the solution set of the inequalities is bounded or unbounded, is readily available.

In the case of unsolvability, information on some of the causes of this solvability can also be easily obtained.

A key fact, from a practical point of view, is that all this information is obtained for free from the standard algorithm. Furthermore, as we shall see, even more information can be obtained with small modifications to the algorithm which entail low overhead.

We start with the case of the empty set as output.

3.3.1 Strong Solvability

It follows directly from the definition of Fourier's elimination that Fourier's algorithm returns the empty set if and only if at one stage during the elimination, at least one of the variables appears in all the remaining inequalities with a coefficient which is always positive or always negative. When this occurs, it is only due to the *left-hand side* of the inequalities, not the right-hand side constants. It is easy to see that changing these constants does not modify the outcome. As Fourier's algorithm is independent of the order in which variables are eliminated, this remark holds for all the inequalities of S. In other words, getting the empty set is independent of the right-hand side constants in *all* the inequalities of S. This leads to the concept of *strong solvability*, which has interesting implications both algebraically and geometrically.

Definition 1 *A set of inequalities* S *is said to be* **strongly solvable** *if and only if any modification of the right-hand side constants of the inequalities of* **S** *results in a new solvable set.*

This is a very strong (no pun intended) characteristic because, if S is strongly solvable, so are all the sets obtained from S by a modification of the right-hand side constants of any inequalities of S. It follows directly from Fourier's elimination that the property is also preserved through the elimination of variables, so that all the intermediate sets obtained by eliminating one or more variables are also strongly solvable.

In geometric terms, a modification of the right-hand side constant of an inequality corresponds to a translation of the hyperplane associated to the inequality. So, the strong solvablity property means that any translation of any of those hyperplanes results in a new non-empty polyhedron. Also, because the geometric interpretation of Fourier's elimination is the projection, this is true of any projections of the polyhedron associated with S.

Strong solvability also implies unboundedness, but as the property is conserved by translation, it is a particular type of unboundedness. This is formalized in the following proposition which also establishes the equivalence between strong solvability and Fourier's algorithm returning the empty set.

Proposition 1 *For a set* S *of inequalities, the following statements are equivalent:*

a *Fourier's algorithm generates the empty set.*

b S *is strongly solvable.*

c *The polyhedral set associated to* S *contains spheres of unbounded radii.*

When Fourier's algorithm returns a set of tautologies, S is still solvable but not strongly solvable. We say that S is *simply solvable.*

If S is simply solvable, there exists a modification of the right-hand side constants that will result in a new non-solvable set. It follows directly from the above proposition that, in this case, the inscribed spheres have a bounded radius. It is easy to see that all bounded polyhedral sets are simply solvable. But some unbounded sets can also be simply solvable like, for instance, the set of points in between two parallel hyperplanes.

Simple solvability is preserved by constants modification, as long as solvability is maintained. In other words, if a modification of the right-hand side constants of the inequalities results in a still solvable set, this new set is again simply solvable.

3.3.2 Implicit Equalities

Inequality constraints in S which can be replaced by equality constraints by simply replacing $\leq$ by $=$ without changing the semantics of S are called *implicit equalities.*

More formally, let $C^=$ denote the equation obtained by replacing $\leq$ by $=$ in the inequality C

Definition 2 *An implicit equality of* S *is an equation* $C^=$ *such that* C *is an inequality of* S *and* $S \rightarrow C^=$.

By abuse of language, C itself is also called an implicit equality.

Example 7

$$S = \{2x_1 - x_2 + x_3 \leq 2,\ x_1 - 2x_2 - x_3 \leq 0,\ -3x_1 + x_2 \leq 0,\ 2x_2 \leq -2\}$$

is equivalent to $\{x_1 = -\frac{1}{3},\ x_2 = -1,\ x_3 = \frac{5}{3}\}$ *and all the inequalities are implicit equalities.* □

From a geometric viewpoint, the information about implicit equalities is fundamental, as it determines the dimension of the polyhedral set associated to S and its affine hull. From a computational viewpoint, implicit equalities are an important part of a number of canonical representations for sets of inequalities and are used for constraint solving and constraint propagation.

A standard method to compute implicit equalities is to run a linear program for each constraint in the set. This is not very efficient, particularly when there are no implicit equalities present, which occurs frequently for a large class of problems. Also, in the case of CLP($\Re$) where backtracking may occur, all this work is wasted. There are far more sophisticated ways of computing implicit equalities by using a single linear program [Freund 85]. However, in these methods, the size of the problem as well as the number of variables are substantially increased. In logic based programming languages, we would rather want to reduce the number of variables than increase it. So these algorithms also lead to a substantial overhead in our setting.

What is needed is an efficient algorithm that answers the existential query first.

Perhaps the most important of Fourier's *hidden* properties stems from the case when S is solvable and the algorithm produces at least one tautology of the form $0 \leq 0$. The presence of $0 \leq 0$, an equality written as an inequality, is an indication that S contains at least two *hidden* or *implicit* equalities.

Modified Fourier's algorithm

Only a trivial change to Fourier's algorithm is necessary to explicitly get the information about implicit equalities. The modification consists in keeping a record of which inequalities of S are involved in producing $0 \leq 0$. This is achieved by associating to each inequality produced by the algorithm the set of the inequalities of S from which it is derived, as follows.

Let C be the inequality obtained from C_i and C_j by the elimination of the variable x. Assuming that x appears in C_i with the negative coefficient $-c_i$ and in C_j with the positive coefficient c_j, then $C = c_iC_j + c_jC_i$. We associate with C the set $S_i \bigcup S_j$, where S_i and S_j are the sets associated with C_i and C_j respectively. Initially, the set $S_k = \{C_k\}$ is associated to each C_k in S. The sets are updated at each step of the variable elimination. Apart from performing this updating, the algorithm behaves exactly as Fourier's. For simplicity sake, we also refer to this algorithm as Fourier's algorithm.

The following theorem provides a direct way to identify the presence of implicit equalities and also establishes the soundness and completeness of the modified algorithm.

We say that an inequality C_k was produced using C'_k if C'_k is in the set S_k associated with C_k.

Theorem 3 *An inequality* C *in* S *is an implicit equality if and only if Fourier's algorithm produces the inequality* $0 \leq 0$ *using* C.

The modified algorithm simply follows an arbitrary sequence of Fourier steps until all variables have been eliminated. The implicit equalities are exactly those original inequalities which are used in producing some occurrence of $0 \leq 0$.

This leads to the following characterization of implicit equalities, which is independent of Fourier's algorithm.

Proposition 2 *An inequality* C *in* S *is an implicit equality if and only if* $0 \leq 0$ *is a positive linear combination of a subset of* S *which contains* C.

Some interesting results both theoretical and practical follow. For instance, it is obvious from theorem 3 that if an initial set of constraints does not contain implicit equalities, none of the sets generated by the elimination of variables will contain implicit equalities. In geometric terms, this means that the projections of a full dimensional polyhedral set are also full dimensional. This remark is useful, as it helps avoid unnecessary computation in a problem of redundancy removal [Lassez et al. 89].

3.3.3 Causes of unsolvability

Finally, when Fourier's algorithm generates a contradiction, S is not solvable. The inequalities associated with the contradiction, that is those whose positive linear combination resulted in the contradiction, give an immediate unsolvable subset of S. This knowledge can be of prime importance when solvability needs to be restored by modifying or removing some inequalities; see [Lassez et al. 90(2)].

3.4 Further Remarks

The extension to Fourier's method is quite useful to establish in a very trivial manner a number of results. We mention here a few examples whose treatment is to be found in the references [Luenberger 73], [Lassez et al. 89], [Lassez and Maher 88]. Sometimes these results may be easy to establish once one has a good grasp of the basics of affine geometry and linear programming, but why use such machinery if there is a trivial proof using this simple extension to Fourier's method?

In a language like CLP($\Re$), constraints are added incrementally to the solver. There arises the problem of determining the implicit equalities in a set $S \bigcup \{C\}$, formed by adding an inequality C to a set S known not to contain implicit equalities. To avoid doing unnecessary computation, one remarks that the new set contains implicit equalities iff C is an implicit equality and, furthermore, if C is an implicit equality, then there is at least one implicit equality in S. So one first tests C for equality: if C is not an implicit equality, the new set does not contain any; if C is an implicit equality we must search S for others, but with a guarantee that some will be found. This useful property is easy to establish, for instance using the mathematics of the simplex algorithm or using geometric arguments [Lassez and McAloon 90], but here the statement is clearly a very trivial consequence of the extension to Fourier's method.

In [Telgen 82], it was proved that, if in a system of equalities and inequalities all implicit equalities are replaced by equalities, the resulting system contains at least one redundant equality. The proof is existential and rests on some non-trivial topological lemmas. In [Lassez et al. 89] it is shown as a direct consequence of theorem 3, that in fact, all the equalities that replace implicit equalities are redundant, which leads to a characterization of the notion of implicit redundancy.

The interested reader will find in [Schrijver 86] a brief history of Fourier's algorithm together with an extensive bibliography. In [Duffin 74] it is shown how, using techniques to reduce the amount of redundancy generated at each step, Fourier's method becomes practical for a class of parametric linear programs.

4 Direct variable elimination problems

Fourier's elimination provides a systematic way of generating sets of constraints directly from an existential specification. We look at three problems that illustrate this property:

1. Finding the convex hull of a given set of points, a typical problem of geometry.
2. Computing the image of a polyhedral set by a linear function.
   This will provide a constructive proof for an alternative to Fourier's elimination presented in section 5.
3. Testing the solvability of a set of constraints whose right-hand side constants are parameters.

Another important application to answering parametric queries is treated in the next section.

4.1 Convex hull

We recall that a point P is in the convex hull of a set of points if and only if the coordinates of P are positive convex linear combinations of the coordinates of the points in this set.

Let $(x_1, \ldots, x_n)$ be the coordinates of P. Let S be the set of points $\{P_1, \ldots, P_m\}$ and $(\alpha_{1j}, \ldots, \alpha_{nj})$ the coordinates of P_j in S. P is in the convex hull H of S if and only if there exist λ_j's such that the system

$$\begin{cases} x_1 = \sum_j \lambda_j \alpha_{1j} \\ \vdots \\ x_n = \sum_j \lambda_j \alpha_{nj} \\ \sum_j \lambda_j = 1 \\ \lambda_j \geq 0 \ \forall j = 1, \ldots, m \end{cases}$$

is satisfied. The representation of H is an equivalent set of relations solely between the x_i's obtained by eliminating the λ_j's.

Example 8 *Let* $S = \{(1,0,0), (0,1,0), (0,0,1)\}$ *and* $P = \{x_1, x_2, x_3\}$. *The linear combinations are:* $\{x_1 = \lambda_1,\ x_2 = \lambda_2,\ x_3 = \lambda_3,\ \lambda_1 + \lambda_2 + \lambda_3 = 1,\ \lambda_i \geq 0\}$. *The elimination of the* λ*'s gives the convex hull as* $\{x_1 + x_2 + x_3 = 1,\ x_1 \geq 0,\ x_2 \geq 0,\ x_3 \geq 0\}$ □

An interesting side effect is that we have a trivial proof of the classic theorem that the convex hull of a finite set of points is a polyhedral set, since Gauss-Jordan reduction and Fourier's elimination do not introduce non-linearities or disjunctions.

4.2 Image of polyhedral set

Let f be a function of R^n into R^m defined by:

$$f(x_1, \ldots, x_n) = \begin{cases} X_1 = \alpha_{11}x_1 + \ \ldots \ + \alpha_{1n}x_n + \beta_1 \\ \vdots \\ X_m = \alpha_{m1}x_1 + \ \ldots \ + \alpha_{mn}x_n + \beta_m \end{cases}$$

The polyhedral set S is represented by the set of constraints $\{\sum_{j=1}^{n} a_{ij}x_j \leq b_i, i = 1, \ldots, p\}$. The image of S is obtained by eliminating all x_i's from the set:

$$\begin{cases} X_1 = \alpha_{11}x_1 + \ \ldots \ + \alpha_{1n}x_n + \beta_1 \\ \ldots \\ X_m = \alpha_{m1}x_1 + \ \ldots \ + \alpha_{mn}x_n + \beta_m \\ \sum_{j=1}^{n} a_{1j}x_j \leq b_1 \\ \ldots \\ \sum_{j=1}^{n} a_{pj}x_j \leq b_p \end{cases}$$

The result is a set of constraints in the space $\{X_1, \ldots, X_m\}$. As a side effect here also we have the trivial proof that the image of a polyhedral set by a linear function is again a polyhedral set.

Example 9 *Let* $f(x, y, z) = \{X = 2x+y+z, Y = x-y+z+3\}$. *The image by* f *of the polyhedral set defined by* $\{x + y + z \leq 1, x \geq 0, y \geq 0, z \geq 0\}$ *is* $\{Y \leq 4, -X + Y \leq 3, 2X - Y \leq 0, -X - Y \leq -3\}$. □

5 The Quasi-dual Method

Based on the properties of Fourier's variable elimination procedure, we develop here a new formulation for variable elimination problems. The *quasi-dual* is a generalization of a classic method of linear programming and provides an efficient alternative to Fourier by allowing variables to be eliminated simultaneously instead of one by one.

The parallel with linear programming is easy to see. Consider the problem of eliminating all variables but one, say x, from a set S of constraints. The projection of S on the space of x is an interval for x. Computing the bounds of the interval can be done with classical optimization methods by maximizing and minimizing the objective function set to x under the constraints of S. This method is far more efficient than Fourier's elimination. If we now eliminate all variables but n, we look for the range of a point in an n-dimensional space. Clearly we need to generalize the notion of objective function to capture this range. We use a parametric query Q to formulate the problem:

$$\exists \alpha, \beta, \gamma, ... \forall x_1, x_2, ... : S \Rightarrow \alpha x_1 + \beta x_2 + ... \leq \gamma?$$

The existentially quantified variables are the variables from S that we want to keep. The set of answers to this query represents the set of constraints implied by the projection of S in the x_1, x_2, ...-space. Since we deal only with projection, we can restrict ourselves to linear combinations rather than quasi-linear. The projection we want to compute will be a minimal set of generators for the set of linear combinations which is the answer to the query. Expressing that the constraint in the query is a linear combination of the constraints in S, we have the following relations:

$$\tag{5.1} \begin{array}{l} \Phi \left\{ \begin{array}{l} \sum_i \lambda_i a_{i_1} = \alpha \\ \sum_i \lambda_i a_{i_2} = \beta \\ \vdots \\ \sum_i \lambda_i a_{i_k} = \gamma \end{array} \right. \\ \Delta \left\{ \begin{array}{l} \sum_i \lambda_i a_{i_{k+1}} = 0 \\ \vdots \\ \sum_i \lambda_i a_{i_n} = 0 \\ \sum_i \lambda_i = 1 \\ \lambda_i \geq 0, i = 1, \ldots, n \end{array} \right. \end{array}$$

The a's are the coefficients of the variables in S and the equalities whose right-hand sides are 0 correspond to the variables to eliminate. We have normalized the coefficients of the linear combination so that their sum is equal to one, without loss of generality. This is in fact more than syntactic convenience. One sees easily that the set of solutions to the above system is closed for non-negative convex linear combinations. In geometrical terms it means that the set of points whose coordinates are the coefficients of the linear combinations is a convex set. A classical theorem states that the set of points in a polytope is the convex closure of a finite set of extreme points. So if we can show that our convex set has a finite set of extreme points we will have a characterization of the set of answers which is a specialization of the subsumption theorem:

Theorem 4 *A constraint C is an answer to the query Q iff it is a quasi-linear combination of the finite set of constraints in G (the set of constraints which correspond to the extreme points).*

In order to establish this result and provide a way of computing G we generalize the optimization function in linear programming in the following way. In (5.1) the set of constraints that are not parameterized represents, but for the lack of objective function, a linear programming problem in standard form. An objective function Φ is a mapping of R^n into R. Let Δ be the polyhedral set associated with the constraints. $\Phi(\Delta)$ is an interval in R, and the linear programming problem is to determine its maximum or minimum (when they exist). That is, we have to compute one or the other of the *extreme points* of the image of a polyhedral set. What we also know is that the value of the maximum or minimum is obtained as an image of an extreme point of Δ. We generalize this picture by taking as objective function a function Φ, from R^n to R^m this time, defined by the parametric constraints in (5.1), and by considering the set of extreme points of $\Phi(\Delta)$ instead of a minimum or maximum. We have again the fact that the extreme points in $\Phi(\Delta)$ are images of the extreme points of Δ, and as Δ is a polytope, $\Phi(\Delta)$ has a finite number of extreme points. This provides an informal proof for the result we needed:

Theorem 5 *Let P be the generalized linear program:*

$$extr(\Phi(\Delta))$$

$$\Phi = \begin{cases} \sum \lambda_i a_{i_1} = \alpha \\ \sum \lambda_i a_{i_2} = \beta \\ \quad\vdots \\ \sum \lambda_i a_{i_k} = \gamma \end{cases}$$

$$\Delta = \begin{cases} \Sigma \lambda_i a_{i_{k+1}} = 0 \\ \vdots \\ \Sigma \lambda_i = 1 \\ \lambda_i \geq 0 \end{cases}$$

where extr *denotes the set of extreme points. The solutions to that program determine a finite set of constraints which defines the projection of* S.

This alternative to Fourier elimination is called the *extreme point method.* Note that if Δ is empty, that is if the system representing Δ is unsolvable, the projection is the whole space.

Example 10 *Let* $S = \{x + 2y + z \leq 1, x - y + z \leq 2, -x + 2y + z \leq 3, -x + y + z \leq 4\}$ *and* x *be the variable to eliminate.*

$$\Delta = \{\lambda_1 + \lambda_2 - \lambda_3 - \lambda_4 = 0,\ \Sigma\lambda_i = 1,\ \lambda_i \geq 0\}$$

$$\Phi = \begin{cases} \alpha_2 = 2\lambda_1 - \lambda_2 + 2\lambda_3 + \lambda_4 \\ \alpha_3 = \lambda_1 + \lambda_2 + \lambda_3 + \lambda_4 \\ \beta = \lambda_1 + 2\lambda_2 + 3\lambda_3 + 4\lambda_4 \end{cases}$$

Δ *has the four extreme points:* $\lambda_A = \{\frac{1}{2}, 0, \frac{1}{2}, 0\}$, $\lambda_B = \{\frac{1}{2}, 0, 0, \frac{1}{2}\}$, $\lambda_C = \{0, \frac{1}{2}, \frac{1}{2}, 0\}$, $\lambda_D = \{0, \frac{1}{2}, 0, \frac{1}{2}\}$ *which give:*

$$\begin{aligned} \Phi(\lambda_A) &= \{\alpha_2 = 2, \alpha_3 = 1, \beta = 2\} \\ \Phi(\lambda_B) &= \{\alpha_2 = \tfrac{3}{2}, \alpha_3 = 1, \beta = \tfrac{5}{2}\} \\ \Phi(\lambda_C) &= \{\alpha_2 = \tfrac{1}{2}, \alpha_3 = 1, \beta = \tfrac{5}{2}\} \\ \Phi(\lambda_D) &= \{\alpha_2 = 0, \alpha_3 = 1, \beta = 3\} \end{aligned}$$

The projection is $\{2y + z \leq 2, 3y + 2z \leq 5, y + 2z \leq 5, z \leq 3\}$. □

Note that in general not all extreme points of Δ map onto the extreme points of $\Phi(\Delta)$; some correspond to redundant constraints in the description of the projection.

The finite set of constraints should be minimized by redundancy elimination to obtain a better representation of the projection of S on the (x, y, ...)-space. As there are algorithms to compute sets of extreme points [Matheiss 80] we can effectively obtain G. Implementation issues are not trivial and will not be addressed here. The reader is referred to [Lassez et al. 93].

6 Fourier's algorithm and the simplex

Here we consider the particular case of the quasi-dual formulation where all variables are eliminated. This case corresponds to Fourier's algorithm for testing solvability. The advantage of the quasi-dual formulation is that it can be executed by the simplex and consequently is far more efficient. It also inherits nice properties from the standard dual simplex, such as good incremental behavior, no need to introduce slack variables and no restriction to have the problem variables positive.

More importantly as a side effect of the solvability test we obtain much information about the algebraic properties of the constraints and the geometric structure of the associated polyhedron. This avoids unnecessary computations, particularly in the case where a set of inequalities does not contain any implicit equality. Such information is essential in a general system to reason about constraints and is used extensively in the projection algorithms [Lassez et al. 93].

We do not provide here formal arguments to substantiate the claims summarized in the table below. It is sufficient to state that proofs are easily derived from the basic properties of Fourier's algorithm [Lassez and Maher 88] and the standard results from linear programming.

When Fourier's algorithm is applied to S, the output Q is either the empty set or a finite set of inequalities of the form $0 \leq d$, where $d \in \Re$. If $Q = \emptyset$, S is solvable. Otherwise S is solvable iff all inequalities in Q are tautologies. S contains implicit equalities iff $0 \leq 0$ belongs to Q. An implicit equality is a constraint in S where $\leq$ can be replaced by $=$ without changing the semantics of S. Since all constraints in Q are of the form $0 \leq d$, it is sufficient to look at the minimum of the d's to determine the solvability of S and the existence of implicit equalities.

Let $S = \{Ax \leq b\}$ where A is the matrix of the coefficients of the variables, x is the vector of the variables and b is the vector of the right-hand side constants, and let $\lambda = \{\lambda_i\}$ the vector of the parameters in the dual space. The quasi-dual formulation which corresponds to Fourier's algorithm is:

$$\Delta = \{A^T\lambda = 0,\ \Sigma\lambda_i = 1,\ \lambda_i \geq 0\}$$
$$\Phi = \beta = b^T\lambda.$$

(^{T} denotes the transpose in the usual matrix notation.)

Here Φ maps $\Re^m$ to $\Re$. Since we want to compute the minimal value of Φ subject to Δ, we need to solve the following linear program:

$$D \begin{cases} \text{minimize} \quad b^T\lambda \\ \text{subject to } \Delta \end{cases}$$

Note that D is a variant of the dual simplex in linear programming.
The dual space here is the space of linear combinations rather than the usual economic or geometric interpretation. There are four possible outcomes:

1. $\Delta = \emptyset$ (D unsolvable)
   This corresponds to the case when Fourier's algorithm gives $Q = \emptyset$. S is solvable and the associated polyhedron is full dimensional. Note that because Q is empty no contradictions can ever be generated regardless of the values of the right hand side constants in the constraints of S. This is why we say that S is *strongly* solvable. It can be shown easily that the polyhedron is unbounded and no projection of S contains parallel facets . Therefore, all inscribed spheres have unbounded radius.

2. $\min(b^T\lambda) > 0$
   Fourier's algorithm generates a non-empty set of tautologies and therefore S is solvable. It is not strongly solvable as different values for b could lead to unsolvability. The associated polyhedron is full dimensional and it is either bounded or one of its projections contains parallel facets. Consequently, all inscribed spheres have a bounded radius.

3. $\min(b^T\lambda) = 0$
   Fourier's algorithm generates at least one $0 \leq 0$. S is solvable and

contains implicit equalities. Consequently, S is not full dimensional and all inscribed spheres are reduced to points (zero radius). We say that S is *weakly* solvable because an arbitrarily small change in b may give unsolvability. The extreme point corresponding to this minimal value gives the first minimal set of implicit equalities in S. To identify all other implicit equalities, we need to generate the extreme points of $\delta' = \delta \bigcup \{\Sigma b^T \lambda = 0\}$. From the extreme points of Δ' we derive the indices of the constraints in S that are implicit equalities.

4. $b^T \lambda < 0$ at some point during minimization
Fourier's algorithm generates at least one contradiction. S is unsolvable. A first minimal infeasible subset is obtained directly as for implicit equalities. To identify all the others, again we consider $\Delta' = \Delta \bigcup \{\Sigma b^T \lambda \leq 0\}$. For simplicity's sake, we use the weak inequality instead of the strict one. Each vertex of Δ' for which $b^T \lambda$ is strictly negative corresponds to a minimal infeasible subsystem of S.

Beringer made two important observations [Beringer]. The first one is that if the constraints in S are appropriately normalized then $min(b^T \lambda)$ (when positive) is in fact the maximal radius of the inscribed spheres. The other is a relation between the quasi-dual formulation and Helly's theorem. Helly's theorem states that a set of $n \geq d+1$ convex sets in $\Re^d$ is unsolvable iff there exists a subset of $d+1$ convex sets which is unsolvable. When D is solvable, the quasi-dual simplex follows Helly's theorem. Each basis corresponds to the selection of exactly $d+1$ constraints. $b^T \lambda$ is a measure of solvability, by minimizing it we therefore search for a subset of $d+1$ constraints which is least likely to be solvable.

These results are summarized in the table in the appendix.

7 Conclusion

As with other problems in linear programming, it is not necessarily so that algorithms with great theoretical complexity cannot be quite efficient in practice. Here we know that the problems we address have substantial theoretical complexity, but they are so recent that we have only partial evidence about practical suitability in our context.

Concerning the implementation in the inequality case several problems need to be addressed.

First, in principle, the number of extreme points can be so large as to be unmanageable. In the practical problems we have encountered, it has not been the case yet. One reason is that for very small or very sparse systems, variants of Fourier's algorithm that include simple forms of redundancy elimination can perform quite well. For systems that are nearly square, that is where the number of variables and the number of constraints are similar, the extreme point method works quite well. These cases are those met most frequently in current implementations. Ultimately, we would rather keep the initial representation than attempt to output an exponential number of constraints. Nevertheless, this problem is being investigated thoroughly; we will come back to it later, for a different type of applications. Elimination of redundancy is a key issue from a practical point of view. Even for simple problems, significant amounts of redundant constraints can be generated. Furthermore, in a projection we deal with constraints that are tangent to the set we construct; consequently, round-off errors can seriously interfere with redundancy elimination. The many algorithms [Matheiss 80] to generate extreme points essentially avoid the issue of degeneracy. These techniques are not suitable in our case. We are currently investigating a promising method due to Kruse [Kruse 86].

In the case of equality constraints, the situation is simpler. The techniques from linear programming can be easily adapted. Also, we know that we can have at most n implicit equalities in a set of n constraints. In practice there will be far less, and each extreme point will give several answers. So we will not face an explosion in the number of extreme points to be computed.

Other problems can be addressed using techniques introduced in this paper. For instance, with constraints being expressed as linear combinations of constraints in S, we could find the causes of redundancy or causes of unsolvability. Techniques of intelligent backtracking could then be applied. A comparison, evaluation and integration of various algorithms can be found in [Lassez et al. 93].

It has also been proposed recently in an important paper [Kanellakis et al. 90] to use constraints in the context of logic databases. An interesting point is that the approach is a bottom up evaluation rather than the traditional top down of logic programs. A consequence is that the number of variables is fixed during execution rather than unbounded. Therefore, methods based on variable elimination might be more successful in that setting. Here, we are applying variable elimination to a restricted type of constraints. One could consider an extension to a symbolic computation system for the full linear case. A major problem to be faced is that even in our simple case, the size of the output may be exponential. There is little need to consider an extension if we cannot solve this problem. The only way out that we can see is to settle for an approximation. Let us propose a simple one: Beringer [Beringer] has proved the very interesting fact that, assuming the constraints are normalized, then the objective function in the quasi dual gives the radius of the largest sphere included in the associated polyhedral set. (If the quasi dual is not solvable, then the radius is not bounded). We can use this fact to obtain an approximation of the set of answers. Geometrically we have a polyhedral set whose projection has a large number of facets; in fact, so large that it makes no sense to attempt to compute it. We want an approximation of the projection that has a simple (small) syntactic representation. Assume that the polyhedral set is such that the spheres it contains have a bounded radius. We can compute via the objective function of the quasi dual the radius of the largest sphere(s) included in the set, (Beringer's theorem). It is then simple to obtain the locus of the centers of the spheres by a simple translation of the constraints. This locus is itself a polyhedral set. The approximation we propose is the projection of this so one simplex is sufficient. If the locus is too costly to project, family of spheres. The radius of a projected sphere remains the same, we can either take a subset or repeat the process by approximating the locus. So this approximation gives us a somewhat central subset of solutions. We can obtain approximations of other areas of the set of solutions by considering subpolyhedra obtained by translations of the constraints. This technique is used in the case where the polyhedral set admits subspheres of unbounded radius. Finally, it may be worth mentioning that a number of important properties of linear constraints related to efficient implementations of negation and canonical representations in a querying system have their counterparts in other domains of computation (term algebras, convex geometry, etc.). An axiomatization of this phenomenon has been reported in [Lassez and McAloon 90].

References

[Achmanov 84] S. Achmanov, *Programmation Linéaire*, Editions Mir, Moscou 1984.

[Arnon 89] D.S. Arnon, *Geometric Reasoning with Logic and Algebra*, in Geometric Reasoning, D. Kapur and J.L. Mundy Eds, MIT Press 1989.

[Arnon 90] D.S. Arnon, *Towards a deductive database for elementary algebra and geometry*, Proceedings of NACLP 90 Workshop on Deductive Databases.

[Beringer] H. Beringer, private communication.

[Bledsoe 75] W.W. Bledsoe, *A new method for proving certain Presburger formulas*, Advance Papers 4th Int. Joint Conf. on Artif. Intell., Tibilisi, Georgia, USSR, Sept. 1975, pp 15-21.

[Borning 88] A. Borning, The Programming Language Aspects of THINGLAB - A Constraint Oriented Simulation Laboratory, *ACM Transactions on Programming Languages and Systems* 3 (1981) 252-387.

[Boissonat and Laumond 88] J.-D. Boissonat, J.-P. Laumond Eds, *Geometry and Robotics*, Springer Verlag Lecture Notes in Computer Science, 1988.

[Brown 90] F.M. Brown, *Boolean Reasoning: The Logic of Boolean Equations*, Kluwer Academic Pub., 1990.

[Buchberger 87] B. Buchberger, *History and Basic Features of the Critical-Pair/Completion Procedure*, in Rewriting Techniques and Applications J-P. Jouannaud Ed., Academic Press 1987.

[Canny 87] J.F.Canny, *The Complexity of Robot Motion Planning*, The MIT Press, 1987.

[Chandru 88] V. Chandru and J. Hooker, *Logical Inference: A Mathematical Programming Perspective*, in AI in Manufacturing:Theory and Practise, Edited by S.T. Kumara, R.L Kashyap, and A.L. Soyster. Wiley 1988

[Chandru] V. Chandru and J. Hooker, Optimization Methods for Logical Inference, *to appear.*

[Chang and Lee 73] C-L. Chang and R.C-T. Lee, *Symbolic Logic and Mechanical Theorem Proving*, Academic Press, 1973.

[Dantzig 73] G.B. Dantzig and B.C. Eaves, *Fourier-Motzkin Elimination and Its Dual*, Journal of Combinatorial Theory Ser. A, 14 (1973) 288-297.

[Davenport and Heintz 88] J.H. Davenport and J. Heintz, *Real Quantifier Elimination is Doubly Exponential*, in D.S. Arnon and B. Buchberger eds., Algorithms in Real Algebraic Geometry, Academic Press, 1988.

[Davenport et al. 88] J-H. Davenport, Y. Siret and E. Tournier, *Computer Algebra, Systems and Algorithms for Algebraic Computation*, Academic Press, 1988.

[Davis 87] E. Davis, *Constraint Propagation with Interval Labels*, Artificial Intelligence, 1987

[Duffin 74] R.J. Duffin, *On Fourier's Analysis of Linear Inequality Systems*, Mathematical Programming Study 1, pp. 71-95, 1974.

[Fourier 1824] J.B.J. Fourier, reported in: Analyse des travaux de l'Académie Royale des Sciences, pendant l'année 1824, Partie mathématique, *Histoire de l'Académie Royale des Sciences de l'Institut de France 7* (1827) xlvii-lv. (Partial English translation in: D.A. Kohler, Translation of a Report by Fourier on his work on Linear Inequalities, *Opsearch* 10(1973) 38-42.)

[Freund 85] R.M. Freund, R. Roundy and M.J. Todd, Identifying the Set of Always-Active Constraints in a System of Linear Inequalities by a Single Linear Program, Technical Report, Sloan School of Management, Massachusetts Institute of Technology, October 1985.

[Hoffman 89] C. Hoffmann, *Geometric and Solid Modelling*, Morgan Kauffmann Pub., 1989.

[Jaffar and Lassez 87(1)] J. Jaffar and J-L. Lassez, *From Unification to Constraints* Logic Programming Conference, Tokyo, Springer Verlag Lecture Notes in Computer Science, June 1987.

[Jaffar and Lassez 87(2)] J. Jaffar and J-L. Lassez, *Constraint Logic Programming*, Proceedings of POPL 1987,Munich.

[Kandri-Rody and Kapur 83] A. Kandri-Rody and D. Kapur *On relationships between Buchberger's Grobner basis algorithm and the Knuth Bendix Completion Procedure*, General Electric Tech report N0 83CRD286, Schenectady New York 1983.

[Kapur et al. 89] A. Kandri- Rodi, D. Kapur and F. Winkler *Knuth-Bendix Procedure and Buchberger Algorithm: a Synthesis*, Proceedings International Symposium on Symbolic and Algebraic Computation, 1989.

[Kanellakis et al. 90] P. Kanellakis, G. Kuper and P. Revesz, *Constraint Query Languages*, Proceedings of the ACM Conference on Principles of Database Systems, Nashville, 1990.

[Kapur and Mundy 93] D.Kapur and J.L. Mundy, *Symbolic and Numeric Computation for Artificial Intelligence*, Academic Press, 1993.

[Kapur and Mundy 89] D. Kapur and J.L. Mundy, *Geometric Reasoning, MIT Press*, 1989.

[Kirchner and Ringeissen 94] H. Kirchner and C. Ringeissen, *Combining Symbolic Constraint Solvers on Algebraic Domains*, Journal of Symbolic Computation vol.18 n.2, 1994.

[Kruse 86] H-J. Kruse, *Degeneracy Graphs and the Neighborhood Problem*, Springer Verlag, Lecture Notes in Economics and Mathematical Systems, No. 260, 1986.

[Lassez 87] C. Lassez, *Constraint Logic Programming*, invited article, *Byte magazine special issue on Prolog*, August 1987.

[Lassez and Lassez 92] C. Lassez and J-L. Lassez, *Quantifier Elimination for Conjunctions of Linear Constraints via a Convex Hull Algorithm*, in Symbolic and Numeric Computation, Kapur and Mundi, Eds, Academic Press, 1992.

[Lassez et al. 90(2)] C. Lassez, J-L. Lassez, T. Huynh and L. Joskowicz, *Reasoning About Linear Constraints Using Parametric Queries*, in *Foundations of Software Technology and Theoretical Computer Science*, Lecture Notes in Computer Sciences, Springer-Verlag vol. 472, December 1990.

[Lassez et al. 90(1)] C. Lassez, J-L. Lassez and T. Huynh, *Fourier Algorithm Revisited*, 2nd International Conference on Algebraic and Logic Programming, Springer-Verlag Lecture Notes in Computer Sciences, 1990.

[Lassez et al. 93] C. Lassez, J-L. Lassez and T. Huynh, *Practical Issues on the Projection of Polyhedral Sets*, Annals of Mathematics and Artificial Intelligence, 1993. IBM Research Report RC 15425, IBM T.J. Watson Research Center.

[Lassez 91] J-L. Lassez, *From LP to LP: Programming with Constraints* Proceedings of Theoretical Aspects of Computer Software, Sendai 91 Springer Verlag. Also in Database Programming Languages, P. Kanellakis and J.W. Schmidt Editors, Morgan Kaufmann 1991.

[Lassez 90(1)] J-L. Lassez, *Parametric Queries, Linear Constraints and Variable Elimination*, Proceedings of DISCO 90, Springer Verlag Lecture Notes in Computer Science, 1990.

[Lassez 90(2)] J-L. Lassez, *Querying Constraints*, Proceedings of the ACM Conference on Principles of Database Systems, Nashville 1990.

[Lassez et al. 89] J-L. Lassez, T. Huynh and K. McAloon, *Simplification and Elimination of Redundant Arithmetic Constraints*, Proceedings of the North American Conference on Logic Programming 1989, MIT Press 1989.

[Lassez and McAloon 88] J-L. Lassez and K. McAloon, *Applications of a Canonical Form for Generalized Linear Constraints*, Proceedings of the FGCS Conference, Tokyo, December 1988, 703-710.

[Lassez and McAloon 92] J-L. Lassez and K. McAloon, *A Canonical Form for Generalized Linear Constraints*, IBM Research Report RC 15004, IBM T.J. Watson Research Center, Journal of Symbolic Computation, 1992.

[Lassez and McAloon 90] J-L. Lassez and K. McAloon, *A Constraint Sequent Calculus*, Proceedings of the IEEE Conference on Logic in Computer Science, Philadelphia 1990.

[Lassez et al. 88] J-L. Lassez, M.J. Maher and K. Marriott, *Unification Revisited*, Foundations of Logic Programming and Deductive Databases, J. Minker ed., Morgan-Kaufmann 1988.

[Lassez and Maher 88] J-L. Lassez and M.J. Maher, *On Fourier's Algorithm for Linear Arithmetic Constraints*, IBM Research Report, T.J. Watson Research Center, 1988.

[Lassez and McAloon 89] J-L. Lassez and K. McAloon, *Independence of Negative Constraints*, Proceedings of the Advanced Seminar on Foundations of Innovative Software Development, Barcelona, Springer Verlag 1989.

[Luenberger 73] D.G. Luenberger, *Introduction to Linear and Nonlinear Programming*, Addison-Wesley 1973.

[Maher 87] M. Maher, *A Logic Semantics for a class of Committed Choice Languages*, Proceedings of ICLP4, MIT Press, 1987.

[Matheiss 80] T.H. Matheiss and D.S. Rubin, *A Survey and Comparison of Methods for Finding All Vertices of Convex Polyhedral Sets*, Mathematics of Operations Research 5 (1980) 167-185.

[Pearl 88] J. Pearl, *Constraints and Heuristics*, Artificial Intelligence, 1988.

[Saraswat 93] V. Saraswat, *Concurrent Constraint Programming*, MIT Press 1993.

[Schrijver 86] A. Schrijver, *Theory of Linear and Integer Programming*, Wiley 1986

[Steele 82] G. Steele and G. Sussman, *CONSTRAINTS - a Constraint Based Programming Language*, Artificial Intelligence, 1982.

[Telgen 82] J. Telgen, *Minimal Representation of Convex Polyhedral Sets*, Journal of Optimization Theory and Application, 38 (1982) 1-24.

[Van Den Vries 89] L. Van Den Vries, *Alfred Tarski's Elimination Theory for Closed Fields*, The Journal of Symbolic Logic, vol.53 n.1, March 1988.

Appendix: Summary of Fourier's Properties

Quasi-Dual D	Fourier algorithm	Properties of S
Unsolvable	$Q = \phi$	• *Strongly* solvable • Full dimensional • No implicit equalities • Unbounded and no projection has parallel facets • Inscribed spheres have unbounded radius
$min(b^T\lambda) > 0$	$Q \neq \phi$ $0 \leq D \in Q \Rightarrow D \in \Re^+$	• Solvable • Full dimensional • No implicit equalities • Bounded or exists projection with parallel facets • Inscribed spheres have bounded radius
$min(b^T\lambda) = 0$	$0 \leq 0 \in Q$ $0 \leq D \in Q \Rightarrow D \notin \Re^-$	• *Weakly* Solvable • Not full dimensional • Exists implicit equalities • An evident minimal subset of implicit equalities • Inscribed spheres have radius zero
$\exists\lambda : b^T\lambda < 0$	$\exists D \in \Re^- : 0 \leq D \in Q$	• Unsolvable • An evident minimal infeasible subset

Proceedings of Symposia in Applied Mathematics
Volume 55, 1998

The Basis of Computer Vision†

Vishvjit S. Nalwa

Abstract: *Computer vision* describes the automatic deduction of the structure and properties of a possibly dynamic three-dimensional world from either a single or multiple two-dimensional images of the world. I provide an overview of the fundamental concepts that underlie computer vision and point briefly to a few important outstanding problems in the field that deserve a fresh look.

1. Introduction

Vision is such an awesome experience that we allude to it time and again in our language. *Seeing* is believing. Love is *blind*. We *see* eye-to-eye, and we *foresee*. We exchange *views*, and we maintain *viewpoints*. It is no surprise that the metaphors abound: Vision is without doubt the predominant mode of human perception. It is fast and accurate; it is reliable and nonintrusive; it simultaneously provides both detail and an overview. After all, it is a picture that is worth a thousand words—not a touch, a sound, a taste, or a smell. This paper is an account of the principles that underlie attempts to automate visual perception.

The plan of this paper is as follows. In Section 2, we shall discuss what computer vision is, and what it is not, and why computer vision is difficult to realize. In Section 3, we shall briefly touch on some noteworthy peculiarities of the human visual system. In Section 4, we shall discuss a plausible schema for realizing a computer-vision system. In Section 5, we shall discuss image formation, whose understanding is

† This paper is adapted directly from *A Guided Tour of Computer Vision*, by Vishvjit S. Nalwa, Addison-Wesley Publishing Company, © 1993 AT&T. Reprinted by permission of Addison-Wesley Longman Inc.

1991 *Mathematics Subject Classification.* Primary 68T99; Secondary 68U10.

key to computer vision. In Section 6, we shall discuss the role of various image characteristics in providing a three-dimensional interpretation to two-dimensional images. We shall conclude with Section 7, where I shall highlight briefly a few important outstanding problems in computer vision that could benefit from a fresh look.

I have kept mathematical symbols and equations to a minimum here as I do not want to distract you from what I consider the core of computer vision, to which, I suspect, most of you have little or no prior exposure. I have adopted this approach despite the continuing fruitful application of a wide variety of mathematical disciplines to computer vision—disciplines ranging from projective geometry to differential calculus, and from the calculus of variations to statistical physics.

2. What Is Computer Vision?

Computer vision, sometimes called **image understanding**, describes the automatic deduction of the structure and properties of a possibly dynamic three-dimensional world from either a single or multiple two-dimensional images of the world. The images may be monochromatic (i.e., "black and white") or colored, they may be captured by a single or multiple cameras, and each camera may be either stationary or mobile. However, the images are almost always sampled in time and in space. That is, the images are almost always "still images"—images acquired at discrete instants of time—that are each represented by its attributes at a discrete set of points on the image. Further, these attributes—typically, brightness and color—at each discrete image point are usually approximated by discrete numbers. Such a discretization of time of image capture, the image plane, and image attributes over this plane reduces images to arrays of digits that are amenable to processing by a digital computer.

Why is computer vision difficult to realize? Because image formation is a many-to-one mapping, with respect to both surface reflectivity and surface geometry: A variety of surfaces with different reflectivities and geometries, possibly under different lighting conditions, could lead to identical images. As a result, the inverse imaging problem for a single image—that is, the problem of inferring from a single image the scene that led to the image—has no unique solution. In other words, a single image of a scene does not sufficiently constrain the imaged scene to allow us to recover the scene. There are two solutions: (1) gather more data (images), and (2) make assumptions about the world. It is, of course, important that all our assumptions be tenable, and that we understand their exact role well. Hence, it is imperative that all our assumptions be explicit.

Even when the inverse imaging problem is sufficiently constrained to allow a unique solution in principle, there remain the twin practical problems of computability and robustness. Is the solution computable using reasonable resources, including computing machinery and time? And, is the solution robust? That is, is the solution insensitive to errors in data (i.e., to signal noise), and to errors in computation (e.g., owing to limited precision arithmetic)? Failure on any of these fronts can render an otherwise promising approach useless in practice.

You might wonder whether computer vision is not a form of image processing or pattern recognition. Although there is some overlap, the differences are distinct. **Image processing** is a generic term for the processing of images to produce new images that are more desirable in some fashion; [Pratt 1991] and [Rosenfeld and Kak 1982] are two standard references for image processing. Image processing encompasses the following: **image enhancement**, which modifies images to improve their appearance to human viewers; **image restoration**, which corrects images for degradations (such as motion blur); and **image compression**, which represents images compactly while maintaining acceptable image quality. **Pattern recognition**, or **pattern classification**, on the other hand, classifies patterns into one of a finite (usually small) number of prespecified categories; [Duda and Hart 1973] is the classic reference for pattern recognition. For the most part, the emphasis in pattern recognition is on two-dimensional patterns—for instance, on the letters of the alphabet. Computer vision, in contrast, is concerned with generating descriptions of three-dimensional scenes—scenes that are not constrained to be members of predetermined sets—from two-dimensional images of the scenes.

The purpose of computer vision is to infer the state of the physical world from the inherently noisy and ambiguous images of the world. If the current state of the art is any indication, such a goal is difficult to accomplish in a reliable, robust, and efficient manner. By the same token, such a goal is challenging. One problem in vision is diversity:

the inherent diversity in any nontrivial domain with respect to the objects and their relative configurations, and the ensuing diversity in the images, each of which may be acquired from anywhere in any given scene. This diversity necessitates opportunism: Of the many possible sources of information in an image, only a few are typically present, and we must do what we can with what we have. In addition to the information provided by the images themselves, at times, we might also be able to bring to bear knowledge about objects, their behavior, and the context. However, we shall not explore the use of domain-specific knowledge here.

We shall adopt a modular approach to computer vision here; an alternative approach, for instance, might seek to perform one grand optimization. We, in contrast, shall endeavor to identify and isolate the various sources of information in an image; these sources include, for instance, brightness discontinuities, shading, and motion. One may use each of these sources of information either individually, or in conjunction with the others, to make deductions about the scene. The benefits of a modular approach are more than pedagogic: A modular approach makes it easier to control and monitor the performance of a system, to debug the system, and to understand and improve it.

Computer vision has several applications, including the following: automation (e.g., on the assembly line), inspection (e.g., of integrated-circuit chips to detect defects in them), remote sensing (e.g., of possibly hostile terrain to generate its relief maps), human–computer communication (e.g., through gesturing), and aids for the visually impaired (e.g., mechanical guide dogs).

3. A Word About Your Sponsor

You might wonder why computer-vision researchers do not simply build systems that emulate the human visual system, especially considering the wealth of literature in neurophysiology, psychology, and psychophysics. Gregory [Gregory 1978] provides a fascinating introduction to the latter topics; see [Levine and Shefner 1991] and [Kaufman 1974] for more detailed treatments, and [Levine 1985] for an engineering perspective. One good reason why computer-vision researchers do not emulate human vision is that what is known about the human visual system beyond the human eye is largely disjointed,

Figure 1 Fraser's spiral. (After [Fraser 1908].)

speculative, and meager. Further, although human vision is certainly adequate for most frequently encountered tasks—or is it that our lifestyles are adapted to tasks that can be accommodated by our perceptual faculties—adequacy must not be taken to imply infallibility. The fallibility of human vision is amply demonstrated by the existence of visual illusions, ambiguities, and inconsistencies.

One visual illusion, the well-known Fraser's spiral, is illustrated in Figure 1. You can easily confirm that the spiral in Figure 1 is illusory by trying to trace the spiral. Figure 2 illustrates six other classical optical illusions. In each of the drawings in Figure 2, geometric truths appear untrue. The illusory effect is so strong that you might wish to have a ruler handy to verify the various assertions. In the Zöllner

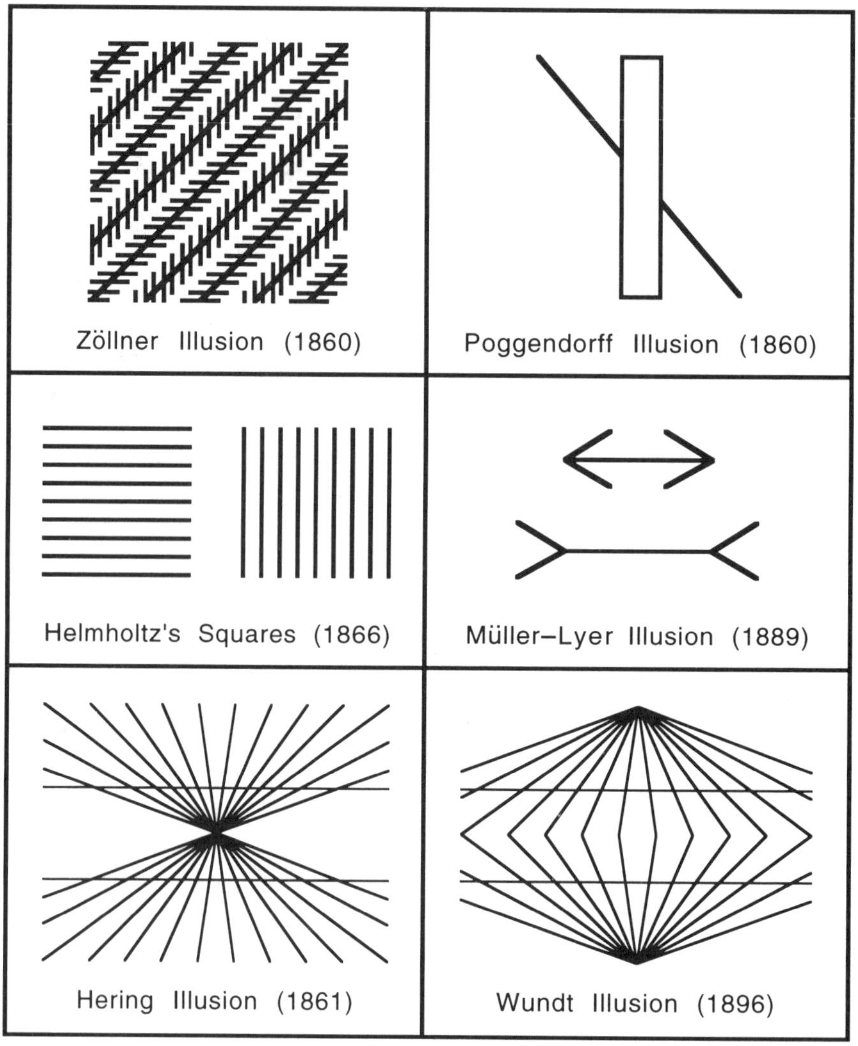

Figure 2 Six classical optical illusions. (See [Boring 1942] for the origins of these optical illusions.)

illusion, the diagonals are parallel, but appear otherwise. In the Poggendorff illusion, the two diagonal straight-line segments seem offset even though they are collinear. Helmholtz's two squares appear rectangular. In the Müller–Lyer illusion, the horizontal line with the reversed arrowheads appears longer than the line with the normal arrowheads, even though both lines have the same length. Finally, in both the Hering and Wundt illusions, the two horizontal and parallel straight lines appear bowed.

Figure 3 Four well-known visual ambiguities. (See [Nalwa 1993] for the origins of these visual ambiguities.)

Figure 3 illustrates four well-known visual ambiguities. In each of the drawings in Figure 3, two interpretations compete for attention. In the young-girl/old-woman illustration, the young girl's chin is the old woman's nose. The interpretation of the vase/faces illustration depends on whether the black region is seen as the background or as the foreground. Finally, the pop-in/pop-out and six-cubes/seven-cubes ambiguities depend on the spontaneous reversal of the perceived concavities and convexities.

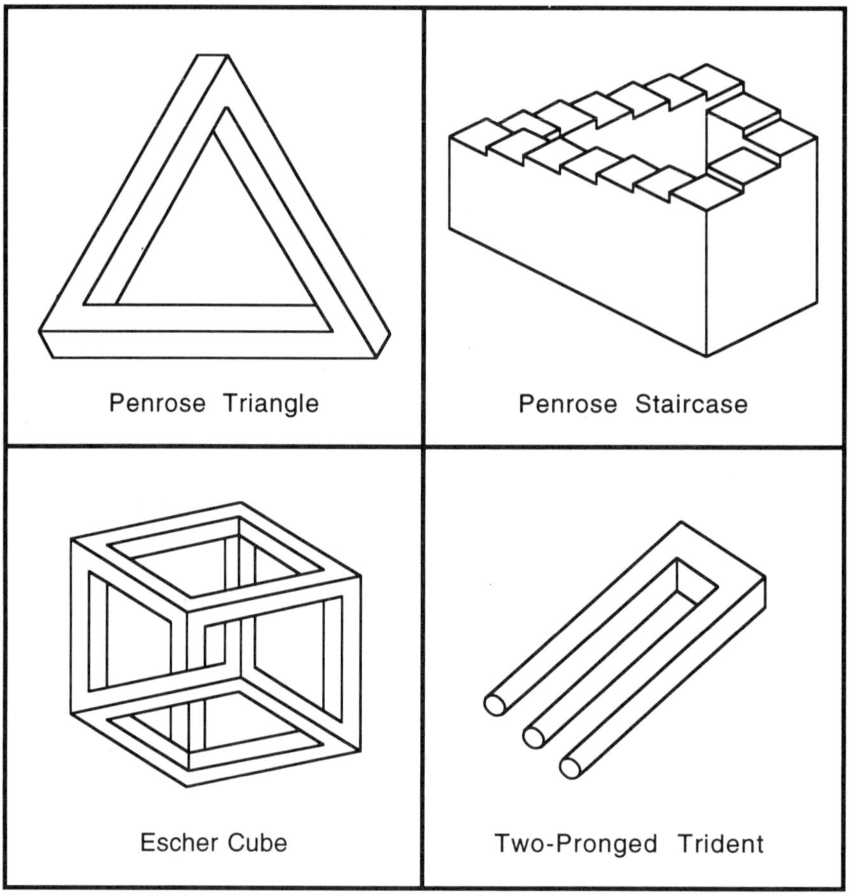

Figure 4 Four well-known visual inconsistencies. (See [Nalwa 1993] for the origins of these visual inconsistencies.)

Figure 4 illustrates four well-known visual inconsistencies. In each of the drawings in Figure 4, geometrical inconsistency makes the perceived object physically unrealizable. The Penrose triangle appears to be a polyhedron, but if it were one, it could not form a closed loop. The Penrose staircase descends (ascends) all the way around to the starting step. The Escher cube has a top that is inconsistent with its base. Finally, the two-pronged trident appears to terminate in three prongs that have circular cross-sections, whereas the base of the trident appears to have only two prongs with rectangular cross-sections.

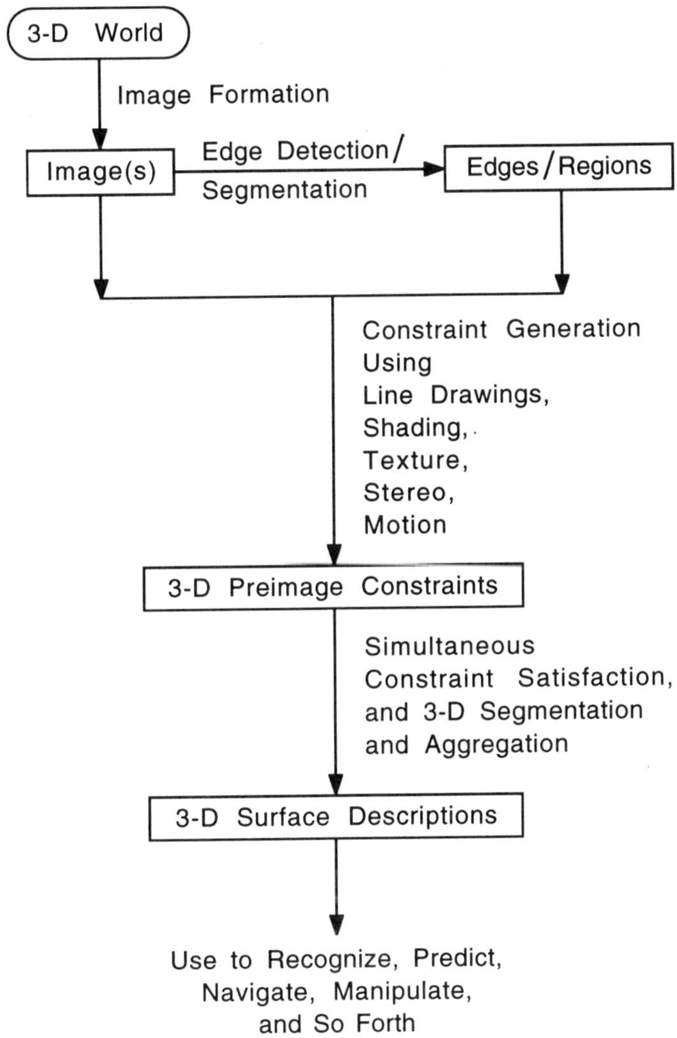

Figure 5 A plausible schema for general-purpose computer vision.

4. A Computer-Vision Schema

Figure 5 provides a sketch of a plausible schema for a general-purpose computer-vision system. By **general purpose** here is meant "without restriction to a particular task or domain." The boxes in the figure represent data, and the arrows indicate processes and the direction of data flow. The computer-vision paradigm in Figure 5 is by far the most common; hence, for purposes of discussion, let us adopt it here too.

In the computer-vision paradigm of Figure 5, the three-dimensional scene is first viewed by one or multiple cameras to produce either monochromatic or colored images. We shall restrict ourselves to monochromatic images here. The images thus acquired are processed so that the brightness discontinuities within the images are detected—these discontinuities are termed *edges*—and perhaps also so that the images are segmented into relatively homogeneous image regions. Then, the images and their edge and homogeneous-region maps are used to constrain the possible interpretations of the imaged world. Currently, the most widely investigated processes used to constrain the three-dimensional world are based on the following image characteristics: line drawings (i.e., edge maps of images), shading (i.e., variation in image brightness), variation in image texture, the disparity between images in stereo image pairs, and image evolution under motion of the camera relative to the scene. We shall examine the significance of edges, shading, texture, stereo, and motion in Section 6. The three-dimensional constraints derived from images may be either local (e.g., the depths, orientations, and reflectances of surface points), or global (e.g., the restriction of a surface to be a surface of revolution). At any rate, once a collection of such constraints has been derived, surface descriptions may be generated by simultaneously enforcing all the preimage constraints (i.e., constraints on the imaged scene) and partitioning the data into sets arising from independent surfaces. These descriptions, preferably simultaneously metric and symbolic, may serve a variety of purposes: recognition, prediction, navigation, manipulation, and the performance of other tasks that require cognition and planning. (The **preimage** of any point in the range of a mapping is the point or collection of points in the domain of the mapping that map onto the particular point in the range—in the context of imaging, the mapping is image formation, whose domain is the three-dimensional world and whose range is the two-dimensional image.)

Although modularity is a convenient design procedure, and the absence of feedback avoids tricky control problems, it is clear that in Figure 5, the strict demarcation between the various processes (and data) and the restriction to forward data flow are both potentially limiting to robustness. For instance, edge detection is likely to proceed better in conjunction with the interpretation of edges. All the processes in Figure 5 could conceivably be modulated by succeeding data; as in all

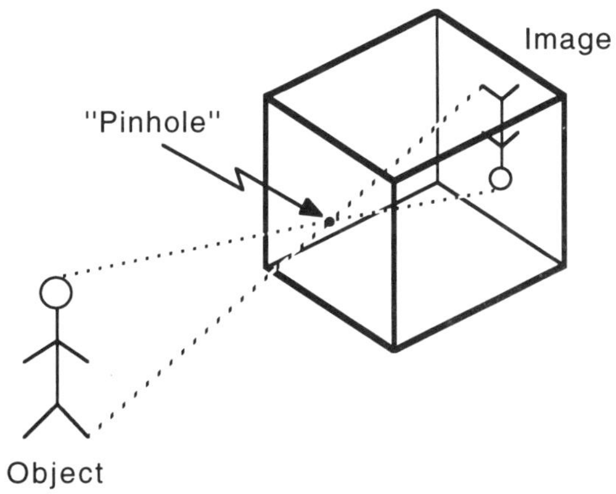

Figure 6 Pinhole camera.

feedback loops, stability would be the primary ensuing concern. Nevertheless, despite its obvious limitations, as Figure 5 does represent the currently most popular paradigm, let us discuss its components.

Let us first discuss image formation, whose understanding is key to computer vision, and then discuss, in sequence, the significance of edges, shading, texture, stereo, and motion. Current computer-vision research is focused largely on the latter topics. Owing to the limited success of researchers in generating robust three-dimensional preimage constraints to this point, simultaneous constraint satisfaction and three-dimensional segmentation and aggregation have received relatively scant attention in the literature. Hence, we shall not discuss these topics.

5. Image formation

Let us now explore the relationship between the three-dimensional world and its two-dimensional image produced by a camera. This relationship is at the heart of every nonheuristic attempt to recover the properties of a scene from its one or multiple images. Hence, it is important that we understand this relationship well.

The simplest imaging device is a **pinhole camera** of the type illustrated in Figure 6. Ideally, a pinhole camera has an infinitesimally small aperture—a "pinhole"—through which light enters the camera and forms an image on the camera surface facing the aperture.

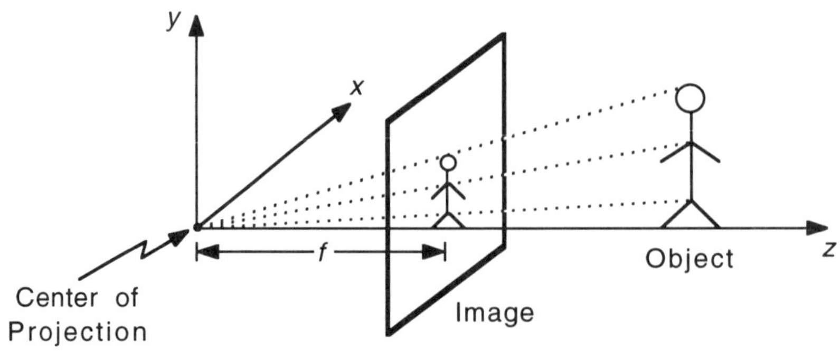

Figure 7 Perspective projection.

Geometrically, the image is formed by straight rays of light that travel from the object through the aperture to the image plane; here, as elsewhere, we use the terms *object* and *scene* interchangeably. Such a mapping from three dimensions onto two dimensions is called *perspective projection*. Specifically, **perspective projection**, also known as **central projection**, is the projection of a three-dimensional entity onto a two-dimensional surface by straight lines that pass through a single point, called the **center of projection**.

As illustrated in Figure 6, the image in a pinhole camera is inverted. As far as analysis goes, this inversion of the image is mildly inconvenient. Hence, it is customary instead to consider the equivalent perspective-projection geometry of Figure 7 in which the image is on the same side of the center of projection as the scene, and, as a result, the image is not inverted. Now, if we denote the distance of the image plane from the center of projection by f, and we denote the object coordinates and the image coordinates by the subscripts o and i, respectively, then it is clear from similar triangles that

$$x_i = \frac{f}{z_o}\, x_o \quad \text{and} \quad y_i = \frac{f}{z_o}\, y_o \,.$$

These equations are the fundamental equations for perspective projection onto a plane.

Now, returning to the pinhole camera, as the size of its aperture is reduced, simple ray tracing would lead us to believe that the image will become progressively sharper. However, the image will become sharper only up to a point. Below a certain aperture size, rectilinear ray tracing is inadequate for purposes of analysis, and we need to consider **diffraction**, a term used to describe the bending of light rays around the edges of objects. In general, the smaller the width of the aperture relative to the wavelength of the incident light, the more pronounced is the diffraction; see [Ruechardt 1958] for an elementary and readable account of diffraction and related optical phenomena. As the aperture size is reduced, in addition to an increase in the image blurring due to diffraction, there is a decrease in the image brightness, the image brightness being directly proportional to the area of the aperture. These considerations lead us to use lenses, the aim of using a lens being to duplicate the pinhole geometry without resorting to undesirably small apertures.

Under ideal circumstances, a lens gathers all the light radiating from an object point toward the lens's finite aperture, and brings this light into focus at a single distinct image point. Let us assume here that the geometry of image formation by a lens conforms to perspective projection, and let us turn our attention to the radiometry of image formation by a lens. That is, let us turn our attention to the relationship between the amount of light radiating from a surface point, called the **scene radiance**, and the amount of light incident at the image of the surface point, called the **image irradiance**. Both scene radiance and image irradiance are informally termed **brightness**.

Without going through the derivation, which is well documented (e.g., see [Nalwa 1993]), the relationship between the radiance of a distant scene point and the irradiance of this point's image formed by a lens is this:

$$\textit{Irradiance} \;=\; \textit{Radiance}\;\frac{\pi}{4}\left(\frac{d}{f}\right)^{2}\cos^{4}\alpha\,,$$

where f is the focal length of the lens, d is the diameter of the circular aperture of the lens, and α is the angle between the optical axis of the lens and the direction from the lens toward the distant object point that is being imaged. This radiometric relation, which is of fundamental importance, tells us that the image irradiance is proportional to the scene radiance. The factor of proportionality is the product of $(\pi/4)$, a constant, $(d/f)^2$, the square of the inverse of the so-called f-number, and $\cos^4\alpha$. The dependence of the image irradiance on $(\pi d^2/4)$, which is the area of the aperture of the lens, is to be expected as the amount of light captured by the lens from a distant object point is proportional to the area of the aperture of the lens. The dependence of the image irradiance on $(1/f)^2$ is also explained easily: The size of the in-focus image is proportional to the distance of this image from the lens, and, for objects that are far away, this distance is the focal length f of the lens; it follows that the image area is proportional to f^2, and, hence, the image irradiance is proportional to $(1/f)^2$. Both the area of the aperture and the focal length of the lens are constant over any image. In contrast, the $\cos^4\alpha$ term—whose physical significance in the radiometric relation is not as immediately apparent—varies over the image. Even the $\cos^4\alpha$ term, however, may be assumed constant when the range of α is sufficiently small. More generally, we can factor this term out by calibrating points on the camera's image plane for their orientation with respect to the optical center of the lens.

6. Image Cues to the 3-D World

Let us now discuss in sequence the role of edges, shading, texture, stereo, and motion in the three-dimensional interpretation of two-dimensional images.

6.1 Edges

When we speak of an *edge* in everyday conversation, we generally refer to a contour in space along which a surface either terminates or undergoes a sudden change in orientation. The concept of an edge in an image is related to this everyday notion: An **edge** in an image is an image contour across which the brightness of the image changes abruptly—perhaps in magnitude or in the rate of change of magnitude. Figure 8 illustrates an artist's rendering of some of the salient brightness edges in a photograph of a sculpture.

Image edges play a central role in computer vision. Let us discuss why. As we saw in Section 5, image irradiance is proportional to scene radiance. Hence, discontinuities in image brightness correspond to discontinuities in the scene radiance. Discontinuities in the scene radiance, in turn, may result from one of several causes, each cause interesting and informative in its own right. Figure 9 illustrates the principal scene events that lead to brightness edges in an image. These events include surface-normal discontinuities, depth discontinuities,

Figure 8 Image edges as a cue to surface shape: An artist's rendering of some of the salient brightness edges in an image of a sculpture gives us a fair idea of the shape of the sculpture.

surface-reflectance discontinuities, and illumination discontinuities. Notice that a depth discontinuity may simultaneously be a surface-normal discontinuity. For glossy surfaces, there also exists the possibility of edges of specular reflections. Although almost never done in practice, it is in principle desirable not only to detect image-brightness edges, but also to distinguish between these edges on the basis of their physical causes.

It is important to distinguish here between viewpoint-independent edges and viewpoint-dependent edges. A **viewpoint-independent edge** is an edge whose location in three-dimensional space *does not* depend on the viewpoint—as is the case with discontinuities in surface

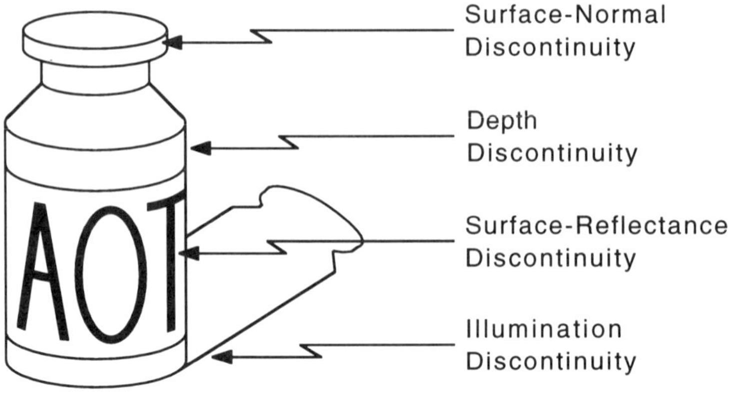

Figure 9 Physical events in a scene that may lead to brightness edges in an image of the scene.

normal, in illumination, and in surface reflectance. A **viewpoint-dependent edge** is an edge whose location in three-dimensional space *does* depend on the viewpoint—as is the case with a depth discontinuity in space across which the surface normal varies continuously. Consider, for instance, the two straight depth discontinuities that lie on either side of the jar in Figure 9 and how the spatial locations of these discontinuities vary as we move about the jar. The distinction between viewpoint-independent and viewpoint-dependent edges is very important because the nature of the conclusions we can draw about the scene from its edges in the two cases is substantially different. For brevity, the terms **limbs** and **apparent contours** are often employed interchangeably for continuous–surface-normal depth discontinuities.

Edges are noteworthy not only because of the scene events that lead to them, but also from a slightly different point of view: an information-theoretic one. Under this view, the more unexpected an event, the more information that event conveys. Edges are important precisely because they represent image nonredundancies—that is, because the image brightness on either side of an edge cannot be predicted by an examination of the other side. This viewpoint was first elaborated by Attneave in his classic paper, "Some Informational Aspects of Visual Perception" [Attneave 1954]; the roots of information theory lie in the seminal paper by Shannon, "A Mathematical Theory of Communication" [Shannon 1948]. The aim of vision is the abstraction

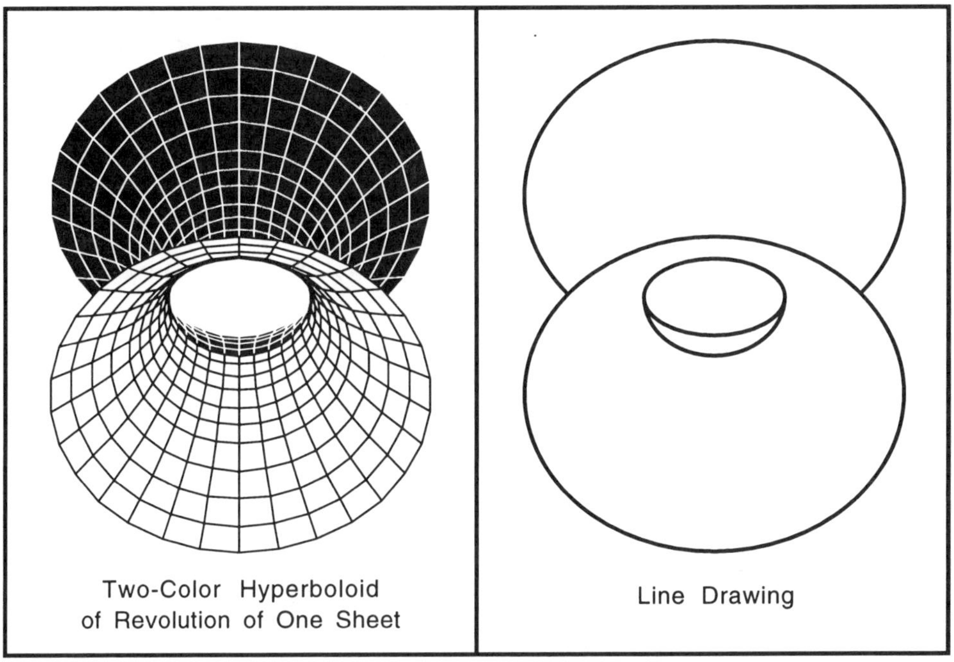

Figure 10 A surface and its line drawing, which evokes an interpretation at variance with the surface. (After [Nalwa 1988].)

of the structure of the world from the world's images, and edge detection is a crucial data-reduction step in almost all proposals to meet this aim.

The importance of brightness edges in images is also borne out by our remarkable ability to infer from a **line drawing**—a term for the representation of the brightness edges in an image—the scene the line drawing represents. This observation is confirmed, for instance, by the line drawing in Figure 8. Although our ability to interpret line drawings is not infallible as demonstrated readily by Figure 10, this ability is quite remarkable in view of the complete loss of depth information under the projection of a scene, this loss illustrated in Figure 11 for perspective projection.

At the heart of the successful interpretation of line drawings as three-dimensional scenes lies the **general-viewpoint assumption**: the assumption that the perturbation of the camera viewpoint would not affect the configuration of the line drawing. When the viewing

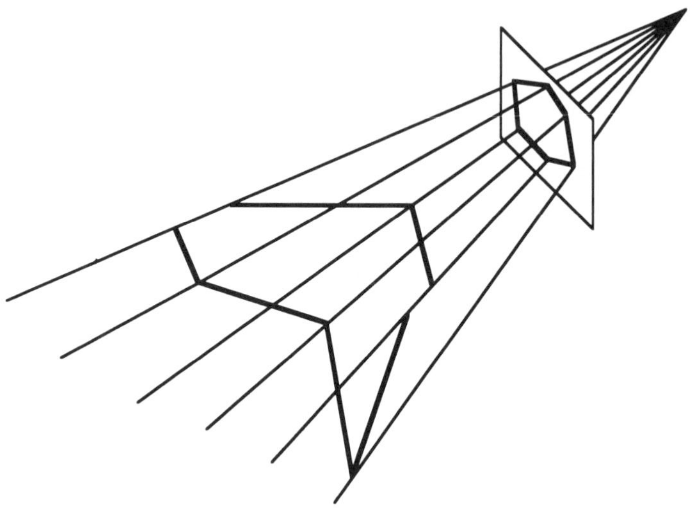

Figure 11 The inherent ambiguity of a line drawing. (After [Barrow and Tenenbaum 1981].)

geometry is modeled by perspective projection, the term *viewpoint* refers to the center of projection. What the general-viewpoint assumption entails is that certain specific properties of the line drawing persist under perturbation of the viewpoint—only such persistent properties can be gainfully employed to make deductions about the imaged three-dimensional world. (See [Nalwa 1988] for a more precise mathematical formulation of the general-viewpoint assumption.) Without the general-viewpoint assumption, meaningful line-drawing interpretation would not be feasible. The hopelessness of the situation in the absence of this assumption may be gauged from the observation that we would then have to allow arbitrary planar curves to project onto straight lines in the line drawing. Worse still, a straight line in a line drawing then need not be the projection of a space curve at all: It could be the projection of a planar patch along some direction parallel to the plane of the patch.

Figure 12 illustrates typical inferences that can be drawn from particular line-drawing configurations under the assumption of a general viewpoint. In the figure, 2-D and 3-D refer to two and three dimensions, respectively. The strength of an inference depends inversely on the size of the set of viewpoints under which the inference may be violated. Although the inferences described in the figure are

Inference Under General Viewpoint	Violation
 Collinearity in 2-D ⇒ Collinearity in 3-D	Collinear points in 2-D are coplanar in 3-D, and are viewed from within common plane.
 Common termination of two or more noncotangent lines in 2-D ⇒ Common termination in 3-D	Common terminations in 2-D are collinear in 3-D, and are viewed from along common straight line.
 Common intersection of three or more noncotangent straight lines (perhaps virtual) in 2-D ⇒ Common intersection in 3-D (perhaps at ∞)	Points along the straight lines (perhaps virtual) at common intersection in 2-D are collinear in 3-D, and are viewed from along common straight line.
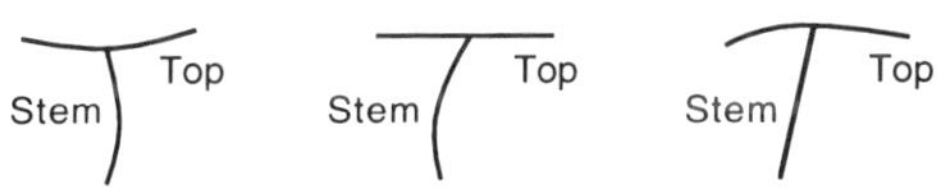 *T-Junctions* Termination in 2-D of one line (*stem*) at another noncotangent line with a continuous tangent (*top*) ⇒ Stem is no closer than the top in 3-D	Points of contact in 2-D are viewed from along a straight line in 3-D that passes through the termination of the stem and a point on the top, all such 3-D lines constituting a cone (or a plane).

Figure 12 Inferences that can be drawn from particular line-drawing configurations under the assumption of a general viewpoint. (After [Binford 1981] and [Lowe and Binford 1985].)

valid for both viewpoint-independent and viewpoint-dependent edges, they are much more difficult to establish when viewpoint-dependent edges are included. With regard to viewpoint-dependent edges that are continuous–surface-normal depth discontinuities, or limbs for short, Nalwa [Nalwa 1988] has established that the canonical singularities of the projection of a C^3 (i.e., thrice continuously differentiable) surface

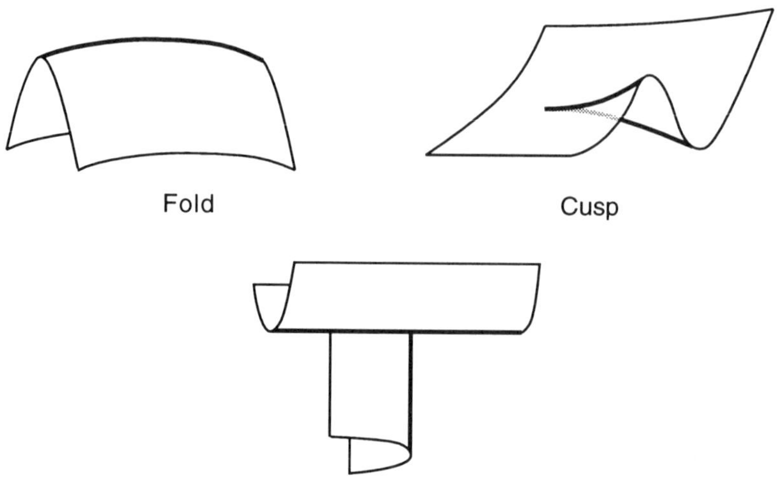

Figure 13 The canonical singularities of the projection of a C^3 (i.e., thrice continuously differentiable) surface under general viewpoint: fold, cusp, and T-junction.

under general viewpoint are folds, cusps, and T-junctions, all illustrated in Figure 13. The projection of a surface is said to be singular wherever the projection direction is tangent to the surface; then, the canonical singularities of the projection of a surface are the simplest surface configurations and their projections to which all instances of singular projection can be reduced without any loss of generality. At a **fold**, the surface folds over to form a continuous-surface-normal depth discontinuity. At a **cusp**, the projection of the limb would cusp—that is, it would undergo a 180° reversal in direction—if the surface were transparent: For an opaque surface, however, only one branch of the cusp is visible in the line drawing, and this branch just terminates freely. Note that it is only the projection of a limb that may cusp, and not the limb itself in space. At a **T-junction**, an opaque fold partially occludes another fold.

6.2 Shading

In the preceding subsection, we were concerned with discontinuities in the image brightness. Let us now turn our attention to continuous brightness variations, better known as **shading**. We all know well that

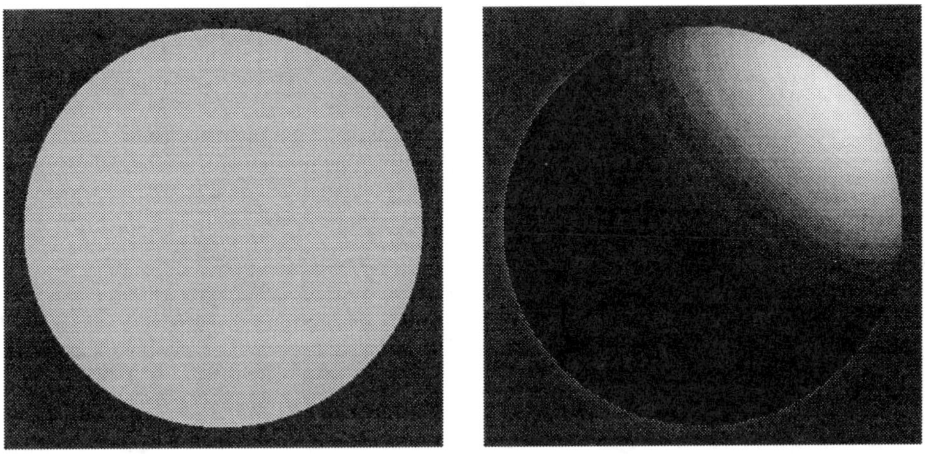

Figure 14 Shading as a cue to surface shape: Whereas the constant-brightness circular region on the left is perceived to be a flat disc, the shaded circular region on the right is perceived to be a sphere. (After [Gibson 1950].)

our perception of the shape of a surface depends on the shading of the surface, as illustrated, for instance, by Figure 14. In the figure, the circle on the left, which is uniformly bright in its interior, is perceived to be a flat disc, whereas the circle on the right, which has varying brightness in its interior, is perceived to be a sphere. Although in either case the image contour across which the magnitude of the image brightness changes abruptly is just a circle, in the image on the left, this circle is perceived to be a surface-normal discontinuity, whereas in the image on the right, this circle is perceived to be a depth discontinuity across which the surface normal varies continuously in space.

Now, we saw in Section 5 that the image irradiance is proportional to the scene radiance. It is the dependence of scene radiance on surface shape that makes image shading useful for shape recovery. For any given homogeneous and isotropic surface that is under homogeneous illumination, this dependence is governed by the incidence, emittance, and phase angles illustrated in Figure 15. The **angle of incidence** of a particular ray of light that is incident on a surface is the angle between the surface normal at the point of incidence and the direction from which the ray is incident. The **angle of emittance** of a particular ray of light that is emitted by a surface is the angle between this ray and the surface normal at the point of emittance. Finally, the **phase angle** is the

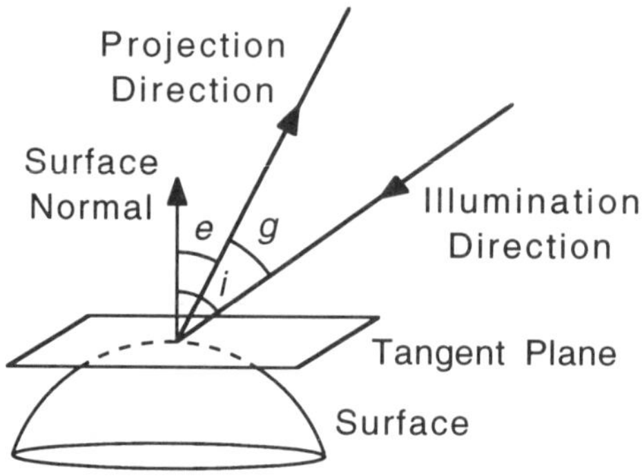

Figure 15 The incidence, emittance, and phase angles, i, e, and g, respectively.

angle between the direction from which a particular ray of light is incident at a surface point and the direction in which a particular ray of light is emitted at the point of incidence as a result. Note that, at any surface point, a given incident ray and a resulting emitted ray together need not share a common plane with the surface normal; that is, the incidence, emittance, and phase angles at a surface point need not be all coplanar.

The brightness of a surface is determined by the rays emitted by the surface toward the camera, or the viewer. A **Lambertian** or **diffuse surface**, which is an idealization of a matte surface, has the property that it appears equally bright from all directions; when such a surface is illuminated from a single direction, its brightness is proportional to the cosine of the angle of incidence. A **specular surface** is a mirror surface, which ideally has the property that it reflects every incident ray only in the single direction for which the angle of incidence is equal to the angle of emittance, and, in addition, the sum of the angles of incidence and emittance is equal to the phase angle.

6.3 Texture

Conceptually, the principal characteristic of a **texture** is the repetition of a basic pattern. That having been said, several clarifications are immediately called for. The structure of the basic pattern may not be deterministic, but rather only statistical, and the repetition of the basic pattern may neither be regular nor deterministic, but rather only statistically regular (e.g., uniformly distributed).

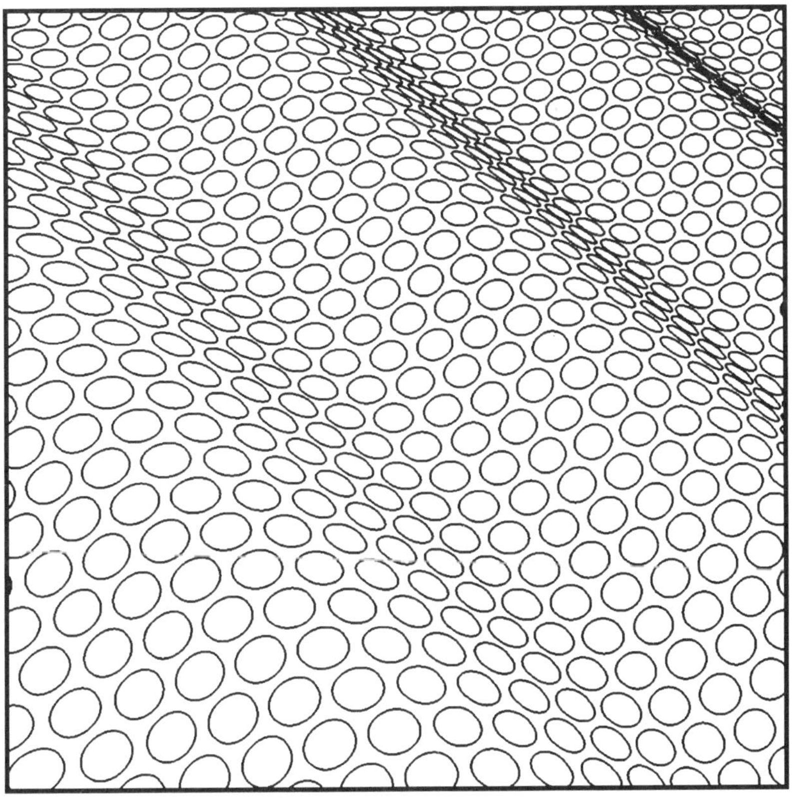

Figure 16 Image textural variation as a cue to three-dimensional shape: The illustrated distribution of ellipses of various shapes and sizes suggests a receding corrugated surface in space.

Furthermore, as is evident from Figure 16, the images of the various instances of the basic repetitive textural pattern in space may not all be identical: These images may be related by geometric distortions. It is these distortions that make texture useful for shape recovery. Variation in the image characteristics of a texture has been long recognized as a cue to surface shape. Ever since Gibson's classic *The Perception of the Visual World* [Gibson 1950], image textural variation as a cue to shape has been the subject of several investigations. In Figure 16, the simple image textural variation of ellipses of various shapes and sizes suggests a receding corrugated surface in space.

The principle that facilitates the recovery of shape from image texture is perspective projection—specifically, the distortion of surface

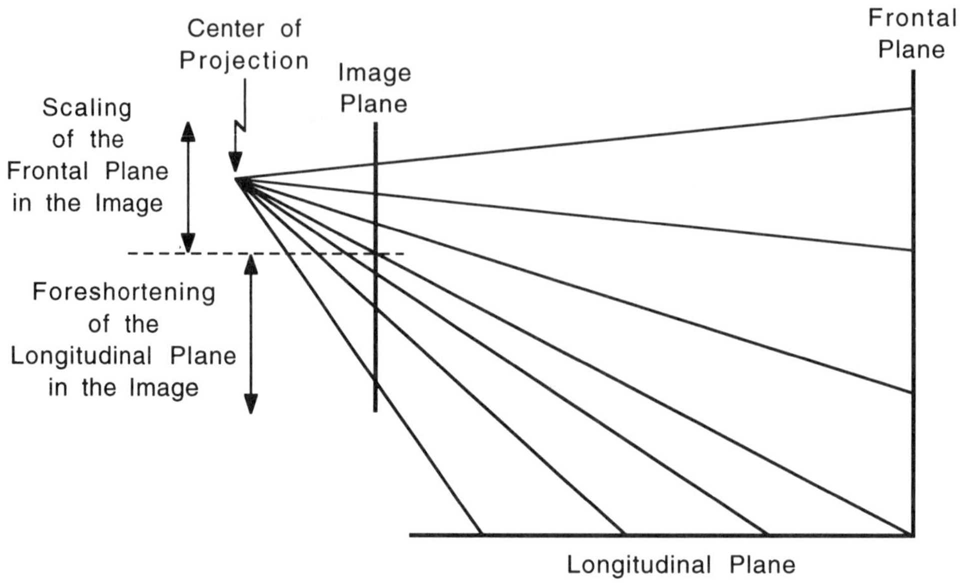

Figure 17 Scaling and foreshortening under perspective projection. (After [Gibson 1950].)

texture under perspective projection. This distortion is typically a combination of scaling and foreshortening, both of which are illustrated in Figure 17. The term *foreshortening* describes the deformation of lines and surfaces that are not parallel to the image plane under projection onto this plane. Whereas the term **scaling** indicates that the proportions of the object are maintained, the term **foreshortening** implies that the fore–aft dimensions of the object are compressed relative to its frontal dimensions. Strictly speaking, perspective projection leads to foreshortening in this sense only when the object lies within that 90° circular cone whose vertex is at the center of projection and whose axis is orthogonal to the image plane.

6.4 Stereo

Stereo—from *stereós*, Greek for solid—is a broad term indicating the involvement of three-dimensional space. However, the use of the term *stereo* in computer vision, as in human vision, has traditionally been restricted to the recovery of a three-dimensional scene from multiple images of the scene. Let us focus here on the recovery of a scene from

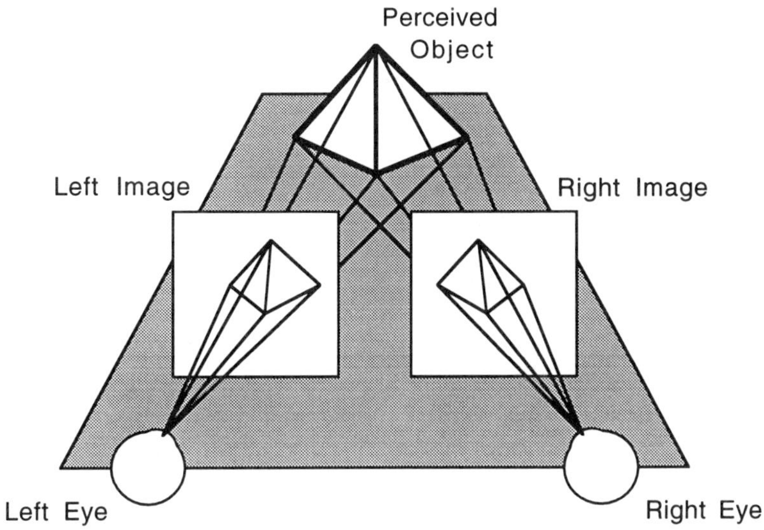

Figure 18 Stereo as a cue to surface shape: Multiple images of a three-dimensional scene, each image acquired from a different viewpoint in space, facilitate the recovery of the three-dimensional structure of the scene in a process known as *stereo*. (After [Gibson 1950].)

two images of the scene that are acquired from different viewpoints. The basis of such a recovery—let us call this recovery **geometric stereo**—is illustrated in Figure 18 in the context of human vision.

The principle that underlies geometric stereo is **triangulation**. As illustrated in Figure 19, under the assumption of perspective projection, each image point is the projection of some point along the ray through the image point and its center of projection—actually, along only that portion of this ray that extends outward from the image point. If the corresponding point in the other image is known, then the object point must also lie on the corresponding ray through that point. Hence, the object point must lie at the intersection of the two rays—the determination of this intersection is called *triangulation*. We are assuming here that every image point is the perspective projection of an object point, and that each image point has at most a single unique matching point in the other image; the latter assumption excludes transparent objects from the scene.

Whereas shape recovery using single-image cues typically depends on the propagation of constraints across image regions, stereo methods

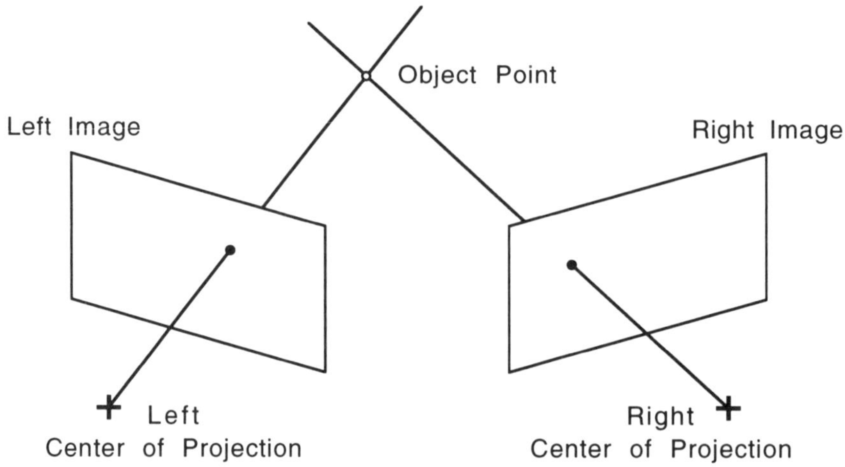

Figure 19 Triangulation as a basis for geometric stereo.

are more local and direct, and, hence, they hold the potential for greater robustness.

6.5 Motion

To this point, we have restricted ourselves to images captured by a stationary camera. Let us now explore the recovery of a three-dimensional scene from multiple images of the scene, these images captured by a camera that is in motion *relative* to the scene. That the recovery of a scene from multiple images of the scene captured by a single moving camera is partially feasible should come as no surprise. Most of us have experienced the feeling of racing through the starry skies—past stars at varying distances from us—while watching science-fiction movies that have stars moving radially outward from our supposed point of approach.

A graphic illustration of precisely this phenomenon is provided in Figure 20. At the top, in Figure 20, are three image frames from a sequence of images that is captured by a camera moving toward the point at the center of images; at the bottom, is the image that results when we superimpose the individual images in the captured sequence. The figure illustrates that, whereas points in the scene that are either distant from the observer, or along the observer's direction of translation, remain relatively clear under translation of the observer—

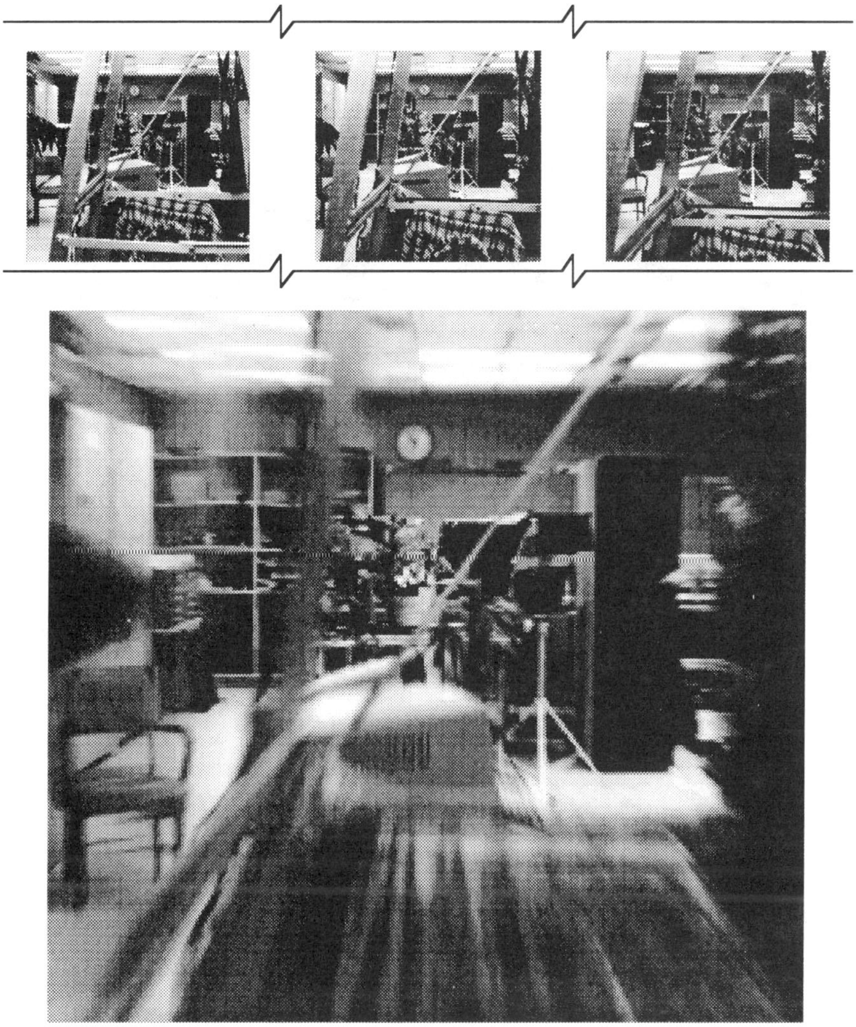

Figure 20 Motion as a cue to surface shape illustrated by a sequence of images acquired by a forward-moving camera: The superimposed sequence is shown below three of its individual frames. (Image sequence, courtesy SRI International.)

that is, the image positions of such points remain relatively unchanged under translation of the observer—other points appear to move radially outward from the observer's point of approach in the image. In general, the magnitude of the image motion of a scene point increases both with a decrease in the distance of the point from the observer, and with an increase in the angle between the direction in which the scene point lies and the direction in which the observer is translating. The notion of

Figure 21 Spatiotemporal image data block comprising a stacked sequence of images acquired under motion of a camera relative to the imaged scene. (After [Bolles, Baker, and Marimont 1987]. Image sequence, courtesy SRI International.)

motion parallax—that of the apparent relative motion between objects that are stationary with respect to one another and at different depths along a common line of sight of an observer who is in motion with respect to the objects—was first outlined by Euclid in his treatise *Optics*, circa 300 B.C. [Euclid c. 300 B.C.].

Image capture under camera motion that includes camera translation provides the image data with an extra dimension: the dimension of a varying viewpoint. For the sake of discussion, let us assume here that the camera has a constant velocity and that the camera is capturing images at equal time intervals. Then, the additional dimension that the camera motion imparts to the image data can equivalently be described as a *temporal dimension*. We thus have intensity variation over the image plane and over time, as illustrated in Figure 21. Let us call this three-dimensional image-intensity variation a **spatiotemporal** variation in the image intensity, where *spatio* in *spatiotemporal* refers to the two dimensions of a single image frame, and *temporal* refers to the time axis over which the image evolves. If we now assume that the scene comprises surfaces that are both temporally unchanging and stationary with respect to one another, then, under relative motion between the camera and the scene, the dimension of the image data will match the dimension of the scene. The third dimension imparted to the image data by the relative motion between the camera and the scene can be expected to make the recovery of the scene easier: At any rate, this additional dimension cannot make the recovery of the scene more difficult as we are always at liberty to restrict ourselves to a single image frame.

Shape recovery using moving-camera imagery is, in a sense, a generalization of geometric stereo. The underlying principle is the same: Every scene point lies on all its projection rays, and, hence, multiple identifiable rays from a scene point determine the spatial position of the point. However, there is one major difference between three-dimensional recovery through stereo (using a calibrated multicamera system) and that through motion. The use of moving-camera imagery to recover shape requires that the relative motion between the camera and the world be determined. It is not difficult to establish that this motion can be determined up to a scale factor.

Now, it is well known that any arbitrary motion can be decomposed into a pure translation and a pure rotation about a line through a fixed point (e.g., see [Nalwa 1993])—a point that we can choose here to be the center of projection of the camera. Then, the net image motion of any scene point, under relative motion between the camera and the scene, can be decomposed into the sum of the individual image motions of the scene point that would occur under each of the two components of the relative camera motion: one component that is purely translational and the other component that is purely rotational about a line through the camera's center of projection. It is easy to see that, whereas image motions of scene points induced by pure camera translation depend on both the camera translation and the scene geometry, image motions of scene points induced by pure camera rotation about a line through its center of projection depend only on the camera rotation, and not on the scene. As a result, it is only the image motions of scene points due to pure camera translation that are useful in determining scene structure.

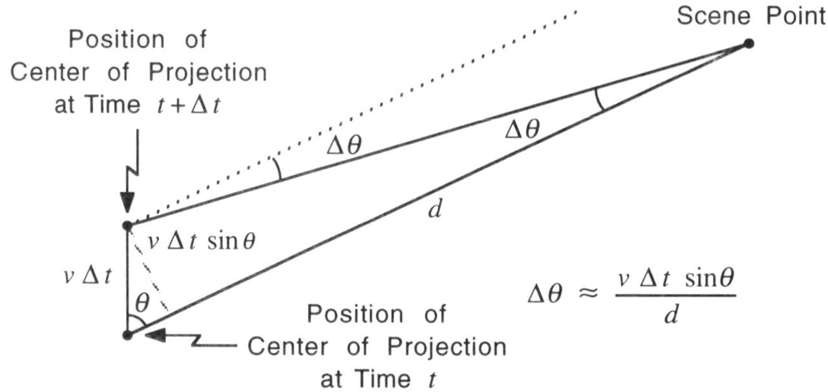

Figure 22 The evolving orientation of a ray from a translating center of projection toward a fixed scene point.

Hence, let us consider a purely translational motion between the camera and the scene here—assuming implicitly that we can decompose the image motions of scene points into components due to pure camera translation and pure camera rotation, a decomposition feasible but beyond the scope of our discussion here. Then, it turns out that the direction of relative translation between the camera and the scene is along the projection ray through that image point from which, or toward which, all the image motion vectors radiate [Gibson 1950]. In Figure 20, this point is seen to be at the center of the superimposed images. The point of the divergence, or the convergence, of all the image motion vectors is called the **focus of expansion (FOE)**, or the **focus of contraction (FOC)**, respectively. The divergence of image motion vectors implies forward motion, and the convergence of image motion vectors implies backward motion.

The phenomenon of radially directed image motion vectors under camera translation is confirmed easily by directly considering the evolution of any projection ray through a fixed scene point and a translating center of projection. Further, with the help of Figure 22, we can easily derive the expression for the angular speed of a ray that originates at a translating center of projection and continues to pass through a fixed scene point. Let θ be the angle between the direction of translation of the center of projection and a ray from the center of projection toward the fixed scene point; let d be the distance of the scene

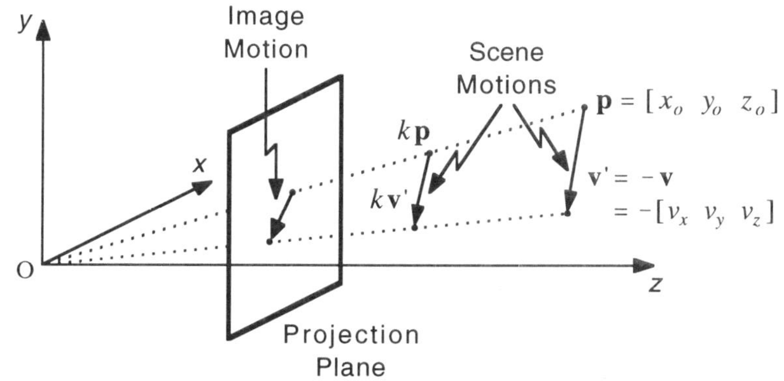

Figure 23 Indeterminacy of up to a scale factor k in both the magnitude of the relative translation $\mathbf{v}$ between the camera and the scene and the positions $\mathbf{p}$ of scene points, given the image motions of scene points.

point from the center of projection; let v be the speed with which the center of projection is translating. Then, it easily follows from Figure 22 that the angular speed of the ray from the center of projection to the scene point is $v \sin\theta/d$. Thus, we see that, given the direction of translational motion of a camera, and the magnitudes of the angular velocities of projection rays through fixed scene points, the distances of these points from the camera can be recovered up to the scale factor v. Equivalently, as illustrated in Figure 23, scaling both the relative motion between the camera and the scene and the structure of the scene by the same scale factor would leave our image observations unchanged. It follows that, if we do not know the structure of the scene a priori, then we can determine the relative translation between the camera and the scene—and, as a result, the structure of the scene—at best up to a scale factor. Determining the relative translation between the camera and the scene up to a scale factor is, of course, equivalent to just determining the direction of relative translation, which we have already seen how to determine.

Given the straightforward relationship between the the angular velocities of projection rays and the velocities of the intersections of these rays with the image plane, it follows from the above expression for the angular speed of the ray from the center of projection to the scene point that, under camera translation, the magnitude of the image motion of a scene point depends inversely on the distance of the point from the camera, and it depends directly on the sine of the angle between the direction in which the scene point lies and the direction in which the camera is translating. Further, if we assume that the image-plane velocities are determinable, as we already know how to determine the direction of camera translation, it is clear that we could also easily numerically derive the structure of the scene up to a scale factor using the above expression for angular velocities.

7. Conclusion

Despite decades of tangible progress in our understanding of our rich visual world, reliable, robust, and general-purpose computer vision remains elusive. There, of course, lies a chasm between gaining an understanding of a mapping and being able to invert that mapping—in the context here, between gaining an understanding of the mapping from the world to its images and being able to reconstruct the world from its images.

Computer vision, as we know it today, has its beginnings in the seminal work of Roberts [Roberts 1965], who developed computer programs to deduce the three-dimensional structure and arrangement of a few simple trihedral-vertex polyhedra from their digital images. Roberts's modest success with his *blocks world* prompted high hopes. Back in the 1960s, the emerging and ambitiously named field, *artificial intelligence*, was arousing spectacular short-term expectations. Soon, however, researchers realized that visual perception is a nontrivial intellectual enterprise, and that techniques developed to analyze polyhedral scenes almost never lend themselves to more general settings. Since the early work of Roberts, substantial time and effort have been devoted to computer vision, and the ensuing results have been documented in several publications. See the following books and the references therein for more on the subject: *Computer Vision* by Ballard and Brown [Ballard and Brown 1982], *Robot Vision* by Horn [Horn 1986], and *A Guided Tour of Computer Vision* by Nalwa [Nalwa 1993].

My aim here was to introduce you to the basis of computer vision. However, I would like to conclude by pointing you to a few salient problems in computer vision that, in my judgment, could benefit greatly from a fresh examination, such as that many of you can provide. These problems, which I discuss at length in [Nalwa 1993], include the following:

- **Edge Detection** We argued that image edges play a central role in computer vision, but it remains a challenging problem to find image edges reliably and accurately; we are a long ways from detecting image edges with anywhere near the quality required to interpret them successfully by the line-drawing-interpretation techniques developed thus far. A large part of the problem is that most edge-detection methods operate locally and noniteratively, whereas the existence of an edge is often a matter of nonlocal context. There have been nonlocal and iterative edge-detection methods, but those proposed to this point—such as the one based on simulated annealing [Geman and Geman 1984]—perform even less satisfactorily than the best available local and noniterative methods, largely because, I believe, the former methods often invoke unsupported assumptions about the image.

- **Line-Drawing Interpretation** Line-drawing interpretation is a challenging and seductive intellectual pursuit that has seen active research since the very beginning of computer vision. However, almost all the techniques developed toward this goal thus far have relied on the availability of perfect line drawings with accurately detected junctions, something not even remotely attainable with current edge-detection techniques. Given that humans can usually interpret the outputs of the better currently available edge detectors quite well and with ease, I wonder if there is not a solid mathematical basis for such interpretations of incomplete and noisy line drawings.

- **Stereoscopic Correspondence Establishment** Whereas the basis of stereo is simple—triangulation—its implementation requires that we establish correspondence between image points in different images that represent the same object point in space. Such establishment of correspondence between image points is nontrivial, and the most interesting approach toward this goal I have seen uses simulated annealing [Barnard 1989], but simulated annealing is a very tedious enterprise using current implementation techniques, and I have seen no follow up to this work. Here, again, the issues are reliability and accuracy.

- **Spatiotemporal Coherence Detection** When it comes to determining scene structure from a sequence of images acquired under relative motion between the camera and the scene, the analog of stereoscopic correspondence establishment is spatiotemporal coherence detection. This latter task entails a rich problem domain, because of the added dimension of varying time, but I have seen little work that exploits this extra dimension well.

- **Surface Representation** This is a very hard and important problem that we did not touch upon at all here. Some of the issues that face us in choosing a representation are the domain of the representation, the uniqueness of the representation, its stability, and, of course, the ease with which we can manipulate the representation and derive useful information from it. When one gets down to designing a representation, as I have tried [Nalwa 1989], addressing these issues effectively turns out to be a tall order, and the most effective and useful representations to this point remain those that are the simplest, and most inelegant.

I look forward to your fresh input on these and other outstanding problems in computer vision.

References

Attneave, F. 1954. "Some Informational Aspects of Visual Perception," *Psychological Review*, Vol. 61, No. 3, pp. 183–193.

Ballard, D. H., and Brown, C. M. 1982. *Computer Vision*, Prentice-Hall, Englewood Cliffs, New Jersey.

Barnard, S. T. 1989. "Stochastic Stereo Matching over Scale," *International Journal of Computer Vision*, Vol. 3, pp. 17–32.

Barrow, H. G., and Tenenbaum, J. M. 1981. "Interpreting Line Drawings as Three-Dimensional Surfaces," *Artificial Intelligence*, Vol. 17, pp. 75–116.

Binford, T. O. 1981. "Inferring Surfaces from Images," *Artificial Intelligence*, Vol. 17, pp. 205–244.

Bolles, R. C., Baker, H. H., and Marimont, D. H. 1987. "Epipolar-Plane Image Analysis: An Approach to Determining Structure from Motion," *International Journal of Computer Vision*, Vol. 1, pp. 7–55.

Boring, E. G. 1942. *Sensation and Perception in the History of Experimental Psychology*, Appleton-Century-Crofts, New York.

Duda, R. O., and Hart, P. E. 1973. *Pattern Classification and Scene Analysis*, John Wiley & Sons, New York.

Euclid c. 300 B.C. *Optics*. English translation from the Greek by H. E. Burton: "The Optics of Euclid," *Journal of the Optical Society of America*, Vol. 35, No. 5 (May 1945), pp. 357–372.

Fraser, J. 1908. "A New Visual Illusion of Direction," *The British Journal of Psychology*, Vol. 2, pp. 307–320.

Geman, S., and Geman, D. 1984. "Stochastic Relaxation, Gibbs Distributions, and the Bayesian Restoration of Images," *IEEE Transactions on Pattern Analysis and Machine Intelligence*, Vol. PAMI-6, No. 6 (November), pp. 721–741.

Gibson, J. J. 1950. *The Perception of the Visual World*, Houghton Mifflin Co., Boston, Massachusetts.

Gregory, R. L. 1978. *Eye and Brain: The Psychology of Seeing*, Third Edition, McGraw-Hill Book Co., New York.

Horn, B. K. P. 1986. *Robot Vision*, MIT Press, Cambridge, Massachusetts.

Kaufman, L. 1974. *Sight and Mind: An Introduction to Visual Perception*, Oxford University Press, New York.

Levine, M. D. 1985. *Vision in Man and Machine*, McGraw-Hill Book Co., New York.

Levine, M. W., and Shefner, J. M. 1991. *Fundamentals of Sensation and Perception*, Second Edition, Brooks/Cole Publishing Co., Pacific Grove, California.

Lowe, D. G., and Binford, T. O. 1985. "The Recovery of Three-Dimensional Structure from Image Curves," *IEEE Transactions on Pattern Analysis and Machine Intelligence*, Vol. PAMI-7, No. 3 (May), pp. 320–326.

Nalwa, V. S. 1988. "Line-Drawing Interpretation: A Mathematical Framework," *International Journal of Computer Vision*, Vol. 2, pp. 103–124.

Nalwa, V. S. 1989. "Representing Oriented Piecewise C^2 Surfaces," *International Journal of Computer Vision*, Vol. 3, pp. 131–153.

Nalwa, V. S. 1993. *A Guided Tour of Computer Vision*, Addison-Wesley Publishing Co., Reading, Massachusetts.

Pratt, W. K. 1991. *Digital Image Processing*, Second Edition, John Wiley & Sons, New York.

Roberts, L. G. 1965. "Machine Perception of Three-Dimensional Solids," in *Optical and Electro-Optical Information Processing*, J. T. Tippett, D. A. Berkowitz, L. C. Clapp, C. J. Koester, and A. Vanderburgh, Jr., Eds., MIT Press, Cambridge, Massachusetts, pp. 159–197.

Rosenfeld, A., and Kak, A. C. 1982. *Digital Picture Processing*, Second Edition, Vols. 1 & 2, Academic Press, New York.

Ruechardt, E. 1958. *Light: Visible and Invisible*, University of Michigan Press, Ann Arbor, Michigan.

Shannon, C. E. 1948. "A Mathematical Theory of Communication," *The Bell System Technical Journal*, Vol. 27, No. 3 (July), pp. 379–423, and Vol. 27, No. 4 (October), pp. 623–656.

Bell Laboratories, Holmdel, NJ 07733
vic@bell-labs.com

Proceedings of Symposia in Applied Mathematics
Volume 55, 1998

Outsearching Kasparov

Monty Newborn*

1. Introduction

For three decades, computers have been competing in tournaments against human opponents. It began in 1967 when Greenblatt's MACHACK competed in the Massachusetts State Championship and performed at the "C" level. It has continued through to today when the best computers are challenging the world's top players and performing admirably. In the coming years, there will be many matches between the world's top players and their cold-blooded challengers. Garry Kasparov, the current world champion, has already battled several computers and this coming February is scheduled to take on IBM's DEEP BLUE in a six-game match that has $500,000 in prize money.** The event is scheduled to take place in Philadelphia as part of the ACM's Computing Week '96. Whether DEEP BLUE wins or loses, it seems to be only a matter of time before man will have to adjust to having a computer as the intellect supreme at chess. For the short term, however, the goal is Kasparov.

Oversimplified somewhat, the game of chess consists of three phases as depicted in Figure 1: an opening phase, a middlegame phase and an endgame phase. The opening phase lasts anywhere from nine or ten moves to as many as fifteen moves and more. Computers have large databases that assist them during this stage, although when playing Kasparov, the opening book can be expected to serve more as a damage control device than as anything else. The computer cannot be expected to outplay Kasparov during this phase. At best, it can only hope to survive with equality and not fall quickly behind upon leaving the book in a position that it finds uncomfortable. Although computers play endgames quite well and probably better than they are given credit for, this stage favors Kasparov since many endgames involve subtle moves that cannot be understood by even the best of the current programs. However, if the endgame is reached with five or fewer pieces, not counting pawns, on the board, it will favor the computer since a database of all 5-piece endgames exists[1,2]. Of course, to reach this phase is no simple matter.

It is during the middlegame that the computer must outplay Kasparov if it is to win, and success here depends on the search capabilities of program. It is these capabilities that are

* School of Computer Science, McGill University, Montreal, Quebec, Canada H3A 2A7.

** This paper was written in late 1995. Kasparov defeated DEEP BLUE in a May 1996 match by a score of 4-2. DEEP BLUE was searching to a depth of about 13 plies.; in a February 1997 match, DEEP BLUE, searching at approximately twice the speed of its first match, defeated Kasparov 3 1/2 - 2 1/2.

*** This work was supported in part by grant O-34588 from the Canadian National Science and Engineering Research Council.

1991 *Mathematics Subject Classification.* Primary 90D40, 90B10.

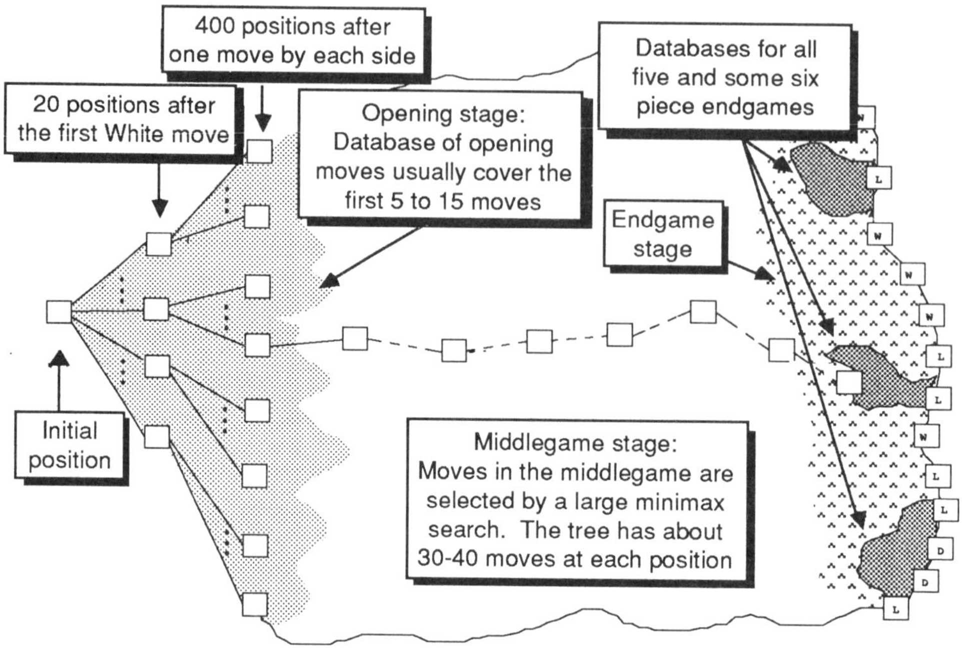

Figure 1. The chess tree

explored in the material that follows. Data is examined that shows the continuing improvement of chess programs and that implies further improvement can be expected. This is followed by a general description of the search algorithms used by computers with an attempt to see whether they are sufficient to match Kasparov.

2. Chess Ratings of Humans

The top players in the world are assigned ratings by FIDE, the International Chess Federation. In addition, most nations where chess is widely played have rating systems of their own. In the United States, ratings are assigned by the United States Chess Federation. Ratings vary somewhat from one group to another but the differences are not of major concern in this paper.

FIDE awards the top players in the world the title of International Grandmasters. Those in the next category are International Masters. Players rated over 2600 are typically IGMs while those over 2400 are IMs although no sharp numerical value distinguishes one group from the other. Titles are awarded based on points won at major tournaments.

The USCF categorizes players as Senior Masters, Masters, Experts, As, Bs, Cs, and Ds. Figure 2 shows the categories, the rating level of the category, an estimate of the number of active players around the world in the category and an estimate of the years of competition required to reach that category.

The top five rated players in the world today, with ratings just below 2800, are Garry Kasparov, Viswanathan Anand, Gata Kamsky, Vladimir Kramnik and Anatoly Karpov. Their ratings differ by less than thirty points.

3. Chess Ratings of Computers

Computers have been receiving ratings for many years. The first program to achieve the level of US Master was Ken Thompson's BELLE; this occurred in 1983. In recent years, computers have won games against the best players in the world, and even Kasparov has been defeated. Kasparov's loses were at the hands of CHESS GENIUS and FRITZ3, although they occurred in games played at speeds faster than the usual 40 moves in two hours or so that is customary at the highest level of play.

Title	Minimum Rating (USCF Scale)	Active Players	Years of Experience
FIDE International GMs	2600	200	15
FIDE International Masters	2400	2000	12
Masters	2200	10000	10
Experts	2000	50000	8
Class A	1800	500000	6
Class B	1600	2000000	4
Class C	1400	10000000	2
Class D	1200	50000000	1

Figure 2. Chess categories, rating and approximate number of players

For many years, commercially-available software was not on a par with that developed at major universities in North America and Europe. In recent years, the situation has changed, and commercial products are now playing on an even footing with the best research efforts. The Swedish Rating List, which has been produced for about a decade, rated the top commercially-available programs in March 1995. The top five on the list are shown in Figure 3 [3]. These ratings may be as much as 100 points below their FIDE ratings according to IM Danny Kopec. Of course, the speed of the computer on which the program executes is very important. FRITZ3, for example, is rated at 2260 when running on a 480/50-66Mhz computer but when running on a Pentium 90Mhz computer earned a rating of 2452 in the Third Godesberg GM Tournament in 1994 [4]. In that event, FRITZ3 scored 2.5/4 against IGMs for the equivalent of a 2652 rating. Its performance against weaker players was not quite as impressive, possibly due to the fact, according to Schulz, that the weaker players prepared more carefully for their encounters.

Program/Computer	Rating
Genius 3.0, Pentium 90 MHz	2440
M_Chess Pro 4.0, Pentium 90 Mhz	2418
Genius 3.0 486/50-66 Mhz	2362
Mephisto Genius 2.0 486/50-66 Mhz	2352
Rebel 6.0 486/50-66 Mhz	2344

Figure 3. Top five programs/computers on the Swedish Rating List

4. On the relation between computer speed and program performance

The relation between computer speed and chess program ratings has been the subject of several papers. [5-8]. In 1978, performance ratings of the programs that had competed in major chess events were plotted as a function of the number of positions searched. Over the range of ratings for which results were available — from about a USCF rating of 1000 to one of 2000 — doubling computer speed seemed to improve play by about 100 points as the graph presented in [5] and reproduced in Figure 4 shows.

Thompson conducted two experiments to confirm this relation [6,7]. Rather than relating rating improvement to the number of positions searched, he related rating improvement to the depth of search. He pointed out that an improvement of 100 points for each doubling of speed was equivalent to an improvement of 250 points for each additional level of search.

In his first experiment, Thompson had one version of BELLE play a series of 20 games against an identical version of BELLE except one version searched to a depth of P levels while the other searched to a depth of P+1 levels. Let the first program be called BELLE(P) and the second BELLE(P+1). The results of this experiment appear in Figure 5a for $3 \leq P \leq 8$.

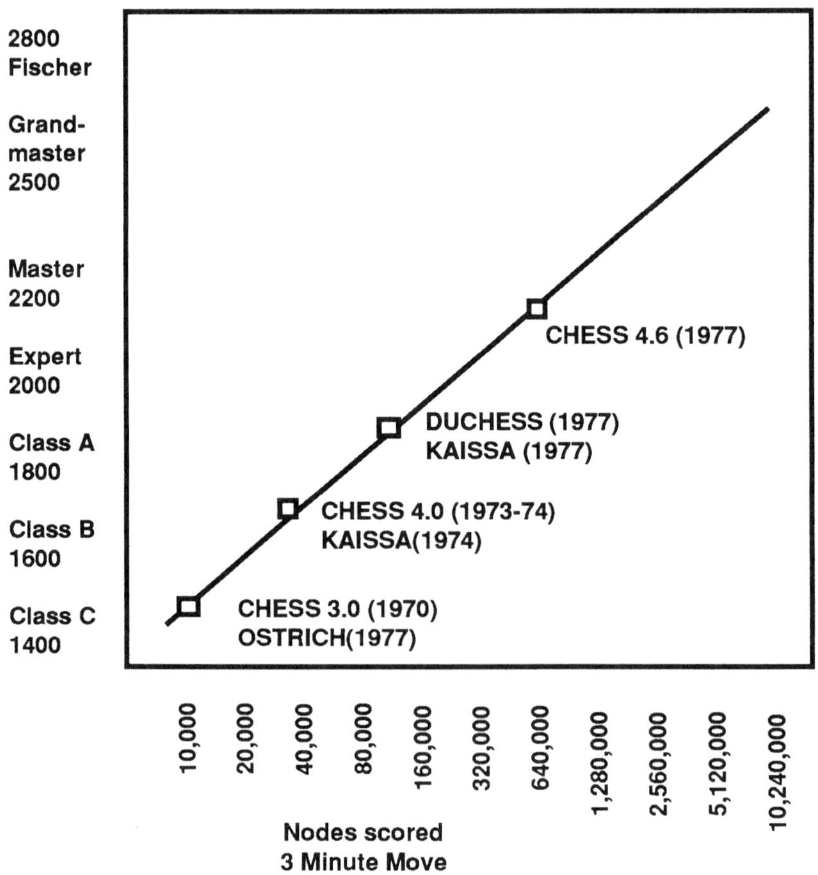

Figure 4. Relationship between the level of play by chess programs and the size of the tree searched during a three minute move.

His second experiment carried out shortly thereafter was more extensive: for 4≤ P,Q ≤ 9 and for P ≠ Q, BELLE(P) played a 20-game series against BELLE(Q). The results are summarized in Figure 5b. The main difference between the results shown in Figure 4 and Thompson's results is that Thompson found that rating improvement drops off from linear at high rating levels, suggesting additional levels of search provide less significant rating improvements. Certainly, eventually the curve approaches a limit but the question is how fast. Thompson evidently did not study deeper search depths because of the large amount of time required to obtain results.

In 1985, the idea that one could obtain rating improvements by a different approach was suggested[8]. It required observing a large number of moves made in random game positions. It was based on the fact that all chess programs of note carry out an iteratively-deepening search when trying to come up with a good move. The paper contended that one could observe the frequency at which a program changed its mind on the best move as a function of the iteration, and that this frequency could be used to obtain a measure of rating improvement.

Consider the following hypothetical situation. Suppose a program that carries out an iteratively-deepening search to a depth of 4 levels, called P(4), has a rating of 1300, and the same program when carrying out an iteratively-deepening search to a depth of 5 levels, called P(5), has a rating of 1550. Now suppose one observes that when making moves in a large number of random game positions, P(5) picks different moves than those picked by P(4) 30%

	BELLE(3)	BELLE(4)	BELLE(5)	BELLE(6)	BELLE(7)	BELLE(8)	Rating
BELLE(3)		4					1091
BELLE(4)	16		5.5				1332
BELLE(5)		14.5		4.5			1550
BELLE(6)			15.5		2.5		1714
BELLE(7)				17.5		3.5	2052
BELLE(8)					16.5		2320

(a)

	BELLE(4)	BELLE(5)	BELLE(6)	BELLE(7)	BELLE(8)	BELLE(9)	Rating
BELLE(4)		5	.5	0	0	0	1235
BELLE(5)	15		3.5	3	.5	.5	1570
BELLE(6)	19.5	16.5		4	1.5	1.5	1826
BELLE(7)	20	17	16		5	4	2031
BELLE(8)	20	19.5	18.5	15		5.5	2208
BELLE(9)	20	20	18.5	16	14.5		2328

(b)

Figure 5. Results of Thompson's two experiments:
(a) first experiment, (b) second experiment

of the time. Furthermore, suppose P(6) picks exactly the same move as P(5) 100% of the time. From this information it seems fair to conclude that the rating of P(6) should be the same as that of P(5); that is, the rating of P(6) should be 1550. This seems straightforward. On the other hand, suppose P(6) picks moves different than those picked by P(5) exactly 30% of the time. In this case, it seems fair to conclude that the rating of P(6) should increase over that of P(5) by the same amount as the rating of P(5) did over the rating of P(4). That is, the rating of P(6) should be 1800.

More generally, if program P(i) and P(i+1) have ratings of R(i) and R(i+1) respectively, and if P(i+1) picks a different move than P(i) F(i)% of the time and P(i+2) picks a different move than P(i+1) F(i+1)% of the time, then it seems reasonable to assign P(i+2) a rating of R(i+2) where:

$$R(i+2) = R(i+1) + (R(i+1) - R(i))*F(i+1)/F(i) \tag{1}$$

In [8], the results of many searches by BELLE were analyzed, and it was found that for $4 \leq i \leq 11$, BELLE(i) picked a different move than BELLE(i–1) with the frequencies shown in column 2 of Figure 6. Given these frequencies, to determine R(i) for a particular i, it is sufficient to know the value of at least one of the Rs, say R(i), and the rating difference between BELLE(i) and its predecessor BELLE(i-1) or its successor BELLE(i+1). Thompson assumed that BELLE(5) had a rating of 1500 in his first paper [6] and 1570 in the second [7]. Since the second paper was written after the first, the value of 1570 is probably more accurate than 1500 and this figure is used in the analysis that follows. For a rating difference, we chose two different values for the difference between BELLE(4) and BELLE(5): 250 and 270 points; Thompson's first experiment found a 168 point difference and his second found a 345 point difference. Averaging these two figures suggests that approximately 250 points is a reasonable compromise. Given that his second experiment may be more credible than his first, the figure is more likely to be 270 than 250. Columns 3-4 show the ratings that follow using (1) a rating of 1570 for BELLE(5), (2) a 250 and 270 point rating difference between BELLE(4) and BELLE(5), (3) the frequencies in column 2 of Figure 6 and (4) Expression (1).

This approach yields in a short time — at least short relative to the amount of time necessary to carry out an experiment like Thompson's — the data necessary to extrapolate Thompson's results by two additional plies. It shows clearly that rating improvement occurs more slowly at deeper levels, but nevertheless, significant improvement still occurs. At ten

i	% of time BELLE(i) picked a different move than BELLE(i - 1)	BELLE(5) = 1570 Rating Diff [BELLE(4) - BEELE(5)] = 250	1570 270
4	.331	1340	1320
5	.331	1570	1570
6	.277	1779	1796
7	.295	2002	2037
8	.260	2198	2249
9	.226	2369	2433
10	.177	2503	2577
11	.181	2639	2725

Figure 6. Percentage of the time BELLE(i) picked a different move than BELLE(i–1) and the corresponding predicted ratings

plies, the ratings are predicted to be 2503 or 2577 depending on the initial assumption that the rating of BELLE(5) is 1570 and the rating of BELLE(4) is either 250 or 270 points less. If one assumes DEEP BLUE(5) is stronger than BELLE(5) and that the difference between the ratings of BELLE(4) and BELLE(5) is closer to 270 points than 250 points, then this analysis comes very near to predicting DEEP BLUE's rating of 2650 for DEEP BLUE(10).

5. Designing to defeat Kasparov

Our results take us only to 11 ply. If one extrapolates the data for an additional three plies, ratings clearly in excess of 2800 seem possible. At the 1993 ACM CCC in Indianapolis, a panel of computer chess experts concluded that a 14-ply search — seven moves for both sides! — in middlegame play when playing at tournament speeds of 40 moves in the first two hours and 20 moves every hour thereafter by the best of existing programs should be enough to compete with Kasparov. Some felt that a 13-ply or even a 12-ply search would be sufficient. At the time of that tournament, the fastest programs were searching 9 to 10 plies in middlegame positions.

It should be pointed out that while computer speed is a very important factor when predicting program performance, there are many other factors that must be taken into account. While it is relatively easy to quantify improvement due to faster computers, it is more difficult to do so for other factors but they are nevertheless very important. Included here are better data structures, improved scoring functions, better use of transposition tables, improved heuristics for varying the depth of search and more efficient use of time. These improvements, as well as many others, have been going on in parallel with advances in hardware speeds.

DEEP BLUE, currently carrying out the most massive searches of all chess programs, is what is generally called a classic brute force plus extended search program. The search guarantees that based on its scoring function, the optimal continuation will be found up to the search horizon. Beyond the search horizon, tactical lines are searched more deeply. Some other programs search as deeply as DEEP BLUE but they carry out some clever pruning of the tree, giving up any guarantee of the correctness of their search.

The remainder of this paper explores how realistic it is to design a program to search to a depth of 12-14 plies in middlegame positions. The issue is really how to design a "computing system" rather than just a program; there are both hardware and software possibilities.

6. The chess tree

In the typical middlegame position, there are about 30-40 moves, about 1000 2-ply continuations and about 1,000,000 4-ply continuations. The chess tree in the middlegame grows quite quickly: every additional two levels of search yields trees with about 1000 times as many terminal positions. Figure 7 shows how many terminal positions a typical middle-

Search depth (plies)	Number of terminal nodes		
12	$\sim 30^{12}$	$=10^{18}$	=10,000,000,000,000,000,000
13	$\sim 30^{13}$	$=3\times10^{19}$	=300,000,000,000,000,000,000
14	$\sim 30^{14}$	$=10^{21}$	=10,000,000,000,000,000,000,000

Figure 7. Search depth and the number of terminal positions scored by the minimax algorithm

game tree would have for search depths of 12, 13 and 14 plies. In the endgame, rather than 30-40 moves, there may be 15-25 moves. A program may be able to search several plies deeper during this stage than in the middlegame. Moreover, as will be explained, in the deep endgame, transposition tables are often very effective and yet deeper searches are possible.

7. The minimax algorithm

Computers that play chess are programmed to search for the best move in a given position by carrying out a depth-first search. The entire chess tree is too large to search in its entirety, so a maximum depth of search, DMAX, must be decided before beginning the search. The value of DMAX, of course, depends on the amount of time allotted to the search. The value of DMAX is hard to set correctly. If DMAX is set too small, a move can be selected based on a shallower search than desired. If it is set too large, an incomplete search can result. Later, we will see that iteratively-deepening search avoids this problem. During the search, the scoring function assigns a score to each position at depth DMAX. Let us not concern ourselves here with the fact that there may be mating positions at depths shallower than DMAX. Positions at which no successors are searched are called terminal positions. Positions with successors are called nonterminal. A score is assigned to each nonterminal position according to the minimax algorithm as follows: at an odd (even) level, back up to the position the maximum (minimum) score of its children.

The minimax algorithm is based on data structures presented in Figure 8 and described in Section 7.1. A pseudo-C version of the minimax algorithm is presented in Figure 9. The algorithm calls five functions, GENERATE, EVALUATE, SUCCESSOR, PREDECESSOR, and SET_PC. These functions are described in Section 7.2. Section 7.3 describes in detail the minimax depth-first search of a specific game tree.

7.1. Data structures used by the minimax algorithm. The following is a simplification of the data structures used by a typical chess-playing program that is based on the minimax algorithm.

BOARD(8,8) represents the contents of the 64 squares of the chess board. White pieces are assigned integers: pawn = 1, knight = 2, bishop = 3, rook = 4, queen = 5 and king = 6. Black pieces are assigned the corresponding negative numbers. A blank square is assigned a 0.

MOVES(128,40) is an array in which the moves at each level in the tree are stored as they are generated. MOVES(128,40) has sufficient space for a search to a depth of 40 plies with up to 128 moves in a position. The squares of the chess board are assigned names as shown on the left in Figure 10a, while the right side of Figure 10a indicates how they might be encoded by a chess program. A move is described, by a "from" square and a "to" square as the partial list of moves for the initial position in Figure 10b shows.

MP(40) is an array of move pointers, where MP(i) points to the move at ply i that is currently under search. For example (See Figure 11), when the terminal position at the end of the move sequence b-c-a-d is reached, the value of the move pointers will be MP(0) = 2, MP(1) = 2, MP(2) = 1 and MP(3) = 1.

SCORE(42) is an array that keeps track of the scores assigned to positions in the search tree. At most one score must be kept for each level in the tree. SCORE(i) maintains the best score found thus far for the position at level i on the continuation under search.

PC(40,40) is a triangular array used to determine the principal continuation. When the search ends, the principal continuation of length, say L, is in the top row of this array, that is, in PC(0,0), PC(0,1), . . . , PC(0,L - 1).

Two additional variables are necessary, DMAX and PLY. DMAX denotes the maximum search depth and PLY denotes the current search depth as the search progresses.

7.2. Functions called by the minimax algorithm. The flow chart in Figure 9 shows that the minimax algorithm calls five function.

EVALUATE(BOARD), the scoring function, takes into account a number of factors to assign a score to a terminal board position called BOARD. Material, pawn structure, king safety, and mobility are the main four, but every program has many other factors that it considers. Factors favorable to White are assigned positive values while those favorable to Black are assigned negative values. The score of a position is usually some non-linear function of the difference in the values of the factors.

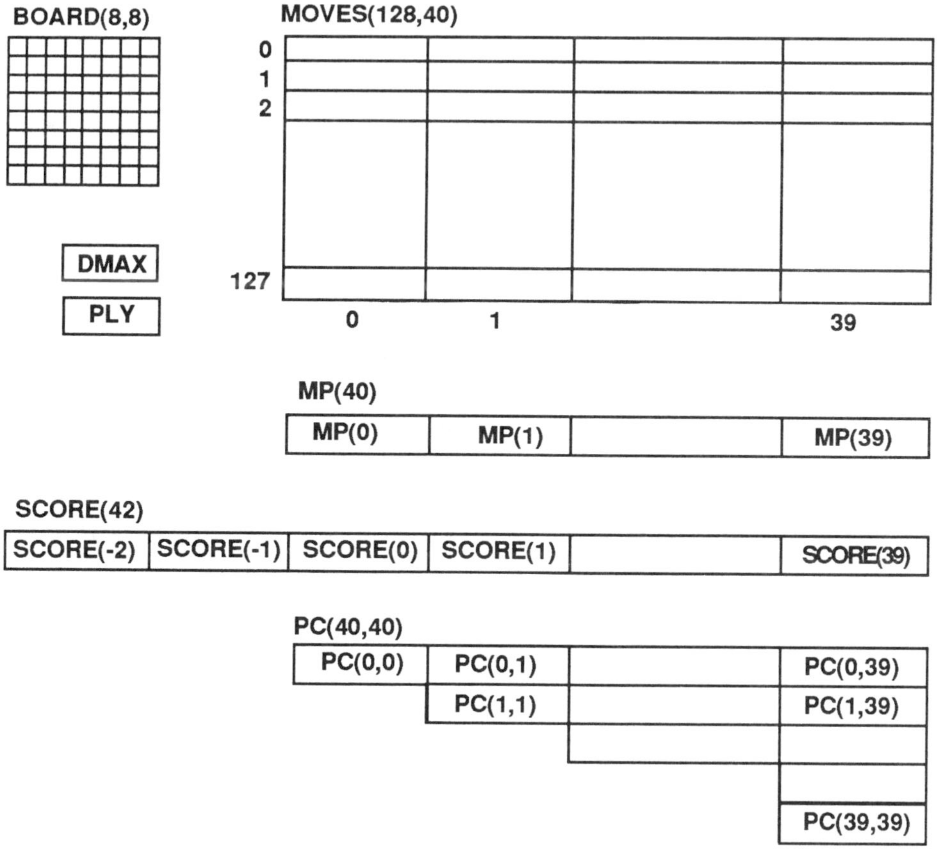

Figure 8. Data structures used by the minimax algorithm

```
/* DATA STRUCTURES */
INTEGER BOARD(8,8), MOVES(40,128), MP(40), SCORE(42),
INTEGER PC(40,40), DMAX, PLY;

/* FUNCTIONS CALLED:  GENERATE(), EVALUATE(), SUCCESSOR(),           */
/* PREDECESSOR(), SET_PC()                                           */

/* INITIALIZE:  ENTER POSITION IN BOARD(8,8), SET MAXIMUM SEARCH      */
/* DEPTH DMAX.  SET INITIAL VALUES OF SCORE(-2) AND SCORE(-1)         */
/* TO EFFECTIVELY MINUS AND PLUS INFINITY RESPECTIVELY                */
PLY = 0; SCORE(-1) = +100000; SCORE(-2) = -100000;

/* A NEW POSITION        ; IF AT MAXIMUM DEPTH, SCORE POSITION */
NEW_POSITION:
IF(PLY == DMAX) GOTO AT_DMAX;

/*  OTHERWISE, GENERATE MOVES, PLACE THEM ON MOVESLIST, BRING */
/* DOWN THE SCORE FROM TWO LEVELS HIGHER IN THE TREE, AND SET */
/* THE MOVE POINTER AT DEPTH "PLY" TO THE FIRST MOVE           */
GENERATE(BOARD,PLY);SCORE(PLY) = SCORE(PLY - 2);MP(PLY) = 0;

/* MOVE FORWARD TO SUCCESSOR POSITION */
ADVANCE:
BOARD = SUCCESSOR(BOARD,MOVES(MP(PLY++),PLY));
GOTO NEW_POSITION;

AT_DMAX:
SCORE(PLY) = EVALUATE(BOARD);

/* MINIMAX NOW:  IF MOVE IS GOOD, SAVE IN PC ARRAY, BACK UP SCORE */
MINIMAX:
IF(((PLY IS EVEN) AND (SCORE(PLY) < SCORE(PLY - 1)) OR
      ((PLY IS ODD) AND (SCORE(PLY) > SCORE(PLY - 1)) {
             SET_PC(MOVES(MP(PLY),PLY),PLY);}

/* BACK UP TO PREDECESSOR POSITION. */
BACKUP:
BOARD = PREDECESSOR(BOARD,MOVES(MP(--PLY),PLY));

/* SEE THERE ARE NO MORE MOVES IN THIS POSITION.  IF SO, GO TO MINIMAX. */
IF(MOVES(MP(PLY) + 1,PLY) == 0) {
      IF(PLY == 0) EXIT;  ELSE GOTO MINIMAX;}

/* THERE ARE MORE MOVES.  GET NEXT ONE, THEN GO TO NEW POSITION */
MP(PLY)++; BOARD = SUCCESSOR(BOARD,MOVES(MP(PLY++),PLY));
GOTO NEW_POSITION;
```

Figure 9. Pseudo-C version of the minimax algorithm

The individual pieces are typically assigned values as follows: pawn = 1, knight = 3, bishop = 3-3.5, rook = 5, queen = 9-10 and the king some large number. These values are somewhat game-dependent. For example, a pawn may be worth considerably more than 1 point if it is on the 7th rank, and a pair of bishops is more valuable than a bishop and knight.

8	a8	b8	c8	d8	e8	f8	g8	h8
7	a7	b7	c7	d7	e7	f7	g7	h7
6	a6	b6	c6	d6	e6	f6	g6	h6
5	a5	b5	c5	d5	e5	f5	g5	h5
4	a4	b4	c4	d4	e4	f4	g4	h4
3	a3	b3	c3	d3	e3	f3	g3	h3
2	a2	b2	c2	d2	e2	f2	g2	h2
1	a1	b1	c1	d1	e1	f1	g1	h1
	a	b	c	d	e	f	g	h

7	70	71	72	73	74	75	76	77
6	60	61	62	63	64	65	66	67
5	50	51	52	53	54	55	56	57
4	40	41	42	43	44	45	46	47
3	30	31	32	33	34	35	36	37
2	20	21	22	23	24	25	26	27
1	10	11	12	13	14	15	16	17
0	00	01	02	03	04	05	06	07
	0	1	2	3	4	5	6	7

(a)

Long Chess Notation (column/row)	Short Chess Notation (new square)	Computer Encoding (column/row)
a2a3---------->	a3----------->	0203
a2a4---------->	a4----------->	0204
b2b3---------->	b3----------->	1213
.		
.		
.		
h2h3---------->	h3----------->	7172
h2h4---------->	h4----------->	7173
Nb1a3-------->	Na3--------->	1002
Nb1c3-------->	Nc3--------->	1022
Ng1f3--------->	Nf3---------->	6052
Ng1h3-------->	Nh3--------->	6072

(b)

Figure 10. (a) Encoding of chess squares and (b) encoding of moves

The pawn structure is carefully analyzed by chess programs and a number of factors are considered. Doubled, isolated and backward pawns are terms that are often used when discussing pawn structure and these are taken into account in one way or another by the scoring function. Pawn advancement, especially to the sixth, seventh and eighth rank are carefully evaluated by the scoring function.

King safety is also taken into account. This rewards castling when appropriate, and keeping defenders near the king and attackers away. The king is encouraged to stay near the edge of the board until the endgame is reached and then the king is encouraged to move to the middle or toward pawns.

Mobility takes into account the number of moves each side can make. In general, the more the better.

Programs typically differentiate between two positions with a precision of approximately 1/100 of a pawn. It turns out that the greater the precision, the more inefficient the search, and thus unless such a precision justifies itself, the programmers would have chosen less. A tree in which all positions have only one of two values corresponding to a victory or loss would be searched very efficiently.

GENERATE(BOARD,PLY) generates moves in a given board position BOARD at ply PLY. The moves are placed on MOVES in column PLY. Generating moves is a costly process and considerable effort is made to optimize this part of the code. It is move generation that has been the primary purpose of special-purpose chess hardware.

SUCCESSOR(BOARD,MOVE) and **PREDECESSOR(BOARD,MOVE)** are used to construct the successor and predecessor of a board position BOARD, respectively, when move MOVE is made or taken back. These functions require only a few lines of code.

SET_PC(MOVE,PLY) saves good moves in the principal continuation array PC in row PLY. Whenever a good move is found at some ply, say PLY, it is placed in PC(PLY,PLY) and the continuation in row PLY+1 is moved up, column for column, to row PLY.

7.3. The depth-first minimax search of a tree. Figure 11 illustrates a depth-first minimax search of a game tree. It shows a tree of depth four with twelve terminal positions. The scores of the terminal positions are shown to the right of the positions. Scores backed up to nonterminal positions are also shown. Arrows show the path of the search. It is a top-down traversal of the tree: terminal positions are encountered from the top of the page down to the bottom. Scores are brought down to each position from two levels higher in the tree and are backed up to each position as shown. The root is eventually assigned a score of 20 and the principal continuation, the line of play that the search concludes is best for each side, is a-c-e-d as the bold line indicates. Figure 12 shows how moves are placed in the array PC as search is carried out. Fourteen calls to SET_PC are made. The nineth call places the continuation a-c-e-d to the top row where it remains.

8. The alpha-beta algorithm

From Figure 7, it should be clear that a program cannot carry out a minimax search to the desired depths in the 180 seconds, on average, allotted to a computer to make a move. The alpha-beta algorithm, however, comes to our rescue! It says, referring to Figure 13a, that if one move, say move C, in position P has been found to refute its predecessor, say move B, it is unnecessary to search any other reply, say move D, in position P. A cutoff of search is said to occur at P.

Refutations are categorized as either shallow or deep. The example given in the previous paragraph illustrates a shallow refutation. A deep refutation is illustrated in Figure 13b. In this position, White can play move A which is assumed to return a score of 10. Then search proceeds out to position Q by the move sequence B-C-D-E. Position Q is assigned a score of 2 by the scoring function. This is less than the score currently assigned to the root, implying that move E is a refutation of move D, and that no other move in position P need be searched. Move E leading to position Q is said to be a deep refutation.

Only minor modifications must be made to the minimax algorithm to incorporate the idea of refutations and the cutoffs they cause. This modified minimax algorithm takes the name of the alpha-beta algorithm and is shown in Figure 14. Note that the pseudo-C code in Figure 14 is identical to that in Figure 9 except for the four additional lines following the label ALPHA_BETA. When the game tree presented in Figure 11 is searched with the alpha-beta algorithm as shown in Figure 15, three moves are found to be refutations.

The effectiveness of the alpha-beta algorithm depends on the order in which moves are searched at each position in the tree. If the best move is always searched first at each node,

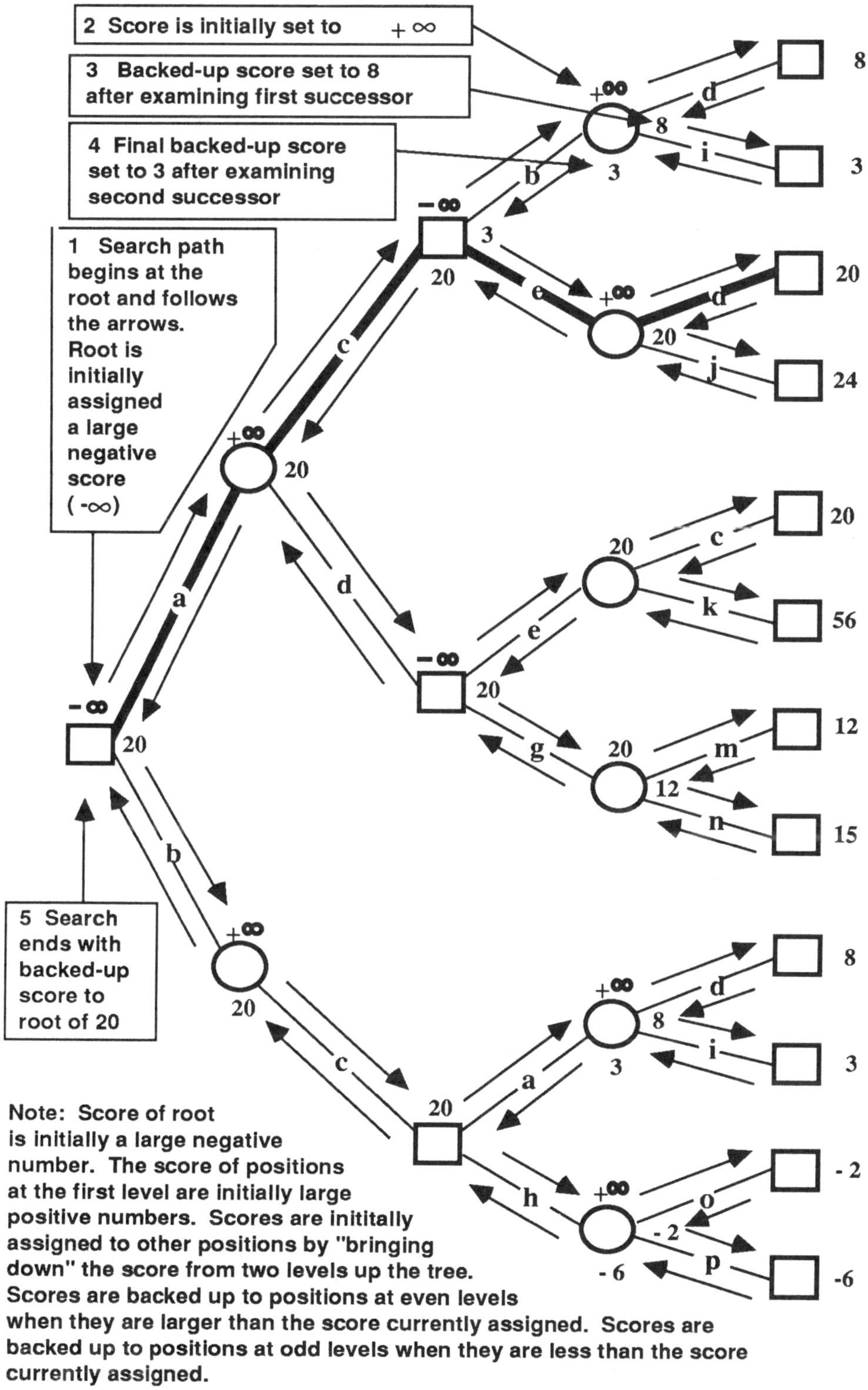

Figure 11. The minimax search of a game tree

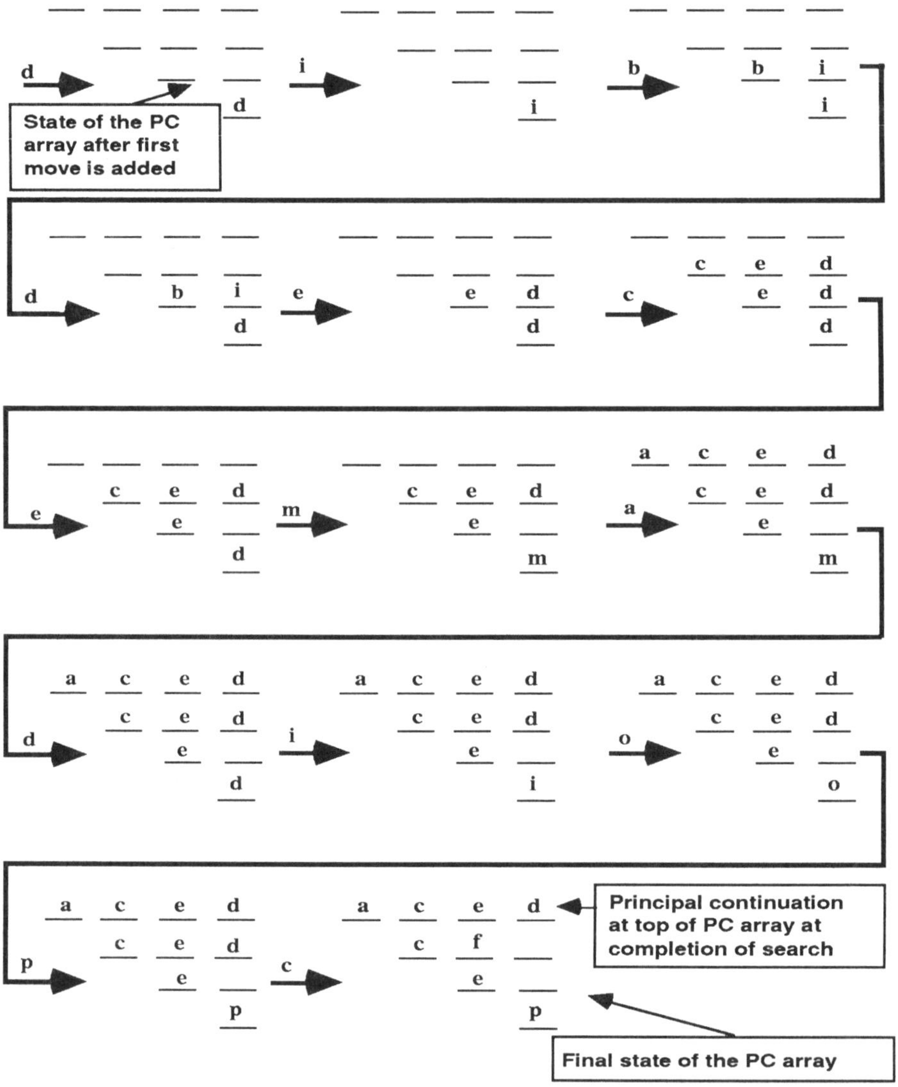

Figure 12. Forming the principal continuation in the PC array

the maximum number of refutations occur and the minimum number of positions are scored. Analysis will show that in a tree with F moves in each position searched to a depth D, the minimum number of terminal positions is:

(2a) $2F^{D/2} - 1$ for D even

(2b) $F^{(D+1)/2} + F^{(D-1)/2} - 1$ for D odd

For D = 12, 13 and 14 and for F = 30, the minimum number of positions that must be scored is given in Figure 16 where approximations have been introduced to keep numbers round.

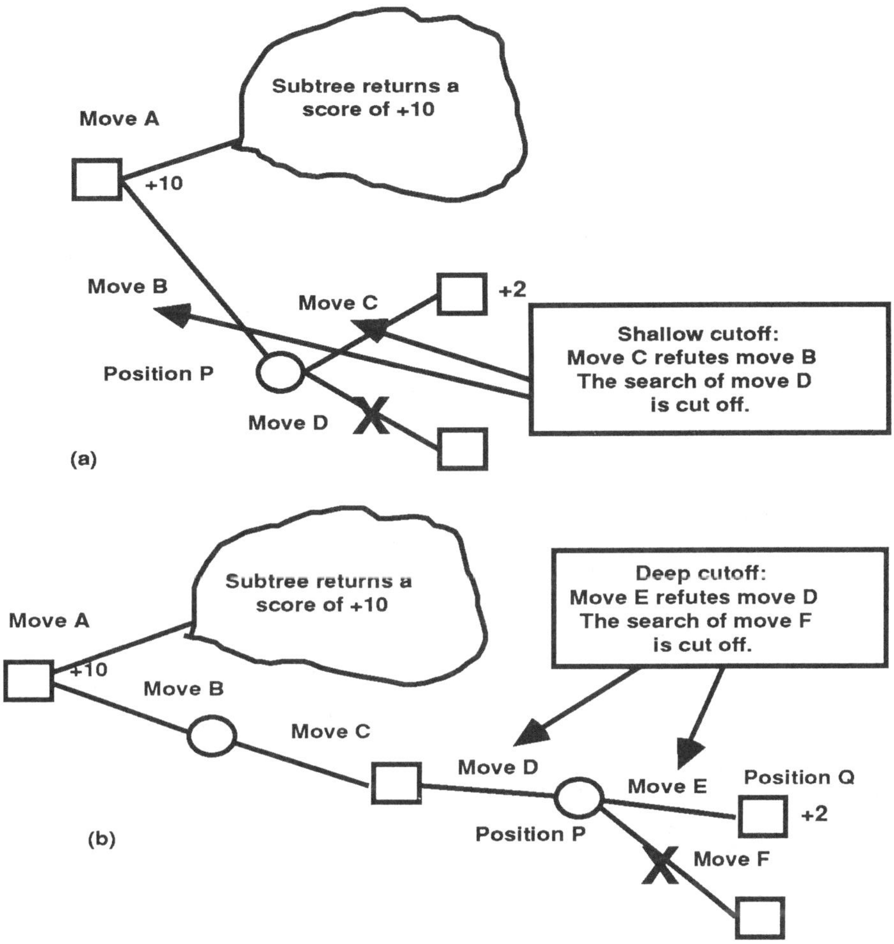

Figure 13. (a) Partially-drawn game tree showing shallow alpha-beta cutoff and (b) partially-drawn game tree showing deep alpha-beta cutoff.

9 Hardware for chess: special-purpose circuits and multiprocessing systems

By using a combination of special-purpose circuitry for generating moves at high speeds and by using a large multiprocessing system, we will see that it is possible to search trees with the number of terminal positions indicated in Figure 16 in the 180 seconds allotted.

9.1. Special-purpose chess circuits. A number of special-purpose chess-playing logic circuits have been developed. The most notable are Thompson's BELLE (120,000 positions/sec.) [7], Ebeling's HITECH (200,000 positions/sec.) [18,19] and Hsu's DEEP THOUGHT and now DEEP BLUE (700,000 positions/sec.) [16,17]. These circuits permit moves to be generated quickly at each node. HITECH is also able to compute the components of its scoring function in parallel. This feature allows additional components to be added to HITECH's evaluation function without increasing the time necessary to evaluate the position. While data on Hsu's newest chip is not yet available, it may evaluate as many as 2,000,000 positions per second.

```
/* DATA STRUCTURES  AND FUNCTIONS ARE THE                          */
/* SAME AS FOR MINIMAX ALGORITHM (SEE FIGURE 8)                    */

/* INITIALIZE:  ENTER POSITION IN BOARD(8,8), SET MAXIMUM SEARCH        */
/* DEPTH DMAX.  SET INITIAL VALUES OF SCORE(-2) AND SCORE(-1)           */
/* TO EFFECTIVELY MINUS AND PLUS INFINITY RESPECTIVELY                  */
PLY = 0;  SCORE(-1) = +100000;   SCORE(-2) = -100000;

/* A NEW POSITION; AT MAXIMUM DEPTH, GO TO SCORE POSITION               */
NEW_POSITION:
IF(PLY == DMAX)  GOTO AT_DMAX;

/*  OTHERWISE, GENERATE MOVES, PLACE THEM ON MOVESLIST, BRING */
/* DOWN THE SCORE FROM TWO LEVELS HIGHER IN THE TREE, AND SET */
/* THE MOVE POINTER AT DEPTH "PLY" TO THE FIRST MOVE                    */
GENERATE(BOARD,PLY);SCORE(PLY)  = SCORE(PLY - 2);MP(PLY)  = 0;

/* MOVE FORWARD TO SUCCESSOR POSITION */
ADVANCE:
BOARD = SUCCESSOR(BOARD,MOVES(MP(PLY++),PLY));   GOTO NEW_POSITION;

AT_DMAX:
SCORE(PLY) = EVALUATE(BOARD);

/* MINIMAX NOW:  IF MOVE IS GOOD, SAVE IN PC ARRAY, BACK UP SCORE */
MINIMAX:
IF(((PLY IS EVEN) AND (SCORE(PLY) < SCORE(PLY - 1)) OR
        ((PLY IS ODD) AND (SCORE(PLY) > SCORE(PLY - 1)) {
                SET_PC(MOVES(MP(PLY)),PLY);}

/* BACK UP TO PREDECESSOR POSITION.*/
BACKUP1:
BOARD = PREDECESSOR(BOARD,MOVES(MP(--PLY),PLY));

/* CHECK FOR ALPHA-BETA CUTOFF  */
ALPHA-BETA:
IF(((PLY is EVEN) and (SCORE(PLY) > SCORE(PLY - 1)) or
        ((PLY is ODD) and (SCORE(PLY) < SCORE(PLY - 1)) {

/* CUTOFF OCCURED; BACK UP TO PREDECESSOR  */
        BACKUP2:
        P = PREDECESSOR(P,MOVES(MP(--PLY),PLY));}

/* SEE IF MORE MOVES IN THIS POSITION.  IF SO GO TO MINIMAX. */
IF(MOVES(MP(PLY) + 1,PLY) == 0) {
        IF(PLY == 0) EXIT; ELSE GOTO MINIMAX;}

/* THERE ARE MORE MOVE.  GET NEXT ONE, GO TO NEW POSITION */
MP(PLY)++; BOARD = SUCCESSOR(BOARD,MOVES(MP(PLY++),PLY));
GOTO NEW_POSITION;
```

Figure 14. Pseudo-C version of the alpha-beta algorithm

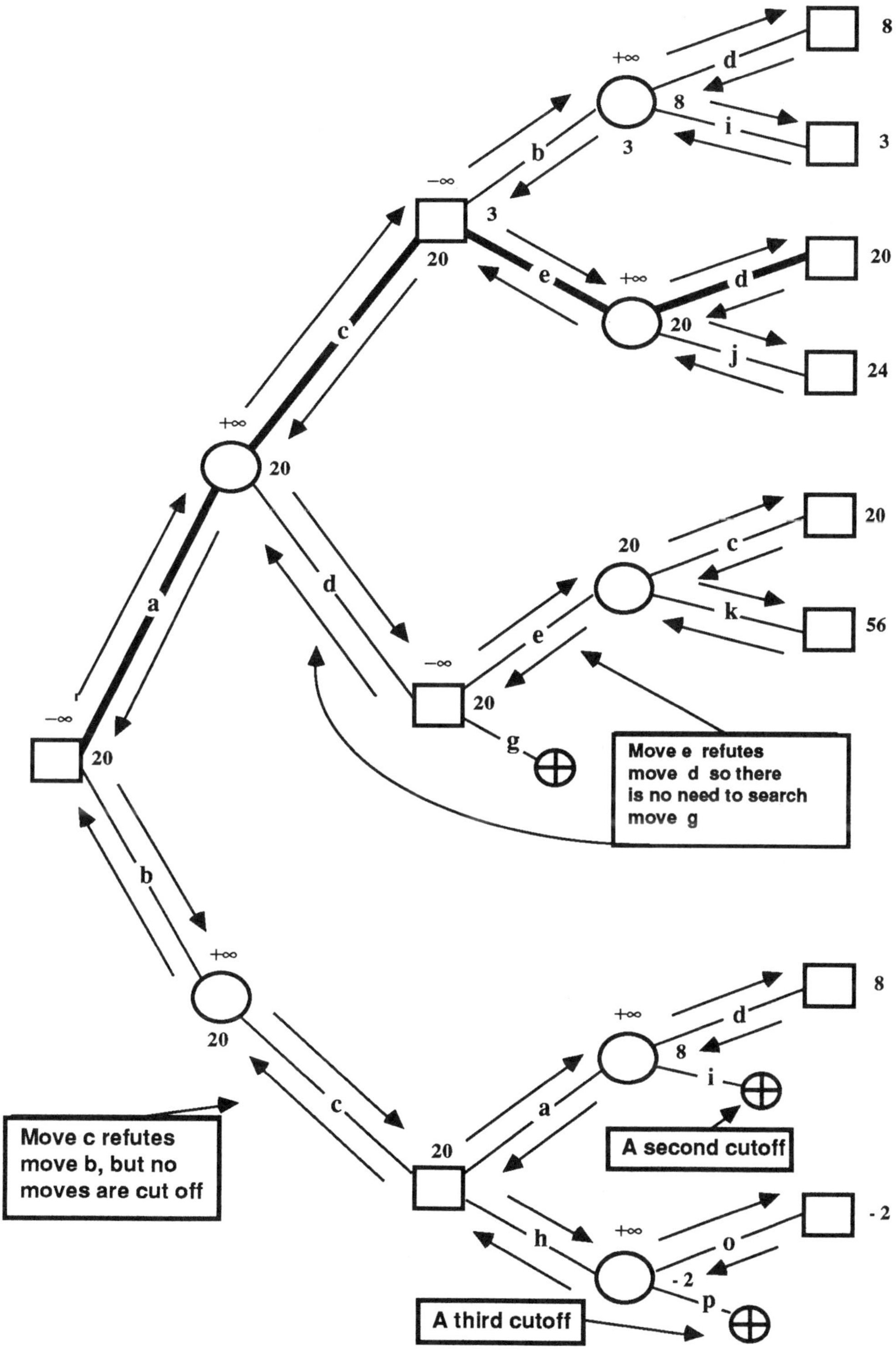

Figure 15. Alpha-beta search of ongoing example

9.2. Parallel search. Multiprocessors have been used by chess-playing computers since 1981 when OSTRICH [14] competed in an ACM tournament using five processors. A year later, it used eight. CRAY BLITZ [11,12], SUN PHOENIX, CHESS CHALLENGER, WAYCOOL, ZUGSWANG [17], STARTECH and later STAR SOCRATES [18] and DEEP BLUE [19] have all competed in tournaments on multiprocessing systems.

Search Depth (Plies)	Minimum number of terminal positions in an alpha-beta search		
12	$\sim 2 \times 30^6$	$= 2 \times 10^9$	=2,000,000,000
13	$\sim 30^7 + 30^6$	$= 3 \times 10^{10}$	= 30,000,000,000
14	$\sim 2 \times 30^7$	$= 6 \times 10^{10}$	= 60,000,000,000

Figure 16. Minimum number of terminal positions scored in an alpha beta search

These systems decompose the tree and attempt to keep all processors busy with useful work. Most programs use the principal variation splitting algorithm or variations of it to divide up the tree. This algorithm essentially finishes the search of the principal continuation found on the previous iteration as quickly as possible and then divides up search of the remainder of the tree. A speedup of approximately 11 on 16-processor systems has been typical. Recently parallel versions of STAR SOCRATES have achieved significant speedups running on yet larger systems. They have obtained speedups of the order of 50 on a 250-processor system and even more on a 1836-processor Paragon system. The newest version of DEEP BLUE is expected to run on a large number of computers as well, and let us assume that it will achieve a speedup of 100.

Search Depth (Plies)	Minimum number of terminal positions	Search time @ 200,000,000 positions/sec.
12	2,000,000,000	10 sec
13	30,000,000,000	150 sec
14	60,000,000,000	300 sec

Figure 17. The relation between search depth, the minimum number of positions scored and search time

9.3. Combining chess circuitry and parallel search. Thus, a system capable of evaluating 2,000,000 positions per second per processor and containing 1000 processors that yield a 100-fold speedup should soon be ready to take on the champion. This system will be capable of processing 200,000,000 positions per second. In Figure 17, it can be seen that when searching trees at this rate and for brute-force searches of 12, 13 and 14 plies, the minimum time required is 10, 150 and 300 seconds, respectively. It thus looks quite feasible to carry out alpha-beta searches of 12 and 13 plies within the allotted time of 180 seconds per move, while 14 ply searches may require a bit of squeezing.

10 But it's not so easy!

The above analysis, however, neglects two important points: alpha-beta search is usually not optimal, and extended search, that is, search beyond the normal maximum search depth, is necessary and accounts for a significant part of the total search time. Moreover, setting DMAX appropriately for a depth-first search is very difficult. The computer searches more than the minimum number of positions when carrying out an alpha-beta search because move ordering at each position is not optimal. Extended search is necessary to follow certain tactical moves such as checks and captures out to their resolution. Slate indicated that his program CHESS 4.0 spent approximately 50% of its time in extended search [20]. The combination of these two factors implies that the times in Figure 17 are underestimates, and may, in fact, underestimate the actual time by a factor of at least 4! Moreover, as said previously, there is also the serious problem in using depth-first search: setting the appropriate depth turns out to be an extremely difficult problem.

10.1 Iteratively-deepening search solves the problem of setting the depth of search. The last of these problems, properly setting the depth of search was solved in 1975 when Slate and Atkin introduced iteratively-deepening depth-first search into their program CHESS 4.5. Rather than attempting to set DMAX at the beginning of search, they programmed CHESS 4.5 to carry out a sequence of depth-first searches, each search being one ply deeper than the previous. The first few searches, when DMAX was 1, 2, and 3 go very fast, of course, while the latter ones take most of the time. Each successively deeper search provides information to the next search that make that search proceed more efficiently. The n-th depth-first search is call the n-th iteration and it returns a principal continuation of length at least n. This continuation is searched first on the next iteration. In addition, a large transposition table is used to keep information about positions encountered and this information is also used on the next iteration. The main strength of this technique is that it can be stopped at any time and the best move found on either the current iteration or on the previous iteration is available for selection. The introduction of iteratively-deepening depth-first search into Slate's program raised the program's level of play from Class B to Expert. It first was used in 1976 in a California tournament, the Paul Masson American Chess Classic, at which wine was available to the participants; the computer's opponents were quick to seize upon the obvious excuse for their defeats. Nevertheless, CHESS 4.5 captured the "B" section title and several months later, won the Minnesota State Championship thus showing that its California success was no fluke. A decade later, the more general artificial intelligence community discovered iteratively-deepening depth-first search could be applied to other problems including automated theorem proving [21,22] as depicted in Figure 18.

10.2 Extended search cannot be avoided. Every strong program incorporates extended search. When designing a chess program, the programmer builds in various criteria for terminating search at each position in the tree. Most programs search all moves to a fixed depth: on the n-th iteration, all moves are searched to a depth of n plies. Moves that are checks and captures are usually searched deeper yet as are pawn advances to the 6th, 7th and 8th ranks. Before the late 1970s, many programs used various heuristics for "forward pruning" but they generally proved unreliable. AWIT was one of the last programs to use extensive forward pruning, and while Marsland invested considerable effort in refining his heuristics and while his program had some success — including finishing second at the 1983 World Championship — this path has received less attention recently.

DEEP BLUE uses what its programmers call the singular extension heuristic. A move in a position is called singular if it is found much better than all the other moves. Whenever such a move is found and if it is likely to affect the outcome of the search if its value changes,

Case of the Missing Kid..........

Look around the yard	Small fast search
Look around the neighborhood	↓
Look around the city	
Look around the country	
Look around the world	Large slow search

Save clues from one iteration to the next to speed up the search.

Iterative deepening depth-first search in the context of chess

Look at all moves one level into the tree

Look at all moves two levels into the tree

. . . .

Look at all moves n levels into the tree

Stop when time runs out

Iterative deepening depth-first search in the context of theorem proving

Look for a proof in one step

Look for a proof in two steps

. . . .

Look for a proof in n steps

Figure 10. Iteratively-deepening depth-first search

the position arising from the move is re-searched one level deeper than previously. The programmers indicate that the added search time is well justified.

At terminal positions, programs use a "swap-off" routine that attempts to carry out an exchange of all pieces that can be exchanged without actually carrying out a search. Some programs simply carry out a swap-off on the square to which the last move was made. This routine provides a cheap and usually improved score for terminal positions.

10.3 Move ordering, windows and transposition tables solve the first problem. Although non-optimal alpha-beta search increases the times in Figure 17, the use of move-ordering heuristics and windowing techniques as well as the use of a transposition table more than compensate for this. By using move-ordering heuristics and windowing techniques, near-optimal alpha-beta search is achieved. The use of a transposition table provides a large speedup in many cases.

Windows were used by BELLE in the late 1970s and are a standard feature of all leading programs today. When using windows, a program begins each iteration by assuming the score that it expects to find will be very near the score found on the previous iteration. It then carries out a search by placing a "window" about the expected score, and this window will cause those parts of the tree with scores outside the window to be cut off. The danger is that if the window is too narrow, the search will fail to find the optimal continuation. In this case, the search must be repeated with a wider window. There are many variations on this basic strategy, and they result in searches that are near alpha-beta optimal.

Crucial to the success of alpha-beta search is effective move ordering at each node in the tree. Move generation can be viewed as a two-stage process: (1) place all legal moves in the position under consideration on a list, and (2) order the moves on the list, placing those that appear best at or near the top. These two steps are generally integrated. Many heuristics are used to develop this ordering and they vary widely from one program to another. They can be classified as static or dynamic and as game-dependent or game-independent. A move-ordering heuristic is static if it is used to order the moves at a node when they are generated. It is dynamic if it is used to reorder moves as they are being searched. For example, if one of the moves in position P at level n can also be made at some position deeper in the tree and is found to be a very good move at that deeper position, then when search returns to P, it can be reordered to near the head of the list of moves if it has not already been searched. Game-dependent heuristics used for chess include placing captures and checks high on the list. Some programs also place pawn moves deep in the opponent's territory high on the list.

The killer heuristic was one of the first game-independent heuristics proposed. It was used in Gillogly's TECH in 1972. When a move is found to be a refutation at ply k, it is placed on a list of "killer moves" for that ply. Let KILLER_LIST(k) denote this list. There is typically one such list for every ply of the search tree. When moves are generated at another position at ply k, KILLER_LIST(k) is scanned for a match with one of the moves, and if a match is found that move is ordered to or near the top of the list of moves.

Many variations on this basic strategy are used. The number of moves on each killer list varies from one program to another. Some programs keep track of how often each move on the list causes a refutation and sorts the list in descending order. If the program attempts to add a move to a list that is full, it will throw away the least successful move and replace it with the most recent refutation. It is unnecessary to keep one list for each level in the tree; two separate lists can be kept, one for White and one for Black. The lists can also record with each refutation the move refuted, and this information can be used when sorting moves.

In the next section, the use of transposition tables will be considered. They can be used to provide near optimal move ordering when coupled with iteratively-deepening search.

11 Transposition tables

Figure 19 shows two continuations that can be played from the initial game position. Observe that moves 1 d4 d5 2 e4 lead to the same position, denoted T, as do moves 1 e4 d5 2 d4. In this case, an identical position arises as a result of a transposition of White's moves. Other sequences of moves such as 1 d4 d6 2 e4 d5 also lead to the same configuration of pieces but in this case, it is White's turn and the position cannot be considered identical. For two positions to be identical, they must have pieces on identical squares and, in addition, they must have identical castling rights, en passant options and the same player on the move. Actually to be 100% identical, it is also necessary to take into account the number of moves since the last capture or pawn advance.

Now suppose the first time position T is searched, it is assigned a score either by backing up a score to it or by the scoring function. Then when T is arrived at through 1 e4 d5 2 d4, it is unnecessary to search beyond T or even score T if the results of the first examination were saved and provide sufficient information. Chess programs use transposition tables, often called hash tables, to save this information. When the computer arrives at each position, it searches the transposition table to see whether this position was previously searched. If it was and if the information saved in the transposition table is sufficient (sufficiency is discussed shortly) then this position need not be searched again. It is considered a terminal position and assigned the score found in the transposition table.

When search of a position in the tree is complete, the transposition table is searched for a match. If no match is found, a new entry is made in the transposition table; if the position is found, the information in the table is updated if appropriate.

In somewhat more rigorous terms, when the computer completes the search of some position P, it knows the following information about P:

(1) The score of P, denoted SCORE(P). This value is either exact or an upper or lower bound,
(2) An indication whether the score is exact or an upper or lower bound, denoted by

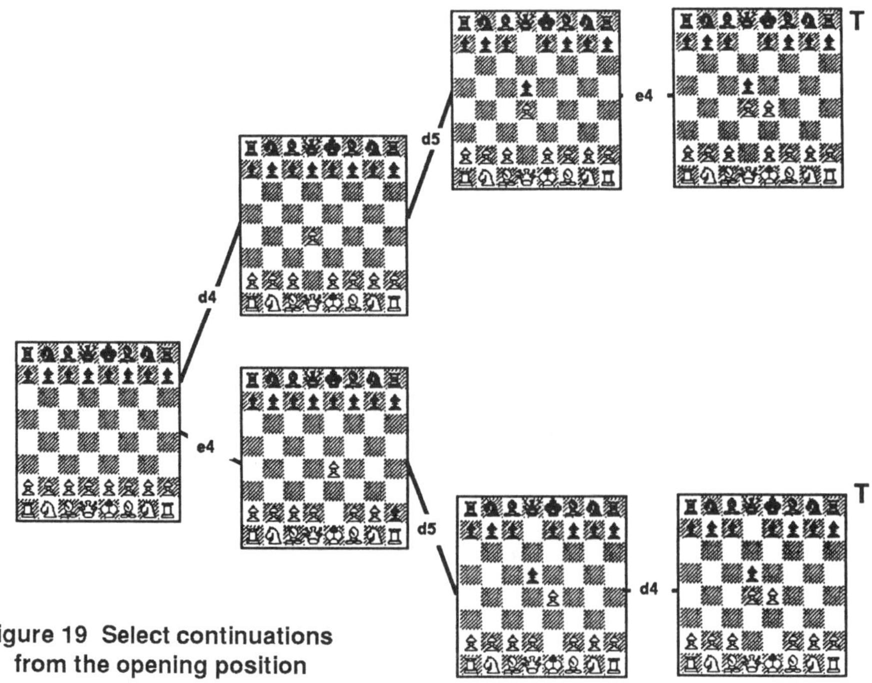

Figure 19 Select continuations from the opening position

BOUND_SCORE(P),
(3) The depth in the tree of P, denoted by DEPTH(P),
(4) The best move to make at P, denoted BEST_MOVE(P),
(5) The hash code of P, denoted HASH_CODE(P). The hash code of P is an encoding of the information used to describe P.

The computer now examines the transposition table to see whether it has previously encountered P. If it has, and if the new information about P is better than that currently stored, the entry in the transposition table is updated. For example, it is possible that BEST_MOVE(P) and SCORE(P) change values and that DEPTH(P) increases. In this case the new move and score are more accurate than the old values.

When the computer arrives at a position, say Q, the transposition table is searched for a match. If successful and if the following two conditions are met by Q, Q is considered terminal and assigned the score recorded with the entry:

(1) DEPTH(Q) ≥ DEPTH(P),
(2) The score in the table is exact, or if not exact, the bound on the score is sufficient to cause the move leading to Q to be inferior to some other choice.

If these two conditions are not satisfied, the computer either scores Q or searches its successors. The move found best the last time Q was searched is in the transposition table and should be searched first on this try.

Figure 20 illustrates various ways that a transposition table can assist during a search. In this contrived example, position T appears five times. When the search of the first appearance of T is completed, the computer knows that is has a score of at most 36, — note that move x refutes move z so that the exact score of T, that is 32, was never determined — that DEPTH(T) is 3, and that BEST_MOVE(T) is x. When search arrives at T the second time, T is found in the transposition table with an upper bound on its score of 36 and since move u leads to a score of 50, search can be terminated at this second appearance. When search arrives at T the third time, the bound of 36 is insufficient to terminate search at T and this time its successors must be searched. When search of the third T is complete, an exact score of 32 is assigned to it. BEST_MOVE(T), which had been x, is replaced with y. When search arrives at T the fourth time, it is at ply 1 in the tree, too shallow to use the information obtained previously to terminate search. If it were used, not all lines in the tree would have been searched to a depth of 4. In particular, the score of this final occurrence of T would be based on a one ply search, an thus the score of the root of the tree would be based on only a two-ply search. After the fourth T has been searched, it will be assigned a score of 36. It is left for the reader to see that search can be terminated at T on its fifth appearance. It is also left for the reader to consider the implications if position W happened to have a score of 24 instead of the 36 indicated.

Figure 21 show the effect of using a transposition table on our continuing example. Moves that transpose are assumed to lead to the same position. For example, move sequence a-c-b leads to the same position as does b-c-a. Two positions, one corresponding to the position at the end of move sequence a-d-e-c and one corresponding to the position at the end of move sequence b-c-a, were found in the transposition table with useful information. In the first case, the information provided a score for the position and in the second, it provided both a score and allowed search to be terminated there.

While the two contrived examples presented in Figures 20 and 21 only show several transposition table hits, in the typical chess tree, there are many hits and search is sped up

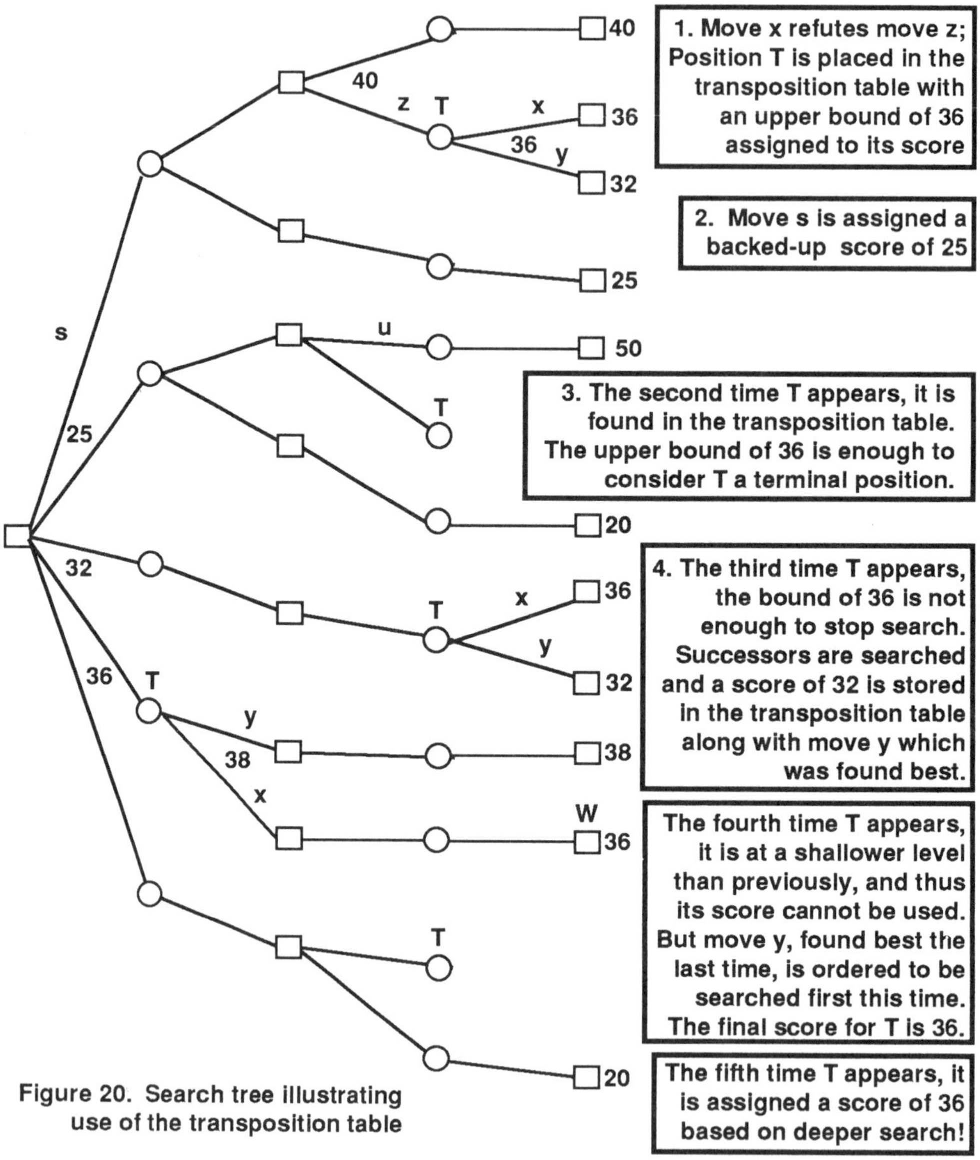

Figure 20. Search tree illustrating use of the transposition table

considerably. In deep endgames, transposition tables are extremely effective. The position shown in Figure 22 cannot be solved without transposition tables; a program with transposition tables can find the correct move in a matter of seconds. In this position, White, to move and win, has only three moves. To each of these moves, Black has five replies. A two-ply search will thus find 15 terminal positions. A three-ply search will find 90 terminal positions but there will only be 45 different ones. It is left for the reader to confirm that an eight-ply search will find only 204 different positions. To see that Ka1b1 is the best move, the program must realize that after 1 Kb1 Kb7 2 Kc1 Kc7 3 Kd1 Kd7 4 Kc2 Kd8 5 Kc3 Kc7 6 Kd3 Black cannot maintain distant opposition. White can eventually capture the pawn on either a5 or f5 and then push a pawn to promotion. To see this, however, requires a very deep search, but within the capabilities of a program using a transposition table!

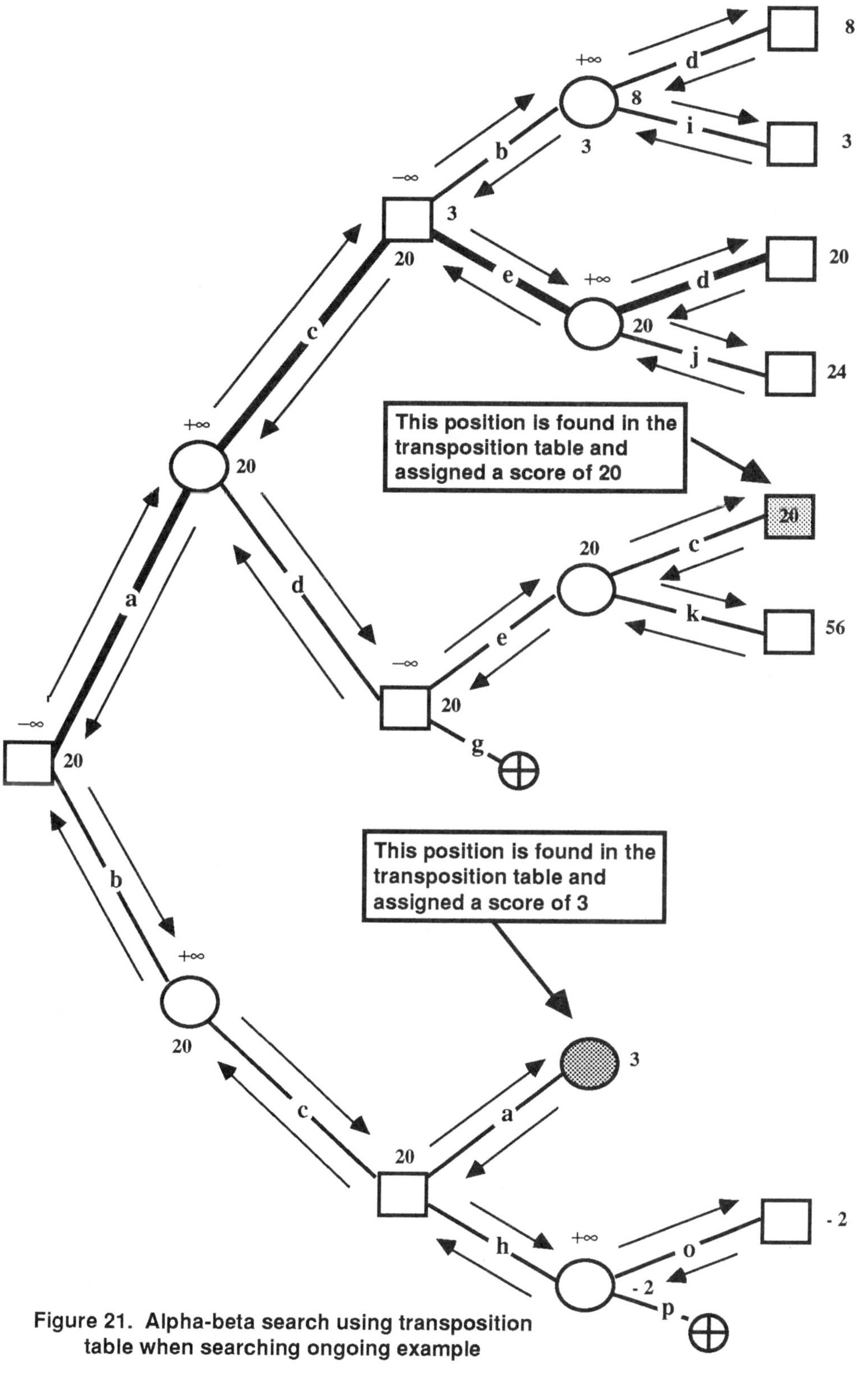

Figure 21. Alpha-beta search using transposition table when searching ongoing example

11.1 Obtaining a hash code for a chess position

When storing information about a position in a transposition table, rather than storing a description of the position itself, a hash code for the position is stored. To uniquely specify a chess position, at least 132 bits are necessary, and this can be done using a Huffman code [23]. Most chess programs use far fewer bits, and thus the possibility exists of having two positions assigned the same hash code. The probability of this occurring is very small when the number of bits is over 48 or so.

The hash code of a position, in addition to being stored along with the other information describing the position, is used to tell the computer where to store the information. Most computers use a transposition table in which the number of entries is a power of 2. Let 2^k denote the number of entries in the table. Then, most typically, the least significant k bits of the hash code are used as the address at which the information about a position is stored. For example, suppose some position has a 16-bit hash code of 0001100011000110, and suppose there are 4K entries in the transposition table. Then the information about this position would be stored in entry 100011000110.

Depth	Search Space	Number of different positions
1	3	3
2	15	3x5 =15
3	90	9x5 = 45
4	405	9x8 = 72
5	~2,000	13x8 = 112
6	~10,000	13x10 = 140
7	~50,000	17x10 = 170
8	~250,000	17x12 = 204
9	~1,250,000	<25x16 ~ 400
10	~6,250,000	<25x25 ~ 625

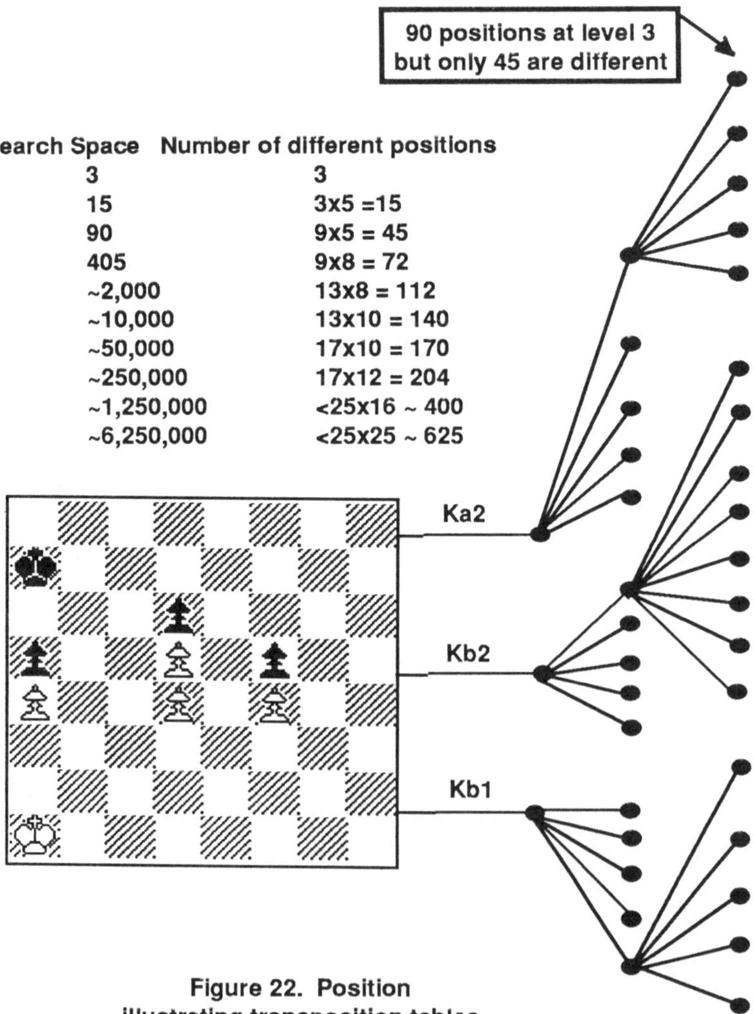

Figure 22. Position
illustrating transposition tables

When searching a tree, it is possible for two different positions to be assigned the same hash code. In this case, a hashing error occurs: the second position is taken to be the same as the first! More often, two different positions may be assigned identical values for their least significant k bits, while the others may be different. In this case, a clash is said to occur, and it is usually resolved most simply by storing the information in the next transposition table entry. Sometimes the next location is also occupied and another choice must be made. A number of tries is often made using a wide variety of strategies.

As the table begins to fill up, and it always does, it becomes necessary to stop entering new positions or to overwrite old ones. Usually, old information is overwritten, and again in this regard, there are many strategies. Often, information entered the longest ago is overwritten, or information least frequently used is overwritten.

Transposition tables in current programs range in size from several hundred thousand to several million entries. Their size is only limited by the size of the computer's memory. There are some interesting design choices that come up when using hash tables in a multi-processing environment [18].

Piece-Square Table

Piece-square	16-bit random number
WK on a1	1001010011110101
WK on b1	1001010001010001
⋮	⋮
WK on c3	0100101000101010
WK on d3	1101000101010111
⋮	⋮
WK on h8	1010010100010111
⋮	⋮
WN on f3	0000100101110101
⋮	⋮
WP on a2	1001001010100101
⋮	⋮
BK on f5	0100111101010001
⋮	⋮
BP on h7	0011010001110101

(a)

Position P

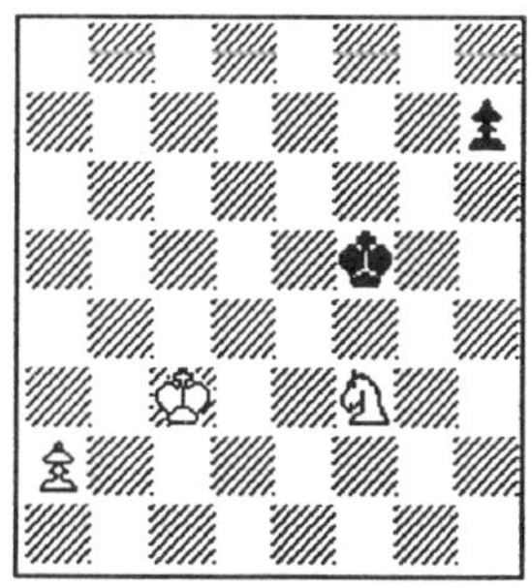

Hash code for this position P as given by piece-square table is:

0100101000101010 (WK on c3)
⊕ 0000100101110101 (WN on f3)
⊕ 1001001010100101 (WP on a2)
⊕ 0100111101010001 (BK on f5)
⊕ 0011010001110101 (BP on h7)
= 1010101011011110

(b)

Figure 23. (a) Piece-Square Table and (b) obtaining the hash code of a position

The technique for assigning a hash code to a position was described by Zobrist [24]. He made use of a piece-square table which held 12 (the number of pieces) times 64 (the number of squares on the board) random numbers. The entries in this table are random numbers, and they are generated before the program begins search. CRAY BLITZ uses 64-bit random numbers, a convenient number to use on the Cray. Based on the entries in the piece-square table, the hash code for a position is determined by a hashing function. It exclusive-ors the random numbers assigned to the appropriate piece-squares. For example, suppose the piece-square table contains the numbers shown in Figure 23a. The position in Figure 23b would then be assigned a hash code by forming the exclusive-or of the five numbers in the piece-square table corresponding to WK on c3, WN on f3, WP on a2 BK on f5 and BP on h7. (We omit considerations related to turn, castling, and en passant.)

The elegance of this hashing function is that given the hash code of a position it is very simple to compute the hash code of a successor. If a move is a transfer of a piece to an open square, it is necessary to carry out two exclusive-or operations: the first removes the piece from its original square and the second places the piece on its destination square. To remove

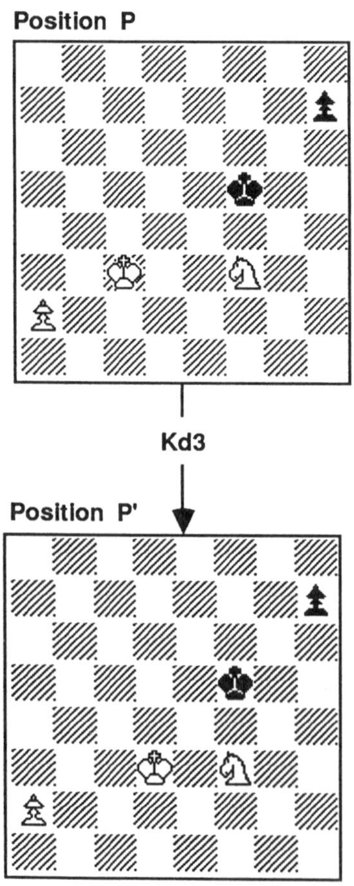

Hash code for this position P as given by the piece-square table is: 1010101011011110

Hash code for successor P' is determined by forming the exclusive-or of the hash code of the predecessor position with the piece-square entries for a White King on square c3 and a White King on square d3. That is:

HASH_CODE(P') =

1010101011011110 (HASH_CODE(P))

⊕ 0100101000101010 (WK on c3)

⊕ 1101000101010111 (WK on d3)

= 0011000110100011

Figure 24. Obtaining the hash code of the successor of a position

a piece from a square, it is only necessary to exclusive-or the original hash code of the position with the entry in the piece-square table corresponding to the original piece and square. To place the piece on the destination square, it is again only necessary to exclusive-or the entry in the piece-square table corresponding to the destination piece-square. Thus two exclusive-or operations are necessary to obtain the hash code of a successor position when given the hash code of the original position. Capturing moves, of course, require three exclusive-or operations.

Figure 24 illustrates how to obtain the hash code of the successor, P', of the position P when Kd3 is played. The new hash code is obtained by forming the exclusive-or of the hash code of the original position with the entries in the piece-square table for WK-c3 and WK-d3.

Hash tables are used in some chess programs to store information other than that about the scores of positions. Some computers hash the value found by the scoring function for each pawn structure found during the search. When the same pawn configuration arises later, the pawn hash table will have its score available. In general, the calculation of the pawn structure component of the scoring function is quite extensive and by using a hash table, significant savings in time can result.

12 Thinking on the opponent's time gives a 50% speedup

Computers gain a speedup of approximately 50% by thinking on the opponent's time. They assume the opponent will play the second move on the principal continuation and then they go on to calculate a reply. If the expected move is made, the computer can then decide whether to continue searching or to stop and save time for another move. Computers correctly guess their opponent's move approximately 50% of the time.

13 Saving time by using the opening book add 33% more speedup

Moves made from an opening book save time for later moves. If the first ten moves are made from this book, then the next 30 moves, the most critical moves of the game typically, can take an extra 33% more time. The combined effect of thinking on the opponent's time and using the book for ten moves results in doubling the amount of time a computer has available for each of the moves from 11 through 40.

14 Summarizing these factors

In Figure 17, the minimum number of terminal positions that must be scored by an alpha-beta search was presented. Assuming terminal positions are searched at the rates indicated, the time required to carry out 12, 13 and 14 ply searches are given. In Section 10, it was pointed out that these times are overly optimistic because: (1) alpha-beta search is not optimal and (2) extended search is necessary.

In Section 10.3, it was pointed out that various techniques could be used to achieve near-optimal move ordering. Further, while extended search slows down the search, the use of other techniques compensates for this. In particular, transposition tables greatly speed the search of many positions. Thinking on the opponent's time and using moves from the opening book also help. In summary, it is reasonable to assume that a program capable of searching 200,000,000 positions per second will be able to search to depths indicated in Table 17 in the times indicated in spite of the problems pointed out in the previous paragraph. A computer searching to these depths should make a match with Kasparov most interesting!

15 Additional reading

Someone interested in more reading material can find it in Marsland and Schaeffer's Computers, Chess and Long Range Planning [25] and Levy and Newborn's How Computers Play Chess [26]. The International Computer Chess Association Journal is required reading of those with serious long-term interests [27]. Advances in Computer Chess has seven volumes filled with important papers [28].

16. References

[1] Thompson, K., Retrograde analysis of certain endgames, ICCA Journal, Vol. 9, No. 3, pp. 131-139, 1986.

[2] Stiller, L. B., Parallel analysis of certain endgames, ICCA Journal, Vol. 12, No. 2, pp. 55-64, 1989.

[3] Karlsson, T., and Grottling, G., The Swedish Rating List, ICCA Journal, Vol. 18, No. 1, p. 60, March 1995.

[4] Schulz, A, FRITZ3 and the Grandmasters, ICCA Journal, Vol. 18, No. 1, pp. 45-48, March 1995.

[5] Newborn, M., Computer chess: recent progress and future expectations, Proc. Jerusalem Conference on Information Technology, North-Holland, pp. 189-192, 1978.

[6] Thompson, K., Computer chess strength, Advances in Computer Chess, (M. R. B. Clarke, Ed.), Pergamon Press, Vol. 3, pp. 55-56, 1982.

[7] Condon, J. H., and Thompson, K., Belle, Chess Skill in Man and Machine, 2nd Edition, (P. Frey, Ed.), Springer-Verlag, pp. 201-210, 1983.

[8] Newborn, M., A hypothesis concerning the strength of chess programs, ICCA Journal, Vol. 8, No. 4, pp. 209-215, December 1985.

[9] Condon, J. H., and Thompson, K., Belle chess hardware, Advances in Computer Chess 3, (M. R. B. Clarke, Ed.), Pergamon Press, pp. 45-54, 1982.

[10] Ebeling, C., All the Right Moves: A VLSI Architecture for Chess, MIT Press, 1987. Originally published as a Ph. D. thesis, Carnegie Mellon University, 1986.

[11] Ebeling, C., and Palay, A., The design and implementation of a VLSI move generator, IEEE 11th Ann. International Symposium on Comp. Arch., Ann Arbor, pp. 74-80, 1984.

[12] Anantharaman, T., Campbell, M., and Hsu, F., Singular extensions: adding selectivity to brute force searching, ICCA Journal, Vol. 11, No. 4, pp. 135-143, December 1988.

[13] Hsu, F., Two million moves/sec CMOS single chip chess move generator, ISSCC Digest of Technical Papers, p. 278, 1987.

[14] Newborn, M., A parallel search chess program, Proceeding of the 1985 Annual Conference of the ACM, pp. 272-277, 1985.

[15] Hyatt, R. M., Suter, B. W., and Nelson, H. L., A parallel alpha-beta tree searching algorithm, Parallel Computing, Vol. 10, No. 3, pp. 299-308, 1989.

[16] Hyatt, R. M., Parallel search on the Cray X-MP/48, ICCA Journal, Vol. 8, No. 2, pp. 96-99, June 1985.

[17] Feldmann, R., Mysliwietz, P., and Monien, B., Game-tree search on a massively parallel system, Advances in Computer Chess 7, (H. J. van den Herik, I. S. Herschberg and J. W. H. M. Uiterwilk, Eds.), Univ. of Limburg, Maastricht, The Netherlands, pp. 203-219, 1993.

[18] Kuszmaul, B., The STARTECH massively parallel chess program, ICCA Journal, Vol. 18, No. 1, pp. 3-19, March 1995.

[19] Hsu, F-h., Large scale parallelization of alpha-beta search, an algorithmic and architectural study with computer chess, TR CMU-CS-90-108, Computer Science Department, Carnegie Mellon University, 1990.

[20] Slate, D. J., and Atkin, L. R., CHESS 4.5 – The Northwestern University chess program, Chess Skill in Man and Machine, (P. Frey, Ed.), Springer-Verlag, pp. 82-118, 1977.

[21] Korf, R., Iteratively-deepening-A*: An optimal admissible tree search, Proceeding of the 9th International Joint Conference on AI, Los Angeles, pp. 1034-1036, 1985.

[22] Stickel, M. E., and Tyson, W. M., An analysis of consecutively bounded depth-first search with applications to automated deduction, Proceeding of the 9th International Joint Conference on Artificial Intelligence, Los Angeles, pp. 1073-1075, 1985.

[23] Knuth, D. E., The Art of Computer Programming, Vol. 1, Fundamental Algorithms, Addison-Wesley, Reading, Mass., 1968.

[24] Zobrist, A. L., A hashing method with applications for game playing, Technical Report 88, Computer Science Department, University of Wisconsin, Madison, Wisc., 1970.

[25] Marsland, T., and Schaeffer, J., Computers, Chess and Cognition, Springer-Verlag, 1990.

[26] Levy, D. N. L., and Newborn, M., How Computers Play Chess, W. H. Freeman, 1991.

[27] van den Herik, H. J., (Ed.) The International Computer Chess Journal, c/o Department of Computer Science, Faculty of General Sciences, University of Limburg, P. O. Box 616, 6200 Maastricht, The Netherlands.

[28] van den Herik, H. J., (Ed.) Advances in Computer Chess, c/o Department of Computer Science, Faculty of General Sciences, University of Limburg, P. O. Box 616, 6200 Maastricht, The Netherlands.

Proceedings of Symposia in Applied Mathematics
Volume 55, 1998

Mathematical Foundations for Probability and Causality

Glenn Shafer

ABSTRACT. Event trees, and more generally, event spaces, can be used to provide a foundation for mathematical probability that includes a systematic understanding of causality. This foundation justifies the use of statistics in causal investigation and provides a rigorous semantics for causal reasoning.

Twentieth-century students of formal reasoning, especially philosophers and mathematicians, have often held causality at arm's length. Their skepticism, embodied by the young Bertrand Russell's denunciation of the law of causality as "a relic of a bygone age," has not yet fully run its course. But causal thinking has always been important in applied statistics and the practical sciences, and in recent years it has enjoyed increasing attention in philosophy, theoretical statistics, and artificial intelligence. In all of these fields, there is now great interest in formalizing and clarifying the idea that an event can change the probability of another event.

Since causality plays out in time, most attempts to formalize its probabilistic aspects have relied, quite naturally, on the best developed formalism for understanding probability in time: the theory of stochastic processes (see, e.g., Eerola 1994 and Spohn 1990). Unfortunately, the resulting theories are cumbersome. In the theory of stochastic processes, all probabilities are explicitly indexed by time, and hence any causal relation must be understood in terms of more basic relations indexed by time. The simple idea of one event changing the probability of another tends, thereby, to lose both its simplicity and its plausibility. For example, the idea that smoking a cigarette raises the risk of a heart attack must be reduced to relations among a legion of events or variables, each representing an act of smoking or a heart attack at some particular time and each supposed to have a precise probability at every earlier time.

This article explores a simpler, more elegant, and more plausible mathematical representation of causality and probability. This representation is based on the event tree, basic to the thinking of Pascal, Huygens, and other pioneers of probability, but long since abandoned in favor of the stronger structures represented by stochastic processes and filtrations. Because they are less structured and more flexible, event trees allow us to represent

---

1991 Mathematics Subject Classification. Primary 60A05; Secondary 62A99, 68T30.

This article has benefitted from the author's conversations with Marty Golumbic, Fred Hoffman, Jan von Plato, and Richard Sherl and from the hospitality of LAFORIA at the University of Pierre and Marie Curie.

causal relations in a straightforward way, without extraneous and implausible assumptions about the extent to which we can probabilize every step in nature's path through the world of possibility. An event tree represents the possibilities for the step-by-step evolution of an observer's knowledge. If that observer is nature, then the steps in the tree are causes. If we add branching probabilities, we obtain a probability tree, which can express nature's limited ability to predict the effects of causes. If we add only expectations that nature has for certain later events or variables, then we obtain a more parsimonious representation of nature's limited ability to predict, a representation liberated from any pretence that nature or anyone else has a complete underlying probabilization indexed by time.

The project of using event and probability trees to understand causality is described most fully in my recent book, *The Art of Causal Conjecture* (MIT Press, 1996). That book emphasizes the causal explanation of statistical structure and begins to explore the role of event trees in causal reasoning in artificial intelligence. This article advances both these enterprises. Its treatment of causal explanation is much less thorough that the treatment in the book, but somewhat simpler. On the side of causal reasoning, it is more ambitious. Starting with the book's abstract concept of an event tree, it develops a new concept, the concept of an event space, which can serve as a transparent semantics for a causal logic.

We begin, in Section 1, with a look at how causal relations in finite probability trees imply statistical associations among events and variables, enabling observed associations to serve as evidence for the causal relations. This connection between causality and statistical association is a cliché, but in the probability-tree setting it acquires, for the first time, a rigorous and detailed expression. Section 2 then explores how a finite event tree can be refined through the addition of more detail and studies the extent to which the causal relations studied in Section 1 are invariant under refinement. Section 3 generalizes the ideas of Section 1 by developing an abstract theory, in which event trees are thought of as partially ordered sets. This abstract approach accommodates infinities and therefore can serve as a foundation for advanced mathematical probability theory. Section 4 shows how probability structure can be added to abstract event trees. This is done using martingales rather than branching probabilities, so that partial probability structures become as natural as complete probability structures. Section 5 analyzes refinement for abstract event trees. Finally, Section 6 develops the idea of an event space, in which events and situations defined at different levels of detail can coexist. Event spaces are sufficiently flexible to serve as a semantics for logics that can be used for probabilistic and causal reasoning, and they therefore provide a framework for the unification of probability modeling and artificial intelligence.

The idea of using branching time as a semantics for a causal or temporal logic is not new. Logics based on branching time have been developed extensively in both philosophy and in computer science (Emerson 1990, Galton 1987, Turner 1984, Vila 1994), and considerable thought has recently been given to combining these logics with probability (Haddawy 1996). But the mathematical representations of branching time used in the models for these logics have the same features that make stochastic processes ill-suited to the study of causality. They represent time explicitly, require unrealistically complete probability assignments, and lend themselves only awkwardly to refinement. The representations developed here, in contrast, allow us to express causal relations without specifying probabilities for the timing of effects, leaving open the extent to which a more refined analysis would reveal regularities in this timing.

The treatment of event spaces in this article is only a beginning. For lack of time and space, I have not begun to explore how partial probability structures can be added to event spaces. Nor have I developed logics based on event spaces. These remain important tasks in the unfinished project of developing and using an understanding of causality based on event trees.

1. Using Probability Trees for Causal Explanation

The idea of a probability tree (an event tree with branching probabilities) can be traced back to the seventeenth-century pioneers of probability theory, especially Christiaan Huygens (see Edwards 1987). A probability tree represents the possibilities for the step-by-step evolution of an observer's knowledge. If that observer is nature, then the steps in the tree represent causes, and the probabilities express nature's limited ability to predict causes and their effects.

In its simplest form, a probability tree is a tree in the sense of graph theory, furnished with branching probabilities, as in Figures 1 and 2. In this section, we show how such trees can be used to define causal relations among events and variables and how evidence for these causal relations can be found in statistical observations.

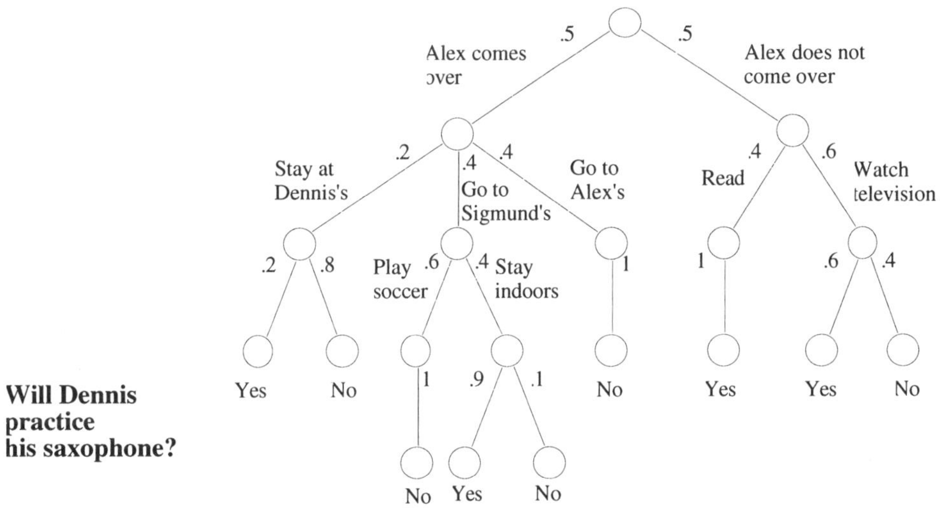

Figure 1 The habits of Dennis and his friends on summer afternoons. The numbers are probabilities for what will happen in each situation (circle).

1.1. Causal Talk. Probability trees for nature provide a framework for a variety of causal talk. We can use Figures 1 and 2 to talk about *singular causation*—why Dennis forgot to practice on a particular occasion or why a particular man is well paid. We can also use them to talk about *average causation*—what makes Dennis likely to practice or why women are poorly paid on average. And we can use them to distinguish between contingent and structural causes.[1] A step or sequence of steps in a tree is a *contingent*

[1]The word "cause" is used here informally. It will not be used as a technical term in this article. This word has so many legitimate uses (in addition to some questionable ones), and it is so often the object of philosophical debates irrelevant to our purposes, that it would be misleading and unnecessarily contentious to assign it a particular technical meaning. (For a contrasting view, see Kutschera 1993.)

cause; Dennis's going to Alex's house is a contingent cause of his forgetting to practice. The habits, preferences, norms, or laws of physics that determine the possibilities and their probabilities are *structural causes*; Dennis fails to practice at Alex's house because he prefers to do other things there.

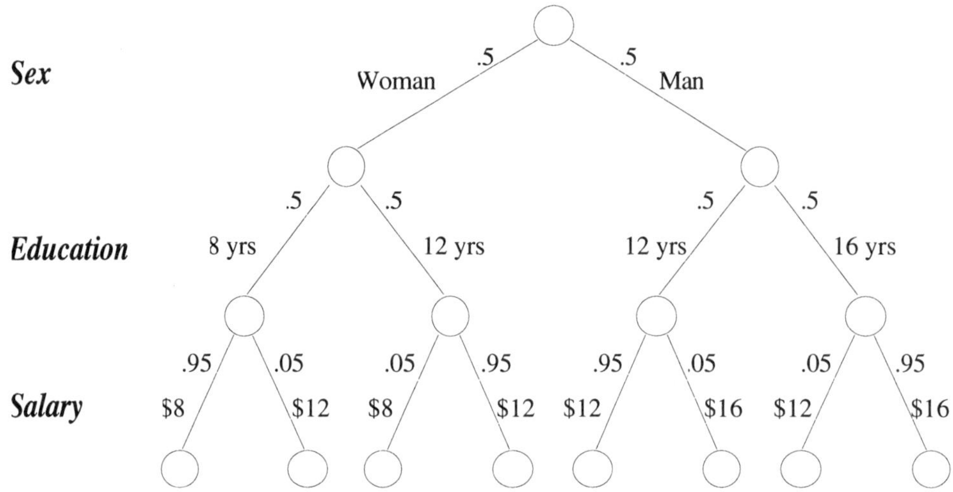

Figure 2 The norms of an imaginary discriminatory society. This society educates men more than women, but there is some overlap. People are usually paid in proportion to their education, but employers may deviate from proportionality for an exceptionally capable or hapless employee, provided they stay within the range of pay customary for the employee's sex.

Most people who have 12 years of education are paid $12, but a few women are paid less and a few men more. Hence women with 12 years of education are paid less on average than men with the same education. Similarly, most people who are paid $12 have 12 years of education, but this group includes a few men with 16 years of education and a few women with only 8. Hence women who are paid $12 have less education on average than men paid the same.[2]

1.2. Probability Talk. It is also easy to talk about probability in a probability tree. The paths through the tree—from the initial situation to the terminal situations—constitute the *sample space*. Following standard practice, we call subsets of the sample space *events*, and we call functions on it *variables*. In Figure 1, the event that Dennis practices is represented by the four paths to terminals situations marked "Yes." In Figure 2, salary is the variable whose value for a path is written next to the last step on the path.

In standard usage, a probability structure is given by a single probability measure on a sample space, but in a probability tree, we have many probability measures, one for each situation in the tree. As Figures 3 and 4 illustrate, each situation has its own probability for every event and its own expected value for every variable. This gives depth to the idea that steps in the tree—steps from one situation to another—are contributing

[2]Situations where discrimination against women is alleged often have similar statistical features. Women are paid less on average than men with the same education but have less education on average than men with the same pay. See Dempster (1988) and Finkelstein and Levin (1990).

causes. Their influence is indicated by changes in the probabilities of events and expected values of variables.

The probability that Dennis practices changes as nature moves through the tree.

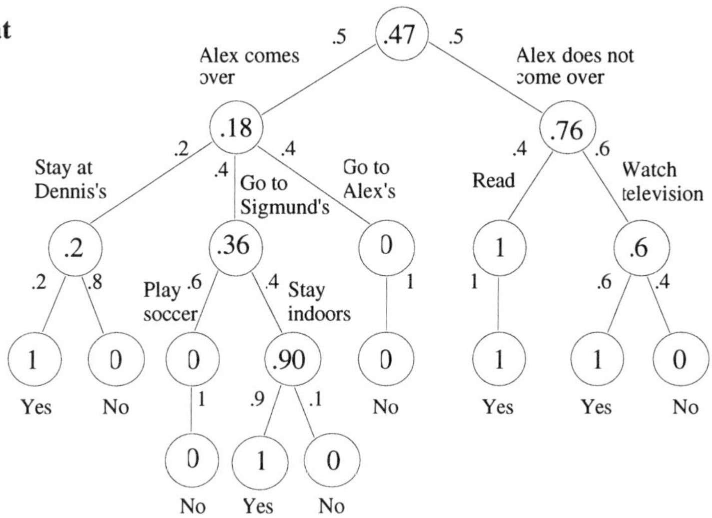

Figure 3 The probability that Dennis practices is shown in each situation.

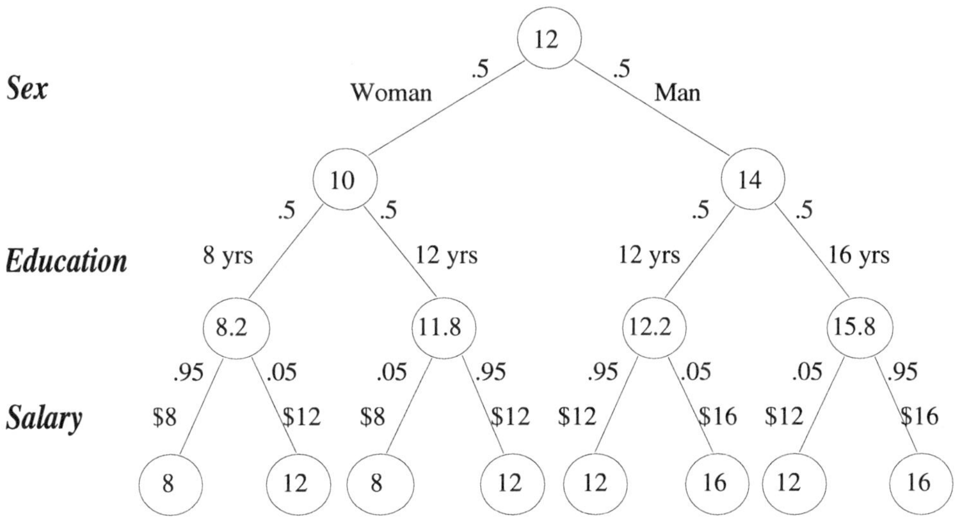

Figure 4 The expected value of salary is shown in each situation.

We will use a notation that makes explicit the dependence of probabilities and expected values on the situation:

- $P_S(E)$ is the probability of the event E in S.
- $E_S(X)$ is the expected value of the variable X in the situation S:

$$E_S(X) := \Sigma x P_S(X{=}x).$$

- $Var_S(X)$ is the variance of X in S:

$$Var_S(X) := E_S([X-E_S(X)]^2).$$

- $Cov_S(X,Y)$ is the covariance of X and Y in S:

$$Cov_S(X) := E_S([X-E_S(X)][Y-E_S(Y)]) = E_S(XY) - E_S(X)E_S(Y).$$

- $P_S(s)$ is probability of a step s in the situation S. If s is below S, $P_S(s)$ is the product of the branching probabilities on all the steps from S to and including s. If s is not below S, $P_S(s)$ is zero.
- $\Delta_s X$ is the change in X's expected value on step s. If s goes from S to T, then
$$\Delta_s X := E_T(X) - E_S(X).$$

1.3. The Analysis of Variance. Analysis of variance is straightforward in a probability tree: we simply apportion $Var_S(X)$, the variance of X in S, among the steps of the tree. The portion assigned to step s is

$$P_S(s) \cdot (\Delta_s X)^2. \tag{1}$$

Figure 5 illustrates this decomposition for Figure 4, with X as salary and S as the initial situation.

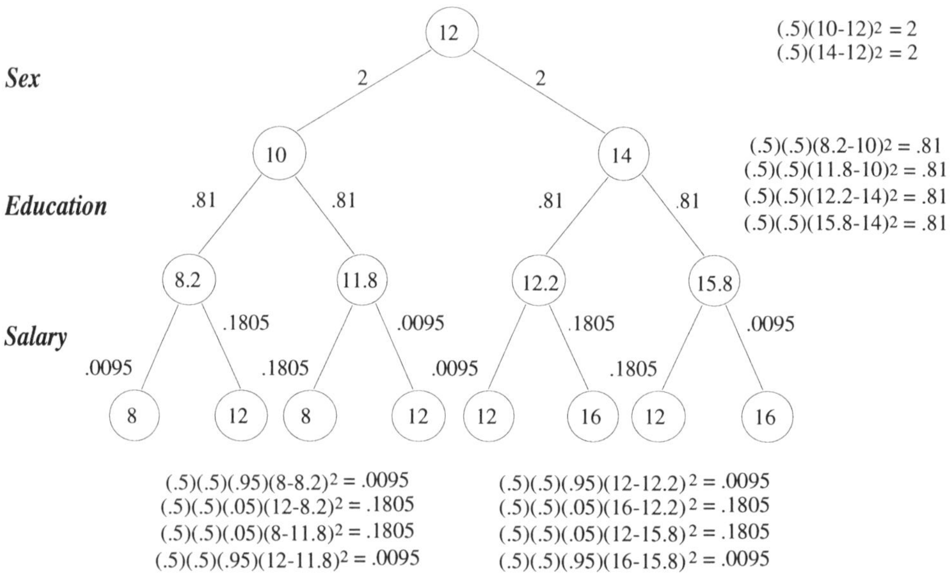

Figure 5 Apportioning the variance for salary. The two steps at which the sex of a child is determined account for 50% of the initial variance of salary (4 out of 8 units). The four steps at which education is determined account for another 40.5% (3.24 out of 8 units). The steps at the bottom of the tree account for the remaining 9.5%.

The rule for apportioning variance among the steps of a probability tree generalizes to covariance;

$$P_S(s) \cdot \Delta_s X \cdot \Delta_s Y \tag{2}$$

is the portion of $Cov_S(X,Y)$ we attribute to the step s. The following proposition establishes that this does indeed define a decomposition.

Proposition 1. *Suppose X and Y are variables in a probability tree, and S is a situation in the tree. Then*

$$Cov_S(X,Y) = \sum_s P_S(s) \cdot \Delta_s X \cdot \Delta_s Y, \tag{3}$$

where the sum is over all steps in the tree.

Proof It suffices to consider the case where S is the initial situation, since any situation is the initial situation in the subtree beginning with it.

In order to prove that (3) holds for the initial situation of every probability tree, we can use induction on the number of nonterminal situations. If there is only one nonterminal situation, as in Figure 6, then (3) reduces to

$$\mathrm{Cov}_S(X,Y) = \sum_{\omega} P_S(\omega)\cdot[X(\omega)-E_S(X)]\cdot[Y(\omega)-E_S(Y)],$$

where the sum is over the elements of the sample space. This is the usual definition of covariance.

In order to complete the proof, consider a probability tree with more than one nonterminal situation, and select a situation U that is neither terminal nor initial. Write

- T for the mother of U,
- $V_1,...,V_k$ for the daughters of U,
- p_0 for the probability of U in T, and
- p_i for the probability of V_i in T,

as in Figure 7. If we remove U, making the V_i daughters of T, then we obtain the tree on the right of Figure 7, which has one less nonterminal situation. This smaller tree has the same terminal situations and hence the same variables as the original tree, and when we assign probability p_0p_i to V_i in T, these variables have the same expected values in all the situations that remain. By the inductive hypothesis, (3) holds for this smaller tree. Hence it suffices to show that the sum on the right-hand side of (3) is the same for the smaller as for the larger tree. But when we reduce the larger tree to the smaller tree, the sum changes only inasmuch as

$$qp_0\Delta X\Delta Y + qp_0\sum_{i=1}^{k} p_i\Delta_i X\Delta_i Y \tag{4}$$

is replaced by

$$qp_0\sum_{i=1}^{k} p_i[\Delta X+\Delta_i X][\Delta Y+\Delta_i Y], \tag{5}$$

where q is the probability of T in the initial situation, $\Delta X := E_U(X)-E_T(X)$, and $\Delta_i X := E_{V_i}(X)-E_U(X)$. Multiplying the binomials in (5), we obtain

$$qp_0\Delta X\Delta Y + qp_0\sum_{i=1}^{k} p_i\Delta_i X\Delta_i Y + qp_0\Delta Y\sum_{i=1}^{k} p_i\Delta_i X + qp_0\Delta X\sum_{i=1}^{k} p_i\Delta_i Y.$$

And the last two terms are zero, because

$$E_U(X) = \sum_{i=1}^{k} p_i E_{V_i}(X) \text{ and } E_U(Y) = \sum_{i=1}^{k} p_i E_{V_i}(Y).$$ ♦

It should be emphasized that Equation (3) is a decomposition, not a representation of $\mathrm{Cov}_S(X,Y)$ as a weighted average. The right-hand side is not a weighted average of the products $\Delta_s X\cdot\Delta_s Y$, because the coefficients $P_S(s)$ do not add to one.

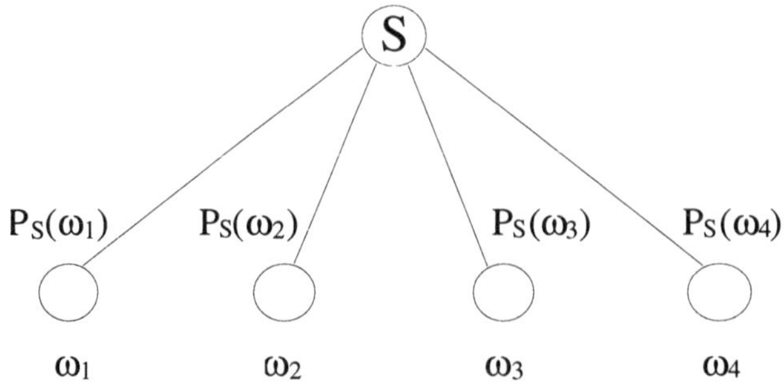

Figure 6 When there is only one nonterminal situation, the steps constitute the sample space, and the branching probabilities are the probabilities of the elements of the sample space in the initial situation.

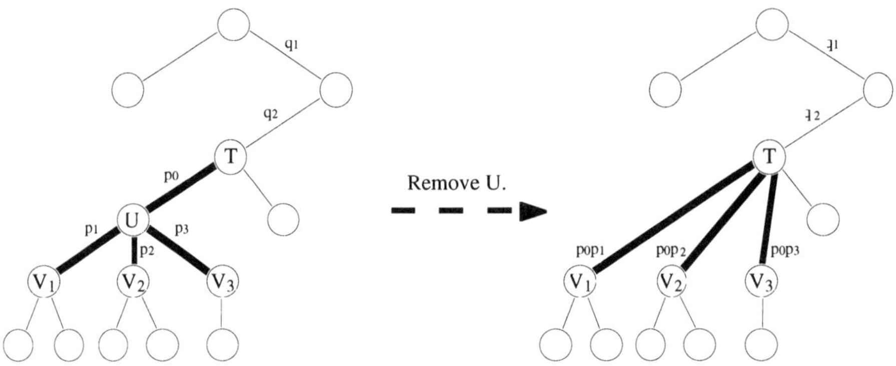

Figure 7 The terms in (4) are the portions of the covariance associated with the four steps marked on the left, while the terms in (5) are the portions associated with the three steps marked on the right. In this example, $q = q_1q_2$.

1.4. Causal Conjecture. The rules for decomposing variance and covariance are rich in implications. Here are a few of them:

Proposition 2. *Suppose X and Y are variables in a probability tree.*

1. *If there is no step in the tree where X and Y both change in expected value, then X and Y are uncorrelated in every situation ($E_S(XY) = E_S(X)E_S(Y)$ for every S).*
2. *If there is no step in the tree where the expected value of X goes up while the expected value of Y goes down, and vice versa, then their correlation is nonnegative in every situation ($E_S(XY) \geq E_S(X)E_S(Y)$ for every S).*
3. *If there is no step in the tree where X and Y both change in probability, then X and Y are independent in every situation ($P_S(X=x\&Y=y) = P_S(X=x)P_S(Y=y)$ for every x, y, and S).*

Proof If X and Y never change in expected value on the same step, then $\Delta_s X \Delta_s Y$ is zero for every step s. It follows from (3) that for every situation S, $Cov_S(X,Y)$ is zero, or $E_S(XY) = E_S(X)E_S(Y)$.

Similarly, if $\Delta_s X$ and $\Delta_s Y$ never have opposite signs, then their product is always nonnegative, and it then follows from (3) that for every S, $Cov_S(X,Y) \geq 0$, or $E_S(XY) \geq E_S(X)E_S(Y)$.

Statement 3 follows from Statement 1, because the probability that X has a particular value is the expected value of the variable that is equal to one when X takes that value and zero otherwise. ♦

These statements illustrate the causal explanation of statistical patterns. If we observe that X and Y are uncorrelated in many different situations, then we may conjecture that they have no common causes—there are no steps in nature's tree that affect them both. If we observe that they are positively correlated in many different situations, then we may conjecture that they consistently have common causes—the events that raise or lower the expected level of one of them also raise or lower the expected level of the other.

We say that X and Y are *causally uncorrelated* when there is no step in nature's tree where they both change in expected value. Thus Statement 1 of Proposition 2 says that causally uncorrelated variables are statistically uncorrelated. Similarly, we say that X and Y are *causally independent* when there is no step in nature's tree where they both change in probability. Statement 3 says that causally independent variables are statistically independent.

We can also provide a causal interpretation for regression coefficients. According to standard theory, the coefficient of X in the linear regression of Y on X is

$$\frac{\mathrm{Cov}(X,Y)}{\mathrm{Var}(X)}.$$

The following proposition reveals that this coefficient is a weighted average of the relative changes in Y's and X's expected values on the different steps in nature's tree.

Proposition 3. *Suppose X and Y are variables in a probability tree, and S is a situation in the tree. Then the regression coefficient of Y on X in S, $Cov_S(X,Y)/Var_S(X)$, is a weighted average, over all the steps in the tree where X changes in expected value, of the ratio of Y's change in expected value to X's. The weight of a step s is the probability of s in S multiplied by the square of X's change in expected value on s. In symbols:*

$$\frac{Cov_S(X,Y)}{Var_S(X)} = \frac{\displaystyle\sum_{s \text{ with } \Delta_s X \neq 0} \frac{\Delta_s Y}{\Delta_s X} P_S(s)\cdot(\Delta_s X)^2}{\displaystyle\sum_{s \text{ with } \Delta_s X \neq 0} P_S(s)\cdot(\Delta_s X)^2}. \tag{6}$$

Proof Equation (6) follows immediately from (3) when we write its right-hand side in the form

$$\frac{\sum_s P_S(s)\cdot\Delta_s Y\cdot\Delta_s X}{\sum_s P_S(s)\cdot(\Delta_s X)^2}.$$

♦

If the ratios $\Delta_S Y/\Delta_S X$ that the regression coefficient averages are quite disparate, then the average is not very interesting, and we will say that the regression coefficient is causally meaningless; it has no simple causal interpretation. But if these ratios are quite similar, then we will feel that the average does have causal meaning. The meaning is clearest when the ratios are all equal. (Figure 8 gives an example.) In this case, the regression coefficient will be the same in every situation, and we will say that there is a stable causal relation between X and Y. This relation deserves a name; I have proposed that we call X a *linear sign* of Y. The concept of linear sign is much more general than the concepts of linear causality usually considered by statisticians and philosophers (see, e.g., Freedman 1991, Humphreys 1989).

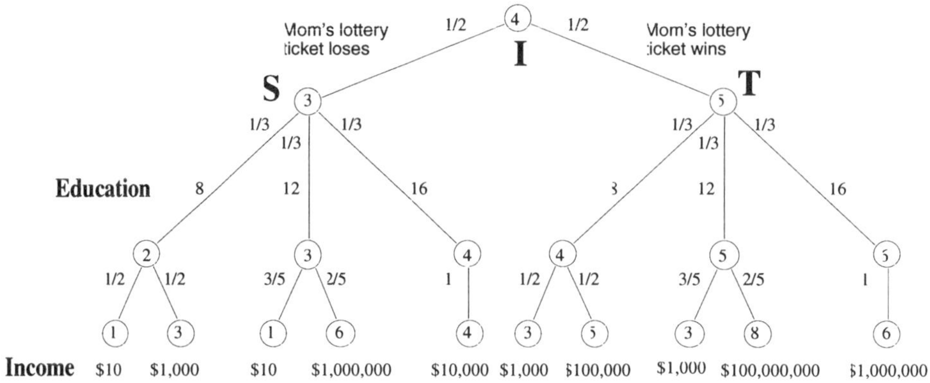

The expected value of $\mathbf{Log_{10}}$(Income) is shown in each situation.

Figure 8 In this society, a person's expected income goes up when the person gets more education. In fact, when the expected value of Education changes, the expected value of the logarithm (to the base 10) of Income changes by exactly one-fourth as much. Consequently, the coefficient of Education in the linear regression of Log_{10}(Income) on Education is 1/4 in every situation where Education is not yet settled. The regression is 1+(1/4)Education in the initial situation I, (1/4)Education in S, and 2+(1/4)Education in T.

Figure 9 summarizes our understanding of causality and statistical observation. Correlation does not prove causality; we cannot deduce a causal relation from a statistical association. But causality does imply statistical association, and hence statistical association can give us grounds for conjecturing a causal relation. Causality can explain correlation.

2. Refinement

Probability trees often seem naive, especially as part of a causal discussion, simply because they necessarily leave aside many issues and factors that might be brought into the discussion. The probability tree in Figure 1, for example, says nothing about the factors that decide whether Alex will come to Dennis's house on a particular afternoon. How can the tree be meaningful and valid if these factors are not taken into account?

The answer is that additional factors can be taken into account without falsifying the assertions made in a particular probability tree. In other words, we can construct a more refined tree that does take more into account but agrees with the assertions already made in the original tree. In order to make a convincing case for probability trees, we obviously need to show that such refinement really is possible. This is the purpose of this section.

This section works in the same finite, graph-theoretical context as the preceding section. In this context, as we will see, any refinement is a composition of elementary refinements, each of which involves interpolation below a single situation. In Section 5, we will study refinement in the more general context of abstract event trees.

Once we have understood the idea of refinement, we will need to look again at the causal concepts of the preceding section. As we will see, they need to be strengthened slightly in order for us to be sure that they will persist when a probability tree is refined.

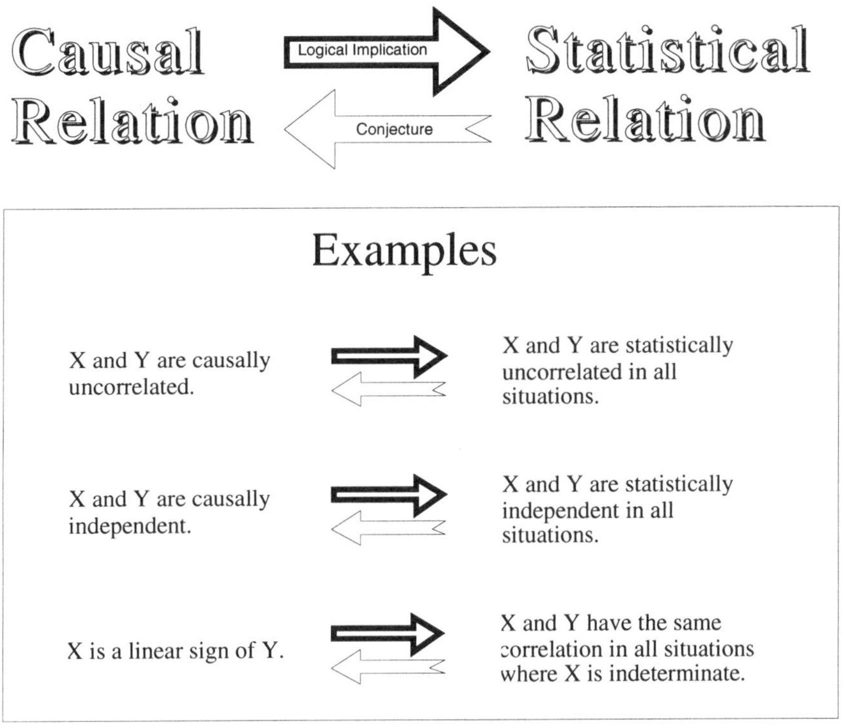

Figure 9 The dual connection between causal and statistical relations. More examples are given in *The Art of Causal Conjecture*.

2.1. Elementary Refinements. When we suppose that a given probability tree represents nature's limited ability to predict, we are not supposing that nature is blindfolded while each step is taken. When we suppose, for example, that nature gives even odds on whether a woman will complete 12 years of education or only 8, we are supposing only that these are the odds at the moment when the woman is conceived (and her sex is determined). As Figure 10 illustrates, the odds may change in the course of the woman's childhood.

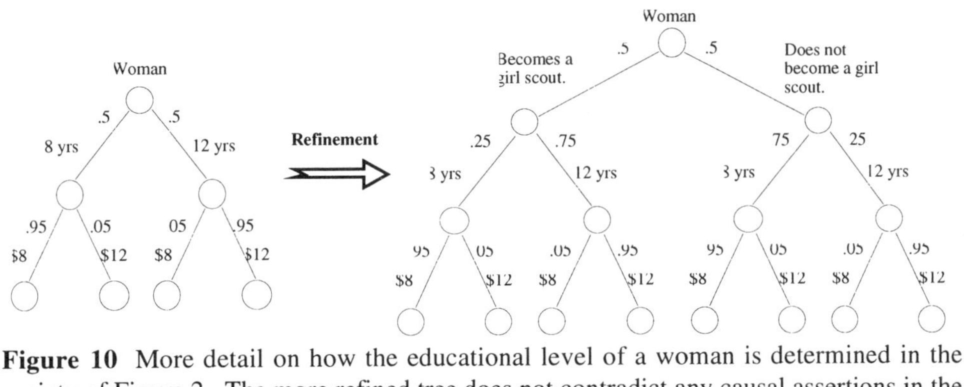

Figure 10 More detail on how the educational level of a woman is determined in the society of Figure 2. The more refined tree does not contradict any causal assertions in the

original tree. It continues to assert, for example, that a woman with eight years of education has only a 5% chance of earning \$12.

We say that the probability tree on the right in Figure 10 is an *elementary refinement* of the probability tree on the left. An elementary refinement involves interpolating a new probability tree between a particular situation S and its daughters. The situation S may be the initial situation (as in Figure 10), a later situation (as when the tree on the left of Figure 10 is considered as a subtree of Figure 2), or even a terminal situation (in this case, we are adding a new tree below S rather than interpolating a tree between S and its daughters). As Figure 11 illustrates, the interpolation proceeds as follows:

1. If S is not terminal in the tree to be refined, remove the subtree below S.
2. Construct a new subtree below S.
3. If S was originally terminal, stop.
4. If S was not originally terminal, assign each terminal situation in the new subtree to one of the original daughters of S, taking care to assign at least one to each original daughter T, and taking care that the probabilities in S of the terminal situations assigned to T add up to T's original probability in S.
5. Then add to each terminal situation in the new subtree the subtree that followed the corresponding daughter of S in the original tree. (In the example, this takes us from the tree on the right in Figure 11 back to the tree on the right in Figure 10.)

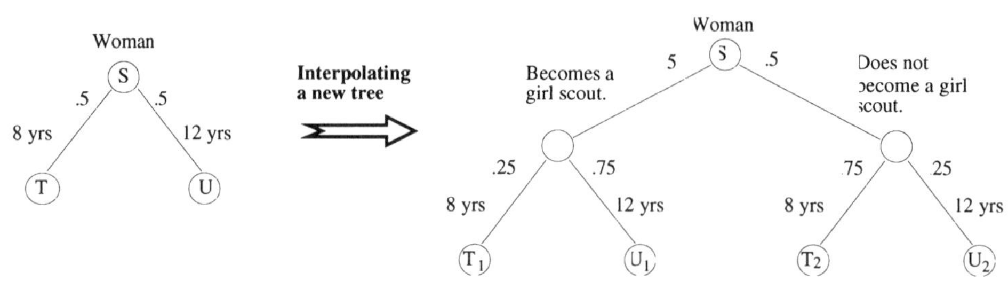

Figure 11 The daughters T_1 and T_2 of S are assigned to T, while the daughters U_1 and U_2 are assigned to U. The total probability of T_1 and T_2 in S is (.5)(.25)+(.5)(.75), or .5, which was T's probability in S. Similarly, the probabilities of U_1 and U_2 add to the probability of U.

Figure 12 shows the elementary refinement of Figure 10 with labels for all the situations in the refined tree that correspond to situations in the initial tree. The two unlabeled situations in the refined tree are not represented in the initial tree; they come into the story only when it is elaborated. Aside from S, all the labeled situations in the refined tree are more detailed versions of situations already present in the initial tree. Situations T_1 and T_2, for example, are different ways of adding detail to T. This means that T_1 and T_2 agree with everything that T already says, including what it says about possibilities and probabilities for future events. We say that T_1 and T_2 *refine* T.

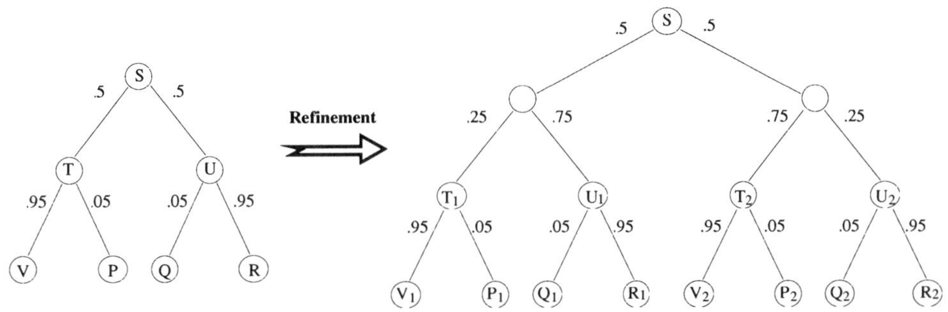

Figure 12 There are two situations in the more refined tree that are not represented in the initial tree.

2.2. Combining Elementary Refinements. We say that one probability tree is a *refinement* of another if it can be obtained by a sequence of elementary refinements. Figure 13 shows a refinement that can be obtained by combining two elementary refinements. In this example, the refinement does not provide more detail for situations already present in the initial probability tree; it merely adds some new situations.

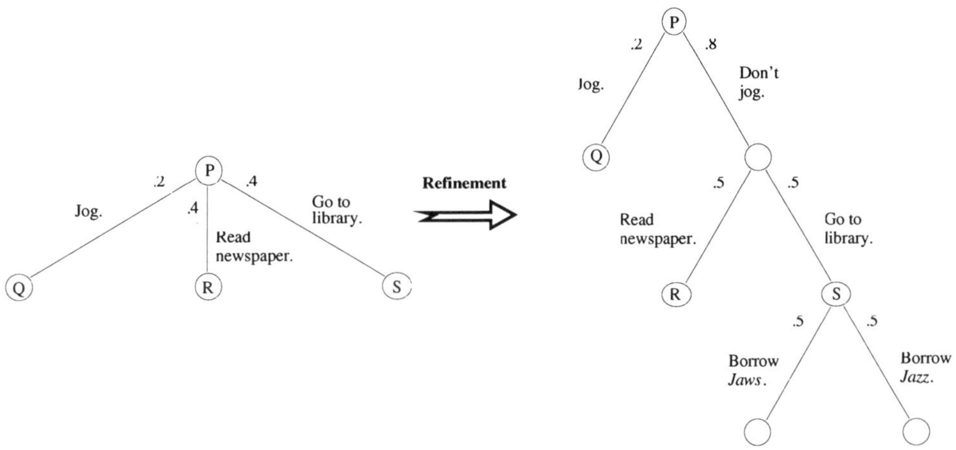

Figure 13 The refinement reveals that the decision whether to jog is taken before a choice is made between reading the newspaper and going to the library. It also shows what can happen at the library.

2.3. Causal Relations Under Refinement. If the concepts that we defined in the preceding section—causal uncorrelatedness, causal independence, and linear sign—are really causal concepts, then they should not be affected by refinement of nature's tree. When we declare that two variables are causally uncorrelated or independent (have no common causes), we do not want to see this judgment contradicted by a closer look at nature's tree.

Unfortunately, the concepts as we have defined them do not quite have this invariance under refinement. Figures 14 and 15 show the difficulty. In Figure 14, the events F and G appear to be causally independent, for there is no step where they both change in probability. But the refinement in Figure 15 shows that there are in fact steps where they both change in probability.

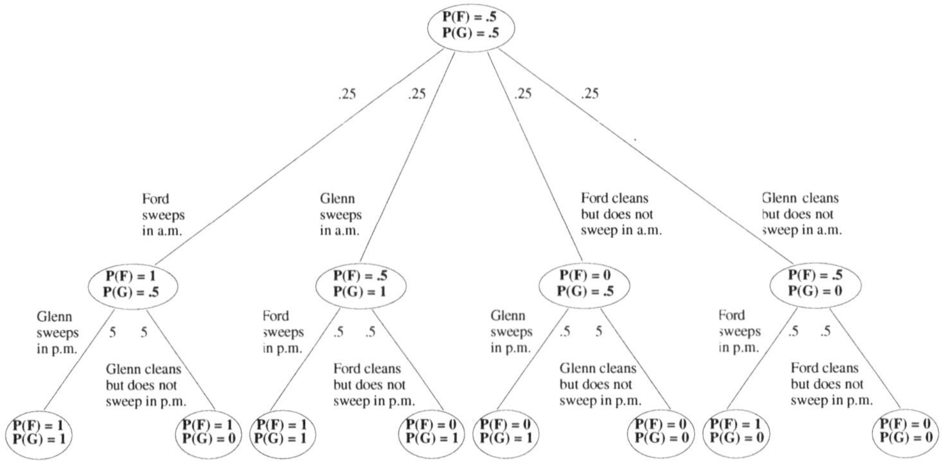

Figure 14 Ford and Glenn clean their room twice a day. One of them cleans in the morning; the other cleans in the afternoon. Sometimes cleaning requires sweeping, sometimes not. We write F for the event that Ford eventually sweeps the room, and G for the event that Glenn does. The probabilities of these events are shown for each situation. (Alternatively, F and G can be thought of as variables, eventually taking the values zero or one, and the numbers in the situations are then their expected values.) According to the definition given in Section 1, the events F and G are causally independent, because their probabilities do not change on the same step of the tree. (Equivalently, the variables are uncorrelated, because their expected values do not change on the same step.)

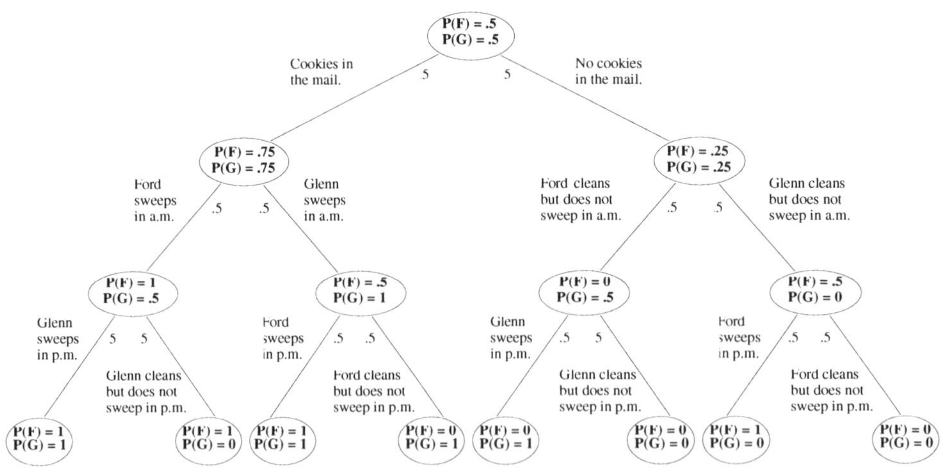

Figure 15 This refinement of Figure 14 reveals that when cookies come in the mail, the probability of sweeping increases in both the morning and afternoon cleanings. The refinement also shows that F and G are not really causally independent, for the step in the tree where cookies come increases the probability of both.

The source of the difficulty in this example is clear. It is true that there are no steps in Figure 14 where both events change in probability, but there are closely related steps—alternative steps—where they do. The step from the initial situation in which Ford sweeps in the morning does not change the probability of Glenn's eventually sweeping, but it has a sister that does. The obvious remedy is to rule this out.

Let us say that a situation in a probability tree *influences* a variable if the variable changes in expected value on at least one of the possible steps immediately after that situation. And let us then revise our earlier definitions as follows:

- X and Y are *causally uncorrelated* if in a sufficiently refined version of nature's probability tree, there is no situation that influences both X and Y.
- X and Y are *causally independent* if all functions of X are causally uncorrelated with all functions of Y.
- X is a *linear sign* of Y with sign coefficient b if X and Y-bX are causally uncorrelated.

We leave it to the reader to verify that these definitions require more than the earlier definitions and that when they are satisfied by nature's tree at one level of refinement, they will be satisfied by nature's tree at any greater level of refinement. (See Chapter 13 of *The Art of Causal Conjecture*.)

3. Event Trellises

So far, our discussion has been based on a graph-theoretical conception of a tree. Trees are rooted directed graphs without cycles. (For simplicity, we have put the root at the top of our trees, directed the arrows downward, and suppressed the arrowheads.) This conception is useful. We can draw small trees of this kind, and even large ones have straightforward computational representations. The intellectual tradition of probability is hardly limited, however, to the finite and discrete. So we need to explore more general ways of understanding probability trees. The first step, which we take in this section, is to formulate a more general and abstract conception of event trees. In later sections, we will study refinement, expectation, and probability in abstract event trees and then move on to a yet more general framework: event spaces.

We actually work with objects slightly more general than trees in this section, objects that we call *trellises*. A trellis is more general than a tree only in that it does not necessarily have an initial situation (see Figure 16). The assumption that we have an initial situation is usually appropriate and always substantively harmless; if we begin with a trellis that does not have an initial situation, we can always add one. But the existence of an initial situation is irrelevant to much of our investigation in later sections (especially Section 6), and the assumption that there always is one would be unnecessarily distracting.

3.1. Event Trees and Event Trellises Defined Abstractly. Abstractly, a tree is a special kind of partially ordered set (see, for example, Jech 1978). In this spirit, consider the following axiom for a set Γ with a partial ordering[3] **precedes**:

Axiom T1 If S **precedes** U and T **precedes** U, then S **precedes** T or T **precedes** S.

---

[3]Recall that a binary relation is a *partial ordering* if it is reflexive, antisymmetric, and transitive. A binary relation **r** is *reflexive* if S **r** S for all S, *irreflexive* if S **r** S for no S, *symmetric* if S **r** T implies T **r** S, *antisymmetric* if S **r** T and T **r** S together imply S = T, and *transitive* if S **r** T and T **r** U together imply S **r** U.

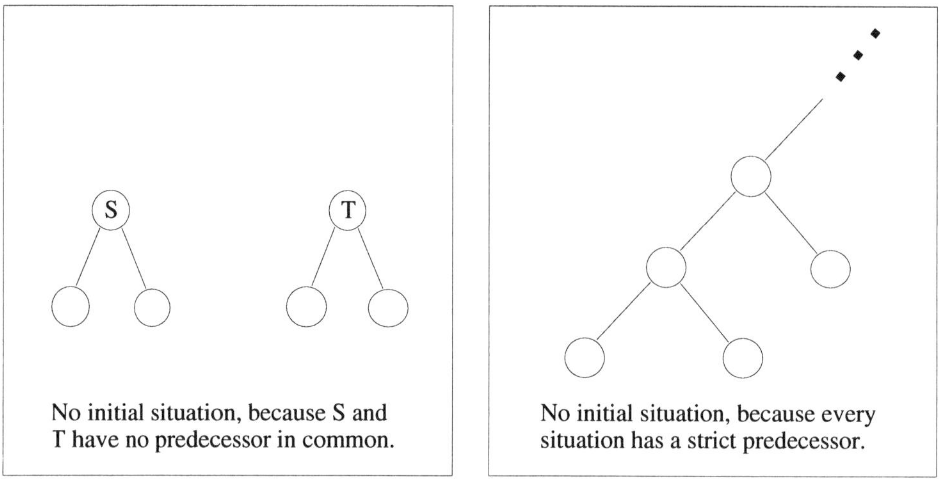

Figure 16 Two event trellises that are not event trees. The trellis on the left consists of two finite but unconnected trees. The one on the right extends infinitely far into the past.

If this axiom is satisfied, we call Γ a *trellis*, and we call **precedes** the *precedence relation* on Γ. When we think Γ's elements as possible situations for some observer, we call Γ an *event trellis*.

If S **precedes** T, we call S a *predecessor* of T, and we call T a *successor* of S. If S **precedes** T or T **precedes** S, we say S and T are *sequenced*. Thus Axiom T1 says that situations with a common successor are sequenced. This is often expressed by saying that the predecessors of a situation are totally ordered.

If S **precedes** T and S ≠ T, we write S **Precedes** T (S *strictly precedes* T). The following proposition spells out how **Precedes** interacts with **precedes**.

Proposition 4.

1. *If S* **precedes** *T and T* **Precedes** *U, then S* **Precedes** *U.*
2. *If S* **Precedes** *T and T* **precedes** *U, then S* **Precedes** *U.*

Proof Suppose S **precedes** T and T **Precedes** U. Then T **precedes** U by the definition of **Precedes**. From S **precedes** T and T **precedes** U and the transitivity of **precedes**, we obtain S **precedes** U.

Since T **Precedes** U, T ≠ U. So S ≠ U. (If S = U, then we have S **precedes** T and T **precedes** S, whence S = T by the antisymmetry of **precedes**. And thus T = U.)

Since S **precedes** U and S ≠ U, S **Precedes** U.

The proof of Statement 2 is analogous. ♦

As we will see more clearly later, **precedes** carries a double meaning: S **precedes** T means that

- T cannot happen unless S happens earlier (or at the same time, in which case S = T),

and

- T is possible (but has not already happened strictly earlier) whenever S happens.

More succinctly: S **precedes** T means that S is a prerequisite for T and allows T. Here we think of S and T not only as situations but also as instantaneous events. The instantaneous event S is the event that happens when and only when the observer moving through the trellis arrives in the situation S.

We call a trellis Γ a *tree* if it has an initial element. This means that in addition to satisfying Axiom T1, it also satisfies the following axiom:

Axiom T0 Γ has an element I such that I **precedes** S for all S in Γ.

The initial element in a tree (the element I required by Axiom T0) is, of course, unique; this is a consequence of the antisymmetry of **precedes**.

As we asserted earlier, we can always turn a trellis into a tree by adding an initial situation. (More precisely, if Γ_0 is a trellis, with precedence relation **precedes**$_0$, and I is an object not in Γ_0, then $\Gamma_0 \cup \{I\}$ is a tree with the binary relation **precedes**, defined by S **precedes** T if either (i) S = I and $T \in \Gamma$, or (ii) $S \in \Gamma$, $T \in \Gamma$, and S **precedes**$_0$ T.) It is also true that if Γ is a trellis and S is an element of Γ, then the subset of Γ consisting of the successors of S is a tree.

The following proposition shows that our abstract definition of a tree is consistent with the graph-theoretical definition.

Proposition 5.

*1. Suppose (Γ,**precedes**) is a partially ordered set satisfying Axioms T0 and T1, and suppose Γ is finite. Then the Hasse diagram of (Γ,**precedes**) is a finite directed tree, with the initial situation as its root. (Figure 17 explains what is meant by the Hasse diagram of a partially ordered set.)*

*2. Conversely, if we begin with a finite tree drawn as in the preceding sections, write Γ for its set of situations, write I for the situation at the root, and write S **precedes** T whenever there is chain of steps downward from S to T, then (Γ,**precedes**) is a partially ordered set satisfying axioms T0 and T1.*

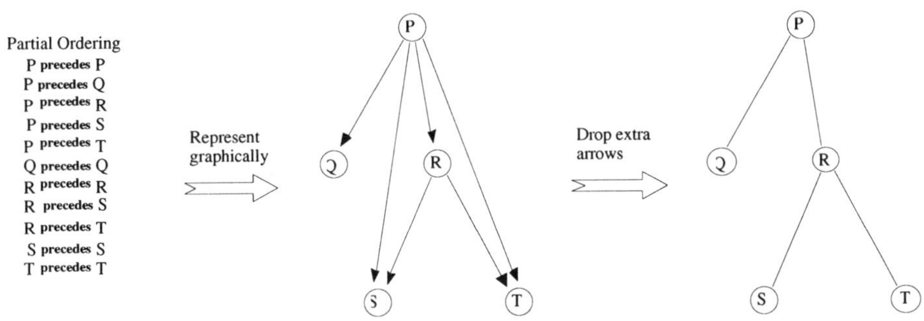

Figure 17 The Hasse diagram for a finite tree. In general, to obtain the Hasse diagram of a finite partially ordered set (Γ,**precedes**), we draw a graph with the elements of Γ as nodes and an arrow from S to T whenever S **precedes** T, and then we delete the arrow from S to T if there is a longer chain of arrows from S to T. (In the figure, we have also deleted all arrowheads, on the understanding that steps are interpreted as arrows pointing downwards.)

Statement 1 may fail when Γ is infinite, because in this case, the journey from a situation S to a later situation T may fail to consist of discrete steps. For example, if we conceive of a different situation for each instant of time between S and T, then a step can always be divided into smaller steps.

Here, in counterpoint, is a simple and familiar example of an infinite tree. Let Γ be the set of all continuous real-valued functions that have closed intervals of real numbers beginning at zero as domains and give the value zero to zero. In other words, each element of Γ is a function S on some closed interval of the form $[0,\tau]$, with $S(0) = 0$. Define the partial ordering **precedes** on Γ by saying that S **precedes** T if T extends S—i.e., if S is a function on $[0,\tau_1]$, T is a function on $[0,\tau_2]$, $\tau_1 \leq \tau_2$, and $T(t) = S(t)$ for all t in $[0,\tau_1]$. The initial element is the function that has only zero in its domain and gives it the value zero.

3.2. Paths and the Sample Space. A *path* in a trellis is a maximal set of sequenced situations—a set ω of situations such that any two elements of ω are sequenced, and no other situation is sequenced with them all. If the trellis is a tree, then every path contains the initial situation. When a path contains a situation, it contains all the situation's predecessors. In a finite trellis, every path contains exactly one terminal situation, and every terminal situation is in exactly one path.

When a situation is in a path, we say the path *goes through* the situation. We speak also of paths from a particular situation: a *path from* S is a maximal set of sequenced successors of S. When S precedes T, we write [S,T] for the set of all situations that follow S and precede T (this includes S and T), and we call [S,T] the *closed interval* between S and T.

The set of all paths is the trellis's *sample space*, which we designate by Ω. A subset of the sample space is a *Moivrean event*, and a function on the sample space is a *variable*.

In Section 1, following the custom in probability theory, we used "event," without qualification, to mean what we now call a Moivrean event, in honor of Abraham De Moivre. The adjective "Moivrean" is introduced here because we need to distinguish the Moivrean concept from other event concepts, including a concept we encountered a moment ago—the concept of an instantaneous event represented by a situation.

3.3. Divergence. Two situations in an event trellis are *divergent* if they have no common successor. By Axiom T1, this is equivalent to their not being sequenced. Divergent situations are instantaneous events that cannot both happen. We write S **diverges** T when S and T are divergent.

We write S **implies** T when every successor of S (including S itself) is sequenced with T. This means that S cannot happen unless T happens (sooner, later, or at the same time).

We write S **foretells** T when S both implies and precedes T. This is equivalent to the requirement that any path through S must later (or at the same time) go through T (see Figure 18). It means that T cannot happen strictly earlier than S but is inevitable (or happens at the same time) when S happens. We write S **Foretells** T when S both implies and strictly precedes T.

S precedes but does not foretell T.

S foretells T.

Figure 18 S foretells T if any path that passes through S must later (or at the same time) pass through T.

The following proposition spells out some properties of the binary relations we have just defined.

Proposition 6.

*1. **diverges** is symmetric and irreflexive.*

*2. **implies** is reflexive and transitive.*

*3. **foretells** is a partial ordering.*

*4. If S **foretells** T and T **Foretells** U, then S **Foretells** U.*

*5. If S **Foretells** T and T **foretells** U, then S **Foretells** U.*

*6. If S **precedes** T and S **implies** U, then T **implies** U.*

*7. If S **implies** U, S **precedes** T and T **precedes** U, then S **implies** T and T **implies** U.*

*8. If S **implies** U, S **precedes** T, but not U **Precedes** T, then S **implies** T and T **implies** U.*

Proof 1. The symmetry and irreflexivity of **diverges** is obvious from its definition.

2. The reflexivity of **implies** is equally obvious; since every successor of S is sequenced with S, S **implies** S.

In order to show that **implies** is transitive, suppose S **implies** T and T **implies** U. Let V be a successor of S, which is therefore sequenced with T: either (i) T **precedes** V or (ii) V **precedes** T. We need to show, in both cases, that V is also sequenced with U.

If T **precedes** V, then it follows from T **implies** U that U and V are sequenced.

If V **precedes** T, then we use T **implies** U to conclude that T is sequenced with U; either T **precedes** U or U **precedes** T. If T **precedes** U, then V **precedes** U by the transitivity of **precedes**. If U **precedes** T, then U and V are sequenced by Axiom T1.

3. Since **precedes** and **implies** are both reflexive and transitive, **foretells** is as well. Since **precedes** is antisymmetric, **foretells** is as well.

4,5. Statements 4 and 5 follows from the Proposition 4 and the transitivity of **implies**.

6. If S **precedes** T, then any successor of T is a successor of S. So S **implies** U implies that any successor of T is sequenced with U—i.e., that T **implies** U.

7. To establish that S **implies** T, we must show that an arbitrary successor V of S is sequenced with T. Since S **implies** U, V is sequenced with U; either V **precedes** U or U **precedes** V. If V **precedes** U, then V is sequenced with T by Axiom T1 (because T **precedes** U). If U **precedes** V, then T **precedes** V by the transitivity of **precedes** (because T **precedes** U).

The additional conclusion T **implies** U follows from Statement 6.

8. Since T is a successor of S and S **implies** U, T must be sequenced with U. Since U **Precedes** T does not hold, we must have T **precedes** U. So the conclusion follows from Statement 7. ♦

3.4. Clades. Let us call a nonempty set of divergent situations in an event trellis a *clade*. The interpretation of individual situations as instantaneous events extends to clades: a clade Ξ is the instantaneous event that happens when and only when the event-trellis observer arrives in a situation in Ξ. A clade, like a situation, can happen only once as the observer moves through the trellis. The various relations we have defined for situations also extend to clades. Some of them (notably **precedes** and **foretells**) unpack in informative ways as they extend.

If S is a situation, then S and {S}, the clade consisting of S alone, represent the same instantaneous event. If the trellis is a tree, we call {I}, where I is the initial situation, the *initial* clade.

When a path and a clade have a nonempty intersection, we say that the clade *cuts* the path, and that the path goes *through* the clade.

When two clades Ξ and Φ are disjoint as sets, we write Ξ **disjoint** Φ. This means the two clades cannot happen at the same time.

We say Ξ and Φ are *divergent* and write Ξ **diverges** Φ if each situation in Ξ is divergent from each situation in Φ. This is equivalent to requiring that Ξ and Φ be disjoint and their union be a clade. It means the two clades cannot both happen. It generalizes divergence for situations: {S} **diverges** {T} if and only if S **diverges** T. If $\{\Xi_\alpha\}_{\alpha\in A}$ are divergent clades (i.e., Ξ_α and Ξ_β are divergent whenever $\alpha \neq \beta$), then the union $\cup_{\alpha\in A}\Xi_\alpha$ is a clade.

Here are six more binary relations for clades:

- Ξ **prerequisite** Φ (Ξ is a *prerequisite* for Φ) if every situation in Φ has a predecessor in Ξ. This means that Ξ must happen before Φ can happen (though they may happen at the same time).
- Ξ **allows** Φ (Ξ *allows* Φ) if every situation in Ξ has a successor in Φ. This means that Φ is possible (but cannot already have happened strictly earlier) whenever Ξ happens. It does not rule out Φ happening without Ξ happening, and it does not rule out Ξ happening without Φ happening.
- Ξ **implies** Φ (Ξ *implies* Φ) if any path through Ξ also goes through Φ. This means that Ξ cannot happen unless Φ happens (sooner, later, or at the same time).
- Ξ **precedes** Φ (Ξ *precedes* Φ) if Ξ **prerequisite** Φ and Ξ **allows** Φ. This means that Φ cannot happen unless Ξ happens first or at the same time, and Φ is possible whenever Ξ happens.
- Ξ **foretells** Φ (Ξ *foretells* Φ) if Ξ **allows** Φ and Ξ **implies** Φ. In other words, if a path goes through Ξ, it goes through Φ later or at the same time. This means that Φ cannot happen strictly earlier than Ξ but is inevitable (or happens at the same time) whenever Ξ happens. It does not rule out Φ happening without Ξ happening.
- Ξ **alw.foretells** Φ (Ξ *always foretells* Φ) if Ξ **precedes** Φ and Ξ **foretells** Φ. In other words, a path goes through Ξ if and only if it goes through Φ, and it always goes through Φ later or at the same time. This means that Φ cannot happen unless Ξ happens first (or at the same time) and is inevitable (or happens at the same time) whenever Ξ happens.

The relation **implies** is reflexive and transitive. The other five relations are partial orderings. The dependencies among the six relations are clarified by the Venn diagram in Figure 19. As this diagram indicates, Ξ **alw.foretells** Φ can be defined from the other five relations in several ways. Instead of saying it means Ξ **precedes** Φ and Ξ **foretells** Φ, we can say, for example, it means Ξ **prerequisite** Φ and Ξ **implies** Φ.

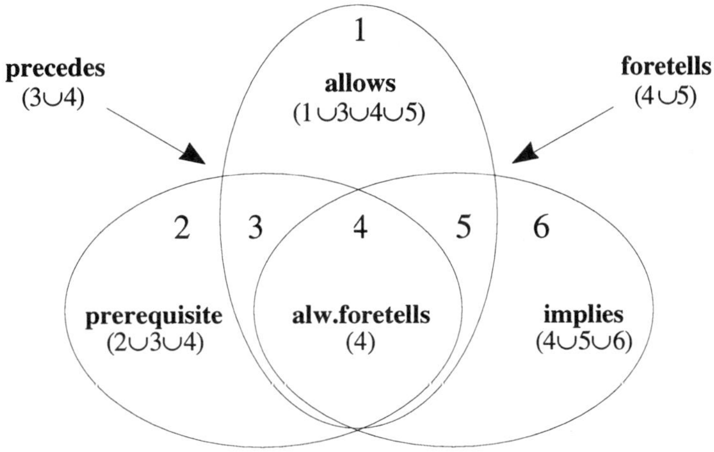

Figure 19 A Venn diagram for six binary relations on clades, thought of as sets of ordered pairs of clades. A Venn diagram for three sets can have as many as seven regions (not counting the region not in any of the sets), but the Venn diagram for **prerequisite**, **allows**, and **implies** has only six, because Ξ **prerequisite** Φ and Ξ **implies** Φ together imply Ξ **allows** Φ. By definition, **precedes** = **prerequisite** $\cap$ **allows** and **foretells** = **allows** $\cap$ **implies**. We can obtain **alw.foretells** in several ways; it is the intersection of either of the pair {**prerequisite**,**precedes**} with either of the pair {**implies**,**foretells**}.

When the clades Ξ and Φ are singletons, say $\Xi = \{S\}$ and $\Phi = \{T\}$, the six binary relations reduce to three. The two relations $\{S\}$ **prerequisite** $\{T\}$ and $\{S\}$ **allows** $\{T\}$ are equivalent to each other and hence to their conjunction, $\{S\}$ **precedes** $\{T\}$. And $\{S\}$ **foretells** $\{T\}$ and $\{S\}$ **alw.foretells** $\{T\}$ are equivalent. (See Figure 20.)

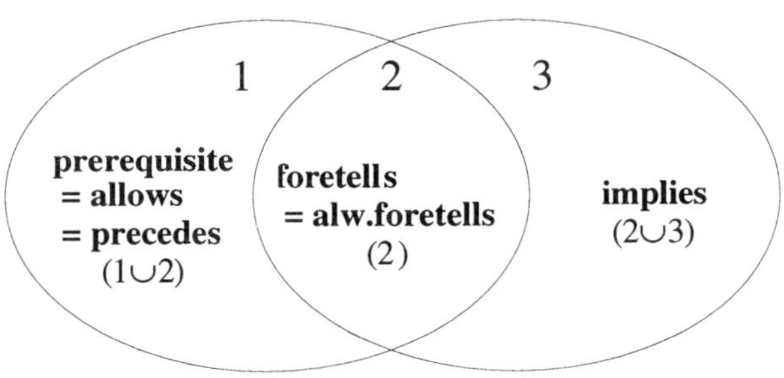

Figure 20 The six binary relations in Figure 19 reduce to three when we consider only individual situations. In this case, **prerequisite** is equal to **allows** and hence to their intersection, **precedes**. And **alw.foretells** and **foretells** are also equal.

We have defined **precedes**, **foretells**, and **implies** separately for clades and situations, but the definitions agree: {S} **precedes** {T} if and only if S **precedes** T, and so on. Hence we can ignore the distinction between {S} and S when talking about relations between clades. The following equivalences are useful:

- Ξ **prerequisite** Φ if and only if Ξ **prerequisite** T for every T in Φ.
- Ξ **allows** Φ if and only if S **allows** Φ for every S in Ξ.
- Ξ **implies** Φ if and only if S **implies** Φ for every S in Ξ.
- Ξ **foretells** Φ if and only if S **foretells** Φ for every S in Ξ.

(The relations **precedes** and **alw.foretells** do not reduce in this way.) Of course, divergence and disjointness reduce completely to relations between individual situations:

- Ξ **diverges** Φ if and only if S **diverges** T for every S in Ξ and T in Φ.
- Ξ **disjoint** Φ if and only if S ≠ T for every S in Ξ and T in Φ.

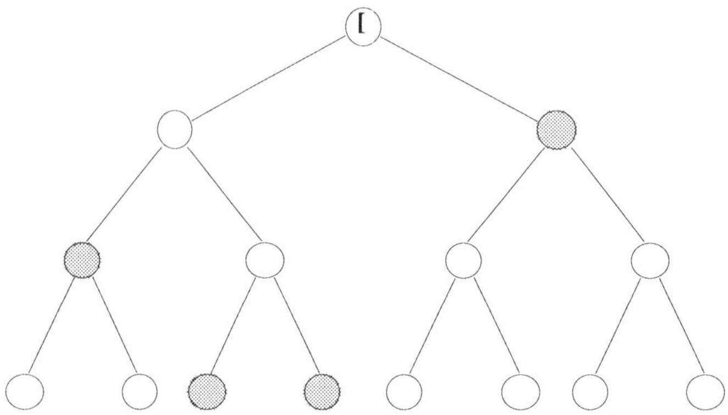

Figure 21 A cut in an event tree.

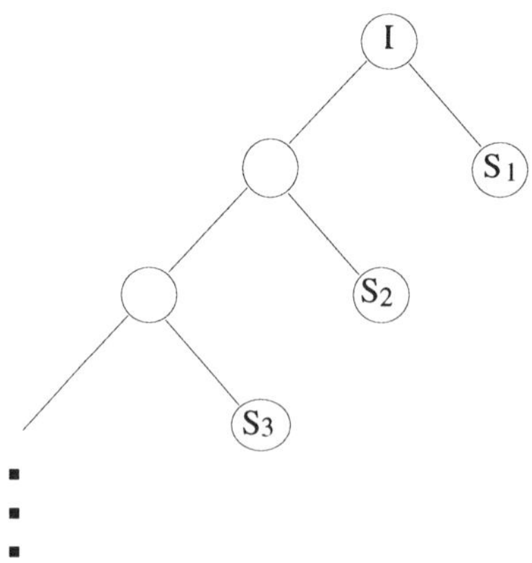

Figure 22 An event tree with one infinitely long path. This path does not go through the clade $\{S_1, S_2, \ldots\}$, which therefore is not a cut, although it is a maximal clade.

3.5. Cuts. When a clade Φ contains cuts every path in an event trellis, we call it a *cut*.[4] Intuitively, a cut is an instantaneous event that must eventually happen (see Figure 21).

A cut is a maximal clade—a clade not contained in any larger clade. In a finite event trellis, the converse is also true: any maximal clade is a cut. But as Figure 22 illustrates, a maximal clade may fail to be a cut in an infinite event trellis. A clade cannot always be enlarged to a cut.

When a clade Φ consists of successors of a situation S, and every path through S also goes through Φ, we say that Φ is a *cut of* S. Intuitively, a cut of S is an instantaneous event that cannot happen strictly before S happens or without S happening but must eventually happen once S has happened. The clade {S} qualifies as a cut of S.

The condition S **alw.foretells** Φ is equivalent to Φ being a cut of S. The condition Ξ **foretells** Φ is equivalent to every situation in Ξ having a cut in Φ. The condition Ξ **implies** Φ is equivalent to every situation in Ξ having either a predecessor or a cut in Φ.

3.6. Humean Events. Thought of as an event, a situation S or a clade Ξ is instantaneous; it is the arrival of the event-trellis observer in S or Ξ. In discussions of causality, we may also be interested in events that are not instantaneous. Such events can be thought of as changes from one clade to another, and hence can be represented as pairs of clades.

Formally, if Ξ **precedes** Φ, then we call the pair (Ξ,Φ) a *Humean event*. The clade Ξ is its *tail*, and the clade Φ is its *head*. The head and tail may be identical; in this case the Humean event is instantaneous. A Humean event is *simple* if its head and tail both consist of single situations, *initial* if its tail is initial, *inevitable* if its head is a cut (in which case its tail is also a cut), *full* if its tail implies its head (since the tail precedes the head, this is the same as requiring that the tail always foretell the head) and *proper* if its head does not include a cut of any of the situations in its tail. Two Humean events are *divergent* if their heads are divergent.

A simple Humean event (S,T) can be identified with the closed interval [S,T]. More generally, any Humean event (Ξ,Φ) can be thought of as the set consisting of all closed intervals that begin in Ξ and end in Φ.

A step from a situation S to a daughter T in a finite event trellis is, of course, a closed interval and hence a Humean event. But individual steps cannot play in a general theory the special role they play when the trellis is finite. A daughter of S is a nearest strict successor—a strict successor of S that has no strict predecessor that is also a strict successor of S. In infinite event trellises, where situations can have strict successors without having nearest strict successors, we must look to Humean events to play the philosophical and mathematical roles assigned to steps in Section 1: Humean events can represent contingent causes, and when we have probabilities, we can sometimes apportion a numerical variable's variance among Humean events.

4. Martingales

Turning an event tree into a probability tree is simple in the finite case: we merely add branching probabilities below each nonterminal situation. This approach does not

[4]This differs from the definition of cut given in Section 11.2 of *The Art of Causal Conjecture*.

always work for infinite trees, for two reasons. On the one hand, there may be a continuum of daughters. On the other hand, there may be no daughters at all, as in the example at the end of §3.1. How can we proceed?

The obvious answer is to shift attention from branching probabilities to expected values. Expected values are assigned to situations, not to branches or steps, and situations remain prominent in our general theory of event trees. Instead of thinking of a probability structure as a collection of branching probabilities, we think of it as a linear space of functions—martingales, we shall call them—that assign numbers (intuitively, expected values for numerical variables) to situations. Instead of axiomatizing probabilities, we axiomatize martingales.

This approach has a number of advantages. Most importantly, it points the way to generalizations that allow probability to play a wider role in causal reasoning. Standard expositions of probability theory insist that probabilities be defined for all events, and in the context of a finite event tree, this means that every step should have a branching probability. But when we think of probability structure in terms of a linear space of martingales, it is no longer natural to insist that the structure be complete in this way. Each martingale is a declaration by the event-trellis observer that certain bets are fair—that they are among the bets the observer can make while expecting to break even—and the observer may have this kind of confidence in only a limited number of bets. The events represented in the trellis may include the observer's own actions, on which it may not be sensible for her to bet. And when the observer is nature, so that the martingales represent regularities that nature can use for prediction, the extent of such regularities should be regarded as an empirical question.

4.1. Martingales Defined. Let us call a numerical function on an event trellis Γ a *process*. A process μ is a *martingale*[5] if it satisfies the following axiom:

Axiom M If $S \in \Gamma$, and Ξ is a cut of S, then there exist situations T_1 and T_2 in Ξ such that $\mu(T_1) \leq \mu(S) \leq \mu(T_2)$.[6]

If the event trellis is finite, this is equivalent to saying that every nonterminal situation S has daughters T_1 and T_2 such that $\mu(T_1) \leq \mu(S) \leq \mu(T_2)$.

For every number a, the process identically equal to a is a martingale. If μ is a martingale, and a is a number, then $a\mu$ is a martingale. More generally, if μ is a martingale, and f is a monotonic function, then $f(\mu)$ is a martingale. On the other hand, as Figure 23 illustrates, the pointwise sum of two martingales is not necessarily a martingale.

---

[5]In the established terminology of advanced probability theory, a martingale is a sequence of random variables $X_1, X_2, \ldots$ together with a sequence of σ-algebras $F_1, F_2, \ldots$ such that X_i is equal to the expected value of X_{i+1} with respect to F_i (see, for example, Shiryayev 1984). This definition has the same intuitive content as our definition, except that it begins with a fully probabilized tree. The sequence of σ-algebras defines an event tree, and the successive variables give the successive values of the martingale as one moves down the tree.

[6]We do not require T_1 and T_2 to be distinct. Thus the condition is satisfied if there exists a situation T in Ξ with $\mu(T) = \mu(S)$.

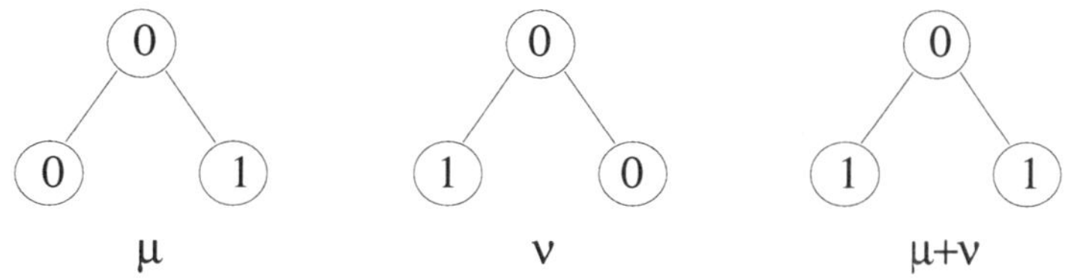

Figure 23 The processes μ and ν are martingales, but the process μ+ν is not.

The expected values of a numerical variable in a finite probability tree obviously form a martingale. More precisely, if X is a variable in a finite probability tree, and we define a process **E**(X) on the tree by setting

(7) $\mathbf{E}(X)(S) := E_S(X)$,

then **E**(X) is a martingale. The variable X is identified by **E**(X); its value on a path is given by **E**(X)'s value on the terminal situation in that path. The abstract concept of martingale does not depend, however, on the event tree having been made into a probability tree by the addition of branching probabilities.

We say a process is *determinate* in a situation S if all T that follow S are assigned the same value as S by the process. We say a process is *terminating* if every path contains a situation in which the process is determinate. If a process is terminating, then it specifies a variable, whose value on each path is the value the process eventually assumes on that path. When the terminating process is a martingale, we may say that it *evaluates* the variable, and we may think of its values as expected values of the variable.

4.2. Catalogs. We call a linear space of martingales on an event trellis a *catalog*. Catalogs provide the principal concept of probability structure in the remainder of this article. Intuitively, a catalog represents all the gambling strategies an observer in the event tree considers fair. The assumption that these strategies form a linear space derives from the judgment that fairness is preserved under the formation of linear combinations. If a given bet is fair, then it is fair to double it, and if two bets are individually fair, then it is fair to combine them.

A catalog can contain at most one martingale evaluating a given variable. (If two martingales in a catalog evaluate the same variable, then their difference, which is also in the catalog and is therefore a martingale, will have the value zero everywhere by Axiom M, and hence the two martingales will be equal.) Whenever the catalog does contain a martingale that evaluates X, we write **E**(X) for this martingale, and we call **E**(X) the *expectation* of X. We write $E_S(X)$ for **E**(X)(S), and we call $E_S(X)$ the *expected value* of X in S.

In the case of a variable E that takes only the values zero and one (an event), we write **P**(E) instead of **E**(E) and $P_S(E)$ instead of $E_S(E)$; we call the martingale **P**(E) the *probability* of E, and we call the number $P_S(E)$ the *probability* of E *in* S. It often happens that a catalog evaluates a variable X without evaluating events of the form $\{X \in A\}$ that interest us. If a catalog does evaluate $\{X \in A\}$ for every Borel set A, we may say that it *probabilizes* X.

In the case of a finite probability tree, the set of martingales $\{\mathbf{E}(X) \mid X \text{ is a variable}\}$, where **E**(X) is given by (7), is a catalog. Such a catalog is maximal; since it already contains a martingale evaluating every variable, it is not contained in any strictly larger catalog. We may call a maximal catalog on any event trellis, finite or infinite, a *probability catalog*.

While probability catalogs are interesting, smaller catalogs are also interesting, even in the case of finite event trees. An important example is the finite decision tree, where branching probabilities are provided for the branchings below *chance* situations, but not for those below *decision* situations. Figure 24 gives an example. If we form martingales by placing bets according to the odds given by the branching probabilities below chance situations, then these martingales form a catalog, which we call the *fair-bet catalog* for the decision tree. Each martingale in the catalog evaluates a variable, but not all variables are evaluated by martingales in the catalog; the evaluated variables satisfy linear constraints imposed by the fact that the martingales are all constant on the daughters of each decision situation. For details, and for an analysis of the structure of all catalogs on finite event trees, see Section 12.2 of *The Art of Causal Conjecture*.

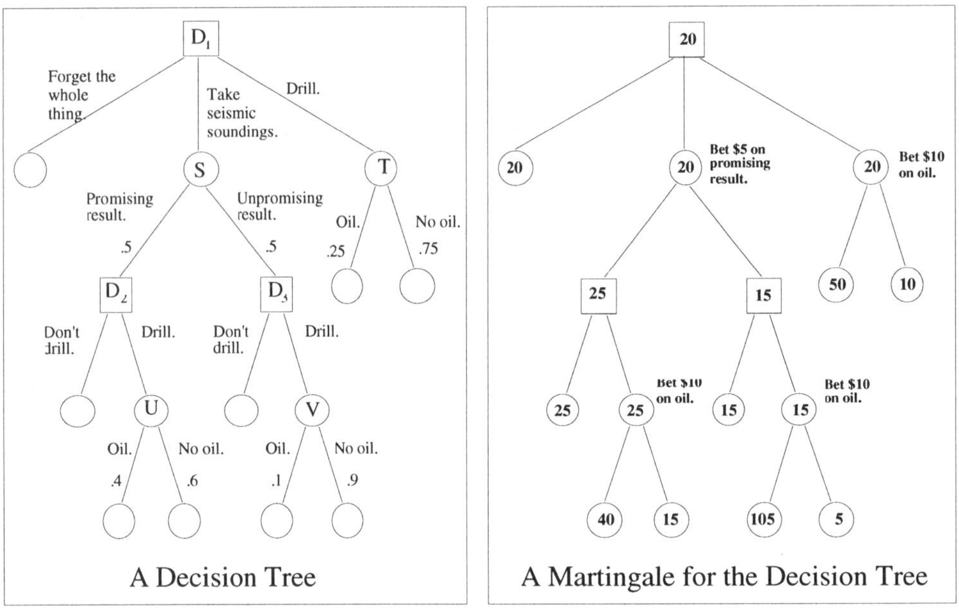

Figure 24 The decision tree on the left is adapted from the problem of the oil wildcatter in Raiffa (1968). There are branching probabilities for the steps following the nonterminal chance situations S, T, U, and V, but no branching probabilities following the decision situations D1, D2, and D3. On picture on the right shows the martingale resulting from one choice of fair bets.

In principle, any catalog can be enlarged to a probability catalog, and we might take the view that a catalog that falls short of being a probability catalog is an incomplete expression of opinion. This seems wrong-headed, however. If we take a constructive view of probability judgment (Shafer and Tversky 1985), then we expect a person's probability opinions to be limited. And if we think of nature's probabilities as reflecting regularities in the world, then we have no reason to believe that such regularities are to be found around every corner.

4.3. Stopping a Martingale. If μ is a martingale, and Ξ is a cut, then we write $\mathbf{E}_\Xi(\mu)$ for the process given by

$$\mathbf{E}_\Xi(\mu)(S) := \mu(\Xi(S)),$$

where

$$\Xi(S) := \begin{cases} S & \text{if } T \in \Xi \text{ and } S \textbf{ precedes } T \\ R & \text{if } R \in \Xi \text{ and } R \textbf{ precedes } S. \end{cases}$$

It is easy to see that $\mathbf{E}_{\Xi}(\mu)$ is a martingale. We call it the *expectation* of μ in Ξ. Intuitively, it is the result of stopping μ in Ξ. Figure 25 illustrates the idea.

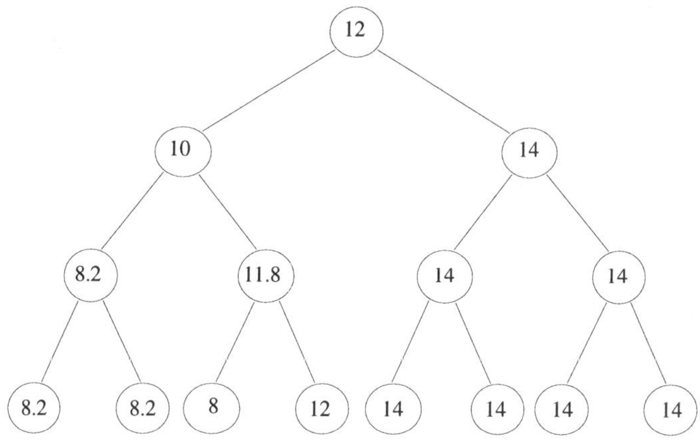

Figure 25 The martingale $\mathbf{E}_{\Xi}(\mu)$, where μ is the martingale in Figure 4, and Ξ is the cut in Figure 21. This martingale agrees with μ down to Ξ and then remains unchanged the rest of the way down the tree.

The expectation of μ given Ξ is determinate in Ξ. If μ is determinate in Ξ, then $\mathbf{E}_{\Xi}(\mu) = \mu$. If Ξ and Φ are cuts and Ξ **precedes** Φ, then

$$\mathbf{E}_{\Xi}(\mathbf{E}_{\Phi}(\mu)) = \mathbf{E}_{\Xi}(\mu).$$

This is an event-trellis form of the *rule of iterated expectation.*

We call a catalog M *Doob* if it satisfies the following axiom:

Axiom V If $\mu \in M$ and Ξ is a cut, then $\mathbf{E}_{\Xi}(\mu) \in M$.

Probability catalogs are Doob, as are the fair-bet catalogs for decision trees. A catalog that is not Doob can always be enlarged to one that is by adding all finite linear combinations of its expectations and its elements. The idea of fairness could justify our incorporating Axiom V into the definition of catalog, but since any linear space of martingales can be enlarged in a canonical way to satisfy them, simplicity and convenience is best served by calling any linear space of martingales a catalog.

4.4. Lower and Upper Probabilities. Consider an event trellis Γ with a fixed Doob catalog M. We say that a process μ on Γ is *eventually* less than or equal to a variable X *after* S, and we write $\mu \leq\downarrow_S X$, if in every path ω from S, there is a situation T such that $\mu(U) \leq X(\omega)$ for all U following T. We define $\mu \geq\downarrow_S X$ similarly.

Given a variable X, we set

(8) $$\bar{E}_S(X) := \sup\{\mu(S) \mid \mu \in M, \mu \leq\downarrow_S X\},$$

and we write $\mathbf{E}^{-}(X)$ for the process given by $\mathbf{E}^{-}(X)(S) := \bar{E}_S(X)$. We call $\mathbf{E}^{-}(X)$ the *lower expectation* of X, and we call $\bar{E}_S(X)$ the *lower expected value* of X in S.

Dual to the idea of lower expectation is the idea of upper expectation. The *upper expected value* of X in S is

$$\overset{+}{E}_S(X) := \inf\{\mu(S) \mid \mu \in M,\ \mu \geq\downarrow_S X\},$$

and the *upper expectation* of X is the process $\mathbf{E}^{+}(X)$ given by $\mathbf{E}^{+}(X)(S) := \overset{+}{E}_S(X)$. Notice that $\mathbf{E}^{-}(X) = -\mathbf{E}^{+}(-X)$.

The ideas of lower expectation and upper expectation are most easily understood in terms of a *house*, an infinitely rich observer in the event trellis, who is willing to make a bet with another observer whenever that bet is in the catalog or is more favorable to herself than one in the catalog. The lower expected value $\overset{-}{E}_S(X)$ is the highest price the house would pay for X in S, while the upper expected value $\overset{+}{E}_S(X)$ is the lowest price she would charge for X in S. If the house were the only betting partner available to us, we would think of $\overset{-}{E}_S(X)$ as the scrap value of X in S, and of $\overset{+}{E}_S(X)$ as the cost of X in S.

Here are some informative properties of lower expectation.

Proposition 8. *Suppose M is a Doob catalog on a finite event trellis.*

1. *The supremum in (8) is attained. In other words, for each S there is a martingale μ in M such that $\mu \geq\downarrow_S X$ and $\mu(S) = \overset{-}{E}_S(X)$.*
2. *$\mathbf{E}^{-}(X)$ is a martingale.*
3. *$\mathbf{E}^{-}(X)$ is the infimum of the expectations of X for the various probability catalogs that contain M. There is a probability catalog containing M for which $\mathbf{E}^{-}(X)$ is the expectation of X.*
4. *If Ξ is evaluated by a martingale in M, so that the expectation $\mathbf{E}(X)$ exists, then $\mathbf{E}^{-}(X) = \mathbf{E}(X)$.*

(See Section 12.6 of *The Art of Causal Conjecture.* We leave it to the reader to formulate the corresponding statements about upper expectation.) According to Statement 3, lower expected values can be thought of as lower bounds. Upper expected values can similarly be thought of as upper bounds. Different ways of completing the definition of the branching probabilities in an event tree with a catalog produce different expected values for X in S, and $\overset{-}{E}_S(X)$ and $\overset{+}{E}_S(X)$ are tight lower and upper bounds, respectively, on these expected values.

If we are in a position to enlarge the catalog to a probability catalog, by taking actions that fix the branching probabilities, then it is appropriate to view lower expected and upper expected values as bounds on expected values. Figure 26 illustrates the point. But when it is not within our power to transform the tree into a probability tree by enlarging its catalog, the idea that the lower and upper expectations are bounds should be treated gingerly. There is no reason to say that there is an unknown expectation between the lower expectation and upper expectation.

When E is an event (a variable that takes only the values zero and one), we write $\overset{-}{P}_S(E)$ for $\overset{-}{E}_S(E)$ and call it the *lower probability* of E in S. Similarly, we write $\overset{+}{P}_S(E)$ for $\overset{+}{E}_S(E)$ and call it the *upper probability* of E in S. The lower probability $\overset{-}{P}_S(E)$ is the highest price the house would pay for a contract that returns \$1 if E happens, while the upper probability $\overset{+}{P}_S(E)$ is the lowest price at which she would sell such a contract.

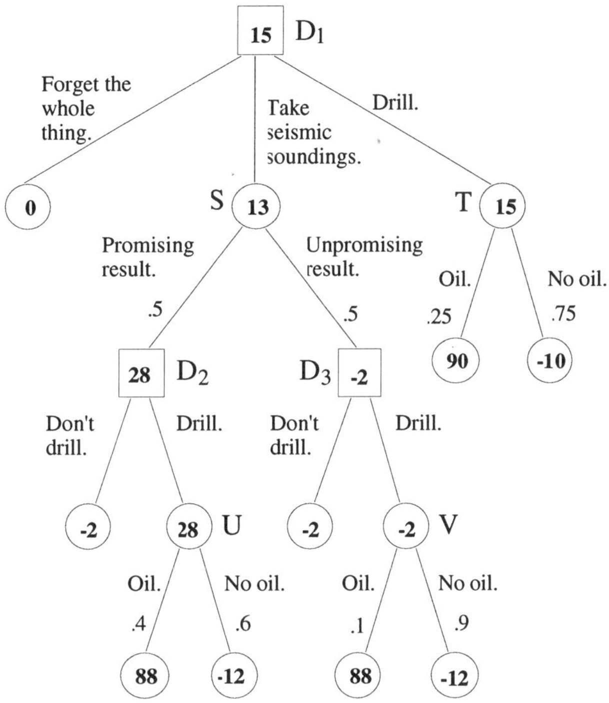

Figure 26 The upper expectation of a wildcatter's payoff. We assume that it costs \$10,000 to drill and \$2,000 to take seismic soundings, and that the wildcatter will earn \$100,000 if she finds oil. This gives the payoff X shown in the terminal situations. The upper expected values of X are shown in the other situations. If the wildcatter wants to choose the branching probabilities in the decision situations so as to maximize X's expected value in the initial situation, then the best she can do is $\mathbf{E}^{+}_{\Omega}(X)$, or \$15,000. This is achieved by drilling in the initial situation with probability one. The choice of branching probabilities for D_2 and D_3 is then immaterial, but in order to achieve the upper expected value in D_2, we should drill with probability one there. Any choice of branching probabilities will achieve the upper expected value in D_3.

4.5. Causality. The theory of causality that we developed in Section 1 can be extended to the general context of event trellises with catalogs provided that we make appropriate regularity assumptions. The simplest adequate assumption, perhaps, is that each path is compact in the interval topology. This means that for any collection of closed intervals (see §3.2) that has ω as its union, there is a finite subcollection that also has ω as its union.

Let us call a Humean event of the form (S,Ξ), where Ξ is a cut of S, an *experiment*, and let us call the set of situations

$$\{T \mid S \textbf{ precedes } T \text{ and there exists } U \in \Xi \text{ such that } T \textbf{ precedes } U\}$$

the *scope* of the experiment (S,Ξ). Let us call a collection of experiments a *cover* if the union of the scopes is equal to the entire event tree.

We say that an experiment *forbears* a martingale if the martingale has the same value on all situations in the experiment's scope. We say that two martingales are *uncorrelated* if there exists a cover, every experiment in which forbears at least one of the two martingales. The following proposition is about uncorrelated martingales is proven in Chapter

12 of *The Art of Causal Conjecture*, the reader may extend it to general event trellises under the regularity condition discussed above.

Proposition 9. *Suppose μ and ν are uncorrelated martingales. Then $\mu+\nu$ and $\mu\nu$ are martingales. More generally, $f(\mu,\nu)$ is a martingale whenever $f(x,y)$ is monotonic in both its arguments.*

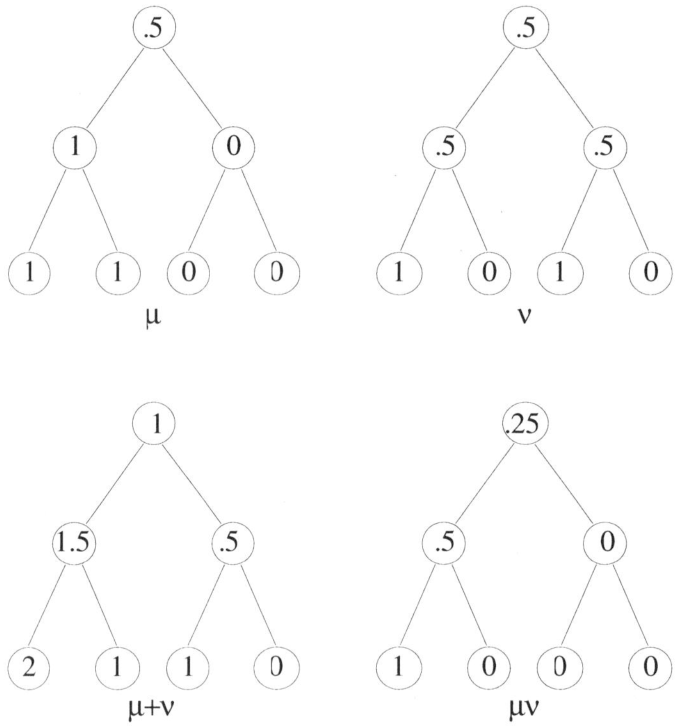

Figure 27 Two uncorrelated martingales, their sum, and their product.

We say that two variables Y and Z are *causally uncorrelated* if they are evaluated and the martingales evaluating them are uncorrelated. The next proposition then spells out within in this general theory the fact, which we discussed for finite probability trees in Section 1, that causal uncorrelatedness implies uncorrelatedness in the usual sense.

Proposition 10. *Consider an event tree with a Doob catalog M.*

1. If μ and ν are uncorrelated martingales in M, then $\mu\nu$ is in M.

2. If X and Y are uncorrelated variables, then the product XY is evaluated, and **E***(XY) =* **E***(X)***E***(Y).*

From the idea of causal uncorrelatedness, we can also construct the other causal ideas that we mentioned in Section 1. For example, we say that two variables X and Y are *causally independent* if they are probabilized and {X=x} is uncorrelated with {Y=y} for all x and y; we can then prove that causally independent variables are independent in the usual sense.

4.6. Limit Theorems. The idea of lower probability is important because it allows us to formulate the traditional limit theorems of probability theory, which assert that various things are almost certain to happen in a long run of trials. We simply interpret "almost certain" as "with very high lower probability."

An example of this approach is provided by the following version of the law of large numbers.

Proposition 11. *For any positive real number K (no matter how large) and any positive real numbers ε and δ (no matter how small), there exists an integer N such that if $n \geq N$ and $X_1, X_2, \ldots, X_n$ are causally uncorrelated variables in an event tree with a Doob catalog, all the X_i have value zero in the initial situation I, all are bounded by K, and $\bar{X}$ is their average, then $\mathbf{P}_I(|\bar{X}| \leq \delta) \geq 1-\varepsilon$.*

The law of large numbers has the same significance in our theory as it does in standard probability theory. It implies that if situations are replicated as nature moves through her tree, we can estimate nature's probabilities in these situations from observed frequencies.

Other limit theorems, including the central limit theorem and the law of the iterated logarithm, have been treated from essentially the point of view taken here by Vovk (1993a,b).

5. Refinement

How can we describe abstractly the relation between an event trellis and a refinement? The examples in Section 2 suggest that we specify, for each situation S in the original trellis, the situations in the refinement that agree with S, in the sense that they represent the same instantaneous event, possibly describing it in more detail. These situations are divergent—i.e., they form a clade, say $\rho(S)$ in the refinement. If we set $\rho(\Xi) := \cup_{S \in \Xi} \rho(S)$ when Ξ is a clade in the original trellis, then $\rho(\Xi)$ is also a clade in the refinement, consisting of situations that agree with and possibly add more detail to some situation in Ξ. The mapping from clades to clades thus defined fully specifies the relationship between the two event trellises.

5.1. An Axiomatization of Refinement. Formally, let us say that a mapping ρ from clades in an event trellis Γ to clades in an event trellis Γ^* *refines* Γ to Γ^* if it satisfies the following axioms:

Axiom R1 Ξ **disjoint** Φ if and only if $\rho(\Xi)$ **disjoint** $\rho(\Phi)$.
Axiom R2 Ξ **diverges** Φ if and only if $\rho(\Xi)$ **diverges** $\rho(\Phi)$.
Axiom R3 Ξ **prerequisite** Φ if and only if $\rho(\Xi)$ **prerequisite** $\rho(\Phi)$.
Axiom R4 Ξ **allows** Φ if and only if $\rho(\Xi)$ **allows** $\rho(\Phi)$.
Axiom R5 Ξ **implies** Φ if and only if $\rho(\Xi)$ **implies** $\rho(\Phi)$.
Axiom R6 If $\{\Xi_\alpha\}_{\alpha \in A}$ are divergent clades in Γ, then $\rho(\cup_{\alpha \in A} \Xi_\alpha) = \cup_{\alpha \in A} \rho(\Xi_\alpha)$.

When ρ refines Γ to Γ^*, we say Γ^* is a *refinement* of Γ, and Γ is a *coarsening* of Γ^*.

Axioms R1-R6 are easy to justify on the understanding that (1) a clade represents the instantaneous event that the observer arrives in a situation in the clade, and (2) Ξ and $\rho(\Xi)$ represent the same instantaneous event. From this perspective, the axioms merely say that the meaning of various relations among instantaneous events (being divergent, one being a prerequisite for the other, etc.) is not affected when we choose to represent the events in greater detail.

We will abbreviate ρ({S}) to ρ(S). By Axiom R1, the clades ρ(S) are all disjoint. When S* is an element of ρ(S), we say S* *refines* or is a *refinement* of S, and S *coarsens* or is a *coarsening* of S*.

Given a subset γ^* of Γ^*, we write $\rho^{-1}(\gamma^*)$ for the subset of Γ consisting of all coarsenings of situations in γ^*.

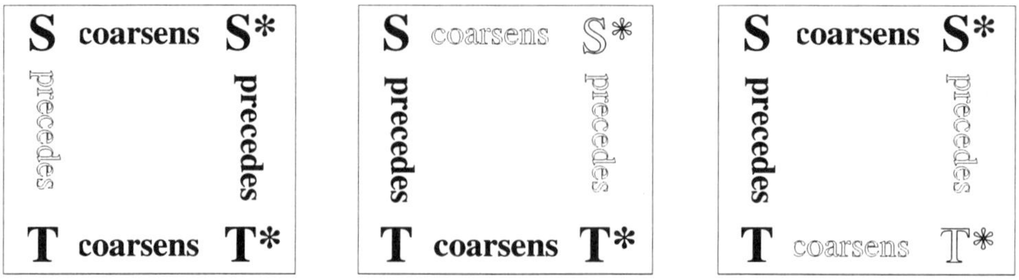

If the relations in bold hold, then the relation in outline holds.

If the relations in bold hold, then there exists S* such that the relations in outline hold.

If the relations in bold hold, then there exists T* such that the relations in outline hold.

Figure 28 Statements 6, 8, and 9 of Proposition 12.

The following proposition clarifies some aspects of refinement.

Proposition 12. *Suppose ρ refines Γ to Γ*, and suppose Ξ and Φ are clades in Γ.*

1. $\rho(\Xi) = \cup_{S\in\Xi}\rho(S)$.
2. *Ξ = Φ if and only if ρ(Ξ) = ρ(Φ).*
3. *Ξ* ***precedes*** *Φ if and only if ρ(Ξ)* ***precedes*** *ρ(Φ).*
4. *Ξ* ***foretells*** *Φ if and only if ρ(Ξ)* ***foretells*** *ρ(Φ).*
5. *Ξ* ***alw.foretells*** *Φ if and only if ρ(Ξ)* ***alw.foretells*** *ρ(Φ).*
6. *Suppose S coarsens S*, T coarsens T*, and S* precedes T*. Then S precedes T.*
7. *Φ contains a cut of S if and only if ρ(Φ) contains a cut of every refinement of S.*
8. *Suppose T coarsens T* and S precedes T. Then there exists a situation S* that refines S and precedes T*.*
9. *Suppose S coarsens S* and S precedes T. Then there exists a situation T* that follows S* and refines T.*

Proof 1. Statement 1 is a special case of Axiom R6.

2. Since the ρ(S) are disjoint, by Axiom R1, Statement 2 follows from Statement 1.

3. Statement 3 follows from Axioms R3 and R4.

4. Statement 4 follows from Axioms R4 and R5.

5. Statement 5 follows from Axioms R3 and R5.

6. By Axiom R2, S and T must be sequenced rather than divergent. So either S precedes T or T precedes S. If T precedes S, then by Axiom R3, there exists a refinement T^*_2 of T that precedes S* and hence T*; since ρ(T) is a clade, this implies that T^*_2 = S* = T*; and so by Axiom R1, S = T. Hence S precedes T.

7. Recall that (1) Φ containing a cut of Ξ is equivalent to Ξ **foretells** Φ and (2) Ξ **foretells** Φ is equivalent to S **foretells** Φ for all S in Ξ. Using these equivalences

and Statement 4, we see that Φ containing a cut of S is equivalent to S **foretells** Φ, which is equivalent to ρ(S) **foretells** $\rho(\Phi)$, which is equivalent to $\rho(\Phi)$ containing a cut of ρ(S), which is equivalent to $\rho(\Phi)$ containing a cut of S* for every S* in ρ(S).

8. Statement 8 follows from Axiom R3.
9. Statement 9 follows from Axiom R4. ♦

5.2. An Alternative Axiomatization. Axioms R1-R6 constitute only one way of axiomatizing refinement; there are many others, some much more austere. For example, instead of thinking of refinement from Γ to Γ^* as a mapping that assigns a clade in Γ^* to each clade in Γ, we can step back to thinking of it as a mapping that assigns a clade of situations ρ(S) in Γ^* to each situation S in Γ, and we can adopt the following axioms:

Axiom R1' All the ρ(S) are disjoint from each other.
Axiom R2' If S **diverges** T, then ρ(S) **diverges** ρ(T).
Axiom R3' If S **precedes** T, then ρ(S) **precedes** ρ(T).
Axiom R4' Suppose Φ is a clade in Γ and S* is in ρ(S). Then Φ is a cut of S if and only if $\cup_{T\in\Phi}\rho(T)$ contains a cut of S*.

As the following proposition shows, Axioms R1'-R4' are equivalent to Axioms R1-R6.

Proposition 13.

1. Suppose ρ is a mapping from clades in Γ to clades in Γ^* that satisfies Axioms R1-R6. Define a new mapping ρ from situations in Γ to clades in Γ^* by setting $\rho(S) := \rho(\{S\})$. Then this new mapping ρ satisfies Axioms R1'-R4'.

2. Suppose ρ is a mapping from situations in Γ to clades in Γ^* that satisfies Axioms R1'-R4'. Define a new mapping ρ from clades in Γ to sets of situations in Γ^* by setting $\rho(\Xi) := \cup_{S\in\Xi}\rho(S)$. Then $\rho(\Xi)$ is a clade in Γ^* for every clade Ξ in Γ, and ρ satisfies Axioms R1-R6.

Proof 1. Axiom R1' follows from Axiom R1. Axiom R2' follows from Axiom R2. Axiom R3' follows Statement 3 of Proposition 12. Axiom R4' follows from Statement 7 of Proposition 12.

2. It follows from Axiom R2' that each $\rho(\Xi)$ is a clade. Axiom R1 follows from Axiom R1'.

It follows from Axiom R2' that if Ξ is divergent from Φ, then $\rho(\Xi)$ is divergent from $\rho(\Phi)$. On the other hand, if Ξ is not divergent from Φ, then there are situations S in Ξ and T in Φ that are sequenced, and hence, by Axiom R3', there are situations S* in ρ(S) and T* in ρ(T) that are sequenced, whence $\rho(\Xi)$ is divergent from $\rho(\Phi)$. This establishes Axiom R2.

Suppose Ξ **prerequisite** Φ. Consider a situation T* in $\rho(\Phi)$. Let T be the situation in Φ that coarsens T*. By the assumption Ξ **prerequisite** Φ, T has a predecessor S in Ξ. By Axiom R3', T* has a predecessor, say S*, in $\rho(\Xi)$. Since T* was an arbitrary situation in $\rho(\Phi)$, this establishes that $\rho(\Xi)$ **prerequisite** $\rho(\Phi)$.

Now suppose $\rho(\Xi)$ **prerequisite** $\rho(\Phi)$. Consider a situation T in Φ. Choose a situation T* in ρ(T). Let S* be T*'s predecessor in $\rho(\Xi)$, and let S be the situation in Ξ that coarsens S*. By Axiom R2', S and T must be sequenced. If T were to precede S, then by Axiom R3' we would have ρ(T) **precedes** ρ(S), which would imply the existence of a situation T_2* in ρ(T) such that T_2* **precedes** S* **precedes** T*, and since ρ(T) is a clade, this would imply that $S^* = T^*$, whence (Axiom R1') $S = T$. So S precedes T. This establishes Ξ **prerequisite** Φ and hence completes the derivation of Axiom R3.

Suppose Ξ **allows** Φ. Consider a situation S^* in $\rho(\Xi)$. Let S be the situation in Ξ that coarsens S^*. Then S has a successor T in Φ. By Axiom R3', S^* has a successor, say T^*, in $\rho(\Phi)$. This establishes $\rho(\Xi)$ **allows** $\rho(\Phi)$.

Now suppose $\rho(\Xi)$ **allows** $\rho(\Phi)$. Consider a situation S in Ξ. Choose a situation S^* in $\rho(S)$. Let T^* be a successor of S^* in $\rho(\Phi)$, and let T be the situation in Φ that coarsens T^*. By the same argument we used in the paragraph before last, S precedes T. This establishes Ξ **allows** Φ and hence completes the derivation of Axiom R4.

Suppose Ξ **implies** Φ. Consider a situation S^* in $\rho(\Xi)$. Let S be the situation in Ξ that coarsens S^*. Then S has either a predecessor or a cut in Φ. If S has a predecessor in Φ, then by Axiom R3', S^* has a predecessor in $\rho(\Phi)$. If S has a cut in Φ, then by Axiom R4', S^* has a cut in $\rho(\Phi)$. This establishes that $\rho(\Xi)$ **implies** $\rho(\Phi)$.

Now suppose $\rho(\Xi)$ **implies** $\rho(\Phi)$. Consider a situation S in Ξ. Choose a situation S^* in $\rho(S)$. Then S^* has either a predecessor or a cut in $\rho(\Phi)$. If S^* has a predecessor in $\rho(\Phi)$, then by a previous argument, S has a predecessor in Φ. If S^* has a cut in $\rho(\Phi)$, then by Axiom R4', S has a cut in Φ. This establishes Ξ **implies** Φ and hence completes the derivation of Axiom R5.

Finally, Axiom R6 follows from the definition $\rho(\Xi) := \cup_{S\in\Xi}\rho(S)$. ♦

For further ways of axiomatizing refinement, see Section 13.3 of *The Art of Causal Conjecture*.

5.3. Consistency with Finite Refinement. We now need to verify that the concept of refinement contained in Axioms R1-R6 agrees, in the case of a finite event tree, with the concept of refinement developed in Section 2.

Proposition 14.

1. Suppose Γ and Γ^* are finite event trees, and Γ^* is a refinement of Γ in the sense of Section 2. For each situation S in Γ, let $\rho(S)$ be the set of situations in Γ^* that refine S. For each clade Ξ in Γ, set

$$\rho(\Xi) = \cup_{S\in\Xi}\rho(S).$$

Then $\rho(\Xi)$ is always a clade in Γ^*, and the mapping ρ satisfies Axioms R1-R6.

2. Suppose Γ and Γ^* are finite event trees, and suppose ρ satisfies Axioms R1-R6. Suppose, moreover, that ρ maps the initial situation I in Γ to the initial situation I^* in Γ^*. Then ρ is a composition of elementary refinements of the kind described in Section 2.

Proof 1. Statement 1 is obviously satisfied by an elementary refinement. To see that it is also satisfied by a composition of elementary refinements, it suffices to notice that composition of refinements means composition of the corresponding mappings: if ρ_1 represents the refinement from Γ to Γ^*, and ρ_2 represents the refinement from Γ^* to Γ^{**}, then $\rho_2 \circ \rho_1$ represents the refinement from Γ to Γ^{**}. It is obvious from the form of the axioms that they are preserved by such composition.

2. We will prove Statement 2 using induction on the number of nonterminal situations in Γ^*. Suppose first that there is only one nonterminal situation in Γ^*, which is therefore initial and has all the terminal situations as its daughters. And consider two cases: (1) there is no situation S in Γ such that $\rho(S)$ contains a terminal situation in Γ^*, and (2) there is such a situation S.

In case (1), ρ maps every situation in Γ to the initial situation in Γ*. But Axiom R1 forbids that ρ should map distinct situations to the same situation. So there is the only situation in Γ, and the refinement is of the form shown in Figure 29. This is an elementary refinement.

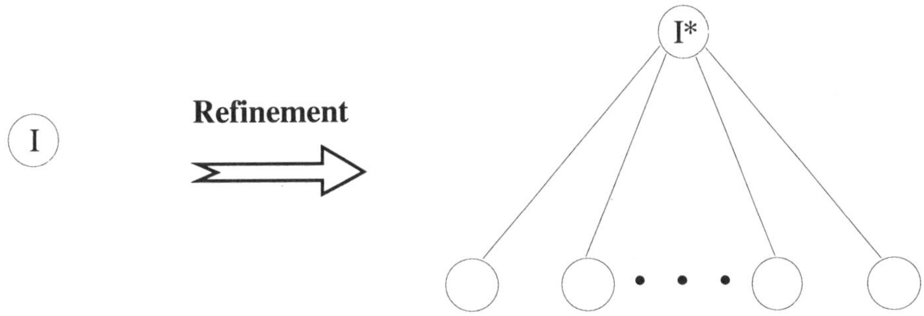

Figure 29 An elementary refinement, in which the original tree consists of a single situation, and the refined tree consists of a situation with daughters.

In case (2), S is distinct from I. By Axiom T0, S follows I. So by Statement 2 of Proposition 5, S is in a cut of I, say Ξ. By Axiom R5, ρ(Ξ) is a cut of I*, and since it is not equal to {I*}, it must consist of all I*'s daughters, the terminal situations in Γ*. So by Axioms R1 and R6, ρ maps the situations in Ξ to disjoint sets of these daughters. This establishes that ρ is an elementary refinement of the type shown in Figure 30, provided that we can show that I and the situations in Ξ are the only situations in Γ. But this is true by Axiom R2.

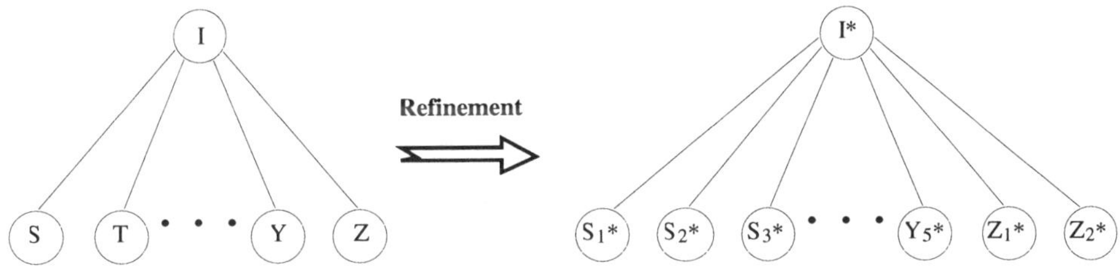

Figure 30 An elementary refinement, in which terminal situations are mapped to clades of terminal situations.

Now suppose Statement 2 holds for refinements with n or fewer nonterminal situations, and suppose Γ* has n+1 nonterminal situations.

We consider three cases: (1) ρ(S) is always a single situation, and every situation in Γ* refines a situation in Γ, (2) at least one situation in Γ* does not refine a situation in Γ, and (3) every situation in Γ* refines a situation in Γ, and at least one pair of distinct situations in Γ* refine the same situation in Γ.

In case (1) ρ maps Γ one-to-one and onto Γ*, and by Axiom R3 (or R4), it also preserves precedence, so that it is the identity mapping from the partially ordered set Γ to itself, and this qualifies as an elementary refinement.

In case (2), choose a situation Z* in Γ* that does not refine a situation in Γ. Let P* be the nearest predecessor of Z* that refines a situation in Γ. By Statement 8 of Proposition 8, P* either has no strict successors that refine situations in Γ or has a whole cut of them. In the first case, we may omit the strict successors of P* to obtain a smaller refinement of Γ, and the addition of the strict successors constitutes a further elementary refinement, so that the proof by induction is complete. In the second case we may choose the cut so that all the situations strictly between P* and the cut do not refine elements of Γ, and Z* will be one of these. Omitting these situations again produces a smaller refinement of Γ, and adding them back again constitutes a further elementary refinement.

Finally, consider case (3), where every situation in Γ* refines a situation in Γ, and at least one pair, say S_1* and S_2*, refine the same situation S. Then there must exist a pair of terminal situations, say T_1* and T_2*, that refine the same situation T. (Choose a terminal successor, say T_1*, of S_1*, and let T be the situation it refines. By Statement 9 of Proposition 12, T is also terminal. By Statement 6 of Proposition 12, S **precedes** T, and by Statement 9 of Proposition 12, there exists T_2* that also refines T and follows S_2*. Since every situation in Γ* refines a situation in Γ, T_2* must also be terminal.)

Now consider any terminal situations T_1* and T_2* that refine the same situation T. Let S* designate the latest common predecessor of T_1* and T_2*, and let S designate the situation refined by S*. Then T is terminal, and S **precedes** T. Moreover, the situations in the closed interval [S*,T_1*] and the situations in the closed interval [S*,T_2*] both correspond one-to-one to the situations in the closed interval [S,T]. Let depth(T_1*,T_2*) denote the number of these situations.

From all the terminal situations that refine the same situation, choose a pair T_1* and T_2* with the least value of depth(T_1*,T_2*). Let S* designate their latest common predecessor. Let R_1*,...,R_k* designate the daughters of S*, and let R_1,...,R_k designate the situations they refine. We may assume that R_1* precedes T_1* and R_2* precedes T_2*, so that $R_1 = R_2$. By the assumption that depth (T_1*,T_2*) is minimal, all the terminal situations following a particular R_i* refine distinct situations. We can therefore deduce from Axioms R3 and R4 that the subtree beginning at R_i* is isomorphic to the subtree beginning at R_i, and hence that the subtrees beginning at R_1* and R_2* are isomorphic. If we remove one of these, say the subtree beginning at R_1*, we will still have a refinement of Γ, and restoring it is an elementary refinement. This completes the inductive step of the proof. ♦

6. Event Spaces

As we learned in Section 3, event trees and trellises pack a great deal of meaning into their apparent mathematical simplicity. There is information in the absence as well as in the presence of branches. This density of meaning is often advantageous, because it allows us to handle underlying logical relationships concisely and quickly, but it is not so helpful when we want to couple probability ideas with other forms of information.

Our study of refining has revealed another shortcoming of event trellises: they do not permit the easy coexistence, in the same conversation, of situations described at different levels of detail. Two situations can coexist in the same event trellis only if they describe earlier events at the same level of detail.

In this section, we generalize from event trellises to event spaces—spaces that can contain situations at many different levels of detail. Like an event trellis, an event space describes possibilities for a single observer. Each element of the space is a situation the observer might find herself in, or alternatively, the instantaneous event that she arrives in that situation. But unlike an event trellis, an event space may contain two situations that can happen simultaneously, perhaps because one is simply a more detailed version of the other.

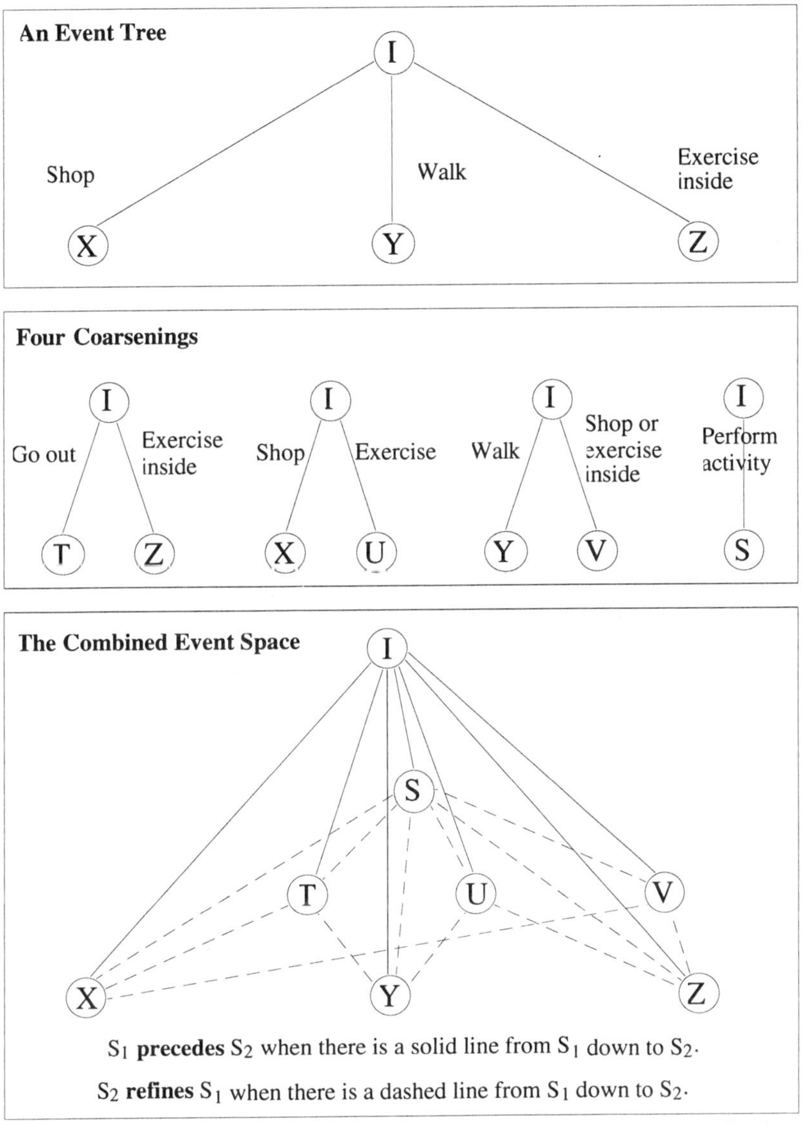

Figure 31 Events trees and an event space for a person who will soon begin to shop, walk, or exercise inside. The second panel shows four ways of coarsening the event tree; the first merges X and Y into T, the second merges Y and Z into U, the third merges X and Z into V, and the fourth merges X, Y, and Z into S. The event space shown in the bottom panel contains X, Y, and Z, together with all the mergers. The two relations shown, **precedes** and **refines**, provide only partial information about how the event space's eight situations are related to each other. A complete account is given in Table 2.

An event space can be thought of, as we shall see, as an event trellis together with additional situations that represent directly the events or situations represented by clades in the event trellis. (Figure 31 provides an example.) But rather than define event spaces in terms of event trellises, we provide a direct axiomatization for event spaces, designed to make clear their potential as a semantics for logics of action and causality. We then prove, from these axioms, that any event space is isomorphic to a space of clades in an event trellis.

6.1. Relations on an Event Space. Consider a set Γ, whose elements we call situations. In order to call Γ an event space, we require certain relations on Γ to satisfy certain axioms. Before listing the axioms, we list the relations, beginning with six primitive ones: **merges**, **overlaps**, **may.Require**, **may.Foretell**, **may.forbear**, and **may.diverge**.

The first primitive relation, **merges**, is a relation between a situation, say S, and a set of situations, say Ξ. Intuitively, S **merges** Ξ means that the single situation S represents the same instantaneous event as the set of situations Ξ.

The other five primitive relations are binary relations—relations between one situation, say S, and another, say T. Their intuitive meanings are listed in Table 1. As this table indicates, each of these relations permits S to happen in a certain way without requiring that it do so. We underline this by calling them *optional* relations. In fact, they are our *basic optional relations*. We will construct from them a number of other relations, some also optional, some mandatory. These relations will include relations with the same names and intuitive meanings as the event-trellis relations we studied earlier.

THE FIVE PRIMITIVE BINARY RELATIONS (BASIC OPTIONAL RELATIONS)

S **1** T	S **overlaps** T (S overlaps T)	S may happen in such a way that T happens at the same time.
S **2** T	S **may.Require** T (S may strictly require T)	S may happen in such a way that T has already happened.
S **3** T	S **may.Foretell** T (S may strictly foretell T)	S may happen in such a way that T must happen later.
S **4** T	S **may.forbear** T (S may forbear T)	S may happen in such a way that T remains only possible.
S **5** T	S **may.diverge** T (S may diverge from T)	S may happen in such a way that T cannot happen.

Table 1 A number, a name, and a verbal explanation is given for each relation. An upper case letter in the name of a relation indicates that it is "strict'—i.e., that it does not permit the two situations to happen at the same time. The strict relations we introduce all have non-strict counterparts.

In order to grasp the intuition underlying Table 1, the reader may wish to think about five ways a situation S* may relate to a clade Φ in an event tree or an event trellis. As Figure 32 shows, S* may be (1) in Φ, (2) below Φ, (3) above Φ, with Φ containing a cut of S*, (4) above Φ, without Φ containing a cut of S*, or (5) divergent from Φ. If we identify the situations S and T in our event space with clades Ξ and Φ in an underlying event trellis, then the situations S* in Ξ are different ways S may happen, and each relates to Φ in one of the five ways shown in the figure.

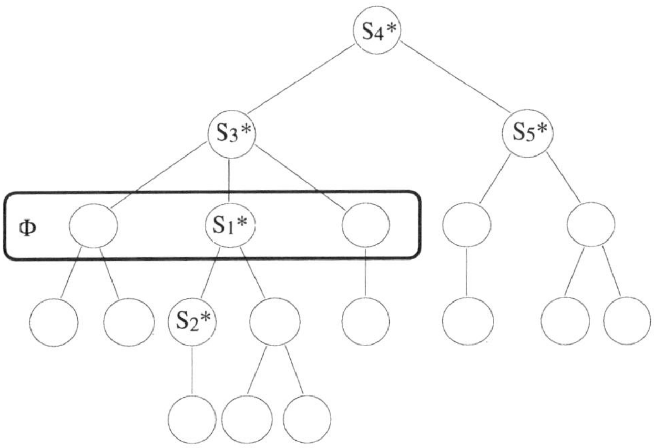

Figure 32 Five ways a situation S* can relate to a clade Φ in an event trellis: (1) S* is in Φ, and so Φ happens at the same time as S*, (2) S* is below Φ, and so Φ has already happened when S* happens, (3) S* is above Φ, and Φ contains a cut of S*, and so Φ must happen after S* happens, (4) S* is above Φ, but Φ does not contain a cut of S*, and so Φ is possible but not necessary after S* happens, and (5) S* is divergent from Φ, and so Φ cannot happen if S* happens.

Table 2 spells out the six primitive relations for Figure 31.

overlaps	(S,S)	(S,T)	(S,U)	(S,V)	(S,X)	(S,Y)	(S,Z)
	(T,S)	(T,T)	(T,U)	(T,V)	(T,X)	(T,Y)	
	(U,S)	(U,T)	(U,U)	(U,V)		(U,Y)	(U,Z)
	(V,S)	(V,T)	(V,U)	(V,V)	(V,X)		(V,Z)
	(X,S)	(X,T)		(X,V)	(X,X)		
	(Y,S)	(Y,T)	(Y,U)			(Y,Y)	
	(Z,S)		(Z,U)	(Z,V)			(Z,Z)
may.Require	(S,I)	(T,I)	(U,I)	(V,I)	(X,I)	(Y,I)	(Z,I)
may.Foretell	(I,S)						
may.forbear		(I,T)	(I,U)	(I,V)	(I,X)	(I,Y)	(I,Z)
may.diverge			(T,U)	(T,V)	(T,X)	(T,Y)	(T,Z)
		(U,T)		(U,V)	(U,X)	(U,Y)	(U,Z)
		(V,T)	(V,U)		(V,X)	(V,Y)	(V,Z)
		(X,T)	(X,U)	(X,V)		(X,Y)	(X,Z)
		(Y,T)	(Y,U)	(Y,V)	(Y,X)		(Y,Z)
		(Z,T)	(Z,U)	(Z,V)	(Z,X)	(Z,Y)	
merges	(S,{S})	(S,{T,Z})	(S,{U,X})	(S,{V,Y})	(S,{X,Y,Z})		
	(T,{T})	(T,{X,Y})					
	(U,{U})	(U,{Y,Z})					
	(V,{V})	(V,{X,Z})					
	(X,{X})						
	(Y,{Y})						
	(Z,{Z})						

Table 2 Primitive relations for Figure 31. These relations describe the event space fully.

The five basic optional relations can be used to form a large variety of further binary relations. For example, we can obtain more optional relations by forming disjunctions of basic optional relations. Since there are twenty-six ways of choosing two or more things from five, this produces twenty-six additional relations. Table 3 lists and names a few of them.

ADDITIONAL OPTIONAL RELATIONS

S **12** T	S **may.require** T (S may require T)	S may happen in such a way that T happens at the same time or has already happened.
S **13** T	S **may.foretell** T (S may foretell T)	S may happen in such a way that T happens at the same time or must happen later.
S **15** T	S **may.align** T (S may align with T)	S may happen in such a way that T happens at the same time or cannot happen.
S **34** T	S **may.Allow** T (S may strictly allow T)	S may happen in such a way that T must happen later or remains only possible.
S **123** T	S **may.imply** T (S may imply T)	S may happen in such a way that T happens at the same time, has already happened, or must happen later.
S **134** T	S **may.allow** T (S may allow T)	S may happen in such a way that T happens at the same time, must happen later, or remains only possible.
S **1234** T	S **compatible** T (S is compatible with T)	S may happen in such a way that T happens at the same time, has already happened, must happen later, or remains only possible.

Table 3 The numbers for each relation list the basic optional relations whose disjunction it represents. For example, S **12** T means that either S **1** T or S **2** T (or both). Notice the non-strict counterparts, **may.require**, **may.foretell**, and **may.allow**, for the strict relations **may.Require**, **may.Foretell**, and **may.Allow**.

We can form yet further binary relations by negating optional relations. This produces *mandatory* relations, relations that restrict the way S can happen. Since there are thirty-one optional relations altogether, there are also thirty-one mandatory relations. Table 4 lists, names, and explains a number of them. We write ¬**o** for the mandatory relation obtained by negating the optional relation **o**. Thus S ¬**45** T is the negation of S **45** T. Since S **45** T means that either S **4** T holds or S **5** T holds (or both hold), S ¬**45** T means that neither S **4** T nor S **5** T hold.

The names and explanations in Table 4 rely on the assumption (which will be a consequence of our axioms) that each time S happens, exactly one of the five possibilities shown in Figure 32 will hold for T—it happens at the same time, has already happened, must happen later, remains merely possible, or cannot happen. This means that denying that some of these possibilities ever arise when S happens is the same as asserting that one of the remaining ones always does. Thus ¬**45** requires what **123** permits. In general, if o is a proper subset of {1,2,3,4,5} and (o) is its complement with respect to {1,2,3,4,5}, then ¬(**o**) requires what **o** permits. We say that ¬(**o**) *realizes* **o**.

BASIC MANDATORY RELATIONS		
S ¬**2345** T	S **refines** T (S refines T)	Whenever S happens, T happens at the same time.
S ¬**1345** T	S **Requires** T (S strictly requires T)	Whenever S happens, T has already happened.
S ¬**1245** T	S **Foretells** T (S strictly foretells T)	Whenever S happens, T must happen later.
S ¬**1235** T	S **forbears** T (S forbears T)	Whenever S happens, T remains only possible.
S ¬**1234** T	S **diverges** T (S diverges from T)	Whenever S happens, T cannot happen.
ADDITIONAL MANDATORY RELATIONS		
S ¬**345** T	S **requires** T (S requires T)	Whenever S happens, T happens at the same time or has already happened.
S ¬**245** T	S **foretells** T (S foretells T)	Whenever S happens, T happens at the same time or must happen later.
S ¬**234** T	S **aligns** T (S aligns with T)	Whenever S happens, T happens at the same time or cannot happen.
S ¬**125** T	S **Allows** T (S strictly allows T)	Whenever S happens, T must happen later or remains only possible.
S ¬**45** T	S **implies** T (S implies T)	Whenever S happens, T happens at the same time, has already happened, or must happen later.
S ¬**25** T	S **allows** T (S allows T)	Whenever S happens, T happens at the same time, must happen later, or remains only possible.
S ¬**5** T	S **tolerates** T (S tolerates T)	Whenever S happens, T happens at the same time, has already happened, must happen later, or remains only possible.

Table 4 Mandatory relations realizing the optional relations in Tables 1 and 3. The numbers for each relation list the basic optional relations it denies. Thus S ¬**45** T means that S **45** T does not hold—i.e., neither S **4** T nor S **5** T holds.

Table 5 shows the basic mandatory relations for Figure 31.

refines	(S,S)	(S,T)	(S,U)	(S,V)	(S,X)	(S,Y)	(S,Z)
	(T,S)	(T,T)					
	(U,S)		(U,U)				
	(V,S)			(V,V)			
					(X,X)	(Y,Y)	(Z,Z)
Requires	(S,I)	(T,I)	(U,I)	(V,I)	(X,I)	(Y,I)	(Z,I)
Foretells	(I,S)						
forbears		(I,T)	(I,U)	(I,V)	(I,X)	(I,Y)	(I,Z)
diverges					(U,X)	(V,Y)	(T,Z)
			(X,U)			(X,Y)	(X,Z)
				(Y,V)	(Y,X)		(Y,Z)
		(Z,T)			(Z,X)	(Z,Y)	

Table 5 Basic mandatory relations for Figure 31. This table follows from Table 2.

The reader will have noted that a good many implications among our binary relations derive directly from the definitions of these relations in terms of the basic optional relations. The following proposition lists a few of these implications.

Proposition 15.
1. *If S* ***requires*** *T, then S* ***implies*** *T. (If S* ¬***345*** *T, then S* ¬***45*** *T.)*
2. *If S* ***overlaps*** *T, then S* ***compatible*** *T. (If S* ***1*** *T, then S* ***1234*** *T.)*
3. *If S* ***allows*** *T, then S* ***tolerates*** *T. (If S* ¬***25*** *T, then S* ¬***5*** *T.)*
4. *If S* ***foretells*** *T, then S* ***allows*** *T. (If S* ¬***245*** *T, then S* ¬***25*** *T.)*
5. *If S* ***Requires*** *T, then S* ***requires*** *T. (If S* ¬***1345*** *T, then S* ¬***345*** *T.)*
6. *If S* ***Foretells*** *T, then S* ***foretells*** *T. (If S* ¬***1245*** *T, then S* ¬***245*** *T.)*
7. *If S* ***Allows*** *T, then S* ***allows*** *T. (If S* ¬***125*** *T, then S* ¬***25*** *T.)*
8. *If S* ***diverges*** *T, then S* ***aligns*** *T. (If S* ¬***1234*** *T, then S* ¬***234*** *T.)*

MORE COMPLEX MANDATORY RELATIONS	
S **precedes** T (S precedes T)	S **allows** T and T **requires** S S ¬**25** T and T ¬**345** S
S **alw.foretells** T (S always foretells T)	S **foretells** T and T **requires** S S ¬**245** T and T ¬**345** S
S **Precedes** T (S strictly precedes T)	S **Allows** T and T **Requires** S S ¬**125** T and T ¬**1345** S
S **alw.Foretells** T (S always strictly foretells T)	S **Foretells** T and T **Requires** S S ¬**1245** T and T ¬**1345** S
S **equipollent** T (S and T are equipollent)	S **implies** T and T **implies** S S ¬**45** T and T ¬**45** S

Table 6 The reader may verify, using the definition of **precedes** given here and the definition of **refines** in Table 4, that the specification of **precedes** and **refines** in Figure 31 agrees with Table 2.

Table 6 defines some further binary relations. These relations are also mandatory, but they are more complex than the mandatory relations in Table 4, because they express constraints directly on both S and T.

For the sake of completeness, we define counterparts of the other relations we used in Section 3: S **disjoint** T means S $\neg$**1** T, and S **prerequisite** T means T **requires** S. We will not make explicit use of these particular relations in the sequel.

We will be interested in sets of situations whose elements are all aligned with or divergent from each other. If Ξ is a nonempty set of situations, and S **aligns** T whenever S and T are in Ξ, then we call Ξ an *alignment*. If Ξ is a nonempty set of situations, and S **diverges** T whenever S and T are distinct situations in Ξ, then we call Ξ a *clade*. Since S **diverges** T implies S **aligns** T, a clade is an alignment.

If Ξ is a clade and S **merges** Ξ, then we say that Ξ *decomposes* S. If Ξ decomposes T and S **alw.foretells** T, then we call Ξ a *cut* of S.

6.2. Axioms for Event Spaces. We call Γ an *event space* if the relations **merges**, **1**, **2**, **3**, **4**, and **5** on Γ satisfy Axioms S1 through S9, listed in Table 7.

The axioms in Table 7 are based on our understanding of clades in a finite event trellis, as illustrated by Figure 32. These axioms reflect the structure of event trellises in the following ways:

- Any event trellis satisfies the first six axioms. If an event trellis is finite, it also satisfies Axiom S9. (See Proposition 16. It is obvious that only event trellises with no divergent situations can satisfy Axioms S7 and S8. Hence event trellises are not, in general, event spaces.)
- The set of all clades in any event space satisfies the first seven axioms. If the event trellis is finite, the set of all clades also satisfies Axioms S8 and S9 and hence qualifies as a event space. (See Proposition 17.)
- Any event space (any space satisfying all nine axioms) is isomorphic to an event space formed by a subset of the clades in an event trellis. (See Proposition 46.)

As a logical analysis of the idea of a finite event trellis, the axioms in Table 7 can be considered definitive. They are satisfied by the clades in any finite event trellis, and any finite space satisfying them is isomorphic to the set of clades in a finite event trellis.

For an infinite event trellis, the story is more complicated. Axioms S1 through S7 are always satisfied by the set of all clades, but Axioms S8 and S9 may or may not. From the viewpoint of classical (nonintuitionistic) mathematics, Axioms S8 and S9 are regularity conditions, which can be weakened or strengthened in any number of ways. From a constructive or logical viewpoint, on the other hand, they are quite natural. Axiom S9 says, roughly, that from an instantaneous event W we can construct a possibly earlier instantaneous event, at which it is first determined that W will happen. Axiom S8 says that we can construct an event at which W is settled one way or another—either it is determined that it will happen or it is determined that it will not happen.

In order to acquire an initial understanding of the axioms, the reader may wish to verify directly that they are satisfied by the relations specified for Figure 31 in Table 2, so that the situations depicted in that figure do indeed form an event space.

Axiom S1 For any two situations S and T, at least one of the basic optional relations S **i** T holds. (S **12345** T.)

Axiom S2 S **may.Require** T if and only if T **may.Allow** S. (S **2** T if and only if T **34** S.)

Axiom S3
a. **refines** is reflexive. (S ¬**2345** S.)
b. **refines** is antisymmetric. (If S ¬**2345** T and T ¬**2345** S, then S = T.)

Axiom S4
a. If S ¬**2345** T and T ¬**1** U, then S ¬**1** U.
b. If S ¬**125** T and T ¬**25** U, then S ¬**1** U.
c. If S ¬**25** T and T ¬**125** U, then S ¬**1** U.
d. If S ¬**1345** T and T ¬**34** U, then S ¬**1** U.
e. If S ¬**345** T and T ¬**134** U, then S ¬**1** U.
f. If S ¬**45** T and T ¬**1234** U, then S ¬**1** U.
g. If S ¬**25** T and T ¬**2** U, then S ¬**2** U.
h. If S ¬**45** T and T ¬**1234** U, then S ¬**2** U.
i. If S ¬**2345** T and T ¬**3** U, then S ¬**3** U.
j. If S ¬**345** T and T ¬**34** U, then S ¬**3** U.
k. If S ¬**45** T and T ¬**1234** U, then S ¬**3** U.
l. If S ¬**45** T and T ¬**234** U, then S ¬**4** U.
m. If S ¬**345** T and T ¬**34** U, then S ¬**4** U.
n. If S ¬**25** T and T ¬**5** U, then S ¬**5** U.
o. If S ¬**5** T and T ¬**45** U, then S ¬**5** U.
p. If S ¬**123** T and U ¬**345** T, then S ¬**3** U.

Axiom S5 Suppose S **i** T, where **i** is a basic optional relation. Then there exists a situation S* that refines S and realizes the relation (S* ¬**2345** S and S* ¬**(i)** T).

Axiom S6 Suppose **i** is a basic optional relation.
a. Suppose S **merges** Ξ. Then S **i** T if and only if S* **i** T for some S*∈ Ξ.
b. Suppose S **merges** {U,V} and T **diverges** U. Then T **i** S if and only if T **i** V.

Axiom S7 If Ξ is an alignment, then there exists a situation S such that S **merges** Ξ.

Axiom S8 If V **requires** S, then there exists W such that V **refines** W and S **alw.foretells** W.

Axiom S9 If V **requires** S, then there exists T such that (i) T **requires** S, (ii) T **alw.foretells** V, and (iii) if U **requires** S and U **alw.foretells** V, then T **alw.foretells** U.

Table 7 Nine axioms for event spaces.

Axiom S2 says that the second of the five basic optional relations can be defined in terms of the third and fourth. We can therefore say, if we wish, that there are only five primitive relations: **merges**, **1**, **3**, **4**, and **5**. In any case, the equivalence between S **2** T and T **34** S enhances our freedom of choice in the formulation of some axioms and definitions. We can replace Axiom S3b, for example, with the assertion that S = T when S

$\neg$**2345** T and T $\neg$**5** S. We can replace Axioms S4j and S4m with a single axiom in the pattern of Axiom S4p:

- If S $\neg$**2** T and U $\neg$**345** T, then S $\neg$**2** U.

Instead of saying that S **precedes** T means

- S **allows** T and T **requires** S (S $\neg$**25** T and T $\neg$**345** S),

we can say that it means

- S **allows** T and T **implies** S (S $\neg$**25** T and T $\neg$**45** S),
- S **allows** T and T **tolerates** S (S $\neg$**25** T and T $\neg$**5** S), or
- S **tolerates** T and T **requires** S (S $\neg$**5** T and T $\neg$**345** S).

And we can play similarly with S **alw.foretells** T:

The reader will have noted that Axioms S4a through S4o resemble assertions of transitivity for mandatory relations. These axioms do, in fact, imply that many of the mandatory relations are transitive (see Proposition 22).

Axiom S6 could be stated more economically. In the presence of Axioms S1 through S5, it suffices to state Axiom S6a for **1** = **1**; the statements for other **i** can then be deduced. Some **i** can similarly be omitted from Axiom S6b.

Axioms S8 and S9 can also be formulated in a number of different ways. These axioms are discussed in Section 6.8.

6.3. Event Trellises and their Clades Satisfy the Axioms. We have claimed that certain of our axioms are satisfied by an event trellis and by the set of clades in an event trellis. In this subsection we formulate these claims precisely. The proofs, which are straightforward but lengthy, are left to the reader.

Proposition 16. *Suppose Γ is an event trellis, with precedence relation* ***precedes***$_0$ *and additional binary relations* ***Precedes***$_0$*,* ***diverges***$_0$*,* ***implies***$_0$*,* ***foretells***$_0$*, and* ***Foretells***$_0$ *as defined in §3.3. Define relations* ***1****,* ***2****,* ***3****,* ***4****,* ***5****, and* ***merges*** *on Γ as follows:*

- *S* ***1*** *T if S = T.*
- *S* ***2*** *T if T* ***Precedes***$_0$ *S.*
- *S* ***3*** *T if S* ***Foretells***$_0$ *T.*
- *S* ***4*** *T if S* ***Precedes***$_0$ *T but not S* ***Foretells***$_0$ *T.*
- *S* ***5*** *T if S* ***diverges***$_0$ *T.*
- *S* ***merges*** *Ξ if Ξ = {S}.*

Then Γ, with these relations, satisfies Axioms S1 through S6. If it is finite, it also satisfies Axiom S9. Moreover, the relations **precedes**$_0$, **Precedes**$_0$, **diverges**$_0$, **implies**$_0$, **foretells**$_0$, and **Foretells**$_0$ agree with the event-space relations **precedes**, **Precedes**, **diverges**, **implies**, **foretells**, and **Foretells** defined in terms of **1**, **2**, **3**, **4**, and **5** in §6.1.

Proposition 17. *Suppose Γ_0 is an event trellis, with precedence relation* ***precedes$_0$*** *and additional binary relations* ***Precedes$_0$***, ***diverges$_0$***, ***implies$_0$***, ***foretells$_0$***, *and* ***Foretells$_0$*** *as defined in §3.3. Let Γ be the set of all clades in Γ_0, and let* ***disjoint$_0$***, ***diverges$_0$***, ***prerequisite$_0$***, ***allows$_0$***, ***implies$_0$***, ***precedes$_0$***, ***foretells$_0$***, *and* ***alw.foretells$_0$*** *be the relations on Γ defined in §3.4. Define relations* ***1***, ***2***, ***3***, ***4***, ***5***, *and* **merges** *on Γ as follows:*

- *S* ***1*** *T if $S \cap T \neq \emptyset$.*
- *S* ***2*** *T if there are situations $S_0 \in S$ and $T_0 \in T$ such that T_0* **Precedes$_0$** *S_0.*
- *S* ***3*** *T if there is a situation S_0 of S such that S_0* ***foretells$_0$*** *T but $S_0 \notin T$.*
- *S* ***4*** *T if there are situations $S_0 \in S$ and $T_0 \in T$ such that S_0* **Precedes$_0$** *T_0 but not S_0* ***foretells$_0$*** *T.*
- *S* ***5*** *T if there is a situation $S_0 \in S$ such that S_0* **diverges$_0$** *T.*
- *S* **merges** *Ξ if $S = \cup\Xi$.*

Then Γ, with these relations, satisfies Axioms S1 through S7. If Γ_0 is finite, then Γ also satisfies Axioms S8 and S9 and hence qualifies as an event space. Moreover, the relations ***disjoint$_0$***, ***diverges$_0$***, ***prerequisite$_0$***, ***allows$_0$***, ***implies$_0$***, ***precedes$_0$***, ***foretells$_0$***, *and* ***alw.foretells$_0$*** *on Γ agree with the event-space relations* ***disjoint***, ***diverges***, ***prerequisite***, ***allows***, ***implies***, ***precedes***, ***foretells***, *and* ***alw.foretells*** *defined in terms of* ***1***, ***2***, ***3***, ***4***, *and* ***5*** *in §6.1.*

Figure 22 provides an example of an infinite event tree for which the set of all clades violates Axiom S8. Indeed, if take V to be the clade $\{S_1, S_2, ...\}$ and take S to be the clade {I}, then V requires S, but it cannot be coarsened to a situation always foretold by S, because $\{S_1, S_2, ...\}$ cannot be enlarged to a cut of S. On the other hand, the set of all clades in this tree does satisfy Axiom S9.

Figure 33 provides an example of an infinite event tree in which the clades satisfy all the axioms except Axiom S9.

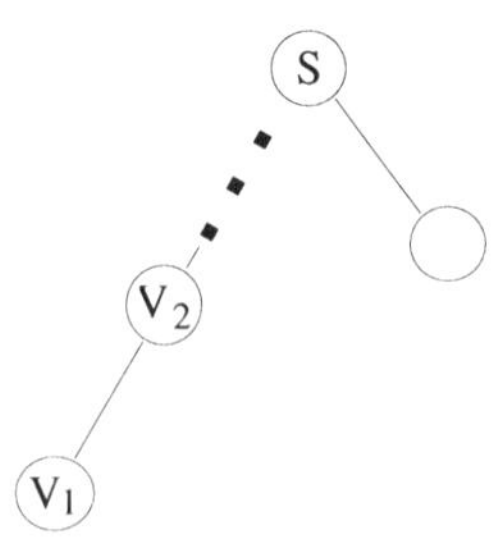

Figure 33 Here V_i **requires** S and V_{i+1} **alw.foretells** V_i, for i = 1,2,...

6.4. Axioms S1 through S5. We now turn to consequences of the axioms. In this subsection, we list some consequences that depend only on the first five axioms and hence do not involve mergers or cuts.

Proposition 18.

1. *Suppose* ***o*** *is an optional relation. If S* ***¬(o)*** *T, then S* ***o*** *T.*
2. *Suppose* ***m*** *is a mandatory relation. If S** ***refines*** *S and S* ***m*** *T, then S** ***m*** *T.*
3. *Suppose* ***o*** *is an optional relation. If S** ***refines*** *S and S** ***o*** *T, then S* ***o*** *T.*

4. *Suppose* **o** *is an optional relation. If S* **refines** S and S* ¬(o) T, then S* **o** *T.*

5. *Suppose* **o** *is an optional relation. If S* **overlaps** S and S* ¬(o) T, then S* **o** *T.*

Proof Statement 1 follows from Axiom S1. Statement 2 follows from Statements a, g, i, l, and n of Axiom S4. Statement 3 is contrapositive to Statement 2. Statement 4 follows from Statements 1 and 3.

To prove Statement 5, we use Axiom S5 to establish the existence of a situation S** refining both S* and S. Since S** refines S*, Statement 2 implies that S** ¬(**o**) T. Since S** refines S, Statement 4 then implies that S **o** T. ♦

Proposition 19. *Suppose* **i** *is a basic optional relation. Then S* **i** *T if and only if S has a refinement S* such that S* ¬(i) T.*

Proof If S has a refinement S* such that S* ¬(**i**) T, then statement 4 of Proposition 18 says that S **i** T. We obtain the proposition by combining this with Axiom S5. ♦

Proposition 20.

1. *S** ***refines*** *S if and only if S overlaps all situations that overlap S*.*
2. *If S and T are overlapped by the same situations, then S = T.*

Proof If S* **refines** S, then T **overlaps** S implies T **overlaps** S* by Axiom S4a. On the other hand, if S* **refines** S does not hold, then S* **i** S for some **i** not equal to **1**. And by Axiom S5 there exists S** such that S** ¬**2345** S* and S** ¬(**i**) S, whence S** **1** S* and S** ¬**1** S, and hence S fails to overlap all the situations that overlap S*.

Statement 2 follows from Statement 1 together with the antisymmetry of **refines**. ♦

Proposition 21.

1. *If S_1 and S_2 both refine T, then S_1 aligns with S_2. (If S_1* ¬**2345** *T and S_2* ¬**2345** *T, then S_1* ¬**234** *S_2.)*
2. *If S_1 ¬(i) T, S_2 ¬(j) T, and* **i** *≠* ***j****, then S_1 ¬**1** S_2.*

Proof 1. By the symmetry of **234**, S_2 ¬**2345** T implies T ¬**234** S_2. And S_1 ¬**2345** T and T ¬**234** S_2 yield the desired conclusion by Axioms S4f, g, and i.

2. If S_1 overlaps S_2, then by Axiom S5, they have a common refinement—a situation S* that refines them both. By Statement 2 of Proposition 18, S* ¬(**i**) T, and S* ¬(**j**) T. But this is prohibited by Axiom S1. ♦

Proposition 22.

1. *The following relations are reflexive:* ***overlaps, may.require, may.foretell, may.align, may.imply, may.allow, compatible, refines, requires, foretells, aligns, implies, allows, tolerates, precedes, alw.foretells, equipollent.***
2. *The following relations are irreflexive:* ***may.Require, may.Foretell, may.forbear, may.diverge, may.Allow, Requires, Foretells, forbears, diverges, Allows.***
3. *The following relations are symmetric:* ***overlaps, compatible, diverges, aligns.***
4. *The following relations are antisymmetric:* ***refines, requires, foretells, allows, precedes, alw.foretells.***
5. *The following relations are transitive:* ***refines, Requires, Foretells, requires, foretells, Allows, implies, allows, precedes, alw.foretells, equipollent.***

6. The following relations are partial orderings: ***refines****,* ***requires****,* ***foretells****,* ***allows****,* ***precedes****,* ***alw.foretells****.*

Proof 1. Axioms S1 and S3a imply that S **1** S—i.e., that **overlaps** is reflexive. It follows that all the optional implications implied by **overlaps**, including **may.require**, **may.foretell**, **may.align**, **may.imply**, **may.allow**, and **compatible**, are also reflexive. Similarly, the reflexivity of **refines** (Axiom S3a) yields the reflexivity of all mandatory relations implied by **refines**, including **requires**, **foretells**, **aligns**, **implies**, **allows**, and **tolerates**. The reflexivity of **implies** yields the reflexivity of **equipollent**. Since S **precedes** S and S **alw.foretells** S are also implied by S **refines** S, **precedes** and **alw.foretells** are also reflexive.

2. The fact that **refines** (¬**2345**) is reflexive means that **may.Require**, **may.Foretell**, **may.forbear**, **may.diverge** (**2**, **3**, **4**, **5**) are irreflexive. From the irreflexivity of **may.Foretell** and **may.forbear**, (**3** and **4**) we obtain the irreflexivity of their disjunction **Allows** (**34**). Finally, the reflexivity of **overlaps** (**1**) implies the irreflexivity of relations that deny **overlaps**, including **Requires**, **Foretells**, **forbears**, **diverges** and **Allows**.

3. Using Proposition 19 with **i** = **1**, we see that S **overlaps** T is equivalent to the existence of a situation S* that refines both S and T. Since this condition is symmetric in S and T, **overlaps** is symmetric. By Axiom S2, **234** and hence its denial, **aligns**, are symmetric. Combining the symmetry of **overlaps** and the symmetry of **234**, we obtain the symmetry of their disjunction, **compatible**, and its denial, **diverges**.

4. Axiom S3b says that **refines** is antisymmetric. By Axiom S2, S **m** T and T **m** S are together equivalent to S **refines** T and T **refines** S, for **m** = **requires**, **foretells**, or **allows**, and hence **requires**, **foretells**, and **allows** are also antisymmetric. Finally, since **precedes** and **alw.foretells** are both stronger than, say, **allows**, they are also antisymmetric.

5. The transitivity of the mandatory relations listed in Statement 6 follows from Axiom S$. To establish the transitivity of **refines**, we use Statements g, i, l, and m. For **Requires**, we use d, j, l, and n. For **Foretells**, we use b, g, l, and n. For **requires**, we use j, l, and n. For **foretells**, we use g, l, and m. For **Allows**, we use b, g, and m. For **implies**, we use l and n. For **allows**, we use g and m. The transitivity of **precedes** follows from the transitivity of **allows** and **requires**, and the transitivity of **alw.foretells** from that of **foretells** and **requires**, and the transitivity of **equipollent** from that of **implies**.

6. Statement 6 follows from Statements 1, 4, and 5. ♦

Proposition 23.

1. *If T* ***requires*** *S* and S** ***refines*** *S, then T* ***requires*** *S.*
2. *If S* ***allows*** *T*, and T** ***refines*** *T, then S* ***allows*** *T.*
3. *If T* ***requires*** *S_1 and S_1* ***diverges*** *S_2, then T* ***diverges*** *S_2.*
4. *If T_1* ***requires*** *S_1, and T_2* ***requires*** *S_2, and S_1* ***diverges*** *S_2, then T_1* ***diverges*** *T_2.*

Proof Statement 1 follows from Axioms S5j, l, and o. Statement 2 follows from Axioms S5g and n. Statement 3 follows from Axioms S4 e, h, j, and l.

To establish Statement 4, apply Statement 3 to T_1 **requires** S_1 and S_1 **diverges** S_2 to obtain T_1 **diverges** S_2. By the symmetry of **diverges**, S_2 **diverges** T_1. A second application of Statement 3, to T_2 **requires** S_2 and S_2 **diverges** T_1, then yields T_2 **diverges** T_1. ♦

6.5. Axiom S6a: Merger. We now turn to the concept of merger. In this subsection, we study the merger using Axioms S1 through S6a. We bring Axiom S7 into play in the §6.6 and Axiom S6b in §6.7.

The relation **refines** is a partial ordering. We can therefore consider the condition that a situation S is the least upper bound of a set of situations Ξ with respect to **refines**. This means that two conditions are met:

(9) S* **refines** S for all S* in Ξ, and
(10) if S* **refines** T for all S* in Ξ, then S **refines** T.

Proposition 24. *If S* ***merges*** *Ξ, then S is the least upper bound of Ξ with respect to* ***refines****.*

Proof Condition (9) follows from Axiom S6a and Statement 1 of Proposition 20.

To demonstrate the contrapositive of (10), suppose S **refines** T does not hold. Then S **i** T for some **i** not equal to **1**, and by Axiom S5 there exists S** such that S** $\neg$**2345** S and S** $\neg$**(i)** T. From S** $\neg$**2345** S, we conclude that S** **1** S, and hence that there exists S* in Ξ with S** **1** S*, and this together with S** $\neg$**1** T implies, by Axiom S4a (or Statement 1 of Proposition 20), that S* **refines** T does not hold. ♦

Since a least upper bound is unique, a merger is as well; if S and T both merge Ξ, then S = T. We write $\oplus\Xi$ for the unique merger of Ξ, if it exists. Statement 1 of Proposition 21 provides a necessary condition for a merger to exist: Ξ must be an alignment.

In the absence of Axiom S7, the converse of Proposition 24 is not true: a least upper bound of Ξ with respect to **refines** is not necessarily a merger of Ξ. The simplest counterexample is provided by a space consisting of four situations, S_1, S_2, S_3, and T. We specify the basic optional relations by saying that S_1, S_2, and S_3 are divergent from each other and all refine T, and we specify **merges** by saying that S **merges** {S} for all S and T **merges** $\{S_1,S_2,S_3\}$. In this space, which satisfies axioms S1 through S6, T is the least upper bound of $\{S_1,S_2\}$ but not its merger.

The next two propositions show how merger interacts with the other optional and mandatory relations.

Proposition 25. *Suppose S* ***merges*** *Ξ.*

1. *If* ***o*** *is any optional relation, then S* ***o*** *T if and only if S** ***o*** *T for some S*$\in\Xi$.*
2. *If* ***m*** *is a mandatory relation, then S* ***m*** *T if and only if S** ***m*** *T for all S*$\in\Xi$.*

Proof These statements follow directly from Axiom S6a. ♦

Proposition 26. *Suppose S* ***merges*** *Ξ.*

1. *T* ***1*** *S if and only if T* ***1*** *S* for some S*$\in\Xi$.*
2. *T* ***2*** *S if and only if T* ***2*** *S* for some S*$\in\Xi$.*
3. *T* ***34*** *S if and only if T* ***34*** *S* for some S*$\in\Xi$.*
4. *T* ***3*** *S if T* ***3*** *S* for some S*$\in\Xi$.*
5. *T* ***4*** *S only if T* ***4*** *S* for some S*$\in\Xi$.*
6. *T* ***5*** *S only if T* ***5*** *S* for all S*$\in\Xi$.*
7. *T* ***precedes*** *S if T* ***precedes*** *S* for all S*$\in\Xi$.*

Proof Statement 1 follows from the definition of merger and the symmetry of **1**. Statements 2 and 3 follow from the preceding proposition together with Axiom S2.

To establish Statement 4, suppose T **3** S* for some S*∈ Ξ. By Axiom S5, there is a refinement T* of T such that T* ¬**(3)** S*. Using Axioms S4b, g, l, and n, we can derive from T* ¬**(3)** S* and S* **refines** S that T* ¬**(3)** S. By Proposition 19, T **3** S.

To establish statement 5, suppose T **4** S. By Axiom S5, there is a refinement T* of T with T* ¬**(4)** S. By Statement 3, there exists S*∈ Ξ such that T* **34** S*. By Statement 4, T* ¬**3** S*. (If T* **3** S*, then T* **3** S, but T* ¬**(4)** S.) So T* **4** S*, and hence T **4** S*.

Statement 6 follows from Axiom S4o. Statement 7 follows from Statements 2 and 6, together with Statement 3 of the preceding proposition. ♦

Recall that a nonempty set of divergent situations is called a clade, and that a clade is an alignment. If all the situations in one clade diverge from all the situations in another, we say that the two clades are *divergent*. The union of two divergent clades is obviously a clade.

Proposition 27.

1. Suppose {T,U} has a merger. If R refines ⊕{T,U} and diverges from T, then R refines U.

2. If U and V diverge from T, the alignments {T,U} and {T,V} both have mergers, and these mergers are equal, then U = V.

Proof 1. Since R **refines** ⊕{T,U}, R ¬**234** ⊕{T,U}. So R ¬**234** U, by the symmetry of ¬**234** and Statement 2 of Proposition 25. So we only need to show that R ¬**5** U.

Suppose R **5** U. Then there exists a refinement R* of R such that R* **diverges** U. Since R* **refines** R and R **diverges** T, we also have R* **diverges** T. Hence, by Statement 7 of the preceding proposition, R* **diverges** ⊕{T,U}, contradicting the assumption that R and hence R* refines ⊕{T,U}.

2. Substituting V for R in Statement 1, we find that V refines U. Symmetrically, U refines V, and hence the two are equal. ♦

6.6. Axiom S7: Merger and Decomposition. We now bring Axiom S7 into play. We assume, throughout this subsection, that Axioms S1 through S5, S6a, and S7 are all satisfied.

In this context, merger is the same as least upper bound with respect to **refines**. All alignments have mergers (Axiom S7), which are also least upper bounds with respect to **refines** (Proposition 24). A set of situations that is not an alignment does not have a least upper bound with respect to **refines** (Proposition 21), and hence does not have a merger (Proposition 24).

Recognizing that merger is now the same as least upper bound, we will write ∨Ξ instead of ⊕Ξ. We will write S∨T instead of ∨{S,T}, and we will use the commutativity and associativity of ∨ without further apology.

The assumption that all alignments have mergers allows us to express Proposition 27 more concisely:

Proposition 28.

1. If T and U are aligned and R refines T∨U and diverges from T, then R refines U.

2. *If U and V diverge from T, and $T \vee U = T \vee V$, then U = V.*

When we are allowed to form mergers freely, we can construct from given situations a wide variety of further situations. Fundamental to this process are mergers based on Axiom S5. As expressed in §6.2, Axiom S5 is nonconstructive. It asserts the existence of an object without specifying the object. Merger allows us to eliminate this vagueness.

Suppose, indeed, that **i** is a basic optional relation, and suppose S **i** T. Axiom S5 says there is at least one situation S* satisfying these two conditions:

(3) S* **refines** S, and
(4) S* ¬(**i**) T.

The set of all such situations is an alignment, by Statement 1 of Proposition 21. Designate its merger by $\mathbf{i}_T(S)$. Then

(5) $\mathbf{i}_T(S)$ ¬(**i**) T (by Axiom S6a),
(6) $\mathbf{i}_T(S)$ **refines** S (by the definition of least upper bound), and
(7) if S* **refines** S and S* ¬(**i**) T, then S* **refines** $\mathbf{i}_T(S)$ (by construction).

In words: $\mathbf{i}_T(S)$ is the coarsest refinement of S that has the relation ¬(**i**) with T.

Proposition 29. *S ¬(i) T if and only if $\mathbf{i}_T(S) = S$.*

We call $\mathbf{1}_T(S)$, $\mathbf{2}_T(S)$, $\mathbf{3}_T(S)$, $\mathbf{4}_T(S)$, and $\mathbf{5}_T(S)$ the *basic constructions.* We write $\text{overlap}_T(S)$ for $\mathbf{1}_T(S)$, $\text{After}_T(S)$ for $\mathbf{2}_T(S)$, $\text{Foretell}_T(S)$ for $\mathbf{3}_T(S)$, $\text{forbear}_T(S)$ for $\mathbf{4}_T(S)$, and $\text{diverge}_T(S)$ for $\mathbf{5}_T(S)$. Thus $\text{overlap}_T(S)$ is the coarsest situation that refines both S and T, $\text{After}_T(S)$ is the coarsest refinement of S that strictly requires T, and so on. Table 8 gives more colloquial readings.

	NAME	ENGLISH READING
$\mathbf{1}_T(S)$	$\text{overlap}_T(S)$	part of S overlapping T (or the overlap of S and T)
$\mathbf{2}_T(S)$	$\text{After}_T(S)$	part of S coming strictly after T
$\mathbf{3}_T(S)$	$\text{Foretell}_T(S)$	part of S strictly foretelling T
$\mathbf{4}_T(S)$	$\text{forbear}_T(S)$	part of S forbearing T
$\mathbf{5}_T(S)$	$\text{diverge}_T(S)$	part of S diverging from T

Table 8 English readings for the names of the five basic constructions. Here, as in Tables 1, 3, and 4, capitalization of a name indicates a strict interpretation of precedence.

When S **i** T does not hold, we say that $\mathbf{i}_T(S)$ does not exist. For example, when S does not overlap T, $\text{overlap}_T(S)$ does not exist.

We write $\text{decomp}_T(S)$ for the set consisting of the $\mathbf{i}_T(S)$ that exist. As the following proposition confirms, $\text{decomp}_T(S)$ is a decomposition of S.

Proposition 30.
1. *The set $\text{decomp}_T(S)$ is nonempty.*
2. *The situations in $\text{decomp}_T(S)$ diverge from each other.*
3. *$S = \vee \text{decomp}_T(S)$.*

Proof 1. Statement 1 simply restates Axiom S1.

2. Statement 2 follows from Proposition 21. (Since the situations in decomp$_T$(S) all refine S, they are aligned, and since they satisfy incompatible mandatory relations, they do not overlap.)

3. If U overlaps one of the situations in decomp$_T$(S), then by Statement 1 of Proposition 20, U overlaps S. If U overlaps S, then by Axiom S5, U and S have a common refinement, say U*. By Axiom S1, U* **i** T for some **i**, and so by Axiom S5 U* has a refinement U** such that U** ¬(**i**) T. Since U** refines both U and **i**$_T$(S), U overlaps **i**$_T$(S). ♦

In general, **i**$_T$(S) is not equal to **i**$_S$(T); in fact, one may exist without the other existing. As the following proposition shows, **1** is an exception: overlap$_T$(S) is the same as overlap$_S$(T).

Proposition 31. *The situation overlap$_T$(S) is the same as the greatest lower bound of S and T with respect to* **refines**. *In other words, overlap$_T$(S) exists if and only if the greatest lower bound of S and T with respect to* **refines** *exists, and when the two exist, they are equal.*

Proof When **i** = **1**, (5), (6), and (7) reduce to

- **1**$_T$(S) **refines** T,
- **1**$_T$(S) **refines** S, and
- if S* **refines** S and S* **refines** T, then S* **refines** **1**$_T$(S).

And this is what is meant by the statement that **1**$_T$(S) is the greatest lower bound of S and T with respect to **refines**. So **1**$_T$(S) exists, it certainly is the greatest lower bound of S and T with respect to **refines**. When **1**$_T$(S) does not exist, S and T have no common refinement, and hence they do not have a greatest lower bound with respect to **refines**. ♦

In light of Proposition 31, we can write S∧T for overlap$_T$(S); the operator ∧ is then commutative and associative and has all the other properties possessed in general by greatest lower bounds in a partially ordered set. For example, if S∧T exists, then T = S∧T if and only if T **refines** S.

The situation diverge$_T$(S) is particularly interesting when it exists (S **5** T) and S is aligned with T (S ¬**234** T)—i.e., when S is aligned with but does not refine T. In this case, we write S\T for diverge$_T$(S). As the notation suggests, S\T plays the role of a relative complement; it is the result, as it were, of subtracting T from S.

Proposition 32. *Suppose S is aligned with but does not refine T. (As we just noted, this implies that S\T exists.) And suppose S* ***1*** *T, so that S∧T exists.*

1. {S∧T,S\T} decomposes S.

2. S\(S∧T) exists and is equal to S\T.

Proof 1. By the assumption that S ¬**234** T, **2**$_T$(S), **3**$_T$(S), and **4**$_T$(S) do not exist. So decomp$_T$(S), which decomposes S, consists of S∧T and S\T.

2. If T refines S, then T = S∧T, and hence it is certainly true that S\(S∧T) exists and is equal to S\T. If T does not refine S, then we can add to the assumptions we have already made (S **5** T and S ¬**234** T) the assumption that T **5** S. And then Statement 2 ap-

plies with S and T interchanged: {S∧T,T\S} decomposes T. A refinement of S diverges from T if and only if it diverges from both situations in this decomposition (Statement 2 of Proposition 25). But any refinement of S diverges from T\S. So a refinement of S diverges from T if and only if it diverges from S∧T. Since S\T is the merger of the former and S∧T is the merger of the latter, the two exist on the same occasions and are equal when they exist. ♦

Proposition 33. *Suppose T refines S and T ≠ S. (This implies that S is aligned with but does not refine T, so that S\T exists.)*

1. *{T,S\T} decomposes S.*
2. *Suppose U refines S and diverges from S\T. Then U refines T.*
3. *S\(S\T) = T.*

Proof Since T = S∧T when T refines S, Statement 1 follows from Statement 1 of the preceding proposition. Statement 2 follows from Statement 2 of Proposition 25. Statement 3 follows from Statement 2. ♦

Proposition 34. *Suppose T and U are divergent, T_1 and T_2 refine T, and U_1 and U_2 refine U. And suppose $T_1 \vee U_1 = T_2 \vee U_2$. Then $T_1 = T_2$ and $U_1 = U_2$.*

Proof By symmetry, it suffices to show that $T_1 = T_2$, and to this end, it suffices to show that if S overlaps T_1, then S also overlaps T_2. If S overlaps T_1, then $S \wedge T_1$ exists, and since it refines T_1, it diverges from U. Since $\{T_1,U_1\}$ and $\{T_2,U_2\}$ have equal mergers, they are overlapped by the same situations, and so $S \wedge T_1$, which certainly does not overlap U_2, must overlap T_2. Hence S overlaps T_2. ♦

Proposition 35. *Suppose T and U overlap and are aligned, so that T∧U and T∨U both exist.*

1. *Suppose U does not refine T (this is necessary and sufficient both for the existence of T\T∨U and for the existence of U\T), then (T∨U)\T = U\T.*
2. *Similarly, if T does not refine U, then (T∨U)\U = T\U.*
3. *If neither U refines T nor T refines U, then the three situations T∧U, T\U, and U\T are divergent and decompose T∨U: T∨U = (T∧U)∨(T\U)∨(U\T).*

Proof Let us begin with the assumption that neither T nor U refines the other. This gives T∨U = T∨((T∨U)\T), by Statement 1 of Proposition 33. By Statement 1 of Proposition 32, T = (T∧U)∨(T\U). So T∨U = (T∧U)∨(T\U)∨((T∨U)\T). By symmetry, T∨U = (T∧U)∨(U\T)∨((T∨U)\U). Both (T\U)∨((T∨U)\T) and (U\T)∨((T∨U)\U) are divergent from T∧U, and hence, by Statement 2 of Proposition 28, (T\U)∨((T∨U)\T) = (U\T)∨((T∨U)\U). Since T\U refines T∨U and diverges from U, it refines (T∨U)\U. Similarly, U\T refines (T∨U)\T. So by Proposition 34, T\U = (T∨U)\U and U\T = (T∨U)\T. This establishes Statement 3, and it also establishes Statement for the case where T does not refine U.

If T does refines U, then T∨U = U and T∧U = T, so that both sides of the equation in Statement 1 reduce to U\T. Statement 2 follows by symmetry. ♦

If we assume only that T and U are aligned, so that T∨U exists, then we can still assert

(11) $$T \vee U = (T \wedge U) \vee (T \backslash U) \vee (U \backslash T),$$

provided that we agree to interpret the right-hand side by omitting any of three situations T∧U, T\U, and U\T that do not exist. At least one of them must exist, and when one or two of them fail to exist, the equation reduces to a relation that we have already established.

Proposition 36. *Suppose S, T, and U are aligned.*

1. If T and U are divergent, and if S refines $T \vee U$ and overlaps both T and U, then S $= (S \wedge T) \vee (S \wedge U)$.

2. More generally, if T and U are divergent, and S overlaps both T and U, then $S \wedge (T \vee U) = (S \wedge T) \vee (S \wedge U)$.

3. If S overlaps T but not U, then $S \wedge (T \vee U) = S \wedge T$.

4. If S overlaps both T and U, then $S \wedge (T \vee U) = (S \wedge T) \vee (S \wedge U)$.

Proof 1. By Statement 1 of Proposition 32, $S = (S \wedge T) \vee (S \setminus T) = (S \wedge U) \vee (S \setminus U)$. By Statement 1 of Proposition 28, $S \setminus (S \wedge T)$ refines U and $S \setminus (S \wedge U)$ refines T. So Proposition 34 yields $S \setminus T = S \wedge U$ and hence the conclusion.

2. We obtain Statement 2 by substituting $S \wedge (T \vee U)$ for S in Statement 1.

3. By Statement 1 of Proposition 28, any refinement of S and $T \vee U$ must refine T. So Statement 3 follows from the definition of greatest lower bound.

4. Consider first the case where S overlaps all three situations $T \wedge U$, $T \setminus U$, and $U \setminus T$. In this case, we can apply Statement 2 to (11) to obtain

$$S \wedge T = (S \wedge T \wedge U) \vee (S \wedge (T \setminus U)),$$
$$S \wedge U = (S \wedge T \wedge U) \vee (S \wedge (U \setminus T)),$$

and

$$S \wedge (T \vee U) = (S \wedge T \wedge U) \vee (S \wedge (T \setminus U)) \vee (S \wedge (U \setminus T)).$$

And this implies the desired result. The cases where S overlaps only some of the three situations are similar. ♦

As the reader will have noticed, we have established most of the properties enjoyed by $\wedge$, $\vee$, and $\setminus$ in a Boolean algebra, but we lack a unit and a zero. It is now easy to see that we obtain a Boolean algebra if we consider only refinements of a particular situation R (so that R serves as the unit) and we adjoin a zero. Designate by Λ the set of refinements of R. Under the partial ordering **refines**, Λ has a unit, namely R, but it has no zero unless R is its only element. In any case, add a zero. In other words, choose an object not in R, say 0, consider the set Λ^+ consisting of Λ together with 0 ($\Lambda^+ := \Lambda \cup \{0\}$), and partially order Λ^+ by setting (i) $S \leq T$ for all S and T in Λ such S **refines** T and (ii) $0 \leq S$ for all S in Λ. Then 0 becomes the greatest lower bound for all pairs of situations that did not previously have one (these situations did not overlap and hence did not have any lower bounds at all), and hence the partially ordered set is a lattice. Statements 3 and 4 of Proposition 36 say that this lattice is distributive. The unit and zero are of course complementary, and Proposition 32 tells us that $R \setminus S$ is the complement of S when S is a proper refinement of R. So all elements of the distributive lattice have complements, and this means that it is a Boolean algebra.

Proposition 37. *Suppose S_1* ***aligns*** *S_2 and T_1* ***aligns*** *T_2.*

1. If T_1 ***requires*** *S_1 and T_2* ***requires*** *S_2, then $T_1 \vee T_2$* ***requires*** *$S_1 \vee S_2$.*

2. If S_1 ***allows*** *T_1 and S_2* ***allows*** *T_2, then $S_1 \vee S_2$* ***allows*** *$T_1 \vee T_2$.*

Proof 1. The situations T_1 and T_2 both require $S_1 \vee S_2$ by Statement 3 of Proposition 23. So $T_1 \vee T_2$ requires $S_1 \vee S_2$ by Statement 3 of Proposition 25.

2. The situations S_1 and S_2 both allow $S_1 \vee S_2$ by Statement 4 of Proposition 23. So $T_1 \vee T_2$ allows $S_1 \vee S_2$ by Statement 3 of Proposition 25. ♦

6.7. Axiom S6b. In this section, we bring Axiom S6b into play. This means that we are now assuming Axioms S1 through S7. Our emphasis will be on the mergers shown in Table 9.

NAME	DEFINITION	CONDITION FOR EXISTENCE
$\text{after}_T(S)$	$\mathbf{1}_T(S)\vee\mathbf{2}_T(S)$ $\text{overlap}_T(S)\vee\text{After}_T(S)$	S **12** T
$\text{foretell}_T(S)$	$\mathbf{1}_T(S)\vee\mathbf{3}_T(S)$ $\text{overlap}_T(S)\vee\text{Foretell}_T(S)$	S **13** T
$\text{Before}_T(S)$	$\mathbf{3}_T(S)\vee\mathbf{4}_T(S)$ $\text{Foretell}_T(S)\vee\text{forbear}_T(S)$	S **34** T
$\text{before}_T(S)$	$\mathbf{1}_T(S)\vee\mathbf{3}_T(S)\vee\mathbf{4}_T(S)$ $\text{overlap}_T(S)\vee\text{Foretell}_T(S)\vee\text{forbear}_T(S)$	S **134** T
$\text{extension}(S\rightarrow T)$	$S\vee\mathbf{5}_T(S)$ $S\vee\text{diverge}_S(T)$	none

Table 9 Additional constructions. In each case, the construction is to be carried out by merging those of the indicated situations that exist. For example, $\text{after}_T(S)$ is equal to $\mathbf{1}_T(S)\vee\mathbf{2}_T(S)$ if both these situations exist, to $\mathbf{1}_T(S)$ if only it exists, and to $\mathbf{2}_T(S)$ if only it exists. Only when neither $\mathbf{1}_T(S)$ nor $\mathbf{2}_T(S)$ exists do we say that $\text{after}_T(S)$ does not exist.

Proposition 38.

*1. If S **allows** T, then S **precedes** $\text{after}_S(T)$. In fact, $\text{after}_S(T)$ is the coarsest refinement of T preceded by S.*

*2. If T **requires** S, then $\text{before}_T(S)$ **precedes** T. In fact, it is the unique refinement of S that precedes T.*

*3. S **allows** T, then $\text{extension}(S\rightarrow T)$ **precedes** T.*

Proof 1. First notice that the hypothesis S $\neg$**25** T implies S **134** T, which is equivalent to T **12** S and hence to the existence of $\text{after}_S(T)$.

To see that $\text{after}_S(T)$ **requires** S, recall that $\mathbf{1}_S(T)$ $\neg$**2345** S and $\mathbf{2}_S(T)$ $\neg$**1345** S, so that $\text{after}_S(T)$ $\neg$**345** S by Statement 3 of Proposition 25.

To complete the proof that S **precedes** $\text{after}_S(T)$, it suffices to show that S $\neg$**5** $\text{after}_S(T)$. To this end, we use the fact that $\mathbf{3}_S(T)$ and $\mathbf{4}_S(T)$ do not exist to decompose T into $\text{after}_S(T)$ and $\mathbf{5}_S(T)$. The conclusion S $\neg$**5** $\text{after}_S(T)$ then follows by Axiom S6b from S $\neg$**5** T and S **diverges** $\mathbf{5}_S(T)$.

Suppose U refines T and requires S. The fact that U refines T means, by the distributivity of $\wedge$ over $\vee$, we can decompose U into its overlaps with the $\text{after}_S(T)$ and $\mathbf{5}_T(S)$, which decompose T. The fact that U requires S means that it does not overlap with $\mathbf{5}_T(S)$. So U refines $\text{after}_S(T)$. Thus we may say that $\text{after}_S(T)$ is the coarsest situation that refines T and requires S. A fortiori, it is the coarsest situation that refines T and is precedes by S.

2. The hypothesis T $\neg$**345** S implies S **12** T, which is equivalent to T **134** S and hence to the existence of $\text{before}_T(S)$.

To see that $\text{before}_T(S)$ **allows** T, recall that $\mathbf{1}_T(S)$ $\neg$**2345** T, $\mathbf{3}_T(S)$ $\neg$**1245** T, and $\mathbf{4}_T(S)$ $\neg$**1235** T, so that $\text{before}_T(S)$ **allows** T by Statement 3 of Proposition 25. Moreover, $\text{before}_T(S)$ is the coarsest refinement of S that allows T, because any refinement of S that does not refine $\text{before}_T(S)$ must overlap $\mathbf{5}_T(S)$, which does not allow T.

To complete the proof that $\text{before}_T(S)$ **precedes** T, it suffices to show that T $\neg$**5** $\text{before}_T(S)$. To this end, we use the fact that $\mathbf{2}_S(T)$ does not exist to decompose T into $\text{after}_S(T)$ and $\mathbf{5}_S(T)$. The conclusion T $\neg$**5** $\text{before}_T(S)$ then follows by Axiom S6b from T $\neg$**5** S and T **diverges** $\mathbf{5}_S(T)$.

We have already established that any refinement of S that allows T must refine $\text{before}_T(S)$. So in order to show that $\text{before}_T(S)$ is the unique refinement of S that precedes T, we need only show that T cannot require any proper refinement of $\text{before}_T(S)$. In fact, if U is a proper refinement of $\text{before}_T(S)$, then S\U must overlap $\text{before}_T(S)$. Thus S\U overlaps at least one of the situations $\mathbf{1}_T(S)$, $\mathbf{3}_T(S)$, and $\mathbf{4}_T(S)$. Hence there is a refinement V of S\U such that either V **1** T, V **3** T, or V **4** T. This implies T **12** V. So there is a refinement W of T such that W $\neg$**345** V. By Statement 3 of Proposition 23, W **diverges** U. Consequently, T cannot require U.

3. Suppose S **allows** T. If S $\neg$**5** T, then (i) S **precedes** T and (ii) $\text{diverge}_S(T)$ does not exist. By (ii), S is the same as extension(S$\rightarrow$T), so that (i) can be read as extension(S$\rightarrow$T) **precedes** T. On the other hand, if S **5** T, then $\text{diverge}_S(T)$ does exist. Since it refines T it certainly allows T, and hence S$\vee\text{diverge}_S(T)$ **allows** T by Statement 3 of Proposition 25.

On the other hand, S **allows** T implies T $\neg$**34** S, so that we can decompose T into $\text{after}_S(T)$ and $\text{diverge}_S(T)$. This first of these requires S by Statement 1, and the second certainly requires itself; hence T **requires** S$\vee\text{diverge}_S(T)$ by Statement 1 of Proposition 37. ♦

It follows from Statement 1 of Proposition 38 that if S **precedes** T and S* **refines** S, then $\text{after}_{S*}(T)$ is the coarsest refinement of T preceded by S*. And it follows similarly from Statement 2 that if S **precedes** T and T* **refines** T, then $\text{before}_{T*}(S)$ is the unique refinement of S that precedes T*. These results can be compared with Statements 8 and 9 of Proposition 12.

We leave it to the reader to formulate strict versions of Proposition 38.

6.8. Axioms S8 and S9: Failure and Resolution. We now come to our last two axioms. Henceforth we will assume that we are working in an event space—a space that satisfies all nine axioms. We leave the proofs in this section to the reader.

Consider Axiom S9: If V **requires** S, then there exists T such that (i) T **requires** S, (ii) T **alw.foretells** V, and (iii) if U **requires** S and U **alw.foretells** V, then T **alw.foretells** U. Because of the antisymmetry of the partial ordering **alw.foretells**, the situation T satisfying the conditions of this axiom is unique. We designate it by Fix(V|S), and we call Fix(V|S) the fixing of V after S. Intuitively, Fix(V|S) is the situation following S where it is first determined that V will happen.[7] Mathematically, it is the least upper bound, in the partial ordering **alw.foretells**, of all the situations that require S and always foretell V.

---

[7]Frantz von Kutschera (1993) calls this instanteous event the *cause* of V.

Proposition 39. *Suppose U and V both require S, and suppose U and V are equipollent. Then Fix(U|S) = Fix(V|S).*

Now consider Axiom S8: If V **requires** S, then there exists W such that V **refines** W and S **alw.foretells** W. The situation W demanded by this axiom is not unique. But as the following proposition shows, we can derive from it some interesting situations that are unique.

Proposition 40. *Suppose V* ***requires*** *S. Suppose, moreover, that* W_1 *and* W_2 *both coarsen V and are always foretold by S. Then Fix(*W_1*\V|S) = Fix(*W_2*\V|S).*

In light of Proposition 41, we write Fail(V|S) for the situation equal to Fix(W\V|S) for all W satisfying V **refines** W and S **alw.foretells** W. Intuitively, Fail(V|S) is the event that V fails after S. The next proposition lists some properties of this event.

Proposition 41. *Suppose V* ***requires*** *S.*
1. *Fail(V|S)* ***requires*** *S.*
2. *Fail(V|S)* ***diverges*** *V.*
3. *Fail(V|S)* ***diverges*** *Fix(V|S).*
4. *If U* ***requires*** *S and U* ***diverges*** *V, then U* ***requires*** *Fail(V|S).*
5. *Fix(V|S) = Fail(Fail(V|S)|S).*

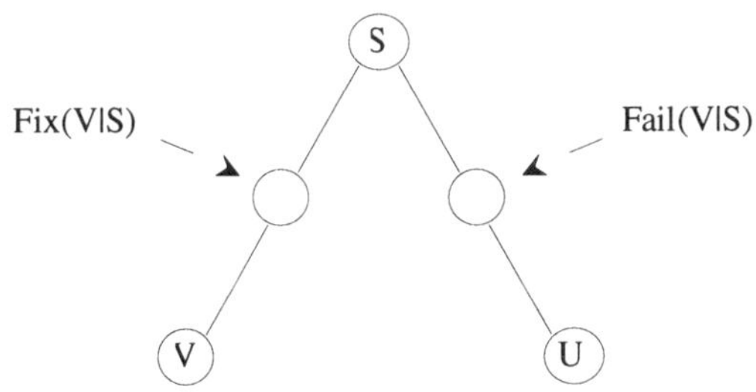

Figure 34 Fix(V|S) is the situation where nature first knows for sure that V will happen; Fail(V|S) is the situation where nature first knows for sure that V will not happen. The situations V∨U and V∨Fail(V|S) both satisfy Axiom S8. (It should not be forgotten that Axioms S8 and S9 apply whenever V requires S. This figure illustrates only the special case where S precedes V.)

We write Resolve(V|S) for the merger Fix(V|S)∨Fail(V|S), and we write Expand(V|S) for the merger V∨Fail(V|S). (Statements 2 and 3 of the preceding proposition assure us that these mergers exist.) Intuitively, Resolve(V|S) is the situation where it is first resolved whether V will happen or fail, whereas Expand(V|S) is the situation where it has actually happened or failed.

Proposition 42. *Suppose V* ***requires*** *S.*
1. *S* ***alw.foretells*** *Resolve(V|S).*
2. *S* ***alw.foretells*** *Expand(V|S).*

3. Resolve(V\S) is the least upper bound, in the partial ordering **alw.foretells**, *of all the situations satisfying Axiom S8.*

In our definitions of **implies** and **foretells** for clades in an event trellis (§3.3), we assumed that a situation with successors in an event trellis must be followed by at least one of those successors; in other words, we took the absence of further alternative successors in the trellis to represent their absence in fact. Axiom S8 requires an event space to provide a more explicit recognition of the exhaustiveness of the successors it provides. It requires, roughly, that any successor of a situation can be coarsened to a single successor explicitly recognized as exhaustive—i.e., as necessary.

Axiom S9, on the other hand, is a regularity condition. It serves to rule out examples such as Figure 33, in which there is an infinite sequence of earlier and earlier situations, each always foretelling the later ones, yet no situation that precedes and always foretells them all.

Table 10 summarizes the constructions based on Axioms S8 and S9.

NAME	ENGLISH READING	DEFINITION
Fix(V|S)	fixing of V after S	unique T satisfying Axiom S9
Fail(V|S)	failure of V after S	Fix(W\V|S), where W satisfies Axioms S8
Resolve(V|S)	resolution of V after S	Fix(V|S)∨Fail(V|S)
Expand(V|S)	expansion of V after S	V∨Fail(V|S)

Table 10 Constructions based on Axioms S8 and S9. These definitions are based on the assumption that V **requires** S. We can generalize from V **requires** S to V **12** S by setting Fix(V|S) in the more general case equal to Fix(after_S(V)|S).

6.9. A More Constructive Axiomatization. The axiomatization in Section 6.2 was formulated classically and hence nonconstructively. Three of the axioms—Axioms S5, S7, and S8, assert the existence of situations satisfying certain conditions without specifying particular situations satisfying those conditions. Our study of the axioms has led, however, to the specification of particular situations in each case. We learned that the basic constructions were the maximal (with respect to refinement) situations satisfying Axiom S5. And we learned that ∨Ξ and Fix(V|S) are the unique objects satisfying Axioms S7 and S9, respectively. And we learned that Expand(V|S) satisfies Axiom S8.

This suggests a more constructive axiomatization for the idea of an event space. We postulate only five primitive relations **1**, **2**, **3**, **4**, and **5** (**merges** is no longer primitive). We adopt Axioms S1 through S4 (omitting S5 through S9). And we complete the axiomatization by adopting the rules of construction and axioms in Table 11.

Rule SA From situations S and T such that S **i** T (**i** being a basic optional relation) construct the situation $\mathbf{i}_T$(S).
Axiom SA
a. $\mathbf{i}_T$(S) **refines** S.
b. $\mathbf{i}_T$(S) ¬(**i**) T.
c. If U **refines** S and U ¬(**i**) T, then $\mathbf{i}_T$(S) **refines** U.

Rule SB From an alignment Ξ, construct the situation ⊕Ξ.
Axiom SB
a. ⊕Ξ **i** T if and only if S* **i** T for some S*∈Ξ.
b. If U **aligns** V and T **diverges** U, then T **i** U⊕V if and only if T **i** V.

Rule SC From situations S and T such that T **requires** S and S **45** T, construct the situation Fail(T|S).
Axiom SC
a. Fail(T|S) **requires** S.
b. Fail(T|S) **diverges** T.
c. If U **requires** S and U **diverges** T, then U **requires** Fail(T|S).

Table 11 Rules of construction and axioms for complete event spaces. (We also adopt Axioms S1 through S4 from Table 7.)

In other words, we replace Axiom S5 with Rule SA and Axiom SA, we replace Axioms S6 and S7 with Rule SB and Axiom SB, and we replace Axioms S8 and S9 with Rule SC and Axiom SC.

From Fail(T|S), we can obtain the other constructions discussed in §6.8 by setting

- Fix(T|S) := Fail(Fail(T|S)|S),
- Resolve(T|S) := Fix(T|S)⊕Fail(T|S), and
- Expand(T|S) := T⊕Fail(T|S).

We can then show that Expand(T|S) satisfies the conditions required of W in Axiom S8 and that Fix(T|S) satisfies the conditions required of W in Axioms S9. This makes it clear that the axioms in Table 10 (together with Axioms S1 through S4) are equivalent to the ones given in §6.2.

In order to make the axiomatization yet more constructive, we might remove Axiom S3b from our list of axioms. We could then define a new binary relation **equals** by writing S **equals** T whenever S ¬**2345** T and T ¬**2345** S. This would put the notion of equality for events inside the theory and would thus put us in a position to formulate the axioms as rules of inference within a logic based on Martin-Löf's type theory, in the manner of von Plato's treatment of elementary geometry (1995). (Axioms SCc and the statements in Axioms S4 should all be cast in a positive form, so that they can be fully exploited within appeal to the law of the excluded middle. Axiom S4a, for example, should be read "S **1** U implies S **2345** T or T **1** U.")

6.10. Isomorphism and Subordination. The axiomatization just formulated leads straightaway to natural concepts of isomorphism and subordination for event spaces. We call a bijection between two complete event spaces, say a bijection ρ between Γ_1 and Γ_2, an *isomorphism* if it preserves the primitive relations and the constructions:

- $\rho(S)\ \mathbf{i}\ \rho(T)$ if and only if $S\ \mathbf{i}\ T$ for $\mathbf{i} = \mathbf{1}, \mathbf{2}, \mathbf{3}, \mathbf{4}$, and $\mathbf{5}$,
- $\mathbf{i}_{\rho(T)}(\rho(S)) = \rho(\mathbf{i}_T(S))$ for $\mathbf{i} = \mathbf{1}, \mathbf{2}, \mathbf{3}, \mathbf{4}$, and $\mathbf{5}$,
- $\vee\rho(\Xi) = \rho(\vee\Xi)$,[8] and
- $\mathrm{Fail}(\rho(T)|\rho(T)) = \rho(\mathrm{Fail}(T|S))$.

If a subset Γ_1 of an event space Γ_2 contains all the constructions for its elements, then it is obviously itself an event space with the inherited primitive relations and these constructions. We say in this case that Γ_1 is *subordinate* to Γ_2, or more colloquially, that it is a *sub* event space.

Combining these two definitions, we have a notion of refinement for event spaces: a mapping ρ of an event space Γ_1 into another event space Γ_2 is a *refinement* if (i) the image $\rho(\Gamma_1)$ is an event space subordinate to Γ_2, and (ii) ρ is an isomorphism between Γ_1 and $\rho(\Gamma_1)$.

6.11. The Underlying Event Trellis. In the introduction to this section, we asserted that event spaces can be understood in terms of event trellises; an event space is essentially a set of clades in an event trellis. We can now express this more precisely: any event space is isomorphic to an event space subordinate to an event space consisting of all clades in an event trellis. We now show how to construct this underlying event trellis.

Suppose Γ is an event space. We call a subset of Γ an *ultrafilter* if it contains the overlap of every pair of its elements and it is maximal with respect to this property. (In other words, S^* is an ultrafilter if (i) $S \wedge T$ exists and is in S^* whenever S and T are in S^*, and (ii) if $S^* \subseteq T^*$ and $S \wedge T$ exists and is in T^* whenever S and T are in T^*, then $S^*=T^*$.) It follows from the axiom of choice (see, e.g., Davey and Priestley 1990 or Kelley 1955) that every situation in Γ is contained in an ultrafilter, and more generally that S^* is contained in an ultrafilter if it contains the overlap of every pair of its elements.

Let Γ^* denote the set of all ultrafilters in the event space Γ.

Proposition 43. *Suppose $S^* \in \Gamma^*$.*

1. If T overlaps every situation in S^*, then $T \in S^*$.

2. If $S \in S^*$ and S ***refines*** *T, then $T \in S^*$.*

3. Suppose $S \in S^*$. If S has no proper refinement, then S^* consists of the situations that S refines. If S has a proper refinement, then S^* contains a proper refinement of S.

4. If $S \in S^*$ and T ***refines*** *S, then S^* contains either a refinement of T or a refinement of $S \backslash T$. (It cannot have both, because the two would not overlap.)*

5. If $S \in S^*$, Ξ is a finite clade, and Ξ decomposes S, then one of the situations in Ξ is in S^*

Proof 1. Suppose T overlaps every situation in S^*. Let T^* be the set of situations obtained by adding T, together with the overlap of T with each situation in S^*, to S^*. It is easily seen that any two situations in T^* overlap and have their overlap in T^*: (i) if S is an element of S^*, then S overlaps T by hypothesis, and this overlap is in T^* by definition, (ii) two overlaps of elements of S^* with T, say $S_1 \wedge T$ and $S_2 \wedge T$, have $(S_1 \wedge S_2) \wedge T$ as their overlap, (iii) an overlap of S^* with T is its own overlap with T, etc. Since S^*

---

[8] $\rho(\Xi)$ denotes, of course, the image of the alignment Ξ; $\rho(\Xi) = \{\rho(S) | S \in \Xi\}$.

was already maximal with respect to this property, it must be equal to T*, and hence it contains T.

2. Statement 2 follows from Statement 1, because when S refines T, T overlaps all the situations overlapped by S.

3. By the definition of ultrafilter, every situation in S* overlaps with S. And in general, when a situation has no proper refinement, every situation overlapping with it is refined by it. So if S has no proper refinement, then every situation in S* is refined by S. On the other hand, every situation refined by S is in S* by Statement 2.

Suppose S does have a proper refinement. Then S* cannot consist just of the situations refined by S, for we could then add the proper refinement to S* without violating condition (i) in the definition of ultrafilter. So S* contains at least one situation, say T, not refined by S. The overlap of S and T, which is a proper refinement of S, is then also in S*.

4. If S = T, then S itself is a refinement of T that is in S*. If S ≠ T, then S\T exists, and by Statement 3, there has to be at least one proper refinement of S in S*. And from the assumption that no such refinement of S in S* refines either T or T\S, we obtain a contradiction: if no such refinement refines either T or T\S, then they all overlap both T and T\S, and consequently their overlaps with T, say, could be added to S* without violating condition (i) of the definition of ultrafilter, contradicting condition (ii).

5. Statement 5 follows from Statement 4. ♦

Proposition 44. *Suppose S* and T* are ultrafilters. Then the following conditions are all equivalent.*

1. *For every S∈S*, there exists T∈T* such that T* **requires** *S.*
2. *For every T∈T*, there exists S∈S* such that S* **allows** *T.*
3. *For every S∈S*, there exists T∈T* such that S* **precedes** *T.*
4. *For every S∈S*, there exists T∈T* such that S* **alw.foretells** *T.*
5. *For every T∈T*, there exists S∈S* such that S* **precedes** *T.*

Proof First we show that Statement 1 implies Statement 2. Suppose Statement 1 holds, and let T be a situation in T*. Choose S_1 in S*, and use Statement 1 to obtain a situation T_1 in T* such that T_1 **requires** S_1.. Designate by T_2 the overlap of T and T_1. Then T_2 is in T* and T_2 **requires** S_1. The condition T_2 **requires** S_1 implies S_1 $\neg\mathbf{2}$ T_2, and hence S_1 decomposes into before$_{T_2}(S_1)$ and diverge$_{T_2}(S_1)$. By Statement 5 of Proposition 43, one of these must be in S*. But diverge$_{T_2}(S_1)$ cannot be in S*; if it were, there would be a situation T_3 in T* requiring diverge$_{T_2}(S_1)$ and hence diverging, by Statement 4 of Proposition 23, from T_2. So before$_{T_2}(S_1)$ is in S*. Moreover, it is the situation we want: by Statement 3 of Proposition 38, before$_{T_2}(S_1)$ **allows** T_2, and hence before$_{T_2}(S_1)$ **allows** T.

Now we show that Statement 2 implies Statement 1. Suppose Statement 2 holds, and let S be a situation in S*. Choose T_1 in T*, and use Statement 2 to obtain a situation S_1 in S* such that S_1 **allows** T_1.. Designate by S_2 the overlap of S and S_1. Then S_2 is in S* and S_2 **allows** T_1. The condition S_2 **allows** T_1 implies T_1 $\neg\mathbf{34}$ S_2, and hence T_1 decomposes into after$_{S_2}(T_1)$ and diverge$_{S_2}(T_1)$. By Statement 5 of Proposition 43, one of these must be in T*. But diverge$_{S_2}(T_1)$ cannot be in T*; if it were, there would be a situation S_3 in S* allowing diverge$_{S_2}(T_1)$, and the overlap of $S_3 \wedge S_2$ would then both allow and diverge from diverge$_{S_2}(T_1)$, which is impossible. So after$_{S_2}(T_1)$ is in T*. It is the situation we want: by Statement 1 of Proposition 38, after$_{S_2}(T_1)$ **requires** S_2, and hence after$_{S_2}(T_1)$ **requires** S.

Statements 3 and 4 each obviously imply Statement 1. To see that they are implied by Statement 1, notice that if T∈T* and T **requires** S, then Resolve(T|S), since it coarsens T, is also in T*; since it is preceded and always foretold by S, it satisfies the demands of Statements 3 and 4.

Statement 5 obviously implies Statement 2. To see that it is implied by Statement 2, notice that if S∈S* and S **allows** T, then extension(S→T), since it coarsens S, is also in S*; since it precedes T, it satisfies the demands of Statement 5. ♦

We define a relation **precedes*** on Γ* by writing S* **precedes*** T* whenever S* and T* are elements of Γ*, and the conditions of Proposition 44 are satisfied. It is evident (by the fact that **precedes**, say, is a partial ordering) that **precedes*** is a partial ordering. The next proposition establishes that Γ*, with the partial ordering **precedes***, is an event trellis.

Proposition 45. *Suppose S* **precedes*** U* and T* **precedes*** U*.*

1. *If S* and T* have a situation in common, then S* = T*.*
2. *If S∈S*, T∈T*, and T **requires** S, then S* **precedes*** T*.*
3. *If S∈S*, T∈T*, and S **allows** T, then S* **precedes*** T*.*
4. *If S∈S* and T∈T*, then Diverge$_T$(S), if it exists, is not in S*.*
5. *Either S* **precedes*** T* or T* **precedes*** S*.*

Proof 1. It suffices to show that an arbitrary situation in T*, say T, is in S*. Let R be a situation common to S* and T*. Since R and T are both in T*, their overlap R∧T exists and is in T*. Thus there exists a situation U_1 in U* requiring R∧T. By Statement 4 of Proposition 43, either R∧T is in S* or else R\(R∧T) exists and is in S*. But if R\(R∧T) were in S*, there would be a situation U_2 in U* requiring it, and this is impossible; two situations U_1 and U_2 in U* must overlap, and Statement 4 of Proposition 23 forbids overlapping situations from requiring divergent situations.

2. It suffices to construct, for an arbitrary situation in S*, say S_1, a situation in T* that requires it. To this end, let S_2 designate the overlap of S_1 and S. Let U_2 be a situation in U* that requires S_2, let T_1 be a situation in T* that allows U_2, and let T_2 designate the overlap of T_1 and T. Since it refines a situation that allows U_2, T_2 also allows U_2, and since it refines a situation that requires S, T_2 also requires S. So we have the following relations: T_2 **requires** S (T_2 ¬**345** S), S_2 **refines** S (S_2 ¬**2345** S), U_2 **requires** S_2 (U_2 ¬**345** S_2), and T_2 **allows** U_2 (T_2 ¬**25** U_2). Using Axiom S4n, we obtain T_2 ¬**5** S_2 from T_2 ¬**25** U_2 and U_2 ¬**345** S_2. We have S ¬**234** S_2 by the symmetry of ¬**234**, and using Axioms S4j and l, we obtain T_2 ¬**34** S_2 from T_2 ¬**345** S and S ¬**234** S_2. So T_2 requires S_2. Since S_2 refines S_1, T_2 also requires S_1.

3. It suffices to construct, for an arbitrary situation in T*, say T_1, a situation in S* that allows it. To this end, let T_2 designate the overlap of T_1 and T. Let U_2 be a situation in U* that requires T_2, let S_1 be a situation in S* that allows U_2, and let S_2 designate the overlap of S_1 and S. Since it refines a situation that allows U_2, S_2 also allows U_2, and since it refines a situation that allows T, S_2 also allows T. So we have the following relations: S_2 **allows** T (S_2 ¬**25** T), T_2 **refines** T (T_2 ¬**2345** T), U_2 **requires** T_2 (U_2 ¬**345** T_2), and S_2 **allows** U_2 (S_2 ¬**25** U_2). Using Axiom S4n, we obtain S_2 ¬**5** T_2 from S_2 ¬**25** U_2 and U_2 ¬**345** T_2. We obtain T ¬**2** T_2 from T_2 ¬**34** T, and using Axiom S4h, we obtain S_2 ¬**2** T_2 from S_2 ¬**25** T and T ¬**2** T_2. So S_2 allows T_2. Since T_2 refines T_1, S_2 also allows T_1.

4. If $Diverge_T(S)$ were in S*, then we would have situations in U* requiring the divergent situations T and $Diverge_T(S)$, which is impossible by Statement 4 of Proposition 23.

5. Choose a situation U in U*, and choose situations S in S* and T in T* that precede U. Decompose S into $S \wedge T$, $Before_T(S)$ and $After_T(S)$, and $Diverge_T(S)$. (This is not to say that all four necessarily exist.) By Statement 4 of Proposition 43, S* contains one of these four situations. So the conclusion follows by the preceding statements. If it contains $S \wedge T$, then S* = T*, by Statement 1. If it contains $Before_T(S)$, which requires T, then T* **precedes** S*, by Statement 2. If it contains $After_T(S)$, which allows T, then S* **precedes** T*, by Statement 3. By Statement 4, it cannot contain $Diverge_T(S)$. ♦

Proposition 46.

1. For each situation S in Γ, the set $\{S^* \in \Gamma^* | S \in S^*\}$ *is a clade in* Γ^*.

2. Designate by Γ^+ *the set of all clades in* Γ^*. *Then* Γ^+ *is an event space. (In other words, addition to satisfying Axioms S1 through S6, like the set of all clades in any event trellis, it also satisfies Axioms S7, S8, and S9.)*

3. Define a mapping ρ from Γ into Γ^+ *by setting* $\rho(S) := \{S^* \in \Gamma^* | S \in S^*\}$. *Then ρ is a refinement.*

Proof Statement 1 is easy to prove; if S* **precedes*** T*, then both S* and T* precede T* and hence, by the first statement of the preceding proposition, S* and T* will be equal if they have a situation in common. Thus S* **precedes*** T* cannot hold when S* and T* are distinct ultrafilters containing S.

We leave the proofs of Statements 2 and 3 to the reader. ♦

6.12. Conclusion. We have formulated a set of relatively constructive axioms, and we have shown that these axioms are essentially equivalent to the mathematically idea of an event tree. The latter step is of fundamental importance, because it is shows that the axioms are complete in the sense that they capture fully, at least in the finite case, the intuitive idea of branching time.

The task of elaborating the axioms into a causal logic remains. This task can be pursued in at least three distinct ways. First of all, the axioms themselves can be reformulated as rules of inference within Martin-Löf's type theory, as suggested in §6.9. Secondly, the mathematical structure can be elaborated in the direction of temporal logic (Emerson 1990). This means adding a domain of individuals, perhaps allowed to vary from situation to situation, together with relations and properties, certainly allowed to vary from situation to situation. The resulting structure would be a very powerful semantics, sufficing not only for temporal logic but also for a logic of events achieving the goals of McDermott (1982), Allen (1984), Kowalski and Sergot (1986), and Galton (1987). Thirdly, since the concept of situation plays a prominent role in our understanding of the axioms, they can also be used as a semantics for the situation calculus (McCarthy and Hayes 1969, Reiter 1991).

7. References

1. Allen, J. F., *Towards a general theory of action and time*, Artificial Intelligence **23** (1984) 123-154.
2. Davey, B. A., and H. A. Priestley, *Introduction to Lattices and Order*, Cambridge University Press, Cambridge, 1990.
3. Dempster, A. P., *Employment discrimination and statistical science (with discussion)*, Statistical Science **2** (1988) 141-195.

4. Edwards, A. W. F., *Pascal's Arithmetical Triangle,* Charles Griffin, London, 1987.
5. Eerola, Mervi, *Probabilistic Causality in Longitudinal Studies*, Springer-Verlag, New York, 1994.
6. Emerson, E. Allen, *Temporal and modal logic.* J. van Leeuwen, ed., Handbook of Theoretical Computer Science, Vol. B, Elsevier, Amsterdam, 1990, pp. 995-1072.
7. Finkelstein, Michael O., and Bruce Levin, *Statistics for Lawyers*, Springer Verlag, New York, 1990.
8. Freedman, David A., *Statistical models and shoe leather (with discussion)*, Sociological Methodology **21** (1991) 291-358.
9. Gabbay, Dov M., Ian Hodkinson, and Mark Reynolds, *Temporal Logic: Mathematical Foundations and Computational Aspects*, Vol. 1, Clarendon Press, Oxford, 1994.
10. Galton, Antony, ed., *Temporal Logics and their Applications*, Academic Press, London, 1987.
11. Galton, Antony, *The logic of occurrence:* Antony Galton, ed., Temporal Logics and their Applications, Academic Press, London, 1987, pp. 169-196.
12. Haddawy, Peter, *A logic of time, chance, and action for representing plans*, Artificial Intelligence **80** (1996) 243-308.
13. Humphreys, Paul, *The Chances of Explanation: Causal Explanation in the Social, Medical, and Physical Sciences*, Princeton University Press, Princeton, New Jersey, 1989.
14. Jech, Thomas J., *Set Theory*, Academic Press, New York, 1978.
15. Kelley, J. L., *General Topology*, Van Nostrand Rheinhold, New York, 1955.
16. Kowalski, R. A. and M. J. Sergot, *A logic-based calculus of events*, New Generation Computing **4** (1986) 67-95.
17. von Kutschera, Franz, *Causation*, Journal of Philosophical Logic **22** (1993) 563-588.
18. McCall, Storrs, *A Model of the Universe*, Clarendon, Oxford, 1994.
19. McCarthy, John, and Patrick Hayes, *Some philosophical problems from the standpoint of artificial intelligence:* B. Meltzer and D. Michie, eds., Machine Intelligence 4, Edinburgh University Press, Edinburgh, 1969, pp. 463-502.
20. McDermott, Drew, *A temporal logic for reasoning about processes and plans*, Cognitive Science **6** (1982) 101-155.
21. von Plato, Jan, *The axioms of constructive geometry*, Annals of Pure and Applied Logic **76** (1995) 169-200.
22. Raiffa, Howard, *Decision Analysis*, Addison-Wesley, Reading, Massachusetts, 1968.
23. Reiter, Raymond, *The frame problem in the situation calculus: A simple solution (sometimes) and a completeness result for goal regression:* Vladimir Lifschitz, ed., Artificial Intelligence and Mathematical Theory of Computation: Papers in Honor of John McCarthy, 1991, Academic Press, San Diego, pp. 359-380.
24. Shafer, Glenn, *Philosophical foundations for causal networks.* Bernadette Bouchon-Meunier, Ronald R. Yager, and Lotfi A. Zadeh, eds., *Advances in Intelligent Computing*, Springer Verlag, New York, 1995, pp. 3-12.
25. Shafer, Glenn, *The Art of Causal Conjecture.* The MIT Press, Cambridge, Massachusetts, 1996.
26. Shafer, Glenn, *The situation of causality.* To appear in Foundations of Science **1** (1996).
27. Shafer, Glenn, and Amos Tversky, *Languages and designs for probability judgment*, Cognitive Science **9** (1985) 305-339.
28. Spohn, Wolfgang, *Direct and indirect causes*, Topoi **9** (1990) 125-145.
29. Turner, Raymond, *Logics for Artificial Intelligence*, Ellis Horwood, Chicester, 1984.
30. Vila, Lluis, *A survey on temporal reasoning in artifcial intelligence*, AICOM **7** #4, 4-28.
31. Vovk, Vladimir G., *A logic of probability, with applications to the foundations of statistics (with discussion),* Journal of the Royal Statistical Society, Series B **55** (1993a) 317-351.
32. Vovk, Vladimir G., *Forecasting point and continuous processes: prequential analysis*, Test **2** (1993b) 189-217.

Department of Accounting and Information Systems, Faculty of Management, Rutgers University, Newark, New Jersey 07102

E-mail address: gshafer@andromeda.rutgers.edu

Home page: http://www.rutgers.edu/Accounting/raw/gsm/shafer.htm

Index

Selected Titles in This Series

(Continued from the front of this publication)

(See the AMS Catalog for earlier titles.)

ISBN 0-8218-0611-4

9 780821 806111